Regional Integration in Early Modern Scandinavia

Chapter 2
The nature of states and regions
Reflections on territory in Swedish historiography

By Peter Aronsson

Questions about the character, size, societal significance, and future role of regions are accentuated in our day by processes which simultaneously suggest a reduced significance for the nation state and an increased nationalism with an ethnic and religious basis.

There are signs suggesting that the development of strong nation states has now reached its zenith after 500 years of almost continuous growth. Economic processes show clear indications of globalization and reduced spatial cohesion, while cultural and political processes show a more complicated picture of several conceivable lines of development. What the two tendencies have in common is that the limits and functions of the old nation states are once again being questioned and debated. One can observe »a growing tension between old decision-making territories and new problem areas«.[1]

The concept of region appears to have been unknown in the Middle Ages. The word itself comes from the Latin *regio*, which means »direction, point of the compass«, but it later developed by association with *regere* »to rule«.[2] The exercise of power and territorial control are linked together in one concept. In political and administrative contexts the word *provincia* (from *vincere* »to conquer«) is used in Latin for areas brought under the control of another power; this usage continued. It is no coincidence that the concept of region in Western Europe did not take shape until the great success of the nation states at the beginning of modern times, from around 1500. The region is conceived of as existing in relation to a centre, not infrequently in opposition to it, perhaps as an alternative national project which failed.

We must eliminate the taken-for-grantedness of our knowledge of 500 years of successful state-building, with relatively stable nation states as the final products, and realize that it was not a given historical mission that was accomplished. This is precisely how it has been seen by many historians ever since the nineteenth century. If we succeed in clearing our vision, we gain several benefits: We can avoid automatically viewing the role of the region as peripheral, as the loser in a struggle for nationhood, and instead question this view. In the study of the dynamics of regions, we can in part employ the analytical tools and concepts used by modern research into the nation state. Finally, both nation-building and regions can be partly viewed in relation to each other

Forskningsråd (The Danish Research Council for the Humanities), Statens Arkiver (The Danish State Archives), Landsdommer V. Gieses Legat, Den Lätterstedtska Föreningen, Fridlev Skrubbeltrangs Mindefond and De Ingwersenske Fonde.

The editors would like to dedicate this volume to the memory of the late Harald Winge, who sadly and tragically died during the production of this book. His contribution to this anthology was one of his last works, showing both his clarity of style and thought, and his great generosity to colleagues and friends. He is greatly missed and fondly remembered.

Notes

1 Cf. W. Wallace (ed.): *The Dynamics of European Integration*, London 1990.
2 An early example is R. Fladby and L. Marthinsen (eds.): *Distriktshistorie. Problemer. Metode. Organisering* (District history: problems, method, structure), Oslo 1979.
3 See especially the lavishly illustrated N.G. Brekke (ed.): *Kulturhistorisk vegbok.* (Roadbook of cultural history) *Hordaland*, Bergen 1993, which is now being taken as a model by other Norwegian counties.
4 See for instance, S. Åkerman and K. Lundholm (eds.): *Älvdal i norr. Människor och resurser i Luledalen 1300-1800* (River valley in the North. People and resources in the Lule valley 1300-1800), Stockholm 1990.
5 Three recent dissertations from Denmark show some of the diversity of regional studies: H.H. Appel: *Tinget, magten og æren* (The local court, the power and the glory), Odense 1999, focusses on economic and social relations and mentalities among peasants in a region of Western Denmark, on the background of regional production patterns and market contacts. P.O. Christiansen: *A manorial world.* *Lord, peasants and cultural distinctions on a Danish estate 1750-1980*, Oslo 1996, is a detailed description and analysis of social relationships on an East Danish estate, also addressing the exchange of goods between Danish rural districts and other parts of Northern and Western Europe in the Early Modern period. S.B. Frandsen: *Opdagelsen af Jylland. Den regionale dimension i Danmarkshistorien 1814-64*, Aarhus 1995, discusses the development of a regional consciousness in the Jutland peninsula in the nineteenth century, delivering an important contribution to the debate on the emergence of the modern national state.
6 J.P. Maarbjerg: *Scandinavia in the European World-Economy, ca. 1570-1625*, New York etc. 1995.
7 Å. Sandström: *Plöjande borgare och handlande bönder. Mötet mellan den europeiska urbana ekonomin och vasatidens Sverige* (Ploughing burghers and trading peasants. The conjunction of the European urban economy and Vasa-age Sweden), Stockholm 1996.
8 Ø. Rian: *Vestfolds historie. Grevskapstiden 1671-1821* (The History of Vestfold. The times of the counts), Larvik 1980; *Bratsberg på 1600-tallet. Stat og samfunn i symbiose og konflikt* (Seventeenth-century Bratsberg. State and society in symbiosis and conflict), Oslo 1997.
9 P. Holm: *Kystfolk. Kontakter og sammenhænge over Kattegat og Skagerrak, ca. 1550-1914* (People on the coast. Contacts and connections across Kattegat and Skagerrak, c. 1550-1914), Esbjerg 1991.
10 A. Døssland: *Med lengt mot havet. Fylkeshistorie for Møre og Romsdal* (With a longing for the sea. County history of Møre and Romsdal), Vol. I, 1671-1835, Oslo 1990; *Strilesoga. Nord- og Midhordland gjennom tidene* (The story of the *Strils*. Northern and Mid-Hordaland through the times), Vol. 3, Bergen 1998; Vol. 4 (with Karl Egil Johansen), Bergen 1998.
11 See also P. Henningsen: *Hedens Hemmeligheder. Livsvilkår i Vestjylland 1750-1900* (The secrets of the moor. Living conditions in Western Jutland 1750-1900), Viborg 1995.

parisons between regions and periods. However, the *Leitmotif* of this anthology is, as its title indicates, integration – in various fields and forms, in different settings, and with different scopes: economic, political, social and cultural integration; within a region, between regions and into state or international structures. In most of the articles, the main focus is on economic integration, into a modern urban, European, or even world economy, in various forms: adaptations to wider market conditions, specialization, commercialization; the development of trade networks, towns and hinterlands, markets and fairs; improved communications and techniques of payment and credit. Along with this economic integration, however, we can observe its concomitant phenomena in the political, social and cultural spheres: the Janus head of fiscal and economic policies, the symbiosis of local administration and commercial enterprise, the mixture of trade and taxation; the doubling of local élites as government officials and private merchants, trading peasants and ploughing merchants; the demographic causes and effects of specialization and commercialization in peasant communities; the »civilizing« and »modernizing« effects of cultural contacts in the wake of trade and shipping. None of these processes were uncomplicated or one-way developments. Even if the general tendency was towards increasing commercialization, urbanization, and market orientation, and although trade volumes tended to increase and the market economy to spread, there were periods of decline as well as growth, setbacks and relics of earlier forms and stages in the most »modern« sectors, and unpredictable and sometimes surprising changes of roles and fortunes in the integration process. Thus, it would be too simplistic, and to some extent even totally misleading, to see the process of regional integration as a steady march in one direction.

Acknowledgements and dedication

The publication of an academic anthology in English, with Scandinavian editors, authors (with the single exception of the Danish-American Professor Maarbjerg), and publishers, would be have been a foolhardy (but far from unheard-of) enterprise without the crucial assistance of a native and professional »language cleaner«. Cand. mag. Maeve Drewsen has performed the unenviable task of translating the »Scandinavian English« of most of the articles into »English English« – a process involving a fair share of creative thinking, sometimes bordering on pure guesswork, and we all – including the readers, who don't know what they have been spared – owe her our most deepfelt thanks!

We would also like to thank stud. mag. Stella Borne Mikkelsen for her great help in preparing the manuscripts for publication and trimming the tables, Birger Bromann for drawing a number of maps, and Thomas Kaarsted and Martin Westergaard of Odense University Press, for the efficient organization of the publishing process.

Finally, we thank the following foundations and institutions for their financial support for this book project, and without whose generous contributions this book would never have seen the light of day: Statens Humanistiske

10), Mikkelsen also introduces another type of region, the nexus of town and hinterland. His is the first of five articles dealing with trade networks and relationships between towns and hinterlands in different parts of Denmark and Norway. Søren Bitsch Christensen (Chapter 11) studies the Norway trade of the merchants of Randers in the 1760s through the account books of one of them, Niels Hasselbalch. He is able to reconstruct both regions affected by this trade: the East Jutland catchment area of Randers and the Norwegian market area for the grain from Randers. In a wide-ranging study of the main town of Northern Jutland, Aalborg (Chapter 12), Poul Holm, a central figure in the Skagerrak-Kattegat project,[9] extends the perspectives of Bitsch Christensen's article, both in time and space. Taking in the whole period covered by this anthology, he places Aalborg both within its hinterland, centered on the Limfjord, and as an international city, and a centre of the entire Skagerrak-Kattegat region. This was originally an internal region within the Union of Kalmar, and later the Oldenborg state, but with the Swedish acquisition of the eastern shores of the Kattegat in the mid-seventeenth century, and the establishment of the personal union of Sweden and Norway in 1814, Aalborg's fortunes and orientation changed dramatically.

Two »Norwegian« chapters each look more closely at the hinterland of one town. Finn-Einar Eliassen (Chapter 13) discusses the changing relationship between the small South Coast town of Mandal and its hinterland from demographic, economic, administrative, political and cultural perspectives, assessing the effects of the crown's policy of privileges, and revealing some surprising changes of roles between town merchants and hinterland farmers in the aftermath of the Napoleonic wars and Norway's »constitutional revolution« of 1814. Atle Døssland, like Øystein Rian the author of two regional histories,[10] and likewise in a good position to conduct comparative research between regions of Western Norway, deals with the nearest hinterland of Bergen (the largest town of early modern Norway), the so-called *Stril* country (Chapter 14). His point of departure is the question of the »Strils« adaptation to the urban market, but he concludes by identifying a counter-culture among the »Strils«, which led them to revolt successfully against an unpopular poll-tax in the 1760s, but which later put them on the sidelines of cultural and political development in Norway.

Cultural integration (or non-integration) of a rural region in the eighteenth and early nineteenth centuries is also the topic of the concluding chapter (15), in which Peter Henningsen studies the »civilizing« process of the peripheral Danish region of Western Jutland in the century before industrialisation.[11] Both Døssland and Henningsen, like Maarbjerg (in Chapter 5) show that peasants of proverbially »backward« regions have been far more rational than they have been given credit for.

Regional integration

As will be apparent from this short overview, there are some thematic overlaps between chapters, and the main topics of some articles may appear as side issues in others, allowing further comthe local administration in regulating and integrating the regional economy in parts of Finland, Sweden and Norway into greater units. Taxation and customs regulations, privileges and general economic and financial policies affected the traditional trading activities of the local peasantry, without however curbing it altogether. John P. Maarbjerg, who has already published a major contribution to the study of the integration of Nordic regions into the developing world economy,[6] focusses (in Chapter 5) on the Finnish region of Southern East Bothnia in a period of economic decline in the late sixteenth century. He shows how the peasants in the region adapted to an international market economy and to the relative price movements (rates of exchange) between goods bought and sold by specializing in the production of salted fish and tar as a response to the economic crisis. Åke Sandström (Chapter 6) in an article bearing the same title as his recent book,[7] studies the role of the state in creating a taxable order in the Swedish market in the sixteenth and seventeenth centuries by regulating the economy through privileges and prohibitions. Merchants in Stockholm and other staple towns were strongly favoured by the crown at the expense of other towns and traders, without, however, the peasant trader becoming completely extinct. In Chapter 7, Øystein Rian compares two neighbouring regions in South-Eastern Norway in the seventeenth and partly in the eighteenth century, on the basis of his own two regional histories.[8] Although close neighbours, the present-day counties of Vestfold (early modern Larvik and Jarlsberg) and Telemark (early modern Bratsberg) present striking contrasts in topography, economy, political structure, and the status of the peasants. His study clearly illustrates the potential of comparative regional history in understanding the social and political processes in a heterogeneous country.

Demographic differences within a region are also dealt with by Maarbjerg, but in Ragnhild Høgsæt's, study (Chapter 8), the connections between population movements and economic change are at the centre of the author's attention. She uses evidence from the small but complex region of Southern Helgeland (Northern Norway) in the late seventeenth century to question an established truism about the connection between population movements and types of production in a pre-industrial agrarian economy. She thus demonstrates the possibilities of regional history for comparisons *within* a region, which would normally be large enough and comprise sufficiently different local communities for this purpose.

Markets and market trading are the topics of two »Danish« chapters. In Chapter 9, Ole Degn provides the first overall view of annual fairs in Denmark in a long-term perspective, from the early seventeenth to the late nineteenth century. Markets and fairs were nodes in the networks of intra-regional and inter-regional trade, and Degn presents the study of fairs as a possible starting-point for regional studies, giving examples of the potential for regional research of the source material relating to fairs. The relationships between towns and markets, and between resident merchants and market traders, are taken up by Jørgen Mikkelsen in the context of the island of Sjælland (Zealand) in the late eighteenth century. In his article (Chapter the individual authors' various approaches to and research interests in regional history. Thus, the 14 subsequent chapters are written from a multitude of perspectives, illustrating some of the most important aspects of Nordic regional history of the early modern period, each covering one, two, or many regions, of various sizes, and within shorter or longer stretches of the period 1400-1850, focussing on different themes and topics. However, they all deal with aspects of what we may loosely call *regional integration* in one form or another, while giving valuable insights into early modern Norden, from a regional perspective. At the same time, they illustrate different theoretical and methodological approaches to regional history. Rather than giving a »full picture« (assuming that such a thing were possible), this collection of articles should demonstrate some of the *possibilities* of a regional approach to Nordic history in the early modern period – and beyond those geographical and chronological limits.

The outer time limits of the present volume are marked by the breakthrough of European market integration and the emergence of a European World Economy in the fifteenth century, and the breakdown of old regions in the wake of the industrial revolution in Scandinavia from the mid-nineteenth century.

Between local and national history

The disposition of this anthology is a mixture of the chronological and the thematic. In two general articles, Peter Aronsson (Chapter 2) and the late Harald Winge (Chapter 3) both address the theoretical and practical aspects of defining a region and studying it in a historical context. Both give a theoretical analysis of the concept and characteristics of a region, but illustrate the theory in different ways. Aronsson, focussing on institutions, functions, identities, and change, is chiefly interested in the regions themselves, as »natural«, »created« or »perceived« entities. He sees Swedish history in a regional perspective, as variations of themes within the country's present borders. Harald Winge, from his vantage point as head of the Norwegian Institute of Local History, gives an overview of Norwegian regional history in the light of his own theories and definitions, seeing regional history as an intermediate level between local and national history. His perspective is historiographical, and his framework is the individual regions as presented in the regional histories.

The other articles follow a roughly chronological sequence, from the Late Middle Ages to the middle of the nineteenth century. More important, however, are the thematic links between successive chapters. Bjørn Poulsen, in Chapter 4, takes us from the Late Middle Ages into the seventeenth century in the company of sailing peasant traders who played a key role in linking together different regions of Denmark, as well as rural areas and towns. Already in this early period, regional specialization and surplus production of commodities like grain, fish and oxen provided the basis for cross-regional trade, peasant shipping providing the vital links in this trade, for a long time unhampered by the crown or by urban merchants.

This study is followed by three chapters (5-7) on the roles of the state and

Eastern Nordic group. On a smaller scale, the Skagerrak-Kattegat region, around the arm of the North Sea between South-Eastern Norway, the Western Coast of Sweden, and Denmark (chiefly Jutland), Trøndelag-Jämtland (in the centre of the Scandinavian peninsula), and the Swedish-Finnish region around the Bay of Bothnia have been among the most important inter-Nordic regions. Finally, parts of the Nordic countries belong to wider regions, incorporating (parts of) countries outside Norden, like the Barents region, *Nordkalotten* (both of which include parts of North-Western Russia), the Baltic or the North Sea regions – all of which have been institutionalized in recent years, with various organs for economic cooperation, cultural exchange, environmental protection, etc., but on a historical background of trade relations, migration, and cultural impulses through the centuries.

Regional history in the Nordic countries

So, many contemporary Nordic regions have a historical ancestry, and in many cases, regional divisions were even more pronounced and had an even greater significance in earlier centuries, when communications were slower and more difficult, state power weaker and more limited, and cultural dominance over greater territories less penetrating. This has long been recognized by Nordic historians, but only in recent decades have individual regions in Sweden, Finland, Denmark, and Norway, become a central field of historical research, resulting in a number of publications, ranging from seminar reports,[2] handbooks,[3] and collections of thematic articles[4] via monographs (often covering a limited period)[5] to multi-volume histories of individual regions from the »earliest times« to the present day. This heterogeneous body of recent and ongoing research provides the foundation and *raison d'être* of the present volume. The editors have brought together a number of the most active and experienced practitioners in this field, inviting them to present some of the most interesting results from their own research and readings in regional history, in a form accessible also to a non-Nordic readership. We decided to concentrate on the early modern period, in a wide sense, ranging from the fifteenth to the mid-nineteenth century. This is both the period which seems to be best covered by research and publications, and, even more important, it is a crucial period in the integration of the Nordic regions into wider economic, cultural and political units and networks – nationally and internationally: the nation-state, the modern world economy, even »civilization« itself!

It is important to state at the outset what this book is not: it is *neither* a regional history of Norden in the early modern period, *nor* a history of the Nordic regions between 1400 and 1850. It does *not* attempt to cover all the major regions, or the main regional variations within Norden in the given period. It does not even allow a systematic comparison between all or most of the regions covered by this volume, either thematically or chronologically. It has not been edited with a fixed set of questions in mind, or based on a common perspective. It is an anthology, reflecting

CHAPTER 1
Historical regions and regional history in the Nordic countries
An introduction

By *Finn-Einar Eliassen, Jørgen Mikkelsen and Bjørn Poulsen*

At the end of the twentieth century, regional consciousness and political regionalism are important, and often problematic, factors in many European countries. Not only individual states, like Spain, Russia, and the UK, but also the European Union has taken the reality of regionalism into account in formulating its policies. There is even the possibility of a Europe where regions are more important than states, some time in the twenty-first century. Already now, »Europe of the regions« is a political slogan with some clout both within and outside the EU.[1]

In the Nordic countries – present-day Finland, Sweden, Denmark, Norway, and Iceland, with the possible exception of the latter – regions and regionalism have played a central role in politics, administration, economic and cultural life for a long time. The differences in voting behaviour, language, religious views, social structure and attitudes between districts, regions, and provinces within each country are often striking. In addition to these internal regions, there are also greater, transnational regions, cutting across state and national boundaries, and incorporating parts of several present-day states. Historically, there is a north-south divide between the thinly populated, less urbanized, less feudal Ice-

Fig. 1.1: The Nordic countries

land, the Faroes, most of Norway and Finland, plus Northern Sweden on one hand, and the more densely populated, urbanized and feudal Denmark, Southern Sweden, South-Eastern Norway, and South-Western Finland on the other. There is also an east-west divide between Iceland, The Faroes, and Western Norway on one side; and Eastern Norway, Denmark, and Sweden on the other, most in evidence in the division of dialects into a Western Nordic and an

7

and seen as a dynamic whole – not as simple opposites nor as a functional, harmonious whole.

The concept of region will not be given a normative definition in this study. The point of departure is the way the concept is used in research and by the historical actors. A discussion of how different definitions have been formed and used and may be further developed will be a result of the study rather than its starting point. There is good reason not only to consider the regions identified by research but also to look at the process whereby intellectuals »produce« regions.

However, a rough delimitation of what should fall within the category of »region« is needed because the explicit word is used only in specific contexts. A region claiming to be a nation and aspiring to be a state would hardly consider itself as a region, but the state might well define this action as a regional problem. By regions we understand, first of all, areas held together by similarities or interactive fields of certain common features in cultural, economic, social, or political terms. These can be found on all territorial levels, but here the discussion is mainly about those which lie above the level of the »place« and the local community but below that of the state. The analytical steps are *place – local community – region – state* and *macro-region*.[3] Many suggestions have been made through the years; regions have been conceived as natural, historically created, or scientifically constructed; demarcated by objective criteria, subjective identities, or instrumental needs.

The upper limit is ambiguous, especially in earlier times, but it is unclear in an interesting way. The Kalmar Union, the Catholic church, and the Hanseatic League are three different examples of regional organizations on a high level, which were real alternatives to the nation state project that gradually amassed the greatest organizational capacity and power. In this perspective, the nation states could be seen as regional projects which triumphed over the Nordic or the Hanseatic projects.[4]

Reflections on the region as a theoretical concept should inquire into how territory is characterized in the following dimensions:

1. Territoriality and institutionalization
What size is the region and what degree of autonomy does it have? Is it seen as a *natural region* on the basis of territorial and geographical conventions, or is it defined with functional, political, social, and economic factors in the centre? In what spheres does it have autonomy? Where and how are the boundaries of the region set? What is its relationship to the process of state formation and national development?

2. Objective criteria: homogeneity or functionality
Is one decisive characteristic singled out, or complex, spatially coinciding patterns? Are these *properties* (the homogeneous region) or *relations* (the functional region)? Are things like ethnic affiliation, commuting to work, or interactive life-modes seen as criteria of region formation? How far is the social applicability of the criteria stretched? Does everyone within the territory belong to the region, or just a few? Is this »membership« confined to a particular class, gender, race or ethnic group?

Regional integration

3. *Subjective criteria: identity*
Does identity formation play a passive or active role in the region? Is identity regarded as an unarticulated precondition, a mentality, based on similar practice and a similar life-mode distinguishing the region from other regions (regionality)? To what extent is self-understanding and the production of symbols considered significant for the development of the region?

4. *Historical change*
How do regions develop and change – through the intervention of the state, through the restructuring of business and industry, or through new discourses – political, cultural, or scientific ones?

These analytical dimensions are to be regarded as a program, presenting an outline of the kind of analysis that has to be done to appreciate the possibilities of a regional perspective. All these analyses cannot be made in a brief survey using secondary literature.

The role of the regions has been emphasized in Swedish historiography mainly in the following contexts, which are here summarized in a roughly chronological order:
- The unification of Sweden: a kindred-based society and the provinces competing for state power.
- The role and development of the administrative framework: provincial self-government versus state centralism.
- Settlement units: the regions of agrarian society, racial theories, and the discussion of Eastern versus Western Sweden.
- The functional regions of industrial society: the geography of proto-industrialization; town and country; regional economy; the geography of civil society; the instrumental regions of regional policy.

The principles for distinguishing regions and the more significant perspectives will be presented briefly under the headings »The regions of the realm« and »The regions of culture and work«. A more dynamic perspective is suggested in »Created regions«.[5]

The regions of the realm

The administrative regions of both the state and the church – the county (*län*), the judicial district (*tingslag*), the municipality (*kommun*), the diocese (*stift*), the deanery (*kontrakt*), the parish (*socken*), etc. – can be considered from two angles. From a purely formal, legalistic point of view, it can be argued that all public political power derives from the state and that all territorial subdivisions express decentralized or devolved state power. From a more historical, practice-oriented point of view, one can see how the territorial arenas, from the parish assembly to the seat of county administration, also function as arenas where different social interests and groups reconcile their positions and resources. Even meetings preceding tax assessments contained elements of negotiation which transformed formally legal measures into micro-politics, and territorial arenas in varying degrees into political forums.

It is possible, however, to distinguish a historical line of development. In the Middle Ages, Sweden was to a large extent a federal realm, held together by bonds of fidelity of varying duration. Negotiations were conducted between a growing central government and local communities in varying groupings at markets, assemblies, and through tests of military might. A number of important regional powers survived for a long time or were divided between the central government and rural assemblies at the level of the province (Old Swedish *land*, Modern Swedish *landskap*) or the *härad* (corresponding roughly to the English *hundred*).

To an increasing extent, the political and judicial game of negotiation between regions and central government was played in organized forms: after the Dacke uprising in the 1540s, the »landsting«, with its right to summon people to arms, was abolished by the central government as being too dangerous. The »häradsting« filled part of the vacuum, with popular influence being exerted through the representatives appointed by the peasants themselves.[6]

Although such crucial functions for the central government as the process of law and the right and obligation to decide in matters concerning war and peace were not wholly monopolized by the state until the eighteenth century, there was a gradual formalization and politicization of relations between the provinces, the regions, and the central government. The peace agreements resolving border disputes, which were concluded without central approval, and sometimes against the will of the government, shrank in territorial scope during the sixteenth and seventeenth centuries; from having encompassed entire provinces, they came down to the level of the hundred and finally the parish. The last popular uprising against the central government's foreign policy was the »Daldansen« of 1742.[7]

Political participation in Sweden developed from the seventeenth century particularly in two arenas: the diet (*riksdag*), linked to the people through the petitions formulated at parish and hundred level and the election of representatives also to the peasant estate, after 1866 to the bicameral parliament; and the parish assembly (*sockenstämma*), later called the municipality, where everyday practice in problem-solving, negotiation, and gradual formalization of decision-making processes became a widespread experience among people of all the estates, especially from the second half of the eighteenth century.

The reintroduction in 1862 of a new arena for regional politics, the *landsting*, this time in the sense of a county council, brought hopes, or fears, of a powerful regionalism. The name evoked the significant provincial assemblies of the Middle Ages, and to some extent the elements of political, communal negotiation at hundred assemblies and county administrations in the succeeding centuries. The hopes vested in the new county councils were soon crushed, however; the arenas where a territorial political awareness developed from the sixteenth and seventeenth centuries were mainly and increasingly the municipal and national ones.

The reason why administrative boundaries have been so little queried by historians, instead being taken as starting points for studies of social processes of various kinds, is probably the long-prevailing view that the important historical processes and actors were to be found at the national level. This view was a product of what was the century of history above all others, the nineteenth century, with its Hegelian state idealism and nationalism. When this view was eroded in the twentieth century, being more and more systematically questioned from the point of view of theoretical criticism and local historical practice, the historical meaning of the administrative boundaries could be discussed in a more multifaceted way.

The question of spatial identity in relation to administrative boundaries has been the subject of little study. My own hypothesis is that in pre-industrial Swedish society, after the break-up of the federal medieval structures, local spatial identities were used to relate to society at large: farm, village, and possibly parish. The next step for really distant relationships was national affiliation, less often provincial origin. The hundred, to a greater extent than the county, had an identification potential and functional relations at a territorial level corresponding roughly to today's municipalities. The nature of interaction in modern municipalities, however, is more like that of the old village and parish levels.

The regions of culture and work

In Sweden it has been more common to adopt a regional perspective in the discussion of agrarian society and folk culture than in narratives about the destiny of the nation. Ethnology, demography, anthropological research, and geography all work with regional divisions of various kinds.

The ethnological concept of the *bygd* (a rural settlement unit constituting a local community) could be used on several territorial levels. The southern limit of transhumance, coinciding with the northern limits of the oak, the ox, and the nobility, is an example of an almost nationally perceived settlement boundary based on both natural and human geography, and with socio-cultural implications (see fig. 2.2).

Swedish ethnologists have been inspired by theories about the diffusion of innovation and, using cartography as a method, distinguished regions based on centres of innovation: a Stockholm-centred Eastern Sweden and a Malmö/Copenhagen-centred Western Sweden. The division into Eastern and Western Sweden (sometimes with the addition of separate divisions for Norrland in the north and Skåne, Halland, and Blekinge in the south) was encouraged in the course of the twentieth century by stimuli from various quarters: demographic observations of differences in birth rate gave rise to attempts to distinguish regions based on ethnic distinctions and later to a debate among historians about differences in social control, family formation, political culture, levels of civilization, churchgoing, club activities, urbanization, and so on. From the eighteenth century Western Sweden was characterized by a tighter social control in a more conservative but egalitarian rural society while Eastern Sweden was more socially polarized and had more urban modernization taking place at an early stage – and more illegitimate childbirths.[8] The question of regional identity has not had a prominent place in these discussions. Perhaps this is because regional identities do not have any great significance for the Eastern and Western Swedish regions which have gradually been perceived as functional regarding the social structure?

The historical provinces were more deliberately emphasized by institutions and associations from the end of the nineteenth century: The Herder-inspired discovery of the people was at the basis of the formation of cultural regions everywhere in Europe. These became institutionalized and historicized in collective memory and education. In projects like the great outdoor park of Skansen in Stockholm, and the elementary school reader, both at the end of the nineteenth century, up till today's tourist brochures, the genuine province has been cultivated, with symbols being produced of a kind and on a scale which the administrative or functional regions cannot match. What this meant for the creation of patriotic sentiment at the turn of the century, and what it means for orientation and identities in the new Europe, are questions that the scholarly community has only just begun to ponder.

The territorial framework of economic history has to a certain extent gone beyond the nation-state as a natural framework. Trade as well as international politics encourages this. But often the nation has nevertheless provided an unreflected frame of reference, also for economic processes. The region as a unit of analysis has been mostly a practicable method to constrain the dimensions of the study of a process conceived of as the growth of a national industry and a national market. Sometimes however, perhaps most clearly so in the study of proto-industrialization, the region has been used as a necessary tool in comparative research, giving significant contribution to the theory itself, resulting in a more complex view of the importance of space.[9]

When industrialization is studied more carefully, it is striking how discontinuously it is distributed in space, even over long periods of time. This fact has been the starting point for a more ambitious discussion of regionality. Sidney Pollard argues that industrialization is a regional process in the first place, which furthermore often draws on an already existing division of labour, e. g. the old exchange between the mining districts and the ones producing grain and other necessary complementary products for the industry. The administrative units cannot be used indiscriminately to analyse this division of labour, or its development over time. The object of study itself demands the development of a more reflective view of territory.[10]

The classical approach, stemming from Mendels, argues that an original regional division of labour was at the root of early industrialization. When it has been established, it reinforces a secondary division of labour between regions where a more differentiated production of more and more of the traded goods is shown to be beneficial. To some degree, this can be seen as a result of rational actors using the naturally available resources in an adequate way: e. g. the fertile plain specializing in grain production, with the woodland developing a more complex internal economy complemented by a diversified agricultural production often with more animals and handicrafts and proto-industrialization. The resulting regionalization does not unequivocally point towards unification or even national integration. Complex and strongly integrated regions, in constant trade with the outside world, are one of the conceivable results.

The specific feature of the economic specialization that is called proto-industrialization is its close link with agriculture: most of the people occupied combine industrial and agrarian skills in a seasonal pattern. Or, rather less abstractly: small peasants or crofters leave their land from time to time to work within industry, or, perhaps more in accordance with the ideal-type, take on work on commission. The rural environment was more than a setting with cheap labour; it was less constricted by the guilds and other monopolistic corporations.[11]

This line of argument could be used at the outset to discuss in what sense industrial structure and social conditions *create* regions in the interplay with political and cultural aspects. When the industrial structure is reshaped the new regions overlap the older ones.[12] A descriptive approach designed to discern regional differences in production develops a concept where the region is an outcome of the dynamics of the industrialization process.

One of the main explanatory challenges that the proto-industrialization theory was designed to meet was to determine what factors made a proto-industrial region take the step into full-fledged industrialization. Why was the metal industry of Gnosjö or the textile industry of Mark, both inland, east of Gothenburg, industrialized, while at the same time the textile industry of Southern Halland or Lower Norrland was de-industrialized? Competition from other industrial regions and a successfully commercialized agriculture are complementary explanations that have been suggested. The relative disadvantage of being an early starter has been recognized as a more structural force, sometimes put forward at least on the national level. The difficulties in modernizing a proto-industrial culture of work or work ethics into a modern disciplined use of time suited for factory production might be evaluated with even greater relevance from a regional perspective.[13]

The original theory has been subjected to many critical remarks and positive comments. Here we will concentrate on the ambiguous role ascribed to the region. On the one hand; if the emphasis is on the local context, tradition and inward interaction, this points towards a local or regional level. On the other hand the role of differentiation and market relations points towards overlapping relations and concentric circles in a constant dynamic which makes the isolation of any definite region an uncertain approach. On the other hand some patterns really seem to be transferred on regional bases, otherwise the stable areas of certain branches would hardly exist. Researchers have great difficulty in discerning the factor that creates this regionality.

In fig. 2.1, some of the more important proto-industrial regions that have been identified in the discussion have been mapped. It is also indicated which of them have successfully transferred their 'capital' into industrial society.

The Swedish word *saluslöjd*, market handicrafts, has preceded and often replaced the imported concept of proto-industrialization in a field of research where this type of occupation is understood as a subsidiary industry to agriculture. This industry increased greatly in the mid-eighteenth century and was at its peak in the 1840s. Two major regions are discernible:
1. South-West Sweden, sometimes divided into a northern and southern part.

Fig. 2.1: Proto-industrial areas in Sweden – and some that disappeared during the phase of industrialization

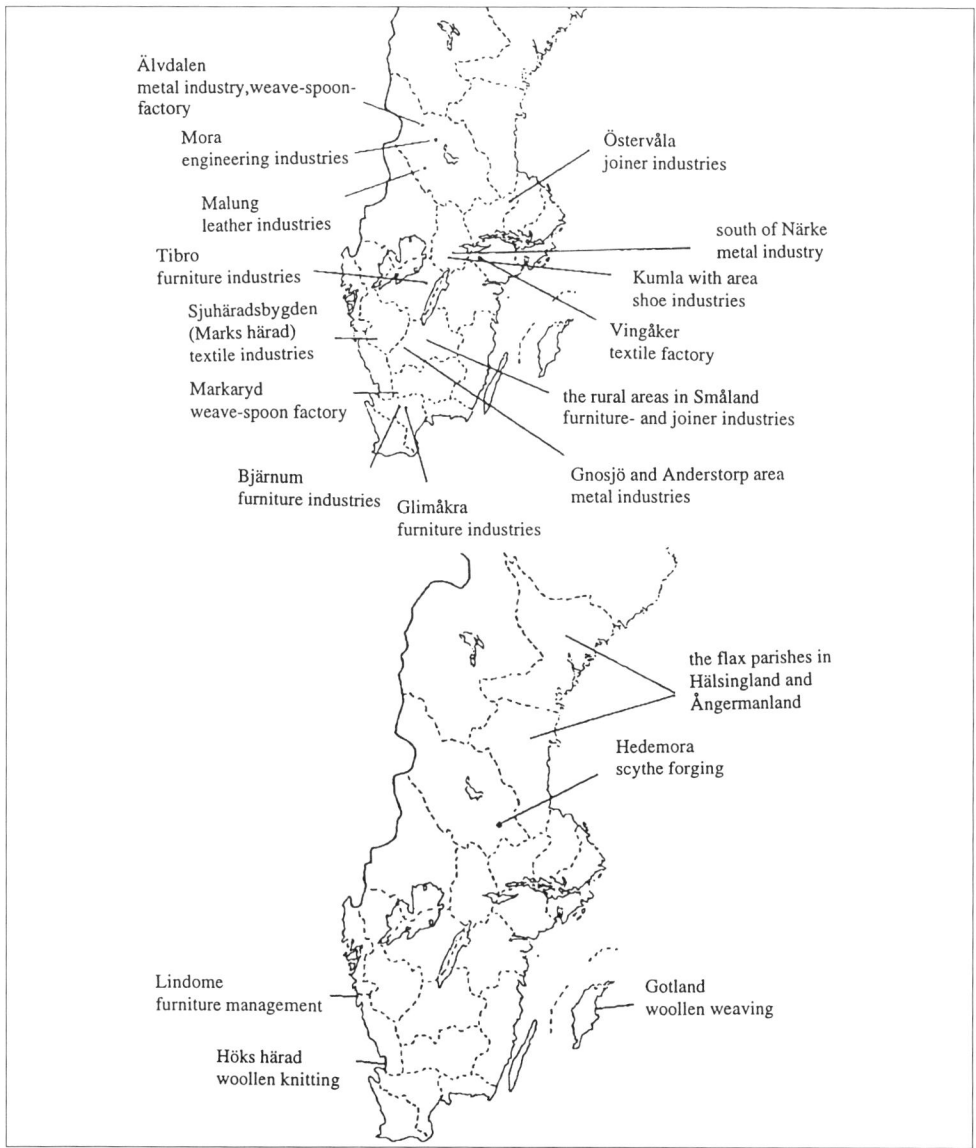

Source: Johansson: *Sveriges protoindustri*, 1993.

Textiles dominate but wooden and iron goods complement the textiles to form a diversified production profile within the region as a whole.

2. In the northern region, the province of Dalarna illustrates an even more noteworthy diversity of production: dressing of fur skins, machine shops, blacksmiths and woodworks were among the more prominent.

Several smaller regions can be distinguished, e. g. the shoemakers of Närke from the 1840s, but the above-mentioned are the most striking. Of course there were rural industries in the other Nordic countries, but they were less pronounced and had less obvious connections to the later industrialization process.[14]

For some obscure reasons, certain occupations have not been in focus as part of the proto-industrial process. Perhaps the sharp focus on the textile industry is linked to the fact that its subsequent development of capital accumulation and industrialization fits so neatly into neo-classical theory? In Sweden the radical transformation of the iron industry during industrialization may have contributed to keeping the early iron industry out of the discussion. They seemed to be two distinct phenomena. If this trade is studied as a long-term process, both the role of the state and the agrarian small-producer seem to be more central than in the idealized textile industry with its more modern capitalists. Vital Swedish industries such as sawmills and iron mills have for a long time been neglected in the proto-industrial discussion.[15]

If the sawmills are taken into account, the extent of proto-industrial activity will be expanded significantly in all Nordic countries except Denmark. There is no reason why these trades should be kept out of the proto-industrial picture in so far as the market was regional rather than local and those employed there worked for periods within the agrarian sector.

The subsequent establishment of the timber industry in areas where there had been a timber trade for centuries is easy to prove. Beside the material conditions of natural resources and market demands, the regional continuity and structure of knowledge can explain how its extremely rapid expansion was possible in the second half of the nineteenth century.[16] The importance of this process in the making of a region is not easy to summarize. The workforce was employed on a seasonal basis, but there was probably no interaction with agriculture: labour was needed in both trades at the same time of the year. A flood of seasonal workers, capital and entrepreneurs from e. g. Western Sweden might counteract the integrative tendency inherent in the regional exchange triggered by the timber and supplementary markets connected to the industry of coastal Norrland.

Not everywhere is the history one of long traditions. It might be suggested that the very rapid economic cycle for the timber industry in Western Jämtland 1880-1900 can be seen as an example of how an exploiting industry which does not meet a developed local counterpart, will have an almost colonial dynamic: a short swing upwards for a mono-cultural economy followed by a long period of more or less chronic crises.[17]

The iron industry should also be drawn into the discussion. It developed from a traditional, widespread and perhaps household-based spare-time occupation using easily accessible ore from mines and lakes to a concentrated industry centred around deep mines, blast furnaces, foundries and ironworks. As a consequence surrounding regions became important as producers of food for the mining communities, even in early modern Sweden. This was not always without tensions. Even if the most important cause of the Dacke rebellion was the rapid rise in state taxation, it was nevertheless ideologically possible and strategically rewarding for Gustav Vasa to blame the cattle-producing farmers of Southern Sweden for the bad conditions of the miners: Since they sold their cattle southwards, to Denmark, the price was higher for their fellow countrymen.[18] The disturbance of the regional distribution of production did not cause the war, but it was important enough to be used by the king to mobilize support to break the rebellion.

The exchange with foreign markets became ever more crucial. The state institutionalized the role of the towns in the interregional trade between *Bergslagen*, the region with the largest iron production in Middle Sweden, and Western Europe. Swedish iron was of major importance, both to Sweden when it was a great power in the seventeenth century and for Europe at large well into the eighteenth century. Sweden was one of the major exporting nations of a product that was central both to warfare and industrialization.

The state took an active part in shaping the regional structure of Bergslagen with privileges, regional/functional jurisdiction and regulation of trade. At the same time the organization of production gave a distinct nodal character to the relationship between the iron mill and its hinterland where peasants and blacksmiths, through a long and complicated development of accumulating debts and struggle over the everyday control of work, lost out to the 'owner' and changed from being a kind of free subcontractors to dependent workers. The tendency did not completely transform the older relations. Small-scale production existed within the more centralized and hierarchic organization until the early nineteenth century.[19]

The dramatic challenge to this order of things came with the new techniques that enabled the use of mineral coal instead of charcoal. The answer was large and self-contained production units and, as a consequence, the regional complexity of the large region of Bergslagen was simplified. The steelworks integrated a smaller region through an accentuated self-sufficiency and put it into direct contact with the world market through liberal market institutions and railways.[20]

This development, to some degree, seems to parallel what many observers describe as the modern scenario: local and regional dependencies interacting with a world market – leaving the national level behind. One difference from contemporary observations on local dynamics was the autocratic ambitions of the Swedish ironworks, the *bruk:* not only was self-sufficiency of food attained but a patriarchal self-contained institution was developed which was, at least superficially, quite the opposite of the flexibility and plurality of local interplay and resources considered relevant today. In fact the old local culture of the »bruk« is often identified as a major obstacle to restructuring a stagnating economy.[21]

Continuity in regional differentiation is striking, even if it is not so clear everywhere: concentration of the modern textile industry in Western Sweden, steelworks in Bergslagen, wood industry with furniture and house production in parts of Småland, and metal manufacturing in other parts. In other regions it is the mill tradition itself that has survived while production changed from iron to paper, pulp or glass.

The East-West distinction in Swedish history has also been discussed by economic historians. One of the subjects of discussion is the shifts in the relative strength of the regions over time. Johan Söderberg puts this dynamic into a model of commercialization. First it was Eastern Sweden which was the leading region of rural and early industrial production. After 1750 the momentum moved over to Western Sweden, a change attributed to the increase in grain production and the relative decline in iron production with Stockholm as a centre of commerce. In the second half of the nineteenth century, Eastern Sweden and Skåne regained the initiative due to the development of commercial agriculture in the plains.[22]

The regions of industrial society are perceived as mainly having an objective foundation, but now related to the demands of a new society. The criteria of a region in this perspective are changed to functional relations of a market character: service, labour, and goods create different regions and relations between town and hinterland, centre and periphery.

In pace with improved communications, and with immaterial value (knowledge) accounting for an increasingly large share of the total production, the concept of the region has met competition from »networks« and »nodes« as the key word for spatial relations.

Scientists, above all geographers, play a very active part in the creation of tools for a new perception of region that is wholly instrumental. Statistical surveys of Sweden draw up regional divisions adjusted to the existing units for data collection; municipalities are amalgamated on the basis of scientific measurements weighing commuting distances, tax base, service index of central places, and so on.

On a more general level, modern regional policy, from the 1960s onwards, has constantly modified its regional development areas in an attempt to refine methods for levelling out the distribution of jobs and incomes. Evaluations of long-term effects of this policy are notoriously difficult to make, since history cannot be re-played. In the economic development itself, there seem to be cyclic forces of concentration and deconcentration. It cannot be doubted, however, that in the present day it is the city regions which contribute via the state budget to the levels of income and service in sparsely populated areas. Whether this should be regarded as a small repayment of previous and current debts generated by »internal colonization« (hydroelectric power, iron ore, timber) or as a result of successful lobbying by skilled politicians from the sparsely populated areas in Norrland is above all an ideological question. But it is also, and not least, a question of historiography.

The creation of regional perspectives has had normative purposes, particularly in relation to the power of the state. Perhaps the efforts have ultimately had an integrative function in the creation of the nation state of Sweden.

Created regions

Without doubt there are regions in the history of Sweden. They do not, however, have an independent existence. Regions must be discovered, invented, or concealed by people or institutions – or by the scholars who are studying them. Historiography has mostly had the negative function of concealment while other cultural sciences have functioned as instruments or inspiration for cultural regionalism. It is evident that a regional cultural struggle arose parallel to nationalism in the second half of the nineteenth century. This process should not be regarded as naturally arising from the soil or from a folk culture, although such threads and arguments can be discovered.

Here I can only make some preliminary observations and interpretations. Federal relations between peripheral regions and the central power are the subject of increasing interest in research. Federal relations were obvious and strong in Sweden in the Middle Ages, after which they were counteracted in a highly systematic way by the central government. A regional opposition, represented by the provincial assemblies, county governors, clergymen, 'immigrant' élites, museum people, and regionally based historians, can be discerned to varying extents throughout history.

Educated regional élites appear to have played a prominent role in the articulation of regional sentiment in the introductory phase of modern nationalism. There were a surprising number of territorial »outsiders«. The initiative taken by the Swedish Finns to form the institutions of Fennoman, a linguistic nationalist movement in Finland, is telling, but only an extreme example of what 'strangers' created of regional identity, from Gothici regional writing by Peter Rudebeck in seventeenth-century Småland to the formation of regional ethnographic societies e. g. in Jämtland and numerous activists in local history societies in the twentieth century.

The local culture and history movement reinforced even more explicitly the patriotic currents at the turn of the century. National forces managed in various ways to take over or lead this cultural struggle along paths which actually strengthened national integration. In the regional history of Jämtland we can clearly see the relationship to the centre and the power of the state becoming one of conflict. Competition with neighbouring regions was a prominent feature already at the start of the twentieth century. In other self-confident regions, e. g. Värend in Småland, this political function was not articulated to the same extent. Generally, cultural regionalism was not politicized in a national context.

A reasonable interpretative context that has been suggested for understanding cultural regionalism is the growing class polarization in the late nineteenth century. Many measures were taken to prevent the established order from collapsing. One of the pictures that emerges in both culture and politics was the necessity of retaining a strong, steadfast, and loyal peasant class. Many nations created images of themselves and their folk identity with a heavy bias towards the agrarian features. This should probably not be seen as nostalgia but as short-term politics which also led to a number of reforms around the turn of the century to support small farms and to encourage the establishment of new owner-occupied smallholdings. Times of crisis caused by a rapid expansion or a sharp decline in population provide a seed-bed for a greater degree of politicization of the regional cultural struggle as could be exemplified by Jämtland both at the beginning and at the end of the twentieth century. We see similar patterns over much of Western Europe in the nineteenth century. The national assembly was seen by Adam Smith and most national liberal politicians who followed his ideas in the nineteenth century as the natural forum for the formulation of economic policy in line with capitalist modernization. In their eyes, regionalism was an obsolete phenomenon which was defended only by reactionary Italian city-states and German principalities.

A slightly different movement, perhaps less antagonistic to the nation than may appear at first sight, was cultural regionalism. The Swedish regional examples mentioned above were also to an important extent constructed, catalyzed and communicated by authors and could be supplemented with examples from Britain: Yorkshire took shape through the destinies of the Brontës and Dorset became a tourist attraction thanks to the novels of Thomas Hardy. Not even in Scotland did the regional literature develop its political potential. According to Harvie, there must be both an interventionist state and a local élite which wants to retain its position if this transformation is to occur. We have good examples of this in Scandinavia; although the Norwegian and Finnish cultural struggles would not have viewed themselves as regional but as national. The Nordic context is in fact not unlike the European examples of Britain or Spain, except that three Nordic regions, Norway, Finland and Iceland, managed to develop or recreate themselves as nations in a comparatively peaceful and definitive manner. Here the Saga literature was utilized both on a regional, national and Nordic level to promote intertwined identities. The German development is perhaps the best example of an intimate and clearly integrative interaction between historiography at regional and national level and the process of state formation.[23]

However, the general conditions necessary for organized regionalism which Seymour M. Lipset and Stein Rokkan formulated in the 1960s were not fulfilled in the Swedish regions on the level discussed here (that is Finland and Norway have not been considered in these terms):
– a spatially concentrated counter-culture;
– a region that is sufficiently separated from the centre quantitatively and qualitatively;
– economic independence of the centres of politics.[24]

Perhaps it is the second point that has the greatest explanatory power for the lack of organized regionalism because of the inclusive nature of Swedish political culture, marked by its ability to create institutionalized interaction between the people and the government. None of the criteria is met even by Norrland, where there has otherwise been a lot of discontent during the last decades. Today's »regionalism of rich regions« has a greater chance of fullfilling all three dimensions. Perhaps it is the region around the capital Stockholm that will be the leading regionalist power, disentangling itself from the state?

Regions stand in relation to each other. How can the power aspect in this be regarded? The German historians Gert

Zang, Wolfgang Hein, and also Michael Hechter have developed a historical materialist approach in which the region not only plays a historical role but will also presumably play an increasingly important role. According to them, it is only as a result of capitalism that regions become provinces, peripheral in relation to an accumulating centre.[25] This is a national specification of the global theories of the ideas of the dependence school.[26]

Christopher Harvie notes that the new bourgeois regionalism that emerged in the 1980s appears to be championed by the strongest who are looking for units other than the old national ones for developing cooperation and in particular their property and strength. In this connection, regions are held up not only as alternatives to the state, as smaller and better states, but also as having a different organization and ethos by viewing themselves as expressions of »civil society« and as such in opposition to the state – as was also seen in the debate in Sweden in the 1980s.[27]

It may be wise to distinguish between the demands of regional movements for political self-determination, state attempts at administrative division, and an analytically defined concept of region. Steen Bo Frandsen suggests *regionalism, regionalization,* and *region* for these three different meanings.[28] It is nevertheless striking how much interplay there is between these three categories: developments in Jämtland once again sum up very well the interaction of the three. This does not mean that they cannot be distinguished analytically, just that a deeper understanding of the links between them is ultimately the most important scientific task.

What is striking about Sörlin's broad survey of Western Europe is how much Sweden deviates from the Continent, in that radical regionalism is so weak in science, art, and literature alike. This judgement is certainly correct in broad outline. However, a slightly different picture has emerged in modern research: popular resistance to central government, arenas for political and judicial action as generators of identity, regional historiography, the local culture and history movement, and commercial strategies are just some examples of regional ambitions which need to be studied more. Just as research into nationalism makes a distinction between cultural, agitational, and massed political phases in the movement, it should likewise be possible to distinguish different degrees of articulation in regionalism. The question should be raised whether the less prominent regional line of argumentation in Swedish political culture can be explained from other perspectives than the predominant one: is the explanation really that the strong Swedish state has centralized power and crushed all resistance? I have argued that an integrationist political culture with strong popular support is a significant part of the explanation.[29]

Region and gender is another field of study that has been little considered, but it has great theoretical potential. Most of the regional boundaries mentioned above are more or less exclusively connected with male activities. It is not yet known what regional patterns can be observed in women's activities and patterns of interaction. It has been pointed out that these shortcomings also have a practical political significance, for example in the shaping of regional policy.

The regions of science

Geography is a sister science to history: it too seeks its identity in its perspective, not in having its object of study objectively fixed. In the chorological perspective the question is: how are things, people, and processes ordered in space? The subdiscipline that is called regional geography originally had its point of departure in postulated regions such as Africa, the Nordic countries, or Sweden, and studied what was characteristic of them, usually matters of physical geography, economy, and population. Relations between these were often, right up to the inter-war years, constructed in the form of natural determinism, or at least with a given point of departure in the perception of physical geographical conditions. An example of the way this school reasoned was the belief that the climate of Western Europe favoured hard work, enterprise, and hence the industrial breakthrough.

Although David Hannerberg, as late as 1971, recognized the justification of the approach because of the real need for descriptions of the situation in existing regions, its status was evidently felt to be problematic: non-systematic, descriptive and with an *a priori* selection of studied phenomena. Others, such as Staffan Helmfrid, saw the perspective as a phase that had been passed, and replaced in research after the 1960s by various instrumental concepts of region.[30] The scientific future lay in two other concepts of region: the *homogeneous* region and above all the *functional* region. The point of departure was still that actual characteristics in space were the basis for regional divisions. The two concepts presuppose this. The instrumental, subjective element comes in the selection of criteria, not as a property of the region in itself.[31]

Homogeneous regions are often described in ahistorical, natural terms, as applicable conditions in a relatively statically perceived early agrarian society. It is no coincidence that most examples of functional regions, which are based on relations between objects, differ from the discussion of homogeneous regions in being taken from modern times: the functions that are usually studied are linked to various aspects of the modernization process: urbanization, differentiation, and the division of labour. A single element in these processes can also be studied, such as commuting, or many elements, such as different types of shopping regions.

A region is homogeneous to an increasing extent the more uniform it is in one or more specific objective properties, the more often they occur, and the more aspects found together in the same space. Both qualitative and quantitative dimensions are thus considered. An example is the division of Sweden into regions according to farm types. A more complex regional division arises when the researcher asks whether farm types can be combined with village types or even more co-varying characteristics, to arrive at different regions of settlement geography. In methodological terms this can be achieved by looking for bundles of isolines for individual features, superimposed on maps. Where several lines are seen to coincide they are taken as a regional boundary defining the features on which the lines are based. Another, fundamentally more positivist approach is to try to correlate, for example, the appearance of farm settlements with explanatory factors of physical geography or climate.

A central model for the emergence of the functional view was Christaller's central place theory, in which a system of hierarchically ordered central places is distributed symmetrically in space. The biggest of these is so by virtue of its centrality, and the hinterland satisfies different functional needs in the interaction between the periphery and the centre. Tendencies to steadily increasing centrality in already large centres and an increasing number of regional centres are two features that have been observed in a long temporal perspective. Variants of this centre-periphery theory which emphasizes global power relations are the development theories developed by scholars such as André Gunder Frank and the world-system approach of Immanuel Wallerstein. Relations between centre and periphery determine the development potential of any region. Peripheral regions are systematically disfavoured by the historical centre in the capitalist world system, although long-term shifts do occur, for example the rise of first a semi-periphery in the Far East, which has since developed into an independent system.[32] This approach has also been used and tested in the analysis of the relation between »disfavoured« or exploited regions, for example, in Northern Scandinavia, and their respective central governments.

The modern tendency to see the region as a result of the scientist's more or less omnipotent choice of perspective can be seen as partly having arisen from the internal shift in the definition of regions in early regional geography: the *landscape region* was perceived as a unit naturally given by topographical conditions. By the turn of the century, the *natural region* had already become more of a framework, for example in the works of Vidal de la Blache, giving certain possibilities which actively deciding human beings could realize or not (so-called possibilism). In pace with the thematization of the cultivated landscape as another part of the landscape region, attention was first drawn to an organically and psychologically perceived relation between space and man. Later, in the inter-war years, it was man's economic functions that were the focus of interest in what was called the *living-space region*.[33] This can be seen as a territorial and also an ideological »little brother« to the term introduced by Rudolf Kjellén, *geopolitics*. It sought to capture the unity and the dynamics between territory, state, and people.[34]

The concepts of »geopolitics« and »living-space« were discredited by their use in political thought and action in Germany. The scientific perspective was redirected towards functionalism after World War II, with the concept of the functional region. Later, with the influence of ethnology and its concept of the region as originally homogeneous, attention was also directed towards the subjective elements, *the perceived region*. With this development, the next step was not hard to take. Not only feelings and subjective identities contain a created, subjective element. Both economic and mental processes in society can be regarded as constructed entities and thus available for reconstruction with deliberate purposes or unconscious desires as the driving forces. Today, finally, attention is increasingly focused on the constructivist elements in region-making.[35] While the earlier theories of the region were based on the assumption that the region actually exists in physical reality, the experience of arbitrariness in the definition and selection of criteria left a lasting feeling that regional division is at least as much produced by the scientist as by reality.

The definition of the concept of region has also become politically interesting, with a demand for regions that are available as objects for political measures. A concept that is too rigidly based on physical geography lacks this potential. Since the 1960s, scientific expertise has been enlisted in connection with reforms of regional divisions, later for regional policy, and today in connection with European integration and economic restructuring.

What place has been given to the region in the historical process and the scientific analysis in the discipline of history? What can be learned from other disciplines? Conversely, what can the historical perspective teach them?

In French historiography, influenced by geography, the regional monograph has long had a strong position in the analysis of early modern times. In Germany, too, traditional *Landesgeschichte* has been developed into a broad current of methodologically conscious regional history. Despite the large volume of research and the elaborate methodology, modern regional historians do not appear to find what they are looking for in the tradition, except as overlooked, latent possibilities. The »Landesgeschichte« of the turn of the century could thus be developed through the idea of *Geschichtslandschaft* in a collaboration between Karl Lamprecht's approach from cultural history and Friedrich Ratzel's insight that other regional boundaries may exist in dynamic tension with administrative boundaries: cultural-historical regions in conflict with the deliberately controlled regionalization of the territory of the state by the central government.

In general, modern historians often criticize earlier traditions for showing the same lack of spatial problematization as the national tradition. This critique, or the alternative that is proposed, is actually based on the same criteria for what is historically interesting! This means that the same processes, the same events are studied and acquire their value through the place they fill in a national historiography. Alternatively, regional history (like local history) is criticized for using the region, automatically and unquestioningly identified with a political territory, as a framework in which to assemble a number of disparate studies. In a more dynamic perspective, the region is presented as a created unit.[36]

The great conflict in Swedish historiography came with the breakthrough of a systematic criticism of sources as a scientific basis for history, led by the Weibull brothers in Lund in the early twentieth century. In this context it is worth noting that, just like the *Annales* school which arose at the same time in France, the movement started in a major provincial university, in opposition to the establishment in the central universities. The conflict made it natural to thematize the role of the province or the regions in scholarly work too: for example the Swedish journal of Scanian history, *Historisk tidskrift för Skåneland*, later prefixed with the title *Ale*, was founded by the Association for the History and Archaeology of the Scanian Provinces in the 1920s, and Lauritz Weibull published monographs on Skåne. Despite this, regional questions did not play any great or lasting role in Swedish historiography. It was instead research in human geography and slightly later in ethnology that used regional and geographical perspectives in a way more in keeping with international currents.

Much later, probably under the direct influence of the French *Annales* tradition, Swedish historiography acquired its first academic regional studies in the 1960s. The 1980s saw the publication of more problem-oriented literature using a rough division into Eastern and Western Sweden in a discussion of differences in the courses of historical change regarding such diverse questions as the civilization process, trade union organization, democratization, and religious culture. Other regions are studied in some works as natural regions with characteristic life-modes, in some cases extending over national boundaries. The »border« itself and border conflict have been treated more thoroughly and theoretically than any actual region in several projects under the leadership of Sven Tägil.[37]

The fact that the municipal reform of 1974 brought town and country together in one administrative unit nearly everywhere has meant that those who commission municipal histories often demand that they cover the whole municipality. A development within various disciplines towards local studies of rural communities shows tendencies in this direction, although they have long been stronger in economic and social questions.

It is perfectly clear, however, that attention to the political life of the countryside has only come at a late stage. In its earliest and fullest form it was seen in parish histories. The local history societies sponsored these at an early stage, sometimes engaging professional historians to write them. A number of such histories, many of them from Småland, were published in the 1980s. A few county histories also give a picture of rural conditions.

Hans Try, who carried out an evaluation of Swedish local history at the end of the 1980s, was struck by the lack of cohesion, the absence of a unifying theme, in most works, especially in the treatment of modern times. When the nineteenth and twentieth centuries are treated it is often on the basis of separate topics such as schools, social welfare, and so on, not infrequently showing an optimistic faith in progress as the only thread running right through the history.[38] The other feature of Swedish academic research in rural local history is how few of the works that are labelled this way, especially when seen in relation to the fairly large amount of traditionally strong urban history. This fact also applies to other countries, with certain exceptions. The »local« is usually seen as instances of a national development.[39]

Development in Norway and Finland has been different, since a local historical awareness had to champion national aspirations *vis-à-vis* a »foreign« government, which more and more people perceived as alien to a true nation state. A stronger and steadier historical interest was, and still is, nourished by this historical context, which is very different from that of Sweden. Yet even in the other Nordic countries there has been no strong movement to liberate the region as an independent unit. It is either the local or the national level that is the focus for identities and historiography. In this respect Denmark is more similar to Sweden. Although the Danish unitary state did not take shape until after 1864, it was nevertheless taken for granted as the frame of reference for historiography, and it is only recently that it has been questioned. It turns out that the tension between the national liberals of Copenhagen and the peasants of Jutland, who for a time were also politically represented in provincial parliaments, was a necessary key to Danish national history![40]

Regional levels in Sweden

The way regions are distinguished in research is influenced by several factors: The definitions of problem complexes have a strong position in contemporary social debate and exert an influence also on research. These complexes in turn are associated with the ongoing historical development of society. An agrarian society is intimately associated with topography and the distribution of soil types. The boundaries between forest and plains, coast and inland, or between climate zones, provide the foundation for the economic and cultural geography of agrarian society.

The greatest economic investments of an industrial society are the relocation of people, and thus of settlement from the countryside to the towns and the consequences of this; new communications make the overlapping networks increasingly free in relation to physical space, access to communications becomes more decisive than distance on the map. The concept of network challenges the region as the basic form of spatial organization.

Internal scientific traditions influence each discipline. The dominant role of nations as the primary and virtually the only legitimate region to study was, until recently, an inescapable maxim in Swedish historical research. As in geography, there is a development from realism and naturalism via instrumentalism to constructivism: regions are first viewed as consequences of physical geographical conditions; later the criteria for regions focus on characteristics (such as demographic differences) or relations (such as commuting to work).

One consequence of the broadening of the criteria is the emphasis on the arbitrary or instrumental way in which boundaries are drawn: the value of the boundaries is determined by how well they answer a question that has been raised. Today subjective aspects of the region are often brought into the argument: identity, culture, and the historical tradition. In one way, some research is once again putting an emphasis on natural regions, but these are now seen as changeable units in slow historical processes. With this in mind, the features of continuity, especially regarding institutions, seem remarkable. Medieval forms of organization, as well as place systems, appear vigorous through their combination of stable forms and flexible content. It is essential to arrive at a better understanding of how this relative continuity is maintained and reconstructed through shifts of identity and changes in the meaning of concepts, and the interaction with the changing demands and opportunities of technology and labour.

Spatial identity is expressed on a number of territorial levels and on the basis of a number of principles: size plays a role, the degree of overlap or the sharpness of the boundaries between regions, the intensity of interaction within and between regions, the degree of institutionalization. Legitimacy and power structures do not just complicate the discussion but are also the reason why the question is interesting in the first place. The number of possible combinations, however, means that the region cannot have a perfectly sharp outline, either in practice or in theory, especially if the ambition is to survey a long time-perspective.

I shall nevertheless attempt to discern a rough pattern, as a tentative summary which can serve as a basis both for discussion and for further research. It has been possible to develop only parts of the outlined argumentation in detail above.

Regional identities can be drawn as a series of concentric circles. This ignores the fact that these are broken by other concentric bases for identification and their inner segmentation: class, gender, etc. Regionality *may* be developed on six different levels:
I. local community (municipality, settlement unit)
II. functional region (market relations etc.)
III. county, province
IV. nation
V. culture circle
VI. mankind

In general it can be said that the predominant factors for identities on a spatial level close to the individual (*region I*) are functional relations and existential living conditions connected with work, neighbourhood relations, organic community, and local self-government. The institutionalization of social bonds can be strong, formal, or informal. For a long time, however, they are expressed in a rich but relatively undifferentiated community such as the diverse but superficially uniform institutions of the church congregation or municipal self-government. Through time the forms of organization of civil society emerge, formally richly differentiated associations and club activities. Actually they are less diversified than might appear. For example, belonging to a sport club involves much more than the activity of, say, football, that it is concerned with. To some extent, municipal politics, sports, the temperance movement, and work can be interchangeable as expressive creators of local community with a scope for what has been called »ideal revival«.[41]

Region II for a long time had a strongly institutionalized form in the district-court area. This could coincide to a greater or lesser extent with the ecclesiastical deanery and the state bailiwicks. The community was not confined to judicial matters but helped to resolve conflicts in a broad spectrum of social issues and in relations between the local community and the state. A regional centre in the form of a town or market allows an opportunity for functional relations of the town/hinterland kind, which can acquire a region-forming character with the declining significance of the district-court area as a generator of community. Later, clubs and associations often form another unit, the district, at this level. With the municipal reforms of the 1950s to the 1970s, the older parish-based institutions were amalgamated and firmly placed into the grid of welfare state policy, the political/administrative level catching up with this development, but on the other hand leaving both higher and lower regional levels with a weak institutional articulation, especially in the political dimension.

It is probable that the county (*region III*), despite its institutional continuity, reinforced by the establishment of the county council and later local radio stations, has not developed into a region to the extent that might have been expected. If this is true, it may be worth bearing it in mind in attempts to create new parliamentary units with broad popular support and involvement.

The province is perhaps the most baffling and most interesting basis of regional identity. From having played a highly significant role throughout the Middle Ages as a competitor of the state, it has, precisely for that reason, been deprived of its political and judicial institutional power in modern times. This level nevertheless appears to be decisive not least for the representation of individual belonging in national contexts which was to be revived in the era of nationalism. Identifying oneself as a Jämtlander, Värmlander, or Smålander is charged with more symbolic meaning than saying that one comes from Östersund, Karlstad, or Kalmar. The constructive and conscious production of symbols plays a much greater role here; a regional historical consciousness is linked to and emphasizes elements in a homogeneous regional perception which especially articulates cultural unity.

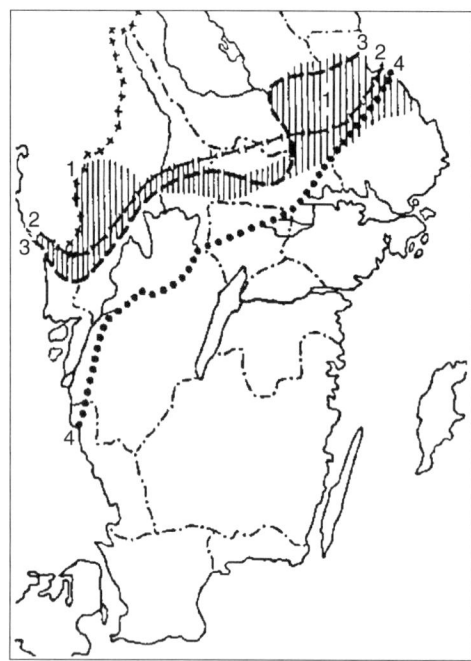

Fig. 2.2: The most important boundaries associated with the *limes Norrlandicus*, the border of the North

Note: The boundaries are seen on the background of the border of the provinces in Southern Sweden: 1. the northern limit of oxen as draught animals, 2. the southern limit of transhumance, 3. the northern limit of double yoke, 4. the northern limit of the four-wheeled wagon.
Source: Erixon: *Kulturgeografiska synpunkter ...*, 1949, p. 158. I have added a line showing the approximate position of the much-discussed boundary between East and West Sweden.

National identity (*region IV*) has been weaker in Sweden since World War II, and more critically articulated than in many countries, perhaps because the country has not been seriously threatened by neighbours for a long time, or perhaps because relative homogeneity or at least an unusually small degree of antagonistic regional identities has developed at lower levels. In an earlier phase a strong nationally oriented culture developed, interacting with a regional cultural struggle led by regional élites. Parts of the national identity and distinctiveness played together in an intensive exchange of opinions around the turn of the century. Such a dynamic national development was not seen again until the 1990s.

In the identification with the culture circle (*region V*), there is in Sweden, as in the rest of Western Europe, a feeling of being specially selected, combined with a profound self-criticism. In earlier decades, this was channelled into a criticism of capitalism, but now it usually takes the form of an environmental awareness. Both these trends open the door to an identification with a global community which, whether one admits it or not, goes hand in hand with the globalization of the economy and of mass-produced culture (*region VI*).

The complexity of relations between local, regional, and national affiliation can be found in every country, but it naturally varies, depending on actual differences between countries, and particularly because of the production of ideologies. France, for example, has on the one hand one of the most centralized political systems in the Western World, with administrative boundaries which demonstratively avoid coinciding with cultural regions, and yet on the other hand possesses regional cultures which have remained alive through the ages, despite the strong emphasis of the educational system, and not least of historiography, on the shared (radical) national destiny. Or perhaps this is precisely why the official national historiography has been so strongly aiming to bridge regional differences. In any case, this cloven soul appears to be reproduced in the social sciences in what C. Harvie has called »academic apartheid«: political science sees no regions, no local politics, while cultural studies are pioneers in the regionalization of knowledge.[42]

Regionality is formed in a complex interplay between structural and dynamic forces. A seemingly permanent structural tension is found between the central government and the local community: competing aspirations to sovereignty, with their different territorial identifications and resource bases, lead to an unfinished tug of war over the drawing of boundaries in a broad sense. The outcome is partly determined by the means or strategies that are chosen or developed in the struggle. Which strategy will dominate: conquest, or integration through participation and consensus?

In a dynamic perspective, developments in society change the contents of regional identity. There have been many attempts to describe this change in detail. Perhaps the classical dichotomy of development from *Gemeinschaft* to *Gesellschaft* is the most apt description of regionality as it has evolved: Close-knit, homogeneous regions are assumed to have been replaced by rationally calculated, negotiated, contract-based relations.

Without doubt, this expresses a dominating development trend. The new ethnic problems of recent years – or rather the ethnicization of recent years' problems – and also the continued role of the province in identity formation, along with the weak position of the county as an administrative unit, make the development of regional identity less easily calculable than might be thought.

Feudal society presupposed, among other things, a complicated network of rights defining the opportunities and obligations of the individual. The modernization process and the growth of capitalism meant that these rights were more and more closely tied together with individual rights of ownership, modern »property rights«. An object or a natural resource could be controlled and handled in all respects by one single owner. This made it possible for private persons to act as individual owners on the market without constant negotiations with a number of interested parties in interwoven and overlapping relationships. Space could increasingly be mastered by means of territorially defined ownership. During this epoch, the state was an absolutely essential body in monopolizing and centralizing the right to settle this struggle between individual and collective rights. In its own exercise of power, territorial principles and rational bureaucracy were two important elements enabling the state to penetrate what had formerly been peripheral territories. The aim was to create a country where everybody was, in legal terms, equally far from each other and equally close to the power of the state. Regions were created and abstracted as a means of gaining territorial control.

At the same time, this provided a model for action which could be used by forces and communities who had other purposes, who wanted to achieve autonomy and satisfy their ambitions through organization at a more local or regional level. A more distinct division between state and region arose, which means that they are often seen as two different organizational principles, as part of the state-society dichotomy.

Developments in the twentieth century have been seen as a refeudalization in more than one way: expanding corporativism, the dissolution of bourgeois public spheres, late-modern tendencies to divide and trade in genes, patented forms, and expectations, are in a way deconstructing the unambiguous and individual property rights once again. Refeudalization can also be observed in the distribution of rights at different levels of society: what type of rights and powers should be associated with which territorial level is no longer as self-evident as it was a few years ago. The internationalization of ties of dependence means that power and regionality are no longer so closely linked. Perhaps we will see the state shedding parts of its »natural« competence to parallel organizations. The idea of a corporative society is slowly being reinvented by social scientists![43]

This does not mean, however, that the ties have ceased to exist. However, the power of regionalism will come less from conflicts between state and society, and will more concern community-creating processes associated with people's views of the good life.[44] This in turn makes what kind of regionality is articulated into a highly subjective, political, and ideological question. It has always been thus, but it will be seen more and more as an objective fact as this process continues. It is no coincidence that it was in the 1980s that nations and nationalism were disclosed as »imagined communities«.[45]

Bibliography

Anderson, Benedict: *Imagined communities*, rev. and extended ed., London/Verso 1991.
Aronsson, Peter: Nations, Provinces and Re-

gions: A Scandinavian Perspective, *Identities, Nations, Provinces and Regions*, eds. Isabel Burdiel and James Casey, Norwich 1999.

Aronsson, Peter: *Regionernas roll i Sveriges historia*, Fritzes 1995.

Aronsson, Peter: Swedish Rural Society and Political Culture: The Eighteenth- and Nineteenth-Century Experience, *Rural History*, vol. 3, 1992:1, pp. 41-57.

Aronsson, Peter (ed.): *The making of regions in Sweden and Germany: culture and identity, religion and economy in a comparative perspective*, Växjö 1998.

Aronsson, Peter: Vem får vara med – och hur? Om delaktighet i historien, *Civilt samhälle kontra offentlig sektor*, SNS 1995. (1995a)

Bandyopadhyaya, Jayantanuja: *North over South. A non-Western Perspective of International Relations*, Brighton 1982.

Berman, Harold: *Law and Revolution. The formation of the Western Legal Tradition*, Cambridge, Mass. 1983.

Björklund, J. & Stenlund, H.: Regionala löner och levnadskostnader i Norrland 1910-1939, *Levnadsnivåns utveckling i Sverige. Två aspekter*, Meddelande från institutionen för ekonomisk historia, Umeå universitet, nr. 4, 1984.

Braudel, Fernand: *The Identity of France. History and Environment*, vol. I, Fontana Press 1989.

Braudel, Fernand: *The Identity of France. People and Production*, vol. II, Fontana Press 1991.

Braudel, Fernand: *Vardagslivets strukturer. Det möjligas gänser. Civilisation och kapitalism 1400-1800*, Band 1, Stockholm 1981.

Burke, Peter: *Annales-skolan. En introduktion*, Daidalos 1992.

Clarkson, L. A.: *Proto-Industrialization: The First Phase of Industrialization*, MacMillan 1991.

Dann, Otto: Die Region als Gegenstand der Geschichtswissenschaft, *Archiv für Sozialgeschichte*, vol. 23, 1983, p. 652-661.

Edquist, Olle: *Guld och gröna skogar. Sågverksepoken i västra Jämtland 1880-1914. En studie av teknik och regional utveckling i skogsbygd*, Fornvårdaren 22, Jämtlands läns museum, 1989.

Eriksen, Sidsel: *Vækkelse og afholdsbevægelse. Et bidrag til studiet af den svenske og danske folkekultur*, Scandia, 1989:2.

Erixon, Sigurd: Kulturgeografiska synpunkter på vår äldsta åkerbrukskultur, *SGÅ*, 1949.

Florén, Anders: *Disciplinering och konflikt. Den sociala organiseringen av arbetet, Jäders bruk 1640-1750*, Studia Historica Upsaliensia 147, Uppsala 1987. (Diss.)

Florén, Anders & Rydén, Göran: *Arbete, hushåll och region. Tankar om industrialiseringsprocesser och den svenska järnhanteringen*, Uppsala Papers in Economic History, Uppsala 1992.

Frandsen, Steen Bo: *Opdagelsen af Jylland. Den regionale dimension i Danmarkshistorien 1814-1864*, Aarhus 1996. (Diss.)

Frank, André Gunder: *On capitalist underdevelopment*, Oxford U.P. 1975.

Gadd, Carl-Johan: *Självhushåll eller arbetsdelning? Svenskt lant- och stadshantverk ca 1400-1860*, Meddelanden från ekonomisk-historiska institutionen vid Göteborgs universitet 64, Göteborg 1991.

Gellner, Ernest: *Nation and nationalism*, 1983. (Blackwell, 1993)

Gidlund, Janerik & Sörlin, Sverker: *Det europeiska kalejdoskopet*, SNS 1993.

Gregory, D.: The production of regions in England's industrial revolution, *Journal of historical geography*, vol. 14, no. 1, 1988.

Gustafsson, Harald: Statsbildning och territoriell integration. Linjer i nyare forskning, en nordisk ansats samt ett bidrag till 1500-talets svenska politiska geografi, *Scandia*, 1991:2.

Hannerberg: *Svenskt agrarsamhälle under 1200 år. Gård och åker. Skörd och boskap*, Stockholm 1971.

Haraldsson, Kjell: Om proto-industri, det industriella genombrottet och industrins lokalisering, *Nordisk samhällsgeografisk tidskrift*, nr. 4, 1986.

Harvie, Christopher: *The Rise of Regional Europe*, Routledge 1994.

Hellquist, Elof: *Svensk etymologisk ordbok*, Liber-Läromedel 1980.

Helmfrid, Staffan: Bruk och missbruk av regionbegreppet. Något om regionindelningsproblem och -metoder, *Region och samhälle*, Ymer 1969.

Herlitz, Urban: *Restadtegen i världsekonomin. Lokala studier av befolkningstillväxt, jordbruksproduktion och fördelning i Västsverige 1800-1860*, Meddelanden från ekonomisk-historiska institutionen vid Göteborgs universitet 58, Göteborg 1988. (Diss.)

Hobsbawm, E. & Ranger, T. (eds.): *The Invention of Tradition*, CUP Canto, 1992.

Hoppe, Göran & Langton, John: *Flows of Labour in the Early Phase of Capitalist Development:*

Regional integration

The Time-Geography of Longitudinal Migration Paths in Nineteenth Century Sweden, Historical Geography Research Series no. 29, Geo Books, Norwich 1992.

Hoppe, Göran & Langton, John: Patterns of Migration and Regional Identity: Economic Development, Social Change and the Lifepaths of Individuals in Nineteenth Century Vadstena, *Naming, Region and Identity*, ed. D. Postles, Leicester University Press 1993.

Hubbard, William H. et al. (eds.): *Making a Historical Culture. Historiography in Norway*, Scandinavian University Press 1995.

Hudson, Pat (ed.): *Regions and industries. A perspective on industrial revolution in Britain*, CUP 1993.

Hutchinson, John & Smith, Anthony D. (eds.): *Nationalism*, OUP 1994.

Isacson, Maths & Magnusson, Lars: *Proto-industrialisation in Scandinavia. Craft Skills in the Industrial Revolution*, Berg 1987.

Isacson, Maths & Magnusson, Lars: *Vägen till fabrikerna. Industriell tradition och yrkeskunnande i Sverige under 1800-talet*, Gidlunds 1983.

Johansson, Per-Göran: *Sveriges protoindustri. En geografisk och bibliografisk översikt 1750-1850*, D-uppsats i historia, Högskolan i Växjö 1993.

Jonsson, Per: *Finntorparna i Mången*, Lund 1988. (Diss.)

Larsson, Lars-Olof: *Bönder och gårdar i stormaktspolitikens skugga. Studier kring hemmansklyvning, godsbildning och mantalssättning i Sverige 1625-1750*, Acta Wexionensia, Serie 1, History & Geography 3, Växjö 1983.

Larsson, Lars-Olof: *Dackeland*, Stockholm 1979.

Lefebvre, Henri: *The Production of Space*, Blackwell 1991.

Lindström, Dag: *Skrå, stad och stat. Stockholm, Malmö och Bergen ca. 1350-1622*, Studia Historica Upsaliensia 163, Uppsala 1991. (Diss.)

Lipset, Seymour & Rokkan, Stein: Cleavage Structures, Party Systems and Voter Alignment, *Party Systems and Voter Alignments*, eds. Lipset & Rokkan, New York 1967.

Lunden, Kåre: Historisk syntese, særleg funksjon i forhold til offentligheita – ukollegiale refleksjonar, *Historien og historikerne i Norden efter 1965*, Studier i historisk metode XXI, Aarhus 1991.

Lundqvist, Karl-Johan & Olander, Lars-Olof: *Sydostregionen. Hemmabas för internationell konkurrens?* Länsstyrelsen i Kalmar län informerar, Meddelande 1993:12.

Mendels, F.: Proto-industrialization: The first phase of the industrialization process, *Journal of Economic History*, vol. XXXII, 1972.

Nordström, Olof: *Lessebo och trakterna kring sjön Läen 1860 till 1940*, Lessebo kulturnämnd 1993.

Nordström, Olof: *Relationerna mellan bruk och omland i östra Småland 1750-1900*, Meddelanden från Lunds universitets geografiska institution, Avhandlingar XXII, Lund 1952. (Diss.)

Ousager, Asger: Nationernes denationalisering, *Scandia*, 1994:1.

Paasi, Anssi: *Territories, boundaries and consciousness*, Chichester: Wiley 1995.

Paasi, Anssi: The institutionalization of regions: a theoretical framework for understanding of the emergence of regions and the constitution of regional identity, *Fennia*, 164:1, 1986.

Pollard, Sidney (ed.): *Region und Industrialisierung*, Göttingen 1980.

Regionalgeschichte: ein Ansatz zur Erforschung regionaler Identität, *Informationen zur Raumentwicklung*, Heft 11, Bundesforschungsanstalt für Landeskunde und Raumordnung, Bonn 1993.

Sjöberg, Maria: *Järn och jord. Bergsmän på 1700-talet*, Stads- och kommunhistoriska Institutet, Studier i stads- och kommunhistoria 9, Stockholm 1993. (Diss.)

Spruyt, Hendrik: *The Sovereign State and Its Competitors*, Princeton University Press 1994.

Strömholm, Stig: »Hugg odjuret Staten i stycken ...«, SvD 94 05 03.

Studying Boundary Conflicts. A Theoretical Framework, Lund studies in international history nr 9, Lund 1977.

Söderberg, Johan: A Long-Term Perspective on Regional Economic Development in Sweden, Ca. 1550-1914, *The Scandinavian Economic History Review*, 1984:1.

Söderberg, Johan: *Civilisering, marknad och våld i Sverige 1750-1870. En regional analys*, Almqvist & Wiksell International 1993.

Sörlin, Sverker: *Framtidslandet. Debatten om Norrland och naturresurserna under det industriella genombrottet*, Umeå (Carlssons) 1988. (Diss.)

Taylor, Charles: *Sources of the Self: The Making of the Modern Identity*, Harvard University Press 1989.

Tilly, Charles: Western State-Making and Theories of Political Transformation, *The Formation of National States in Western Europe*, ed. Charles Tilly, Princeton University Press 1975.

Try, Hans: Lokal og regional historie, *Historia i belysning. Sex perspektiv på svensk historisk forskning. En utvärdering av svensk historisk forskning utförd på uppdrag av humanistisk-samhällsvetenskapliga forskningsrådet och universitets- och högskoleämbetet*, ed. Rolf Danielsen et al., Uppsala 1988.

Tägil, Sven (ed.): *Europa – historiens återkomst*, Gidlunds 1992.

Törnqvist, Gunnar: Europa – territoriet och den nya rörligheten, *Närhet och nätverk – regionernas återkomst*, eds. Sven Tägil, Hans-Åke Persson and Solveig Ståhl, Meddelanden från Erik Philip-Sörensens Stiftelse 5, 1994.

Wallerstein, Immanuel: *The Modern World-system*, I-III, Academic Press, New York 1974-1989.

Weber, Eugen: *Peasants into Frenchmen. The modernization of Rural France, 1870-1914*, Stanford University Press, 1976.

Wehner, Burkhard: *Nationalstaat, Solidarstaat, Effizienzstaat*, Darmstadt 1992.

Winberg, Christer: Öst och Väst i svensk samhällsutveckling, *Lokalt, Regionalt, Centralt – analysnivåer i historisk forskning*, ed. Ingrid Hammarström, Stadshistoriska Institutet, Studier i stads- och kommunhistoria, 3, Stockholm 1988.

Ylikangas, Heikki: The Historical Connections of European Peasant Revolts, *Scandinavian Journal of History*, 1991:2.

Ågren, Katarina: För överlevnad och till lyst. Den svenska slöjdens regionala betydelse, *Den regionala särarten*, eds. Barbro Blomberg & Sven-Olof Lindqvist, Studentlitteratur 1994.

Ågren, Maria: *Jord och Gäld. Social skiktning och rättslig konflikt i södra Dalarna ca 1650-1850*, Studia Historica Upsaliensia 166, Uppsala 1992. (Diss.)

Österberg, Eva: Agrar-ekonomisk utveckling, ägostrukturer och sociala oroligheter: de nordiska länderna ca 1300-1600, *Scandia*, 1979:2.

Österberg, Eva: Social Arena or Theatre of Power. The courts, crime and the early modern state in Sweden, *Maktpolitik och husfrid. Studier i internationell och svensk historia tillägnade Göran Rystad*, Lund 1991.

Notes

1. Tilly 1975, Hutchinsen & Smith 1994, cit. Törnqvist 1994, p. 23.
2. Hellquist: *Svensk etymologisk ordbok*.
3. Cf. Tägil 1992, p. 17 and Harvie 1994, who uses the political interaction between the nation and the next sublevel to define a region. Gidlund & Sörlin 1993.
4. Cf. Spruyt 1994. Berman 1983 on the stateness of early church institutions; Lindström 1991 on the Hanseatic League and Gustafsson 1991.
5. Most of the text is compiled and revised from Aronsson 1995, where more elaborate references and a more thorough theoretical argumentation are given.
6. The rebellion in the south of Sweden led by Nils Dacke in the 1540s and the last major peasant uprising, the War of Clubs in Finland in the 1590s, were the major challenges to the increased taxation and centralized government of Sweden in the early modern period. The military force of the provinces was to some extent utilized by the king in the formation of the provincial regiments. Larsson 1979, Ylikangas 1991, Österberg 1979.
7. On the balance between local and central power see Österberg 1991 and Aronsson 1992.
8. Winberg 1988, Söderberg 1993.
9. Florén & Rydén 1992, p. 89ff.
10. Pollard 1980; Hudson 1993, Dann 1983, Haraldsson 1986; Gadd 1991.
11. Mendels 1972; Hoppe & Langton 1992, 1993; Florén & Rydén 1992 deal with the overlooked importance of the iron industry in proto-industrialization; Gadd 1991 treats the crafts in a broad perspective; also Isacson & Magnusson 1987; Clarkson 1991. Regional diversity in wages seems to be equalised only when the centralized wage negotiations take place in the 1930s. E.g. Björklund & Stenlund 1984.
12. Lefebvre 1991; Gregory 1988, taken from Florén & Rydén 1992, p. 92ff.
13. Isacson & Magnusson 1983.
14. Isacson & Magnusson 1987, p. 25-37. A more ethnografic perspective in Ågren 1994.
15. Florén & Rydén 1992.
16. Haraldsson 1986.

17 Edquist 1989.
18 Florén & Rydén 1992, p. 95ff; Larsson 1979.
19 Florén 1987; Ågren 1992; Jonsson 1988; Florén & Rydén 1992; Sjöberg 1993; Larsson 1983; Nordström 1952.
20 Florén & Rydén 1992, p. 104ff. Nordström 1952, Nordström 1993.
21 Lundqvist & Olander 1993.
22 Herlitz 1988, p. 82-95, 100f; Söderberg 1984.
23 Harvie 1994, p. 18ff; Aronsson 1999. Recent German research findings in, e.g. *Regionalgeschichte: ein Ansatz zur Erforschung regionaler Identität* 1993.
24 Lipset & Rokkan 1967, cited here from Sörlin 1988, p. 257.
25 Dann 1983; Tägil 1992, pp. 26f.
26 Frank 1975, Wallerstein 1974–1989.
27 Aronsson 1995; Harvie 1994.
28 Frandsen 1996.
29 Aronsson 1992.
30 Hannerberg 1971, pp. 133f; Helmfrid 1969.
31 A somewhat different description of the difference between regional geography before and after World War II is given by Anssi Paasi, who stresses how the object-defined region is connected with chorological thinking which focuses on territorial differentiation, while the functional, interactive perspective focusing on distance/nearness is characterized by spatial thinking. Paasi 1986, p. 115.
32 Frank 1975; Wallerstein 1974-1989; Braudel 1981; Bandyopadhyaya 1982.
33 Paasi 1986, pp. 137f. Also Paasi 1995.
34 Geopolitik in: *Svensk uppslagsbok*.
35 Paasi 1986.
36 Burke 1992. *Regionalgeschichte: ein Ansatz zur Erforschung regionaler Identität* 1993; Dann 1983.
37 See e.g. *Studying Boundary Conflicts: A Theoretical Framework* 1977.
38 Try 1988.
39 A search in the international database Historical Abstracts for »rural & politics« gives 126 matches, but the majority concern the Third World, and the second largest group comprises early modern conditions in Central Europe, France, and England. A few works thematize politics in the German countryside in the Nazi period. The rest are on diverse topics.
40 Frandsen 1996; Hubbard et al. 1995. My survey is far from total, and I will gladly be contradicted on this point. A tendency towards an increasing number of commissioned works at county and district level may possibly be observed today. Perhaps institutions whose relevance is being questioned are trying in this way to obtain historical legitimacy. See the German development in *Regionalgeschichte: ein Ansatz zur Erforschung regionaler Identität* 1993.
41 Eriksen 1989.
42 Harvie 1994, pp. 37 and 58; Weber 1976; Braudel 1989 and 1991.
43 E.g. Wehner 1992, discussed by Strömholm 1994.
44 Taylor 1989. See also the discussion and references in Aronsson 1995a.
45 Hobsbawm & Ranger 1992; Anderson 1991; Gellner 1993. Cf. Ousager 1994, who is more critical of the constructivist approach which has otherwise been so triumphant in the academic world, and more favourably disposed to a substantial perspective. See also Lunden 1991.

Chapter 3
Regions and regional history in Norway

By Harald Winge

This article presents a brief and general survey of Norwegian regional history, as it has been written by historians, against a background of general reflections with regard to the concept of »region«. These reflections are based mainly on knowledge of Norwegian history and natural features, which means that I shall mostly be referring to regions at a sub-national level. When nothing else is said, I am usually referring to early modern times.

I. *The concept of region*

Terminology

The word region, as well as the word district, has so far had no established technical definition among Norwegian historians, and both words seem to have been used rather indiscriminately in the past. Here I will apply the following definitions:

The word *district* will be used to describe any sub-national area larger than one local community (municipality), without saying anything about possible topographical, historical or cultural distinctiveness or coherence. A district is simply a geographical area smaller than the country but greater than individual municipalities. The term *region*, on the other hand, will be used to denote an area which can be delimited on the basis of cultural criteria. The boundaries of a region may coincide, totally or partly, with natural or administrative boundaries, but they do not have to do so; a region is primarily a culturally defined and delimited area.

Essential characteristics of a region

Normally a region consists of a continuous area with a culture, in a broad sense of the word, that shows some sort of basic homogeneity, and which at the same time is clearly distinguishable from the culture of other, adjacent, regions. The whole world, of course, consists of cultural regions.

The cultural criteria that may serve to distinguish a region from its surroundings must refer to traits sufficiently conspicuous or basic to allow the observer of today, or the historian analyzing the past, to identify the region. The process of identification will demand the use of comparative methods that will allow the historian to establish cultural boundaries between the region in question and its surroundings. In principle, cultural traits of all kinds may contribute to the constitution of a region, but clearly cultural elements of some »weight« have to be involved.

These basic elements will often have to be sought in the economic life of an area, or they will be most conspicuous there. But they may also, possibly, be related primarily to social conditions or to the organization of society, or they may perhaps be connected basically to religious practice or even to the prevailing mentality among the inhabitants. In most cases, however, the distribution of natural resources in the area and the exploitation of these resources by the people living there, i.e. the ecosystem, will play a decisive part in the formation of regions.

Homogeneity versus diversity

Normally, cultural homogeneity is thought of as the fundamental criterion of a region. Every region thus characterized will be topographically and economically homogeneous, with similar or nearly similar living conditions in all the associated communities. Typical examples in Norway are farming districts like Jæren or Romerike, or fishing districts along the coast.

However, even certain kinds of cultural diversity may have considerable regionalizing effect. In these cases the area will be topographically varied, and will consist of communities utilizing different kinds of resources. Taken as a whole, however, the communities involved will complement each other in such a way that together they make up an interdependent, coherent unit. I shall call complementary cultural diversity *integrational diversity*, as opposed to disintegrational diversity, which, of course, will cause an area to fall apart into independent regions.

In Norway, each of the greater valleys in the southeastern part of the country and every fjord area along the coast may be regarded as a distinctive region, but this is certainly not because the culture is homogeneous from one end of a certain valley or fjord to the other. On the contrary, it is easy to observe considerable cultural differences between lower, middle and upper parts of valleys, and between inner, middle and outer parts of most fjords, differences that are mainly due to variations in natural resources. One may therefore be justified in regarding, in some connections, any valley or fjord of some length as consisting of not one, but two, and sometimes even three separate, individually homogeneous regions. However, the cultural differences that exist between these adjacent parts will normally be complementary, the result being a functional division of labour between the areas involved. As an example, coastal areas will frequently have little or no woodland, and will therefore need regular supplies of timber, wooden goods and wood fuel from inner fjord districts, usually in exchange for fish products.

On the other hand, the outer, coastal part of a fjord may be regarded in other connections not as part of a fjord region, but of a wider coastal region, including the outer parts of several neighbouring fjords.

All this should be taken as a reminder of the fact that the regional pattern of an area will never be indisputable. It will always be possible to establish alternative patterns.

Regions and regional history in Norway

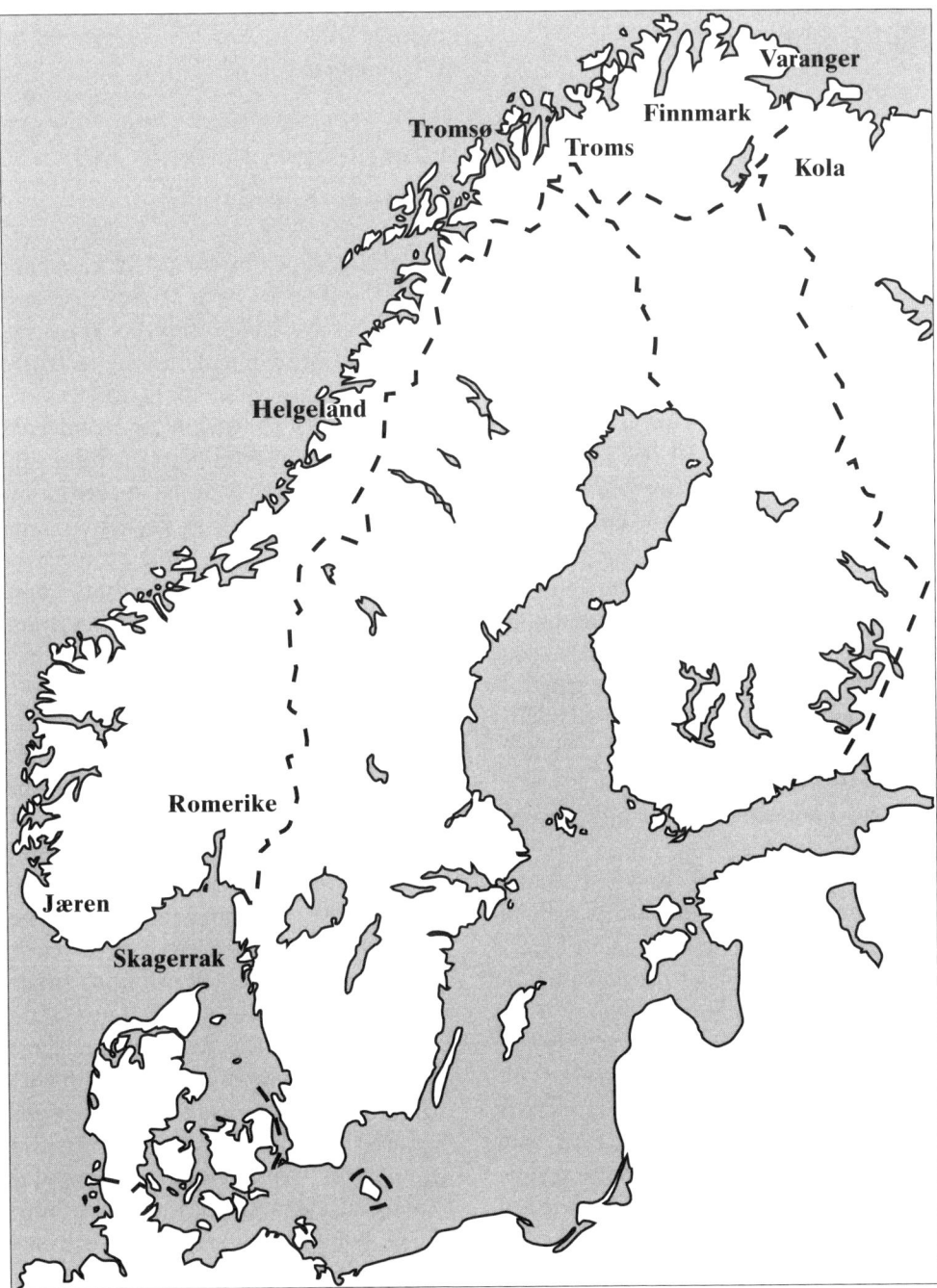

Fig. 3.1: Some Norwegian regions

Multi-ethnic regions

Another kind of cultural diversity carrying integrational power may be found in regions inhabited by two or more ethnic groups, living more or less intermingled. This has been the case throughout large areas of Northern Norway for many centuries, where Lapps and Norwegians, and even people of Finnish origin, have lived in the same area.

In some cases each ethnic group in a multi-ethnic area will utilize only certain parts of the natural resources, leaving other parts to other groups. The outcome of this may be a functional coexistence, where the groups are mutually interdependent economically, socially or in other respects, perhaps exchanging goods and services on a regular basis and according to rules generally adopted by the parties involved. This does not always imply purely friendly relations; even expressions of hostility may be channelled into socially accepted forms.

It should be noted, however, that a multi-ethnic area will not necessarily be regarded as one coherent region by the groups involved. They will most often be more inclined to talk about two or three different cultures existing separately.

By mutual agreement co-existing cultures will rarely be regarded as socially equal. In most cases one or the other of the cultures represented, and the people subscribing to it, will regard itself as superior. This may, or may not, be acknowledged by the group labelled »inferior«. Frequently, both or all cultures will regard themselves as superior to the other(s). In any case, an area which from the outside may look like one, multi-ethnic region, may be experienced in quite a different way when observed by the people involved.

Complexity of culture and cultural boundaries

A culture does not consist of elements picked at random from a vast repertoire somehow available. On the contrary, some cultural elements are more likely to stay together than others, and to form *cultural complexes* within the total culture of a society. And even the total culture of a society will be regarded by many social scientists as a system of mutually dependent parts functioning as a whole. This view implies that when changes occur in one part of the system they will inevitably have a certain impact even on other parts.

Mutual dependence, then, is a characteristic of the elements forming a cultural complex, and, to a certain extent, of all elements constituting a total culture. The strength of the mutual dependence will vary. Elements belonging to the same cultural complex will be more strongly connected with each other than with elements from other sectors of the same society. Thus, agriculture is likely to favour specific forms of social structure in a society, different from, for instance, the social structures favoured by fishing or mining. But the interconnection between agricultural and social elements within the culture will probably be less strong than the mutual bonds connecting elements within the agricultural sector as such. Generally speaking, the predominant way of making a living in a society is a fundamental cultural trait, which will affect all other sectors of culture, material sectors like diet, style of building and clothing, as well as immaterial sectors like folklore, mentality etc. It should be noted, however, that there is no determinism involved; it is only a case of more or less distinct tendencies.

As a consequence of the interdependence of cultural elements and groups of elements, single cultural elements will only exceptionally have a geographical distribution unlike those of all other elements. Normally, several cultural elements will show identical or nearly identical distributional patterns, and if mapped, the borderlines delimiting the areas where these elements are found, will largely coincide.

This means that a cultural boundary of some significance will never consist of a change in one cultural element only, be it ever so fundamental, but rather of changes in a group of interdependent elements.[1] Where topographical conditions enforce uninhabitable areas between habitable areas, as for instance a mountain range will do, many borderlines, each delimiting the distribution of one cultural element, will concur, and thus establish a conspicuous and sharply defined cultural border.

On the other hand, major cultural borders may be found even in areas which are geographically more continuously inhabited. In such cases, however, it may be that the lines delimiting the distribution of individual cultural elements are not all run closely together. The main reason for this is that there are degrees of interdependence between the cultural elements of any coherent culture. A culture will always allow a certain variation as regards combination of elements, especially when it comes to elements of minor or peripheral significance to the basic cultural forms. For example, animal husbandry will require certain types of farm buildings, which are different from those of a mainly crop-growing society. The difference in principal industry will also have a rather strong effect on diet, for instance, and, perhaps, on rules of inheritance, but it may only slightly effect several other aspects of life, such as clothing and funeral rites. In this case, the regional boundary, when mapped, will therefore appear not as a number of individual cultural borderlines all running closely together, but only as a certain congruence of individual lines, while others run along separately at varying distances from the main stream.

Regionalizing effect of administrative activity

In a country like Norway, the natural boundaries between different parts of the country are in many cases very distinctive, being made up of conspicuous natural formations such as mountain ranges, or other uninhabited areas like forests or wilderness. Naturally, districts that are separated from their surroundings by these kinds of borders, will obviously be considered convenient administrative units. Norwegian administrative units therefore tend to coincide with areas that are clearly delimited by natural boundaries.

Regardless of natural boundaries, distinct or not, the actual administration of any area will have a certain regionalizing effect in the long run. This impact will be recognizable in several ways.

On one hand, the administrative unit will be given a name that will be used in many connections and over a long period of time. This will implant in the inhabitants a habit of thinking of the area as a unit, a habit which may eventually create a sense of belonging, and even an accompanying mental line of division towards neighbouring districts and their inhabitants. On the other hand, a comprehensive, intra-regional, administrative activity, performed by ecclesiastical as well as secular bureaucracies, will contribute to strengthening the view that the area is a unit separate from other districts. The many routines of the administration will create innumerable personal and institutional links, connecting individuals and sub-districts in different ways and on many levels.

Further, the existence of an administrative centre will create a certain demand for commodities and services from the surrounding area, which may lead to the development of infrastructural elements, especially as regards communication, strongly favouring internal economic integration. Earlier, integration of this kind mostly occurred spontaneously, as it was beyond the capacity or the scope of the regional authorities to play an active part in the development. A high degree of internal integration will, of course, be achieved faster today than previously, because such great importance is attached by the authorities to the development of communications and other infrastructural factors through public involvement. For instance, the construction of bridges connecting inhabited islands to the mainland along the western coast of Norway has certainly led to convenient and frequent connections between areas that used to be somewhat less accessible to each other, and has favoured a process of demographic and economic integration.

The factors just mentioned imply that the existence of administrative units favours the establishment and maintenance of regions by strengthening regional coherence. However, the areas in question were most probably cultural units even before they were subject to centralised administration. The question is whether administrative activity in itself can create genuine regions.

This is unlikely. There certainly has to be a primary basis of economic and cultural homogeneity or integration. Possible concurrences of administrative units and cultural regions should therefore not mislead any one to believe that administration as such has a regionalizing power strong enough to bring about regions in the cultural sense of the word. Nevertheless, the authorities of new administrative units will usually aim at a regionalizing effect, and will want to arrange for this by a wide variety of means, extending from infrastructural remedies to rhetoric. A recent example in Norway is the »region« of Tromsø. In 1964 the municipality of Tromsø and several surrounding, rural municipalities were amalgamated into one, large municipality. The authorities of today, in the resulting municipality, frequently talk about »the Tromsø region«, clearly indicating that the centralised administration has had a decisive regionalizing effect.

This assumption is not necessarily correct. The fishing districts along the coast outside the town of Tromsø have been part of a larger coastal cultural region for centuries. In the same way the inner districts belong to a wider fjord-culture region. At the same time, however, the area around Tromsø has had the town as its economic centre ever since its foundation in 1794, that is, long before the amalgamation of 1964. The bonds connecting the town and the different parts of the surrounding, rural area may have become stronger during the last 30 years, because of the development of the communication system within the new municipality and other factors related to the existence of an administrative centre, as mentioned above. But a similar development, though perhaps not so rapid, might very well have occurred even if the former independent municipalities had not formally joined, simply because of the city's economic importance. The conclusion should be that, to some extent, one may regard Tromsø as an example of administrative activity and infrastructural adjustment enforcing a regionalizing process already in progress, but the effect of administration should certainly not be overestimated.

Hierarchies of regions

The area covered by individual regions may vary greatly, the size depending, among other things, on the preciseness of the distinctive cultural criteria applied when the boundaries are drawn. If these criteria are made very comprehensive and very precise, the result will be that only a small area can be included in the region. As the criteria are made less and less precise, we move from smaller to larger regions. The larger the region, the vaguer the distinctive criteria involved.

There are no established rules about how to draw cultural boundaries, and no one can say exactly how many or what kind of cultural differences are needed before a regional boundary becomes indisputable.

At no time, therefore, will there exist a fixed number of regions, for instance in Scandinavia, with established boundaries that are unanimously recognized.

On the contrary, the number and the extension of regions will at all times be a matter of discussion, and it will often be possible to distinguish regions within regions, and to establish hierarchies of regions, with several steps leading from smaller to larger units.

An example of this can be found in Northern Norway, which is frequently regarded as a single region, especially when viewed from the southern part of Norway. On the other hand, a number of relatively small areas like Varanger or Helgeland, which are only minor parts of Northern Norway, are also categorized as regions in some connections, as well as one or two or even more levels of regions of intermediate sizes, leading step by step to the main region of Northern Norway as a whole. Thus Varanger, for instance, may be said to belong to the somewhat larger East Finnmark region, which again may be regarded as part of the Finnmark and Northern Troms region, which in its turn clearly belongs to the region of Northern Norway.

Similar examples may be found anywhere in Norway, and indeed in any country. And of course, there are hierarchical steps even above the national level. Norway for instance may be said to be part of a Scandinavian or Fenno-Scandinavian region or a Northwest European region.

Sub-national regions crossing international boundaries

Sub-national regions do not always stop at international boundaries, because these boundaries are usually a result of political decisions and power structures which do not always take full account of existing cultural units and divisions.

In spite of 70 years of absolutely no contact across the Soviet Union border coastal Finnmark may still be regarded in certain ways as part of a Finnmark-Kola region. This became obvious recently, when the border was reopened and contacts were re-established.

In the same way, Finnmark in many respects belongs to a region consisting also of Northern Sweden, Northern Finland and adjacent parts of Northern Russia, as these areas are all inhabited by the Sami people, but their »nation« is divided between four countries today. As for the eastern group of Lapps, earlier inhabiting and exploiting an area consisting of South Varanger in Norway and adjacent parts of Finland and Russia, their possibilities of pursuing their traditional, semi-nomadic way of life were very much restricted by the 1826 border agreement between Norway and Russia.

In some connections historians will recognize a circumpolar region of vast dimensions, including all inhabited areas north of a certain latitude, usually the Arctic Circle. The natural conditions prevailing in these areas tend to enforce identical or similar cultural solutions, although there may be no direct contact between the different groups living there.

At the southern end of Norway, a trans-national region around the Skagerrak, including Danish, Swedish and Norwegian territories, has recently been brought to public attention by historians. They have demonstrated comprehensive cultural similarities between the areas involved, at least during the nineteenth century, and have established the distinctive criteria and the historical background of a cultural region that was previously only vaguely recognized by the people living there. The culture shared by the groups involved includes material as well as immaterial elements, as is clearly demonstrated by the publications resulting from the project. They include 17 books, covering topics like trade and shipping, religious revivals and associations, fishing, migration, etc.[2]

Another, and much larger, trans-national region, which has recently attracted more attention, is a Baltic Sea region. After the fall of the Iron Curtain, closer contact has been established between historians from Estonia, Latvia and Lithuania, and adjacent parts of the neighbouring western countries, which has encouraged a regional approach to the history of the area.

Several aspects of a Baltic region through the centuries were discussed at a congress of Nordic historians in Oslo in 1994.[3]

As is only too well known, the existence of trans-national as well as sub-national regions has recently been, and still is, a source of violent conflicts in certain parts of Europe. This is because national boundaries do not always coincide with ethnic or cultural boundaries, for reasons which have already been mentioned.

Obvious and hidden regions

At any given time, every country will have a number of rather obvious regions, whose existence no one questions. They are recognized as such by the people living in the area that constitutes the region, as well as by people living outside it. The recognition is usually based on the observation that the inhabitants of the area show points of strong resemblance in respect to a multitude of cultural traits, displaying what seems like an inner cultural homogeneity, which clearly sets them apart from their surroundings.

At the same time a more or less hidden system of relationships may exist in an area, discernible only through analysis, contemporary or historical, of the distribution of cultural elements. For the most part, possible non-obvious regions can be disclosed through an analysis of economic relations, which will sometimes reveal close connections between adjacent districts and even between non-adjacent districts. It is true that these relations may not always develop into regions in the full cultural sense, and certainly not if the areas involved are geographically non-adjacent, like the Norwegian city of Bergen and Northern Norway, which for centuries maintained close economic contact, but nevertheless remained culturally widely separated.

In other cases an important economic relationship will in the long run entail comprehensive cultural contact, enabling the formation of a region in the cultural sense. Possible examples of this may be cities and their hinterlands, as already discussed in the case of Tromsø, even perhaps mines and their circumferencial areas, provided they are maintained over a long period of time.

Changes in regional patterns

Most regions show great stability over the centuries. Nevertheless, they do not usually last for ever. Regions will rise and fall, and their borders will sometimes change, because of alterations in the culture, brought about by innovations or by the adoption of cultural elements from the outside world, for instance technological devices enabling exploitation of natural resources previously unexploitable. Regional boundaries may also be altered when new markets evolve, by royal foundation of cities, by changes in climate, and so on. Mass migration will be likely to affect the culture of two areas, the emigration area as well as the immigration area.

In seventeenth and eighteenth century Norway, the sawmills and their demand for timber, the mines and their demand for supplies, probably created economic relations that lasted so long and were so comprehensive that in some cases they may be said to have contributed significantly to the formation of regions in a cultural sense. The great winter cod fisheries of Northern Norway and even the herring fisheries farther south can be mentioned as other examples. But the ways of the herring being unpredictable, this makes any »herring area« quite unstable, and not likely to evolve into a lasting region.

Variations in climate are known to have caused changes in the distribution of cultural elements. An example is the northern boundary of grain production in Norway, which – from the information provided by tithe accounts – seems to have fluctuated a great deal during the seventeenth century.[4] Climatic variations became crucial because the area was marginal for grain production even in »normal« times.

II. Norwegian regional history

Origin and genres of local history in Norway

Modern local history research in Norway dates back to the first decades of the twentieth century.[5] Norwegian historians played an important part in this development. Around 1905, or shortly afterwards, when the union with Sweden had been peacefully dissolved, the focus of historical research in Norway turned, to a certain degree, from national political history to economic and social history, subjects that were well fitted for studies on a local or regional basis. At the same time there was great popular interest in local history, especially among middle-class urban dwellers and, above all, among well-to-do sections of the rural population. The outcome of all this may be regarded as an alliance between historians and the local history movement, which has lasted to this day, and which sets Norway apart from other countries in this respect.

From the beginning of the century, written local history in Norway consisted of certain fixed genres, which have been maintained to the present time. The major works of local history may be grouped in three categories.

On the one hand, there are the farm and family history books of rural communities, containing the individual history of each farm and its inhabitants, from as far back as sources will permit and up till today. This kind of work is likely to result in several large volumes for any rural municipality. The family history related to the farm will usually make up the greater part of these books. Every person known to have lived on the farm is presented with name, year of birth and other vital information, along with wife or husband and children.

Secondly, we have the genre of general history of rural or urban municipalities. Books of this kind will give the history of the community as a whole, and will usually aim at a »total history«, that is they cover what are regarded as the main sectors of life, usually including demographic, economic, social, political, cultural and religious history. The books may be organized by topics or chronologically.

Finally, we have the genre of regional history, which I shall term, for the moment, district history, as it remains to be seen whether the areas involved are real regions as defined in this article. District history in Norway is of the same age as local history in general, and is written in much the same way as the general history of local municipalities.

In addition to the main genres just mentioned, there are a growing number of local and regional history periodicals, and a large and miscellaneous selection of literature consisting of minor works about special subjects, such as local school history, local church history, the history of local industry, family history, the history of local associations, local biographies, etc. etc. These minor works are usually written by persons or private institutions from within the local community. The authors will frequently work without payment.

History research projects belonging to the main genres are normally instigated locally, often by local historical associations, and these works are usually publicly financed and administered. Money covering authors' fees and cost of printing is voted by the local or regional councils. Authors are hired for a specified period of time, and are expected to do a pre-determined amount of work within these limits, for instance to present one volume of farm and family history, or the general history of the area for a certain period of time. Authors are paid monthly, and, if they are historians, they expect to receive a salary commensurate with their normal income as for instance college or university lecturers.

The time needed to write the general history of a rural or urban municipality, or a region, from the oldest times till today, may vary greatly, depending on many factors, such as the type of society involved, the source situation, the qualifications of the author or authors engaged, and – above all – the ambitions of the project: one, two, or several volumes? Based on a very comprehensive or somewhat less comprehensive source foundation? Organized topically or by periods, and written by amateurs or historians?

Historians and amateurs

Local and district history writing has been practised by amateurs as well as historians throughout the twentieth century. It is a distinctive feature of Norwegian historiography, which sets it apart from that of other countries, that so many historians participate in local history research. While historians in other countries occupy themselves with urban history, they seem to avoid becoming involved in rural local history. Norwegian historians, however, frequently undertake to write farm and family history as well as general local history, i.e. historical works aimed primarily at local readers, and therefore written in a popular style. In fact, the percentage of historians among local history authors has been increasing recently, and has never been higher than today. In the 1990s, two thirds of all authors engaged in projects within the main genres of local history are historians or persons with a related educational background.

The amateurs who have been involved as authors of main genre works have mostly written farm and family history and general history of rural communities. With regard to district history and urban history, historians have always had nearly a monopoly, as they certainly have today.

The number of district histories in Norway

Around 40 different districts in Norway have a written history of some kind at the present time. These works are more or less comprehensive, covering all eras or specific parts of history. Some districts have had their history, or part of it, written more than once, and therefore the number of district history projects, completed or still in progress, is somewhat higher, amounting to around 50, including between 80 and 90 volumes.

District history books have been produced in all decades of the twentieth century, but three periods display a greater frequency of publications than the rest – viz. the 1930s, 1950s and the 1990s. The many works during the 1930s can be attributed to the centenary celebrations of local and district self-government in 1937, which gave rise to a considerable number of local and district history projects. The peak in the 1950s is more difficult to explain, and certainly has no single cause.

Today, district history has a stronger position than ever, and the 1990s will no doubt see an all-time record number of volumes published. The reason to some extent may be found in the fact that the 150th anniversary of the establishment of local and district self-government occurred in 1987; some of the historical works which were initiated in connection with the celebration were delayed and did not appear until the turn of the decade. In addition, however, there seems to be a growing interest in district history at the present time, among historians as well as among the public. Some possible reasons for this will be discussed below.

What kind of districts?

For reasons which I have discussed above, it is not always easy to distinguish geographically between administrative units and cultural regions. A rough estimate, based on the titles of the existing district history books, seems to indicate that among the 50 works which we have categorized as district history, nearly twenty are explicitly concerned with the history of administrative units, and, in fact, concentrate on the administrative history of these units.

The rest of the works do not seem to deal primarily with administrative history. On the contrary, according to the titles they embrace a wide spectrum of economic, social and cultural history. However, the geographical areas which they cover nearly always coincide with actual administrative units. This means that almost all works of Norwegian district history refer to areas that are, or have been, administrative units.

Nevertheless, because the administrative divisions of Norway are mostly founded upon ancient cultural differences, these works may be regarded in many cases as regional. The administrative unit setting the limits for district history projects may very well be, at the same time, a region. The problem is that the districts chosen as objects of study are not chosen primarily because they are regions, but because they are administrative units, and the boundaries are not discussed or even questioned.

The advantages of studying administrative units

There are three main reasons for historians preferring to study units that are, or have been, administrative units, instead of trying to establish and to study culturally delimited units. Two of these reasons have to do with conditions of today.

The first one is that district-history projects in Norway in most cases are initiated by the regional administration itself, and in these cases it is regarded as a matter of course that the work should deal with precisely the administrative unit of today. This has been the case with all anniversary books, not only those commemorating the local and district self-government of 1837, but even some works that appeared around 1914, celebrating the centenary of the Norwegian constitution.

In these cases all expenses were voted by the regional councils, and this, in fact, is the case with regard to nearly all other district-history projects that have been launched, even those which are not primarily concerned with administrative history. No other funding possibilities are normally available. And of course, no district history will ever appear without considerable financial support. The historians employed will demand a reasonable salary, commensurate with their normal wages in other employments, and the book has to be printed; only a portion of the total expenses will be covered by income from the sale of the books. Regional councils seem to be much more inclined to vote money if the administrative unit as a whole will benefit from the project. Thus it is much easier to raise public money in connection with research on contemporary administrative units as wholes than to finance research on any other conceivable units. This is the second reason why most district history is confined to administrative units.

Thirdly, it will usually be somewhat less demanding or time-consuming for the historian to study administrative units than any other units. This is because administrative units are also source-producing units, and since the archives of today consistently apply the provenance principle, keeping together sources which were produced by one and the same office, it follows that it is easier, in practice, to examine the sources concerning a whole administrative unit than to collect information regarding any non-administrative or cross-administrative area. In addition, the sources produced by any administration will largely give information about the actual administrative unit as a whole, information which only with difficulty, and sometimes not at all, can be subdivided by the historian wanting to study specific parts of this unit.

Administrative units as regions

Nevertheless, because most administrative units are cultural regions as well, we do have at least some genuine regional history in Norway. But one has to look closely at each work to recognize it as such. This could be more easily ascertained if the historians would engage themselves more consciously in discussions regarding the relationships between the administrative units they are paid to study and the actual cultural regions which they are, probably, studying at the same time.

All historians doing district-history research should continuously be asking themselves: in what ways, and to what degree is this administrative or geographical area also a discernible cultural region? Is this area one region? Or two or more? Or is it rather not a region in itself, but perhaps a part of some larger region? Questions of this kind will help the historian to find or to define the cultural criteria which will allow him to separate »his« region or regions from the surroundings, and in my opinion the research will benefit greatly from the pursuit of these questions. The outcome is likely to become more interesting, for the readers too. A few historians have been doing this recently, and their works demonstrate that this contributes greatly to transform the history of an administrative unit into the history of a cultural region.

I will now discuss briefly a recent work about Northern Norway as an example of this kind of approach.

The cultural history of Northern Norway

This work, which was published in 1994 in two volumes, *The stubborn landscape* and *The many-sided people*, is in my opinion the most successful example so far of how fruitful this kind of approach can be.[6] The main hypothesis of this work is that there are some basic cultural traits which are exclusively North Norwegian, and common to all inhabitants of the region, regardless of place of residence, age, ethnicity etc. These traits are believed to consist, above all, of a common mentality or outlook on life, arising from certain fundamental experiences which everybody in the area, today or in the past, has had.

First, there are experiences originating from the people's relationships to nature, »the stubborn landscape«, characterized by an »abundance that could not be harvested without suffering«. Secondly, the inhabitants are believed to have common experiences stemming from relationships to »the Southerners« and the national authorities, who have always regarded Northern Norway as culturally backward, and who have dominated and exploited the area. These two factors together are thought to have resulted in a permanent stubbornness among the inhabitants of the north, making them fall out of step with the rest of the country, and causing a distinct »culture of rebellion« among all inhabitants.

The work does not give a clear answer as to whether this is really the case. The idea is to present a hypothesis, and to let each of the 49 (!) authors examine his/her subject in the light of the main hypothesis. In doing this, the authors convey a variegated multitude of descriptions and carry through many exciting analyses of past and present life in Northern Norway. They do not, however, draw any conclusions. Neither do the editors. Instead, it is mostly left to the readers to draw their own conclusions.

The basic hypothesis is essential. If the editorial board had not from the beginning presented their vision of a possible North Norwegian cultural particularity, the work would never have reached either its high professional level or attracted such a wide circle of readers. The lack of an unambiguous answer is not to be regarded as a fault of the work. The crucial thing is to pose a question, and to discuss possible answers. Whether the hypothesis is verified or modified or falsified is less essential.

Regional history in contemporary Norway

The early 1990s have so far witnessed the publication of more district or regional history than any previous half-decade. And there is more to come. It would seem justifiable, therefore, to maintain that this branch of history is today the subject of considerable interest. This applies to historians as well as the people in the local areas who commission such books.

Perhaps one may discern an increasing tendency today among historians themselves to initiate regional-history projects, while until now most of the initiative has come from other quarters. This may imply that the question of regional culture and regional borders will be in focus more frequently in regional history in the years to come, and that the historians will no longer be content to accept tacitly the contemporary administrative borderlines as inassailable confines.

Funding problems may certainly cause future district-history projects to be confined within the safe borders of existing administrative units. But if the historians insist on paying proper attention to the question of regions, the outcome may nevertheless be quite satisfactory, as proven by the history of Northern Norway mentioned above.

Hopefully, we shall even get genuine regional history, that is history totally liberated from regional administrative units, as seems to be the case with the history of the »Stril« region in Western Norway, which is now being published.

Notes

1. Examples of distinct as well as diffuse cultural borderlines are mapped in Sigurd Erixon (ed.): *Atlas över svensk folkkultur*, Stockholm 1957.
2. The publications appeared in the years 1982-1991. The address of the project is: The Kattegat-Skagerrak Project, Museum of Fisheries and Shipping, Tarphagevej, DK-6710 Esbjerg V, Denmark.
3. Kåre Tønnesson (ed.): *Norden og Baltikum*. The report may be purchased from: IKS, Department of History, University of Oslo, P.O.Box 1008, 0315 Oslo.
4. The cultural processes connected with this situation are discussed theoretically by the Norwegian ethnologist Knut Kolsrud in: Diffusjon og grense, *Kultur og diffusjon*, ed. Arne Martin Klausen, Oslo 1961. (Report from a Nordic meeting of ethnographers)
5. A presentation of local history in Norway is given in Harald Winge: Local History, *Making a Historical Culture. Historiography in Norway*, eds. William H. Hubbard et al., Scandinavian University Press 1995, pp. 240-260. See also Ola Alsvik: *The Norwegian Institute of Local History, and Local History in Norway*, Oslo 1993 (free copies can be ordered from the Norwegian Institute of Local History, Kronprinsens gate 9, 0251 Vika, Norway).
6. Einar-Arne Drivenes, Marit Anne Hauan, Helge A. Wold (eds.): *Nordnorsk kulturhistorie*, I-II, Oslo 1994.

CHAPTER 4
Middlemen of the regions

Danish peasant shipping from the Middle Ages to c. 1650

By Bjørn Poulsen

Typically, the pre-industrial European peasant went to the nearest market town when he wanted to sell his products. To borrow an expression from geography, in doing so he was part of a central place system.[1] In this article I intend to give examples of market relations of quite another and much less hierarchal type: I shall focus on Danish producers who traded directly with the largest centres and thus bypassed the neighbouring central places.

An important precondition for bypassing the central structure is the possession of ships and the existence of navigable waters. The trade which will be studied here is therefore sea trade.[2] This is even more justifiable given the central role played by shipping in Danish transport history due to the country's many islands and its long coastline. Fundamentally, of course, it is the possibilities of the market which determine a peasant population's allocation of land and time. It is my goal to show how the direct involvement of agrarian producers in sea trade furthered regional specialization and how it created different land-use regions. There is also a discussion of whether this regional specialization was reflected in the creation of regional identities. In the following I will examine the development of a number of economic regions from c. 1200 to c. 1650, primarily in the kingdom of Denmark.

Commercialization and markets

The local commercialization of Denmark in the Viking Age has seemingly been underestimated. Quite recently, archaeologists have in fact located a number of »beach markets« dating back to the eighth century; inland local places of exchange have also been found.[3] As has now been shown, as early as the eighth and ninth centuries foreign goods were widely used in Danish villages. For instance, quern stones of basalt lava from the Rhine area from that time seem to have reached every farm and village of Western Jutland. Presumably, the town of Ribe was already functioning as a distributor of international commodities, which were brought to local, agrarian consumers. Of course, these consumers must have supplied the city with agrarian products in return.[4] Recent archaeological excavations of the site of Lundeborg on the island of Funen even make it possible to speculate on the existence of local market trade as early as 200-500 AD.[5]

On the other hand, we must insist

that a qualitative leap in economic development occurred about 1100-1200, making the trade in agrarian products much more widespread than it had been before. From this time and until the last years of the thirteenth century a number of Danish towns arose under royal suzerainty and the urban pattern became almost complete in the years before the mid-fourteenth century.[6] Money was now increasingly the universal binding material of society. Lords and peasants started to produce for local markets in the towns which, as the urban pattern became more closely meshed, were normally located within the convenient travel distance of 10 to 15 km. At the same time, the number of artisans multiplied and they were found to a larger extent inside the towns, which made going to town to buy the necessary manufactured goods more and more inevitable. In the towns a strengthened group of merchants emerged, profiting from the trade between town and country. The growth of Danish towns was contemporary with and, of course, not without connection to the changes on the southern coast of the Baltic. In the twelfth and early thirteenth centuries, a string of vigorous port towns arose here, taking older Slavonic settlements as their starting point. Up sprang towns like Wismar, Rostock, Stralsund, Greifswald, Stettin, Danzig, Elbing – and first and foremost the city of Lübeck, which from c. 1230 had the status of the metropolis of the Baltic. It can be asserted quite rightly, that from this time and up through the following centuries the kingdom of Denmark was, economically and demographically, only a sub-system in the superior region of Lübeck.[7] The Hanseatic towns became markets for Danish agrarian products. Already in the first decades of the thirteenth century Danish grain exports to German towns were of such dimensions that an older Nordic system of measuring grain in *mark*, *øre* and *ørtug* gave way to the German measures of *Last* and *Pfund*, which were closely related to shipping measures (*skibslæsten*).[8]

In the fourteenth century and up into the fifteenth century Danish and Baltic trade experienced a decline which was probably connected to a crisis in the traditional production of grain.[9] But from the late fourteenth century and during the fifteenth century a new trend of development emerged. The peasants as producers came forward, strengthened after the late-medieval agrarian crisis.[10] A general decline in large-scale seigneurial production gave peasant producers a chance, peasants who now possessed far larger farms than before the crisis. This meant that the peasants could sell a larger surplus and that their need for foreign goods increased. On the demand side important developments also occurred. As part of a European division of labour Denmark became an exporter of beef cattle (oxen) to Northern Germany and, in time, to the Netherlands too. The first quantification of the oxen export to the south from Denmark is from 1485.[11] That year duty was paid on 13,020 oxen at Gottorp, the customs post where nearly all Danish and most Schleswig cattle passed. As the importance of the Dutch market grew so did the number of cattle exported from Denmark; in 1501, 28,300 oxen were registered at customs points and in the 1540s the export had reached about 35,000 animals. At that time Denmark could be considered integrated in the European world market economy both with regard to prices and production: Danish oxen were then, in fact, semi-manufactured articles for the Dutch market.[12]

From around 1500, sea trade also grew, and from 1560 it multiplied. Grain shipments to the South Norwegian, North German and Dutch markets increased dramatically during the sixteenth century.[13] Serious economic problems did not arise again before the beginning of the seventeenth century.

This, then is the broad framework in which Danish trade and regional development is to be understood. During this period a number of specialized agrarian regions crystallized.

There were areas characterized by a surplus of agrarian production. Important among these were Southern Denmark including the islands of Tåsinge, Langeland, Lolland and Falster along with a number of smaller islands as well as parts of Southern Zealand. This area was connected to the so-called Wendish Hanseatic towns via the Baltic Sea. It is an open question whether the island of Fehmarn should also be included in this region.

Another »surplus area« is, unquestionably, to be found on the west coast of Southern Jutland and Schleswig, which via the North Sea was connected to North German and Dutch towns. As a region characterized by a weak agrarian (that is, grain) economy the province of Blekinge should be mentioned, linked by sea to the rest of Denmark and Northern Germany. This also applies to the province of Halland and Southern Norway which via Kattegat-Skagerrak was connected to Northern Jutland and other parts of Denmark.

Surplus areas

The integration of markets did not develop at the same pace everywhere. Commercial links were developed from the North Frisian areas on the west coast of Schleswig to areas in the south at an early date. As early as the thirteenth century the peasants of the west coast were selling products to Hamburg and the Netherlands. The early phase of these transactions is best illuminated from the southern part of the coast where the North Frisians lived. Already in 1261 the Frisians living in Utland promised the merchants of Hamburg that they could come to them without being robbed or taken captive, and in 1284 the people of Eiderstedt were given trade privileges in Bremen.[14] At the same time contacts to Flanders developed. In 1314 Duke Erik of Southern Jutland asked Count Robert III of Flanders to help some of his Frisian subjects. They had been robbed in France on their way to Flanders and had lost goods to the value of 2000 large florins.[15] During the fourteenth century several letters testify to contacts between the west coast areas of (Nord)strand, Edoms Harde and Eiderstedt, and Hamburg, Bremen, Holland and Flanders. A complaint of 1360 records ships from Hamburg which had sailed to small harbours on the West Schleswig islands of Föhr and List.[16]

The West Schleswig contacts became increasingly intense in the following centuries, and because of its low degree of urbanization, peasant trading was more important here than anywhere else. At the same time the situation of the area close to the Netherlands, the core area of the fledgling world eco-

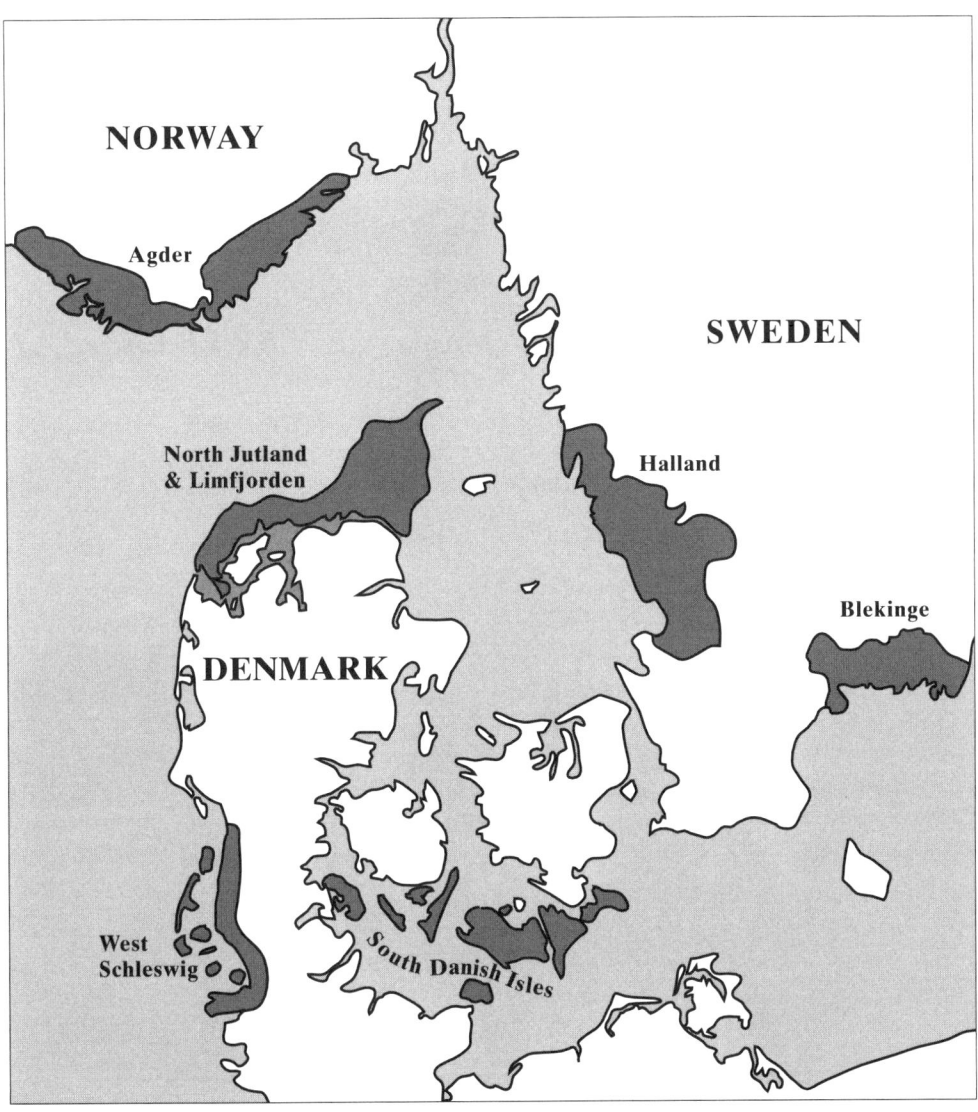

Fig. 4.1: Main regions of peasant shipping

nomy, afforded the peasants unique opportunities for market access. For instance, in a record of judgments from the years 1444-49 from the islands of Nordstrand and Eiderstedt, 11 peasants are mentioned whose ships were seized during local disturbances. Some of these sailing peasants were evidently active in the ongoing trade in North Frisian salt.[17]

Others, such as the peasant Maie Odenson from Eiderstedt, who had 30 *Tonnen* rye and wheat, 1 Tonne beans and 1 Tonne of peas in his ship, were trading with customers in the south. He and other grain exporting peasants found their buyers in Hamburg, in Bremen and in Dutch towns. Eventually beef cattle also came aboard the peasant vessels. In

Regional integration

Fig. 4.2: Location of areas, isles and towns involved in the peasant trading network

1512, when war interfered with land transport, for instance, the large farmer Frodde Brodersen from the village of Toftum in Viding Harde sailed to Holland with a cargo of beef cattle, hides, feathers and homespun cloth. Soon live cattle became a major article of export. In 1576 the trade in live oxen constitut-

ed such an integrated part of the economy of the peasants of Schleswig that the inhabitants of the small island of Föhr maintained that it would ruin them if they were not allowed to export oxen abroad.[18] On the other hand, quite early on, the nearly treeless areas of Schleswig and Western Jutland had to import tim-

Table 4.1: Ships in West Jutland villages, 1642-43

Locality	Vessels	Ship lasts
Højer	7	252
Rudbøl	2	50
Møgeltønder	7	374
Sejerslev	5	137
Emmerlev	15	176
Hjerpsted	3	61
Ballum	7	155

Note: 1 ship last (læst) = c. 2600 kg
Source: N.H. Jakobsen: *Skibsfarten i det danske Vadehav* ... 1937, p.22

ber and wood from other regions, for example beginning from Norway in the sixteenth century. Thus, cattle products were exported to the south while timber was imported from the north. In the sixteenth and seventeenth centuries the islands of Rømø and Föhr as well as a number of small harbours on the west coast of Jutland gained considerable influence in this pattern of exchange. A customs duty which was collected on the west coast in the years 1642-43, the so called *List Strømtold*, gives us an impression of the size of the merchant fleets present in some of these West Schleswig coastal villages (table 4.1).[19]

By Danish standards, these are considerable numbers, and there is no doubt that they reflect the fact that the villages like the rest of area were deeply involved in shipping. The close market relations between the west coast and the European cities resulted in agrarian specialization, especially with regard to cattle farming, and gave rise to particular agrarian systems such as the marsh agriculture in Schleswig and the Jutland *græsmarksbrug* (agricultural use of grass meadows).[20]

However, we leave this West Danish region in order to address the development of another area. The commercial links between Southern Denmark and the North German Hanseatic towns go back to the thirteenth century, when the islands of Fehmarn and Falster were the first Danish areas to adopt the German grain measures. The wreck of a relatively small vessel, a so-called *skude*, found on Falster near the village of Gedesby and dated to the last quarter of the thirteenth century, should probably be regarded as early evidence of trade with this area.[21] Furthermore, already at that time traders from the neighbouring island of Langeland are mentioned in the German town of Wismar.[22] The written sources indicate that trade with these southern islands of Denmark was growing from the latter part of the fourteenth century, that is, in the very same years when trade from the Mecklenburg coast in the south also flourished.[23] Small »peasant« harbours in the South Zealand county *Bårse herred* are observed in this period, and it is noted in the cadasters that the peasants of the island of Møn owned ships so that they could deliver their rent where their lord wanted – *in casu*, the Zealand town of Køge.[24] And a customs account of 1368, a *Pfundzollbuch*, from Lübeck shows us how the peasants of the island of Fehmarn were engaged in fairly large-scale shipping of victuals, especially grain, to Lübeck. All in all, in 1368, 43 vessels sailed from Fehmarn to Lübeck.

From the early years of the fifteenth century the Southern Danish towns backed by royal power launched a fight against the commercial activities of the agrarian districts which would continue for centuries. After the crushing of a peasant rebellion under King Christoffer III, a number of royal decrees were issued. In 1442 the peasants on the island of Lolland were forbidden to trade elsewhere than in towns and they were also forbidden to use small »illegal harbours« and to act as traders.[25] In 1445 the king emphasized that it was illegal for the peasants from Lolland to trade directly with foreign countries.[26] In 1447 King Christoffer issued a decree which would force all inhabitants of the island of Langeland to seek their markets in the only town of the island, Rudkøbing, and at the same time would ban the shipping of goods from »illegal harbours«.[27] The same year the king acted as mediator between bishop Ulrik of Aarhus and the peasants of the island of Tåsinge on the one hand and the townsmen of Svendborg on the other.[28] In this case a contract was drawn up allowing the bishop to sail to Germany and buy what he needed for his own manor house on Tåsinge and giving the peasants of the same island freedom to export horses, oxen and cows to Germany. But the peasants, according to the contract, had to take their own grain, flour, butter, honey and other such goods to the market of Svendborg. They were not allowed to trade in the goods bought in Germany.

This was the beginning of a long battle between townsmen and peasants over who was to have the profitable role of middleman between the producers and the larger centres. On the 30th of September 1475, King Christian banned in general peasants from sea trade with Germany and at the same time the laws became more and more geographically extensive.[29] In 1480, for instance, the inhabitants of Tåsinge were again forbidden to trade to the detriment of Svendborg, and this applied to all the tiny islands around Tåsinge: Skarø, Thurø, Drejø, Hjortø, Birkholm, Strynø, Strynø Kalv.[30] Evidently the problem was the same as in 1447 – the peasants were not allowed to sail to Germany with oxen, cows or butter on their own vessels. The goods had to be taken to the market of Svendborg. This decree was stressed again by King Christian II in 1521.[31] The constant repetition of the bans gives ground to believe that the decrees were mostly ineffective. In 1516 King Christian II totally banned peasant shipping from Southern Zealand, Lolland, Falster and Møn and evidently this ban was observed.[32] Already one year later, however, the ban was removed, and, according to a chronicler from Lübeck, in two days 200 small peasant vessels, »skuder«, arrived in Lübeck – although the temperature was already below zero. It seems that it was not until the years 1547 to 1550 that the townsmen achieved some success, as it was prescribed that the rural population of Lolland, Falster and Møn should only ship grain to the German towns in the period from May 1st to September 8th and from November 1st to February 2nd.

The constant complaints of the townsmen, however, show that this regulation was only followed to a certain degree and there are also indications that the peasants of Southern Denmark became increasingly involved in trading horses and cattle which they bought in Scania and on Zealand. Traditionally, the peasants stuck to the sale of grain, meat and wood. These are the goods mentioned in all privileges and bans, and there is concrete evidence that the peasants also normally exported such goods. In 1539, for instance, the town of Haderslev in the Duchy of Schleswig was called on by several peasant skippers from Langeland, Lolland-Falster, two from the tiny island of Askø, three from Ærø and one from Fehmarn.[33] Onboard their vessels, the »skuder«, almost only grain was found. A skipper arrived from Fehmarn with a cargo of wheat. A man from Langeland, however, arrived with 3 sheep on his ship and the skippers from the island of Askø also had 4 sides of bacon besides rye.

Starting in the 1570s, however, there were also people from the South Danish islands such as Langeland at the horse markets in Zealand and the province of Scania.[34] Apparently, they exploited their trade privileges to engage in professional trade. In the customs accounts of the Scania towns of Landskrona and Helsingborg, dating from the years between 1591 and 1651, for instance, there are a number of peasants from Langeland, buying up horses every year. In the case of the market of Landskrona it can be seen that the trade peaked in the 1620s and 30s (table 4.2).

It is clear that some of the horses bought were taken to Langeland and from there sailed by ship to Northern Germany. In addition to barley, peas, vetch, salted fish, wood, oxen, swine, bacon and sheep, rural skippers also exported horses from Langeland to German harbours in 1605-6. And in the fiscal year 1618/19, 764 horses were shipped from the harbour of Rødby on Lolland.[35]

An analysis of the *certificationes*, which note all the destinations of ships sailing from Lübeck 1579-81, permits us to look at the significance of the individual rural districts in the trade with Lübeck. The lists show that of the total number of 1982 ships which left the harbour of Lübeck in 1580, 1149 were headed for Danish ports. Of these, 134 cited Fehmarn as their destination, 133 Lolland or Falster, 63 Langeland. Trade between the South Danish islands and Lübeck can thus without exaggeration be described as intense. If one takes a closer look at Langeland, Lolland and Falster and take away the skippers specifying towns on the islands as their destinations, one presumably has the skippers from the rural areas. In 1579-80 their journeys were distributed as shown in table 4.3.

The traffic was clearly heaviest in the autumn months when the harvest was in. Looking at this distribution one must doubt whether the royal order to sail with grain only in the period from May 1st to September 8th and November 1st to February 2nd had any effect, and the suspicion is confirmed by a royal decree of 1585, again stressing the proper periods for the shipping of peasant grain.[36]

Table 4.2: Number of horses bought by peasants of the island of Langeland at the market in Landskrona, 1591-1649. Ten-year averages.

Year	Number of horses
1591	29.0
1600-09	45.5
1610-19	178.2
1620-29	176.0
1630-39	137.5
1640-49	60.7

Source: Vilh. Lütken: *Bidrag til Langelands Historie*. 1909, pp. 578-80.

Regional integration

Table 4.3: Ships sailing from Lübeck, presumably to »peasant harbours« on Langeland, Lolland and Falster

	Langeland	**Lolland**	**Falster**
September 1579	7	2	2
October 1579	10	11	0
November 1579	7	23	1
December 1579	6	8	1
January 1580	0	0	0
February 1580	1	4	0
March 1580	1	13	5
April 1580	5	10	1
May 1580	6	12	2
June 1580	8	8	5
July 1580	5	11	4
August 1580	15	7	1
September 1580	4	5	0
October 1580	8	3	0
November 1580	6	17	0
December 1580	4	4	0

Source: Archiv der Hansestadt Lübeck. Altes Senatsarchiv. Certificationes, 1579-81.

The table also makes it clear that Lolland played a far larger role for the Lübeckers than Falster. In addition, in 1580 a number of ships sailed to Lübeck from the smaller islands of the South Danish area: 10 vessels from Ærø, 2 from Møn, 2 from Fejø and 1 from Askø.

Presumably, what we are observing here are old patterns, for the trade between Denmark and Lübeck was rather stable, even though it changed in accordance with the changing trends of the Lübeck market. The traffic in the harbour of Lübeck was undoubtedly larger in 1580 than was the case in the 1490s and it was far larger than in the minimum year of 1380. But for centuries the traffic of Danish peasant ships to Lübeck was heavy and constant.

This trade became the precondition of agricultural specialization. The cash crop of wheat was normally grown to a fairly small extent in Denmark. But already in the thirteenth century wheat was grown in some quantities on the islands of Fehmarn, Falster and Møn as well as on Samsø.[37] In the following centuries Lolland along with the Schleswig island of Als became the main wheat-growing areas in Denmark. Presumably in the sixteenth century a special and very intensive open-field system of four to five fields developed on Lolland, probably modelled on parallel systems in Mecklenburg and Pomerania.[38] As in Mecklenburg, the peasant was able to export peas as well as malt made out of barley to North German town markets thanks to the new field system. It is not surprising that the sources show that it is on the islands of Lolland and Falster that the long-handed scythe replaces the older short scythe as a grain-reaping instrument for the first time in Denmark.[39] This seems to have occurred in the late fifteenth century and, presumably, was part of the intensified grain production on the South Danish islands. Apparently new methods of cultivation and agrarian technology came with the increasing integration of the market.

Areas of deficit

From the second half of the fifteenth century and onwards Halland along with Southern Norway became increasingly involved in exchange with other agrarian areas.[40] A number of royal decrees from the late fifteenth century indicate a certain amount of shipping by Halland peasants and at this time it was

Table 4.4: Number of ships in the harbour of Aalborg, 1583

Origin	Denmark	Halland	Norway	Sweden	Lübeck	Rostock	Emden	Holland	Scotland
Number	198	23	53	5	(20)	(7)	12	4	1

Note: The number of ships enclosed by parentheses indicates the use of supplementary material. The number of Danish ships does not include ships from Halland.
Source: Landsarkivet for Nørrejylland. Bropengeregnskab, Aalborg.

already common for Norwegian timber vessels to enter the Northern Zealand Isefjord.[41] In 1489, for instance, two Norwegian skippers sailed into the Isefjord, anchored their »skude« near the coast of Horns herred, a North Zealand county, and began to sell timber to local peasants. However, the Norwegians were attacked by townsmen from Roskilde, who considered that their privileges had been violated, and totally stripped the ship, drank the beer they found, and took off with the sail of the vessel. Connections were also established between Funen and Norway and Halland around 1500. In 1509, in the harbour of Odense, Queen Christina bought 100 pieces of timber (*lætter*) from a *Bagge*, that is, a Norwegian, and in 1519 it was noted in the customs accounts of this town that 17 vessels (»skuder«) from Halland and Norway arrived with limestone and departed with grain.[42]

In 1539 the peasants of Halland were given the privilege of exporting timber and stone, »stok og sten«, and of importing what they needed for their own farms.[43] However, it seems that no real breakthrough in the local Kattegat-Skagerrak trade took place before the mid-sixteenth century. This is made clear by a comparison between two customs accounts of the North Jutland town of Aalborg. From this town, the largest in the area, the ships which called at the harbour in 1583 can be found in so-called *bropengeregnskab* (toll accounts). There are certain problems with the number of ships coming from Lübeck and Rostock, but here other sources can help elaborate the picture (table 4.4).

If one takes a closer look at the home ports of the Danish skippers, including those of the province of Halland, it is clear that the areas close to Aalborg were very important. A total of 121 vessels came to Aalborg from the Limfjord area, just outside the town. Around the Limfjord, the towns of Skive (9) and Thisted (26) as well as its rival Hovsør[44] (17) were predominant, but one also frequently finds small localities without any sort of town privileges such as Harboør (10) and Aggersund (11); other villages are less represented such as Hals (4) and Heltborg (4), and there are also many tiny settlements noted from which one or two ships came, such as, for instance, Ginnerupgård in the parish of Heltborg or Kobberrø in the parish of Refs. Many of the peasants who paid the customs must have arrived with herring from the fjord in their vessels, but others arrived with local products or they were fishermen with eel from the parts of the fjord with brackish water. Especially on the days around the large Easter market, lasting for 14 days, the influx of vessels was large.

Fifty names from the customs account of Aalborg are from other parts of

Jutland. Some of these had their home port in the towns of the Skaw (Skagen) (3), Sæby (13), Grenå (2), Mariager (2) and Aarhus (2); but others were from »peasant harbours« and fishing localities: they came from Voerså in the parish of Albæk (9), from Hov (4), from the parish of Ferring (2), from the parish of Jerslev (2), from the rural districts of Northern Djurs (10) and Southern Djurs (1). Ships from Funen, Zealand and Scania came only from towns.

The situation is quite different with regard to Norway and Halland. In the 1583 accounts from Aalborg, a total of 53 vessels came from Norway and 23 from Halland.[45] In the traffic from Halland the rural harbours totally dominate, as is the case with regard to Norway. From the parish of Släp in Halland, for instance, 7 persons arrived, and 8 persons came from the county of Nedenes in South-Eastern Norway. However, some Norwegian towns are represented, namely Oslo (11 persons), Kongelv (12), and Marstrand (2), as well as the newly founded Fredrikstad (2). From Sweden, from Nya Lødøse among other places, only 5 ships arrived. The 1583 accounts do not reveal much about the goods traded from Halland and Norway; in fact, we are only told that 4 people from Halland had horses on their ship and a man named Peder Suendsen of the parish of Släp had three horses in his vessel. Accounts from the year 1587 are more telling and mention several horses as well as iron on board vessels from Halland and Sweden, and in the accounts of the following years many horses on the Halland »skuder« are mentioned.[46] We can safely assume that there was also timber on board their ships.

A comparison with older accounts from Aalborg from the year 1518 shows us that the situation in 1583 was new. In the year of 1583, 76 ships coming from Halland and the South Norwegian coast called at Aalborg; in 1518, there were none from these areas. Apparently, during the 65 intervening years a decisive breakthrough had taken place in the Kattegat-Skagerrak trade. The accounts show that starting in the 1580s and for the next hundred years this trade continued structurally unchanged and with steady growth.[47]

The involvement of Northern Jutland in the Kattegat-Skagerrak trade by the middle of the sixteenth century was presumably also followed by a stronger integration of other parts of Denmark and Southern Norway. We hear of a »harbour« where Norwegians sold timber to local peasants at Næsbyå on the western coast of Zealand for the first time in 1562.[48] In 1568 and 1571 it is mentioned that people from Halland and Norway entered the Limfjord area and that on the island of Mors timber was sold in return for payment in grain.[49] In 1568 the peasants of Halland officially obtained confirmation of their earlier permission of 1539 to sail with and trade timber, but at the same time officials were worried that the vessels the peasants were building were too large, so they fixed an upper limit to their size.[50] At least from the 1590s the northern part of the west coast of Jutland and Southern Norway were involved in trade, largely carried on by peasants. In 1596-97 a total of 58 Norwegian vessels arrived at the coast of Thy.[51] The peasants of Southern Norway, of the so-called *Nedenes len*, were now given royal permission to sail to Jutland and buy grain, and from 1630 North Jutland peasants also took up shipping. In several lawsuits from these years and onward the North Jutland town of Thisted tried to block the peasant trade but without success.[52] The capital of Denmark, Copenhagen, which was growing strongly around 1600, primarily attracted »skuder« from Halland. In 1615, 110 vessels from Halland called at the port of Copenhagen, corresponding to 11 % of the total number.[53]

The intensive export of horses from markets in Scania to the South Danish islands of Lolland and Falster around 1600 has already been mentioned. Undoubtedly, a large number of these animals originated in Halland, like the horses imported by ship to Aalborg from the mid-sixteenth century. Already in 1553 horses (*bagge-øg*) from Halland and Norway were common in Aalborg.[54] Grain, however, was the fundamental basis of the Kattegat traffic. The grain was exported north to parts of Norway (especially the interior of Agder) as well as Halland, which in return sold timber and other sorts of wood.[55] This kind of exchange is mentioned in all the relevant decrees from the mid-sixteenth century and onward.[56] Further, it is often mentioned that the peasants of Halland, the Norwegian southwest county of Bohuslen as well as the interior of Agder needed bread, herring, salt and German beer, which was imported on their own ships.[57] It is evident that the buyers of the south were in need of timber, especially building timber, while in the northern areas there was a deficit in grain. Evidently, wood could be supplied in large amounts from the northern parts of the Kattegat area. From the early and mid-sixteenth century the number of buyers expanded. Now peasant skippers also headed for Norway for the timber needed for houses and dikes. It is quite typical that in 1562 the inhabitants of the village of Møgeltønder were permitted to buy oak timber in Norway for their sluices and houses.[58] Or that in 1573 the inhabitants of the North Frisian village of Bredstedt on the west coast were licensed to send five duty-free ships to Norway and from there to import 50 cargoes of timber because their village had burned down.[59] In Norway the exploitation of the forests intensified when the use of water-powered saws spread after c. 1520, and trade increased explosively when Dutch demand started in the mid-sixteenth century. In fact, for a while many Southern Norwegian peasants became small-scale capitalists, specializing in forestry for an international market.[60] Resources, however, were not unlimited. Already in the late sixteenth century Halland began to re-export Swedish timber, and from around 1600 the forests in the Norwegian county of Bohuslen were over-exploited and timber was brought from far inland in Sweden.[61] No doubt, these areas were not particularly suitable for grain production, but studies indicate that the concentration on timber export further lowered agricultural productivity. As pointed out by Øystein Rian, for instance, agriculture in the Norwegian region of Vestfold stagnated in the sixteenth and seventeenth centuries as a consequence of the growth in forestry.[62] At the same time, there is no doubt that Danish peasants, from Northern Jutland among other places, adjusted their production in order to be able to produce a grain surplus for export to the wood-supplying regions.[63]

The development of the Northern

Kattegat region was not unique. From the northwestern parts of Scania a brisk trade in firewood to Copenhagen evolved in the late sixteenth century, much of it coming from tiny »harbours« such as Båstad and Grytehamn.[64] Furthermore, the province of Blekinge, situated on the Baltic Sea, also assumed a central position as a supplier of wood and importer of grain from around 1500. In the first decades of the sixteenth century one sees the towns of the island of Bornholm selling grain to Blekinge and importing timber from there, and we know that the peasants of Blekinge were active skippers at that time.[65] In 1514, for instance, King Christian II banned the peasants of Blekinge both from carrying out foreign shipping and receiving visits from foreign merchants in their harbours. Only if the foreign merchants could not get a »full cargo« in the local towns were they permitted to go to a limited number of »harbours« in the countryside, where they were allowed to buy timber, wood, and firewood for cash.[66] This order was stressed in 1521 but abolished already the following year as a consequence of the king's dethronement.[67] When, in 1538, the inhabitants of the towns of Blekinge tried to persuade the king to ban the local peasants from shipping, the peasants stated, »that there was little grain in the countryside, so they had few chances to earn a living, barring what they could garner from the woods and the shores,« and they told the king that if this should be taken from them, their most important livelihood would be gone. The king, however, decided that the peasants of Blekinge were not allowed to export goods from their province.[68] The same matters were discussed in 1550 when the towns of Ronneby and Lykå and the peasants of Blekinge complained together over a royal embargo on timber. As a consequence, the king lifted the embargo but stressed the decision of 1538: that peasants should only ship their goods to domestic harbours.[69] The following year it becomes clear that there was lively traffic of Danish and German merchants in the small »country harbours« of the region and we see that the peasants were constantly trying to get their own shipping to Germany legalized.[70] And, in fact, the legalization of peasant foreign trade was achieved in 1568 and confirmed in 1582.[71] During the following years certain limitations were imposed, but, basically, peasant shipping from Blekinge remained free until the area was surrendered to Sweden in 1658.

The many ordinances make it clear that originally timber was exported from Blekinge, but from the late sixteenth century it was only legal to ship firewood of alder and birch. At that time fish apparently was also an important export item. Import goods were, according to the ordinances, mainly grain malt, hops, iron, salt and beer.[72] A number of customs accounts give more details about the goods traded in the small »harbours« in the countryside of Blekinge and the ships calling at these places.[73] It is clear that firewood was exported in large quantities, first and foremost from the small harbours of Bodekull and Pukavik, while goods such as grain, malt, peas and beer were imported. The South Danish islands of Lolland and Falster played a surprisingly large role in trade at this time, confirming the fact that this was an area specialized in the export of agricultural products. In 1652, for instance, Mickel Staffer of the town of Sakskøbing called at the tiny Blekinge »harbour« of Hjortahammar loaded with 18 barrels of peas. Important partners in this trade were in addition Copenhagen and the island of Bornholm as well as German towns on the Baltic like Rostock, Stralsund, Greifswald and Kolberg. It may safely be assumed that this export influenced the production of Blekinge. Even if the important role of fishery is not forgotten, only a specialized forestry production would have made possible the demographic growth which characterized this infertile area from the sixteenth century. As the peasants repeatedly stated in their letters to the central administration, their grain production was extremely limited, and they had to buy grain from outside. The pressure for wood and its diminishing availability also furthered the trade across the border with Swedish peasants, which had been active from the late Middle Ages. In 1582 it is expressly mentioned that wood was among the goods which the peasants of Blekinge bought in Sweden.[74] However, unlike in Norway and Halland, the forests of this area were not over-exploited in the seventeenth century.[75]

Market geography and peasant trade

Fundamentally, Scandinavian agriculture is divided into pastoral and agrarian zones or regions, but it is often characterized by the fact that other trades play a prominent role. The development of different land-use regions has clear preconditions in natural conditions and the regionalisation known from pre-historic times should presumably be explained on the basis of natural variations. On the other hand, examples have been given above that illustrate the decisive role of markets in creating regions characterized by different productions.

Considerations of the geographic pattern of regional specialization could take their point of departure in von Thünen's classic work *Der isolierte Staat in Beziehung auf Landwirtschaft und Nationalökonomie* from 1826. Here he introduces the theory that the distance between land and market determined both the income from the landed property and how the land was used. According to von Thünen, the main determining factor was to be found in the costs of transport to get from the place of production to the inhabitants of cities. On this assumption, production around the imagined »city« would be divided into circles. In the inner circle vegetables were grown, then came a circle of forestry, then a very broad circle of grain production, and finally an outer circle producing cattle for slaughter. We do not need to consider the concrete attempts to use this model on a North European reality made by Wilhelm Abel, Marion Malowist – and for that matter Immanuel Wallerstein – as they are not very useful in a Danish context.

If we stick to von Thünen it becomes evident that two factors exist in Denmark which create deviations from his constructed ideal situation, that is, variations in the quality of the land and the conditions of transport. The location of the South Danish grain zone may very well be explained according to von Thünen's ideal situation. The neighbouring German market in connection with easy transport by sea should theoretically have given the appropriate conditions for grain export from Southern Denmark, as it did in fact. Forestry should, according to von Thünen, take place close to the centre core. The explanation for the deviation from this ideal situation with regard to peripheral regions of Halland and Norway is found in the poor, rocky soils found here, which restricted agrarian production, and, on the other hand, in the excellent shipping conditions in these areas.

Maritime transport was a precondition for breaking out of the natural regions and creating larger economic regions. Of course, this form of transport could not function without entrepreneurial persons ready to cross the sea.

Middlemen of the regions

From the thirteenth century onwards, the towns aimed at trade monopolies under the leadership of their merchants, and gradually many of the old sites of trade and shipping along the coasts in their vicinity were abolished.[76] Total monopoly, however, was never achieved by the towns. In the countryside of the regions sketched above, both skippers and harbours were found, and they could absolutely dominate trade, as in 1605/6 on the island of Langeland, where the local town, Rudkøbing, was only responsible for 1/3 of total exports.

In many cases, the peasants themselves acted as skippers, using their own ships to market their own production. An investigation of a customs account from the island of Ærø shows that export was mainly in the hands of skippers from the villages.[77] Of the 29 vessels sailing from the island in that year, only two were from its small town. These vessels were sailed by 26 men, which means that the owners of them normally only shipped goods once a year. That this should be interpreted as an indication that they were full-time farmers with shipping only as a sideline is supported by studies of the cadasters, which list many of the skippers as solid, rent-paying peasants. Studies of the small harbours of Blekinge have also shown that as a rule sea trade was not done by professional skippers. Skippers of the regions were, evidently, peasants who owned a boat they used only a few times a year to transport goods, either on their own account or for other people.[78] The same is true for Halland, where skippers did not give up farming but instead invested their profits from shipping in land.[79] In Halland, as in Northern Jutland, shipping was based on part owners. In Halland in 1569, we hear of a case where a local peasant, Mikkel Nielssen from Råø, shared a vessel with a Lübeck citizen, Jakob Griis.[80] In Northern Jutland in the seventeenth century, normally two or three part owners were found per vessel, generally peasants from the coastal area but with some townsmen from local towns among them.[81]

During the sixteenth century a real professional maritime culture based on fishing and trade evolved in the Danish countryside. One could now meet full-time agrarian skippers and seamen. One of them, a peasant son called Anders Ogels from the west coast of Schleswig, trading in the years 1544-45, left his account book.[82] It shows us how he had commercial transactions with 106 persons to whom he sold cloth, hops, flax, salt, beer, spices as well as other products during these two years. His export goods to the Danish town of Ribe and to Hamburg predominantly consisted of fish. Ogels' account book makes it clear that he must have been sailing with his ship most of the year. Only for shorter periods did he live with his father, a wealthy peasant in the Schleswig village of Højer. Another account book from West Schleswig was written in the 1570s by a peasant from the small village of Maas, outside the town of Husum. One of this peasant's projects was to build a vessel to be sailed by an employed skipper who undertook many journeys, one of them to Bremen with a cargo of beef and linen.[83] Mortensøn has been able to demonstrate the existence of a professional class of skippers from around 1600 in the rural districts of the island of Lolland who were not dependent on agriculture. In some cases they were sons of peasants, possibly like Ogels, who sailed as a step in a career aiming towards positions as peasants. However, Mortensøn has also shown how shipping on the island of Langeland gave way to specialized maritime settlements. During the last part of the sixteenth century and until the 1620s two fishing villages without any land existed here, inhabited by the »rural skippers« of the island.[84] They sailed for the wealthiest peasants, who functioned as suppliers of goods and buyers of imported goods and who paid the necessary customs to the authorities. At other places in the country the same development took place and small fishing villages became the sites of export shipping.[85]

In fact, a number of very small islands in Denmark became what one might designate as transport centres. This is the case for some of the South Danish islands, which from around 1400 had taken part in the trade with Germany, as well as a couple which first took part in the sixteenth century: Læsø and Samsø, two islands very different from each other. Læsø was characterized by a grain deficit which also slowly turned into a wood deficit. As early as 1446 the inhabitants of the island were allowed to buy grain anywhere in the Denmark, and this privilege was regularly renewed during the following centuries.[86] In the sixteenth century the island was still a centre of salt fabrication from sea water, the salt functioning as payment for the necessary grain import.[87] But while all the woods of the island were being cut down to be used in the manufacture of salt in the sixteenth century, the Norwegian timber export grew. A specialized carrying trade now evolved in which vessels from Læsø took timber from South Norwegian saw mills in return for the sale of their grain. The timber was then sold in Jutland, on Funen and in Western Zealand. The trade seems to have culminated in the year 1671, when 81 vessels could be counted on the island.[88]

Samsø, on the other hand, was a grain producer; however, in the sixteenth century it was faced with the same problem as Læsø, that is, a lack of wood on the island. From the second part of the sixteenth century a number of royal privileges took note of this situation and secured the inhabitants of the island the right to sail to the town of Aarhus as well as other towns and to buy building timber, fuel, coal, wheels and other necessary items.[89] It was stressed that the inhabitants were not allowed to buy grain, butter and the like in rural areas in order to trade.

However, this more limited trade only constituted one side of the Samsø trade. The people of Samsø became involved in the carrying trade in the Danish realm, and in 1602 when it was stressed by the king that they should pay customs duties on beer from Rostock and Wismar, these products were most likely directly imported from their North German places of production.[90] In the Lübeck »certificationes« of 1579-81 one sees that Samsø played a significant role among the Danish destinations listed. In 1580, 19 skippers sailed from Lübeck to Samsø. The fact that this mostly occurred September through October underscores the link between shipping and the sale of the annual harvest. In a few Danish agrarian areas specialization of the transport sector occurred during the sixteenth and seventeenth centuries so that shipping became one of the most important occupations; however, coastal sea transport undeniably became very important to many regions. In light of this, first of all it hardly seems justifiable to operate with such a sharp division between town and country, as it is often the case, and, second, to regard the agrarian skippers as central entrepreneurs in an increasingly more clear-cut regional specialization.[91]

Regional identities?

Exchange and regionalization had their economic consequences. They forced local production to adjust to the possibilities for export; they were the expression of a growing commercialization and, in the areas of agrarian surplus, could lead to increased monetization.

From around 1200, agrarian Denmark was generally monetized, although certain regions were different in this respect. This was the case in the North Frisian and West Schleswig areas, which were already much more monetized than was the norm in the fifteenth century. In 1438 the peasants of a number of districts (*herreder*) (Sønder Gos herred, Nordstrand, Eiderstedt) paid a considerable share of their taxes in gold coins. There is also evidence from the same region of widespread late-medieval credit transactions among peasants, local churches, ecclesiastical institutions and local townsmen. In the sixteenth and seventeenth centuries a rather highly developed credit economy existed among the peasants, who kept their own account books to maintain order in their loan transactions.

The peasants of Southern Denmark also acquired cash money via their trade with German towns, even though goods were often traded in return for other goods: for instance, in 1528 the peasants of Langeland received confirmation of their privileges to sail to German Hanseatic towns with their own cattle and grain and to buy hops, salt and steel there because the local town of Rudkøbing was unable to supply them with these necessary goods.[92] However, the monetary economy of this area became closely linked to the local shipping to certain German harbours, as is made clear in a number of negotiations between King Christian II and townsmen and peasants of the island of Lolland in the year 1516. The king had ordered the peasants to stop their shipping, but they came to him and proved that their land rent (*landgilde*) was predominantly fixed in cash money and that they would be unable to earn the money necessary to pay it if they were not allowed to sail to Germany. According to the peasants, the townsmen of the local towns of Lolland were only able to offer them goods for their freight.[93] It seems that the peasants of this area had achieved a degree of monetization, just as high as the towns. From time to time the sources also give an impression of individual ship-owning peasants and their wealth. A peasant from Lolland had 13 gold coins, *rhinegulden*, when he returned from a trip to Germany in 1505, and if one took a closer look at his rooms much wealth could be discerned: for instance, coats and cloaks of cloth from Bruges, Deventer, England and Hagen in Westphalia. This man, who also operated in Northern Jutland, was in no respect inferior to a wealthy townsman.[94]

Trade not only developed regional economies, to some degree it must have also furthered regional identities. Medieval society was made up of communities negotiating terms with the governing hierarchies. Typically, these negotiations concerned the size of the rent and villeinage given by the peasants to the king and other lords, but also trade rights were, in fact, an important matter of negotiation. The right to trade in rural areas, desired by the towns, was always negotiated with the inhabitants of certain limited areas. As a rule, recipients of privileges were single districts or islands like, for instance, Lolland, Falster, Blekinge, and more rarely, parts of islands such as »herreder«. It could even be a very small island. Two peasants, Jep Nilssen and Jep Olssen, inhabitants of the tiny island of Rågø, negotiated a royal privilege in 1570 so that they, like the people of larger islands, could sail with their vessels, their »skuder«, and earn their living in this way.[95] Common interests were the basis of communities that needed to negotiate a successful result with the royal chancellery. The sources show the general pattern that the monopolies of towns and the rights of towns came as the result of a dialogue between the two parts. One had to achieve results with which both parts could live. In 1561 it is recorded that the peasants of Blekinge drew up a formal contract regulating the number of ships to be sailed by the peasants.[96]

In the cases of which we are aware, the king was normally drawn in as an arbitrator.[97] Already in 1447 it can be seen that the trade rights of Tåsinge were the result of an agreement brought about by the king to end a fight between the townsmen of Svendborg on the one hand and the peasants of Tåsinge with their lord bishop Ulrik of Aarhus on the other.[98] In 1460 the trade rights of Lolland peasants were fixed after a meeting in the town of Kalundborg, where King Christian I had heard the mayor of the Lolland town of Nakskov speak on behalf of the Lolland towns and some peasants who spoke for the local peasantry of the island.[99] Of course, in the end royal policy was quite a determining factor in the solutions of the conflicts over trade rights in which he was involved. Under the reign of King Christian II the royal »compromises« were normally to the benefit of the towns and the disadvantage of the peasants, but under the reign of the following kings of the sixteenth century, the situation was evidently much more open. Indeed, there was a real dialogue in which arguments counted, and the peasants' emphasis of the fact that only trade made it possible to survive economically most certainly made an impression on the largest landowner of the country, the king. The peasants' most important argument, however, was the privileges they had already achieved, and the letters which constituted proof of this were carefully kept and if necessary could always be presented. As the king wrote in a letter on the peasants of Sønderherred (the southern part of Lolland) in 1537, »they have been at our court with sealed parchment letters and privileges.«[100]

The common goal of the peasants and their common negotiations must have furthered regional identities, geographically identical with the natural regions. Increased communication was thus not only creating homogeneity and harmonization in this region, but was also the precondition of cultural regionalization.

Concluding considerations

It is possible to identify different economically specialized regions of the kingdom of Denmark from 1200 to 1650. Some of these had a surplus of agrarian production, first and foremost of grain, but lacked wood, while others lacked agrarian products but had easy access to wooded areas.

Only to a certain degree did this reflect an original, prehistoric regionalization arising from the ecological basis.[101] Of course, the strong points of the natural conditions were developed. Norway, Halland and Blekinge had no chance at all to develop into large producers of grain. But the regional specializations became unmistakably evident in the late medieval and early modern period.

The development seems to have taken place in two stages. While what we can label surplus areas, at least from around 1400, were heavily engaged in transactions with other regions, the development was slower in other areas. Not until the sixteenth century do the areas marked by agrarian deficit enter the transaction scene.

In respect to supply conditions the first phase can be explained by changes in the agrarian social structure with a change from large-scale farming to peasant farming. In respect to the market conditions there is reason to point to the fact that demand from the Dutch market was felt both in the Baltic and in the North Sea areas.

The second phase is linked to demographic growth in Denmark: the recovery following the late-medieval crisis. The density of settlements and the size of the cultivated area increased again in the central Danish agrarian districts. Inevitably this reduced the commons, and the grain regions experienced an escalating demand for supplies of fuel and timber. In the fifteenth century, wood could normally be obtained fairly close by. In 1475, for instance, peasants of Funen sailed to the fjords of Eastern Jutland to buy fuel and house timber.[102] Around 1500, the west coast of Jutland and Schleswig was still supplied with firewood and small timber from the east coast of Jutland. When it was forbidden to export timber from the town of Ribe in 1480, the Schleswig islands of Sylt, Föhr and Eiderstedt were explicitly excepted from the prohibition. A customs account from the West Schleswig castle of Schwabstedt of 1504 registered that large cargoes of inland wood were sent out to the marshes, even a cargo destined for the island of Helgoland. But everywhere the local wood resources became exhausted and in a royal decision of 1558, *Den koldingske reces*, it was generally stated that all Danish peasants were free to buy wood in their local areas outside the towns »from those who import it by ship to the towns«.[103] Now Norway, Halland and Blekinge got their chance, and here the sale of wood to the grain areas in the south became the basis of an economic and demographic growth matching the general growth of the time. Thanks to commercialization, the population of these areas could grow more than local food production allowed. It could even, as was the case in Norway, lead to a neglect of the inadequate agriculture in favour of commercial forestry. In the Norwegian case international trade was added to the regional exchanges, intensifying the development. But in general it was the regional trade and the ships of local peasants which were the foundation of continued growth. That this could lead to deforestation, as occurred in Southern Norway, Halland and, for instance, on the island of Læsø, is another matter.

The growing regional trade must be regarded as a decisive factor in the increasing commercialisation of rural areas even if one should not forget the international development and the integration into larger economies or, for that matter, the consequences of the increase in the levying of customs and taxes so characteristic of the sixteenth to the eighteenth centuries. There was always money to be saved by evading city customs, and of course the profit made by shipping without customs from local country harbours was growing just as fast as the customs duties escalated. For instance, the flourishing sea trade of the Ducal island of Ærø in the seventeenth and eighteenth centuries was especially based on profits from smuggling.

The changes in the local trade of the seventeenth and eighteenth centuries are not, however, the topic of this article. The surrendering of the provinces of Scania, Halland and Blekinge as well as the Norwegian Bohuslen to Sweden by the mid-seventeenth century seriously damaged the established systems. On the South Danish islands the power of the towns grew, and to a certain degree they successfully took over trade from the peasants. Here and elsewhere the fisheries experienced a general decline. At the same time, the position of Lübeck as a totally dominating centre dwindled and the exchanges gradually concentrated more and more on the national centre, Copenhagen. Thus, in 1618 the peasants of Langeland were ordered not to ship their products to Germany. Legal places of sale were now only found in the local town of Rudkøbing – and Copenhagen.[104] Likewise, in 1623 the peasants of Blekinge were told to sell their firewood only to merchants of Copenhagen.[105]

Danish agrarian shipping is quite a complex matter, but it seems to be a fact that from around 1200, and especially during the period 1400-1650, we must regard it as a fundamental factor in the economic development and commercialization of the rural areas, and the economic regionalisation of the entire country.

Abbreviations:

DD: *Diplomatarium Danicum*, ed. Det Danske Sprog- og Litteraturselskab, Copenhagen 1938ff.

DGK: *Danmarks gamle Købstadslovgivning*, I-IV, ed. Erik Kroman, Copenhagen 1951-61.

Rep.: *Repertorium Diplomaticum Regni Danici Mediævalis*, ed. Kr. Erslev, William Christensen and Anna Hude, Copenhagen 1894-1939.

Notes

1. Cf. Walter Christaller: *Die zentralen Orte in Südwestdeutschland*, Jena 1933.
2. See Hermann Kellenbenz: Bäuerliche Unternehmertätigkeit im Bereich der Nord- und Ostsee vom Hochmittelalter bis zum Ausgang der neueren Zeit, *Vierteljahrsschrift für Sozial- und Wirtschaftsgeschichte*, 49, 1962, pp. 1-40; Nils Friberg: *Stockholm i bottniska farvatten: Stockholms bottniska handelsfält under senmedeltiden och Gustav Vasa*, Stockholm 1983; G. Kerkkonen: *Bondesegel på Finska Viken. Kustbors handel och sjöfart under medeltid och äldsta Wasatid*, Helsingfors 1959; Åke Sandström: *Plöjande borgare och handlande bönder. Mötet mellan den europeiska urbana ekonomin och vasatidens Sverige*, Stockholm 1996; Karl Koppmann: Zur Geschichte der Mecklenburgischen Klipphäfen, *Hansische Geschichtsblätter*, 14, 1885, pp. 103-60.
3. Jens Ulriksen: Teorier og virkelighed i forbindelse med lokalisering af anløbspladser fra germanertid og vikingetid i Danmark, *Aarbøger for Nordisk Oldkyndighed og Historie*, 1990, pp. 69-101; P. Birkedahl Christensen and E. Johansen: En handelsplads fra yngre jernalder og vikingetid fra Sebbersund, *Aarbøger for Nordisk Oldkyndighed og Historie*, 1991, pp. 199-229; T. Nilsson: Stentinget. En indlandsbebyggelse med handel og håndværk fra yngre jernalder og vikingetid, *Kuml*, 1990, pp. 119-32; Merete Binderup, Jørgen Christoffersen, Ole Crumlin-Pedersen, Bente Holmberg, Niels Nielsen, Erland Porsmose and Henrik Thrane: *Atlas over Fyns kyst i jernalder, vikingetid og middelalder*, ed. Ole Crumlin-Pedersen, Erland Porsmose and Henrik Thrane, Odense 1996, pp. 194-200.
4. Stig Jensen: Handel med dagligvarer i vikingetiden, *Hikuin*, 16 (Handel og udveksling i Danmarks Oldtid), 1990, pp. 119-38.
5. *Atlas* ... (see note 3), pp. 194-97.
6. Anders Andrén: *Den urbana scenen: Städer och samhälle i det medeltida Danmark*, Malmö 1985.
7. Josiah Cox Russell: *Medieval Regions and their Cities*, Newton Abbot, 1972, pp. 106-111. Cf. Jan de Vries: *European Urbanization 1500-1800*, London 1984, pp. 40-43.
8. Poul Rasmussen: *Mål og vægt*, Copenhagen 1967, p. 13; Poul Enemark: Kornhandel, *Kulturhistorisk Leksikon for Nordisk Middelalder*, vol. 9, pp. 147-54.
9. Michael North: *Geldumlauf und Wirtschaftskonjunktur im südlichen Ostseeraum an der Wende zur Neuzeit*, Sigmaringen 1990.
10. Erland Porsmose: Middelalder o. 1000-1536, *Det danske landbrugs historie*, 1, ed. Claus Bjørn, Odense 1988, pp. 341-43.
11. Poul Enemark: Oksehandelens historie ca. 1300-1700, *Sortbroget kvæg*, ed. Aksel Pedersen, Poul Enemark, E. J. Ipsen and Vagn Bro, Aarhus 1983; Ian Blanchard: The Continental European Cattle Trades: 1400-1600, *Economic History Review* 39, 1986, pp. 427-60.
12. John P. Maarbjerg: *Scandinavia in the European World-Economy, ca. 1570-1625: Some Local Evidence of Economic Integration*, American University Studies, Ser. IX, History vol. 169, New York 1995.
13. Ole Feldbæk: *Dansk økonomisk historie 1500-1840*, Viborg 1993, p. 33.
14. DD, II, 1, no. 334, no. 490. DD, II, 3, no. 100.
15. DD, II, 7, no. 142.
16. DD, III, 5, no. 387.
17. On North Frisian salt production and trade, see Bjørn Poulsen: Wirtschaftliche und rechtliche Aspekte des nordfriesischen Salzes im Spätmittelalter und in der frühen Neuzeit, *Das Salz in der Rechts- und Handelsgeschichte*, ed. Jean-Claude Hoquet and Rudolf Palme, Schwaz 1991, pp. 279-92.
18. V. A. Secher: *Forordninger, Recesser og andre kongelige Breve*, vol. 2 (1576-95), Copenhagen 1889-90, p. 25, no. 38.
19. N. H. Jacobsen: *Skibsfarten i det danske Vadehav: En Erhvervsgeografisk Studie*, Copenhagen 1937, p. 22.
20. Karl-Erik Frandsen: *Vang og tægt: Studier over dyrkningssystemer og agrarstrukturer i Danmarks landsbyer 1682-83*, Esbjerg 1983; Karl-Erik Frandsen: Danish Field Systems in the Seventeenth Century, *Scandinavian Journal of History*, 8, 1983, pp. 293-317; Bjørn Poulsen: Agricultural Technology in Medieval Den-

mark, *Medieval Farming and Technology: The Impact of Agricultural Change in Northwest Europe*, ed. Grenville Astill and John Langdon, Leiden, New York, Köln: Brill, 1997, pp. 115-45.
21 Jan Bill: Gedesbyskibet: Middelalderlig skude- og færgefart fra Falster, *Nationalmuseets Arbejdsmark*, 1991, pp. 188-97.
22 *Urkundenbuch der Stadt Lübeck*, 2, Lübeck 1858, no. 745.
23 Karl Koppmann (see note 2).
24 DD, IV, 1, no. 133. *Danmarks middelalderlige regnskaber, Roskildebispens Jordebog*, ed. C.A. Christensen, Copenhagen 1956 p. 139.
25 DGK, III, p. 409.
26 DGK, III, pp. 409-10.
27 DGK, III, pp. 607-08.
28 DGK, III, pp. 538-39.
29 An injunction from 1486 preventing Møn's peasants from sailing to Germany with anything but their homegrown goods is cited in Kr. Erslev and W. Mollerup: *Danske Kancelliregistranter 1535-50*, Copenhagen 1881-82, pp. 246-47.
30 DGK, III, pp. 541-42.
31 DGK, III, pp. 551-52.
32 DGK, III, pp. 371-73.
33 Bjørn Poulsen: Skibsfart og kornhandel omkring de slesvigske kyster ved det 16. århundredes begyndelse, *Historie*, 1995, 1, pp. 38-58.
34 L. Laursen (ed.): *Kancelliets Brevbøger 1571-75*, Copenhagen 1898, p. 151; L. Laursen (ed.): *Kancelliets Brevbøger 1584-88*, Copenhagen 1906, p. 495.
35 Ole Mortensøn: *Renæssancens fartøjer: sejlads og søfart i Danmark 1550-1650*, Rudkøbing 1995, p. 170.
36 V. A. Secher: *Forordninger, Recesser og andre kongelige Breve*, vol. 2 (1576-95), no. 407, pp. 401-06.
37 Johannes Steenstrup: *Studier i Kong Valdemars Jordebog*, Copenhagen 1873-74, p. 253.
38 Karl-Erik Frandsen: *Vang og tægt* (see note 20).
39 Bjørn Poulsen: Agricultural Technology … (see note 20).
40 On the boat trade between Northern Jutland, Halland and Norway, see among others Johan Hvidtfeldt: Skudehandelen i det 17. aarhundrede, *Jyske Samlinger*, ser. 5, 2, 1935-36, pp. 29-79; C. Klitgaard: Den jyske Skudehandel, *Jyske Samlinger*, ser. 5, 1, 1932-43, pp. 383-92;

C. Klitgaard: Nordjylland og det norske Sørland. Skudehandelens Indvirken paa Befolkningsforholdene, *Historisk Tidsskrift*, ser. 10, 5, 1939-41, p. 625-57; C. Klitgaard: Den vendsysselske Skudehandel, *Vendsysselbogen*, 1953, pp. 301-13; Poul Enemark: Skudehandel, *Kulturhistorisk Leksikon for Nordisk Middelalder*, vol. 16, pp. 1-3; Bjarne Stoklund: Tømmerskuderne fra Læsø. Et kapitel af skudehandelens historie i Danmark, *Årbog 1972. Udgivet af Selskabet »Handels- og Søfartsmuseets Venner«*, pp. 153-98; Albert Sandklef: Halländsk sjöfart i danska arkiv, *Årbog 1966. Udgivet af Selskabet »Handels- og søfartsmuseets venner«*, pp. 239-259; Gunnar Jedeur-Palmgren: Skutefarten i Onsala före Skånska kriget, *Forum navale. Skrifter utgivna av Sjöhistoriska Samfundet*, no. 27, pp. 24-41; Poul Holm: *Kystfolk. Kontakter og sammenhænge over Kattegat og Skagerrak ca. 1550-1914*, Esbjerg 1991.
41 Rep., II, 12549. DGK, I, pp. 291-95.
42 W. Christensen: *Dronning Christines Hofholdningsregnskab*, p. 325. Rigsarkivet (Copenhagen), Reg. 108A, Gl. pk. 24, no. 1. Cf. the fact that in 1531 a tradesman from Odense had *»bagge rafter«* (Norwegian timber) lying in his basement: Jørgen Olrik: Et borgerligt Inventar fra Middelalderens Slutning, *Fra Arkiv og Museum. Studier og Aktstykker*, vol. 1, Copenhagen 1899-1902, pp. 429-32 (p. 431).
43 Tegnelser over alle Lande, *Danske Magazin*, III, 6, p. 279.
44 In 1528-42 Hovsør was developing into a market town, cf. Anders Andrén (see note 6), p. 159. Up until the eighteenth century it maintained its position as Thisted's winter harbour, cf. J. P. Trap: *Danmark*, fifth ed., VI, 2. Copenhagen 1961, p. 578.
45 These tradesmen and their appearance in the toll accounts is transcribed by C. Klitgaard in: Pinsemarkedet i Aalborg 1583 og 1594. Markedshandlende fra Halland og Bohus Len, *Varberg Museum. Årsbok*, 1957, pp. 9-14. Albert Sandklef examines Aalborg's toll accounts from 1575-83 for Hallanders in: Halländsk sjöfart … (see note 40). Cf. Albert Sandklef: *Allmogesjöfart på Sveriges västkust 1575-1850*, Lund 1973.
46 On horses in the accounts from the following years, see Sandklef: Hallandsk sjöfart … (see note 40), p. 247.

47 Poul Holm (see note 40), p. 74. On Norwegian traffic to Aalborg in the years 1676 to 1709, see Wenche Hervig: Sjøfarten fra Sør-Norge til Ålborg omkring 1700, *Heimen*, 1995, 4, pp. 241-56.
48 L. Laursen (ed.): *Kancelliets Brevbøger 1561-65*, Copenhagen 1893-95, p. 388.
49 L. Laursen (ed.): *Kancelliets Brevbøger 1566-70*, Copenhagen 1896, pp. 357-88. L. Laursen (ed.): *Kancelliets Brevbøger 1571-75*, pp. 31-32.
50 L. Laursen (ed.): *Kancelliets Brevbøger 1566-70*, pp. 192, 311, 490-91. L. Laursen (ed.): *Kancelliets Brevbøger 1571-75*, p. 416.
51 Johan Hvidtfeldt (see note 40), p. 31.
52 Ibid.
53 Ole Mortensøn (see note 35), p. 173.
54 Poul Enemark: Hestehandel, *Kulturhistorisk Leksikon for nordisk Middelalder*, vol. 6, p. 529.
55 For an analysis of the Kattegat-Skagerrak »system« throughout 400 years, see Poul Holm (see note 40).
56 See, for instance: L. Laursen (ed.): *Kancelliets Brevbøger 1561-65*, esp. p. 388; L. Laursen (ed.): *Kancelliets Brevbøger 1566-70*, pp. 311 (Halland) and 357-88; L. Laursen (ed.): *Kancelliets Brevbøger 1571-75*, pp. 31-32 (Norway).
57 L. Laursen (ed.): *Kancelliets Brevbøger 1566-70*, pp. 296 and 490-91.
58 L. Laursen (ed.): *Kancelliets Brevbøger 1561-65*, p. 168.
59 L. Laursen (ed.): *Kancelliets Brevbøger 1571-75*, p. 251.
60 Stein Tveite: *Norsk skogbrukshistorie*, vol. 2, Oslo 1971; John P. Maarbjerg (see note 12), pp. 248-49.
61 *Bohusläns Historia*, ed. Erik Lönnroth, Göteborg 1963, pp. 171-78; Poul Holm (see note 40), p. 74.
62 Øystein Rian: Kan regionhistorien gi oss ny innsikt?, Rolf Fladby og Liv Marthinsen (eds.): *Distriktshistorie: Problemer, metode, organisering*, Oslo 1979, p. 16. See also chapter 7 in this volume.
63 Poul Holm: Havskab og kystkulturer, *Den jyske historiker*, 68 (Regionen i historien), Aarhus 1994, pp. 37-50.
64 Margareta Swensson: Bondehamnar i det nordvästra Skåne och Blekinge under 1600-talet, (Dansk) *Historisk Tidsskrift*, ser. 12, vol. 4. 1969, pp. 47-95.
65 DGK, IV, pp. 243-44.
66 DGK, IV, pp. 330-32.
67 DGK, IV, pp. 365ff.
68 Kr. Erslev and W. Mollerup (see note 29), p. 73.
69 Op. cit., p. 453.
70 Margareta Swensson (see note 64), p. 47; L. Laursen (ed.): *Kancelliets Brevbøger 1561-65*, p. 73.
71 Margareta Swensson (see note 64), p. 47; L. Laursen (ed.): *Kancelliets Brevbøger 1571-75*, pp. 673-74; L. Laursen (ed.): *Kancelliets Brevbøger 1580-83*, Copenhagen 1903, p. 521.
72 Kr. Erslev and W. Mollerup (see note 29), p. 453; L. Laursen (ed.): *Kancelliets Brevbøger 1571-75*, pp. 673-74; L. Laursen (ed.): *Kancelliets Brevbøger 1588-92*, Copenhagen 1908, p. 719; L. Laursen (ed.): *Kancelliets Brevbøger 1616-1620*, Copenhagen 1919, p. 188; V. A. Secher, *Forordninger, Recesser og andre kongelige Breve 1558-1660*, vol. 6 (1651-60), Copenhagen 1918, no. 289, p. 339.
73 Margareta Swensson (see note 64), pp. 65-92. Cf. Ole Mortensøn (see note 35), p. 164. Leifh Stenholm: *Ränderna går aldrig ur: en bebyggelseshistorisk studie av Blekinges dansktid*, Lund Studies in Medieval Archaeology, 2, Lund 1986, pp. 106-109.
74 L. Laursen (ed.): *Kancelliets Brevbøger 1580-83*, Copenhagen 1903, p. 521.
75 S. Bjørnsson: *Blekinge. En studie av det blekingske kulturlandskapet*, Lund 1946.
76 Cf. Orla Vestergaard: Forkøb, landkøb og forprang i middelalderlig dansk handelslovgivning, *Middelalderstudier tilegnede Aksel E. Christensen*, Copenhagen 1966, pp. 185-218; *Atlas ...* (see note 3), pp. 194-200.
77 Bjørn Poulsen: Skibsfart og kornhandel ... (see note 33), pp. 40-43.
78 Margareta Swensson (see note 64), p. 92.
79 Poul Holm (see note 40), p. 74.
80 L. Laursen (ed.): *Kancelliets Brevbøger 1566-70*, pp. 487 and 525.
81 Hvidtfeldt (see note 40).
82 Bjørn Poulsen: Die ältesten Bauernanschreibebücher: Schleswigsche Anschreibebücher des 16. und 17. Jahrhunderts, *Bäuerliche Anschreibebücher als Quellen zur Wirtschaftsgeschichte*, ed. Klaus-Joachim Lorenzen-Schmidt and Bjørn Poulsen. Neumünster, 1992, pp. 89-105; Bjørn Poulsen: *Bondens penge: Studier i sønderjyske regnskaber 1400-*

1650, Odense 1990, pp. 50-77.
83 Bjørn Poulsen: *Bondens penge ...* (see note 82), pp. 93-96.
84 Ole Mortensøn (see note 35), p. 169.
85 On late medieval development, see Bjørn Poulsen: Land og by i senmiddelalderen, *Danmark i senmiddelalderen*, eds. Per Ingesman and Jens Villiam Jensen, Aarhus, 1994, pp. 196-220; Ole Munksgaard: Lollands Albue: fiske(r)leje, udskibningshavn og krigshavn i tiden 1524-1648. Træk af udviklingen fra fiske- og handelsplads til støttepunkt under kampen om Østersøherredømmet, *Lolland-Falsters Historiske Samfund*, 1994, pp. 45-57; Ole Mortensøn: Fordi der liden fisk vanker, *Skalk*, 1981, 5, pp. 18-26.
86 *Diplomatarium Viborgense*, ed. A. Heise, Copenhagen 1879, p. 225 (1446 6/12; 1541 5/7); L. Laursen (ed.): *Kancelliets Brevbøger 1571-75*, p. 255 (1573 9/5); V. A. Secher: *Forordninger, Recesser og andre kongelige Breve*, vol. 3 (1596-1621), Copenhagen 1891-94, no. 47, p. 45 (1596 24/12).
87 Jens Vellev: Die Salzproduktion in Dänemark – besonders auf der Insel Læsø, *Das Salz in der Rechts- und Handelsgeschichte*, eds. Jean-Claude Hocquet and Rudolf Palme, Schwaz 1991, pp. 413-38.
88 Bjarne Stoklund (see note 40), pp. 153-98; Jørgen Steen Jensen og Bjarne Stoklund, Skatten fra Læsø, *Skalk*, 1984, 4, pp. 3-9.
89 L. Laursen (ed.): *Kancelliets Brevbøger 1580-83*, p. 522; L. Laursen (ed.): *Kancelliets Brevbøger 1596-1602*, Copenhagen 1913, p. 261; V. A. Secher: *Forordninger, Recesser og andre kongelige Breve*, vol. 4 (1622-38), Copenhagen 1897, p. 574; Jens Holmgaard: *Kancelliets Brevbøger 1648*, Copenhagen 1991.
90 V. A. Secher, *Forordninger, Recesser og andre kongelige Breve*, vol. 3 (1596-1621), p. 155.
91 Cf. H. Kellenbenz: Die Unternehmerische Betätigung der verschiedenen Stände während des Übergangs zur Neuzeit, *Vierteljahrschrift für Sozial- und Wirtschaftsgeschichte*, 44, 1957, pp. 1-25.
92 Kr. Erslev og W. Mollerup: *Kong Frederik den Førstes danske Registranter*, Copenhagen 1879, p. 168.
93 Kong Christian II. aabne Breve Fyn angaaende, *Samlinger til den danske Historie*, ed. P. F. Suhm, vol. 2,2, Copenhagen 1782, pp. 70ff.
94 Rep., II, 10330, 10357, 10358, 10365. H. Zangenberg: En lollandsk Gaards Inventar i 1505, *Lolland-Falsters Historisk Samfunds Aarbog*, 16, 1928, p. 36-50. Cf. Rep., II, no. 11746.
95 L. Laursen (ed.): *Kancelliets Brevbøger 1566-70*, pp. 631-32.
96 L. Laursen (ed.): *Kancelliets Brevbøger 1561-65*, p. 73.
97 Ibid.
98 DGK, III, Svendborg, no. 9, pp. 538-39.
99 Rep., II, 1193.
100 Tegnelser over alle Lande, *Danske Magazin*, III, 6, pp. 150-51.
101 Mortensøn discussed the sixteenth-century Danish system of exchange in light of the ethnological division of the cultural landscape into areas dominated by either forests or agriculture or combination of the two (*skov, slette- og risbygd*). Ole Mortensøn (see note 35).
102 Erland Porsmose: *De fynske landsbyers historie*, Odense 1987, p. 90. At the same time people from Zealand sailed to Funen to buy wood. Rep., II, vol. 5., no. 8469.
103 Cf. Florian Martensen-Larsen: *Hav, fjord og handel: En studie i handelsveje i Nordjylland i tiden indtil 1850*, Herning 1986, p. 20.
104 L. Laursen (ed.): *Kancelliets Brevbøger 1616-1620*, Copenhagen 1919, p. 402; V. A. Secher: *Forordninger, Recesser og andre kongelige Breve 1558-1660*, vol. 3 (1596-1621), no. 498, Copenhagen 1891-94, pp. 544-45.
105 L. Laursen (ed.): *Kancelliets Brevbøger 1621-23*, Copenhagen 1922, p. 607; V. A. Secher: *Forordninger, Recesser og andre kongelige Breve*, vol. 4 (1622-38), no. 66, Copenhagen 1897, p. 75.

CHAPTER 5
Trade from Southern East Bothnia from 1560 to c. 1600[1]
An analysis of responses to economic stress

By John P. Maarbjerg

Throughout the later Middle Ages and into the early modern period, the Bothnian region was closed to the otherwise complete Hanseatic penetration of the Baltic. Not that the products of this region were without commercial interest to those inveterate traders, but the remoteness of the region and the efforts of Swedish rulers had combined to establish Stockholm, and to a lesser extent Åbo/Turku, as staple markets for its products. The region, consisting of the coastal areas of present-day Sweden and Finland bordering on the Gulf of Bothnia, extended 650 km from the Åland archipelago in the south to the mouth of the Torne river in the north. It encompassed significant geographical diversity. Ecology, distance, sub-regional specialization and established markets had given rise to a number of economic sub-regions, or economic landscapes, each with its specific economic links with the larger Baltic trading system.[2]

The trade of this region has been the subject of two recent monographs by Friberg (1983) and Sandström (1990).[3] These are focused on Stockholm and cover the periods from the late Middle Ages to 1560 and from 1600 to 1650, respectively. The intervening four decades

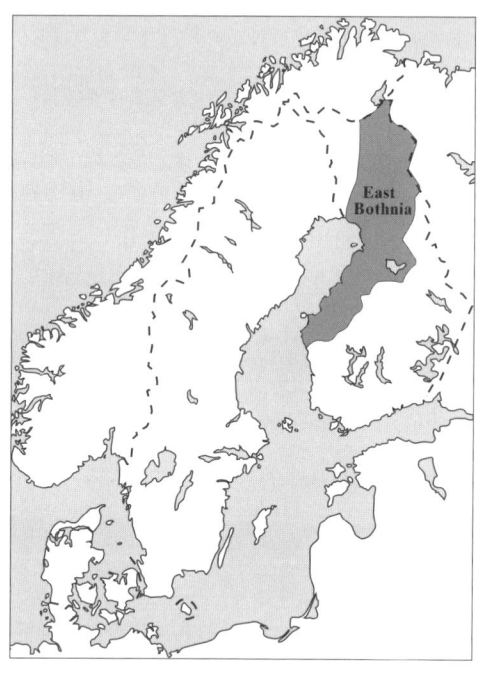

Fig. 5.1: The region of East Bothnia. The map shows the present frontiers. In the sixteenth century Finland was a part of Sweden.

represent a critical epoch in the history of the region, however, covering its growing integration into the larger European economy and the beginning transformation of Sweden into a militarized »tax-state.« While the merchants of Stockholm and South-West Finland

Fig 5.2: East Bothnian parishes c. 1570

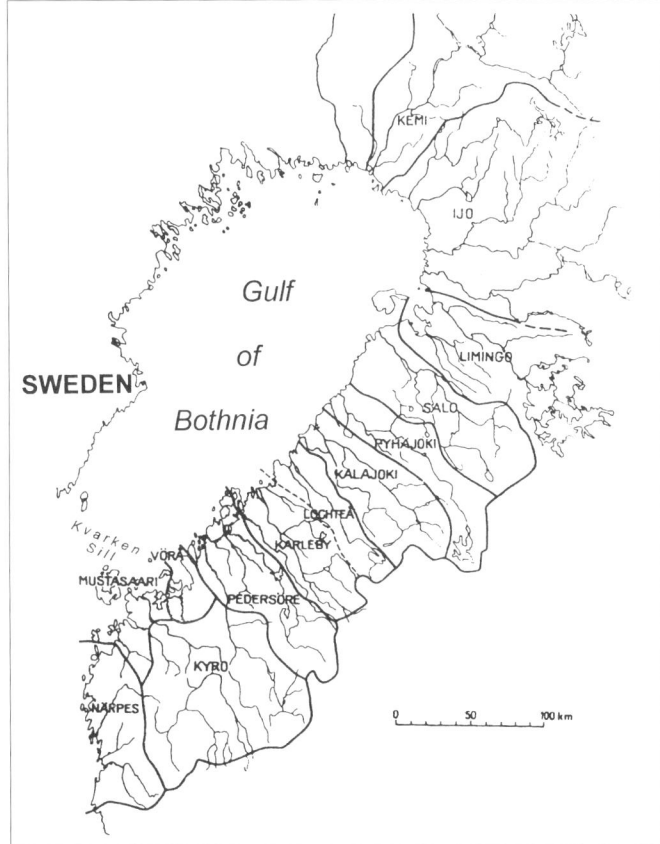

were affected by these developments, the peasant communities of the region bore the brunt of the changes. The purpose of this study is to analyse the transformation of peasant trade from the three coastal parishes, Mustasaari, Vörå and Pedersöre, in one such economic landscape in Southern East Bothnia during the last four decades of the sixteenth century.

The study by Friberg, as well as the present one, is based on the Stockholm Castle customs rolls, *slotstullen*, which cover Bothnian imports to Stockholm. Sandström has questioned the inclusiveness of these rolls, so it is appropriate to examine how representative they are of the East Bothnian peasants' trade in this period. Sandström's examination of a later customs roll, *lilla tullen*, imposed after 1622, which specifies that all goods »quick and dead« be subject to duty, reveals that livestock, among other items, was omitted by the earlier rolls.[4] Livestock was a major export from the southwestern provinces of present-day Finland, but made only occasional appearances in the rolls for East Bothnia.[5] The only other commodity that has gone unregistered in »slotstullan« appears to have been feathers, a low value item, which were gathered from sea-fowl, cleaned and shipped in barrels.[6]

Until 1605, Stockholm was the only port in the region imposing duty on the Bothnian trade, and with the exception of the East Bothnians' voyages to the north of their own province we are ignorant of their possible trade with other areas in the region. Below, I argue for the economic rationale for the East Bothnian traders' preference for Stockholm and the Mälar region. Furthermore, Friberg has found few appearances of East Bothnian traders elsewhere in Bothnia in the period under review.[7] This pattern is confirmed by the post-1605 custom rolls; the town of Hudiksvall (chartered in 1582) was the only port in Northern Bothnia to have a regular, but limited trade with East Bothnia. Its trade was almost exclusively with the parish of Karleby, however, and points north.[8] Thus, the trade of Mustasaari, Vörå and Pedersöre was still focused on Stockholm, and it is safe to conclude that Stockholm was the only important port of destination in the previous half-century as well. Accordingly, the customs rolls of »slotstullen« give us a reliable picture of the changes in the trade of Mustasaari, Vörå and Pedersöre.

While the southern areas of the Bothnian region were self-sufficient in cereals, cultivation in Northern Bothnia, commonly called *Norbotten*, was an uncertain undertaking. As a consequence, the northern agrarian communities focused on activities with more dependable outcomes, relying on trade to supplement their own fluctuating cereal output as well as to supply them with the other critical commodities they needed to sustain life. As Olaus Magnus wrote in 1555: »The inhabitants of Norbotten live mainly by fishing. Not that their fields are barren, but they have such an abundance of good fish, that it suffices amply in trade for all essentials.«[9]

He might have added that many of these fields were used for grazing livestock, which supplied meat, hides and dairy products, much of which was also traded and, in the case of butter, used to pay taxes. Given the abundance of fish in the entire region, heavy reliance on fishing and animal husbandry extended far south along the coastal communities on both sides of the Gulf. Consequently, the Bothnian region was characterized by a lively exchange of goods, as these populations traded their surpluses of fish, animal products and articles from the many cottage industries (such as textiles, lumber, wooden containers and small boats) for salt, cereals and iron. Involvement in this exchange, however, and the specific mix of commodities traded by the peasant societies varied greatly along the 2,000 kilometer long coastline of the Gulf of Bothnia.[10] A broad spectrum of traders, from city-based merchants at the one extreme to peasant traders at the other, were engaged in the commerce of the region. Between these two extremes, we glimpse the activities of rural-based merchants, the *lanthandlare*, whose largely illegal trade in goods of third parties was the object of alternating persecution and taxation by the Swedish crown. These categories were quite fluid, however, and individuals moved from one to the other as circumstances, such as economic conditions and the erratic persecution by the state, dictated.[11]

As noted above, Stockholm was the main focus of the Bothnian trade, but other towns in Sweden and South-West Finland, notably the town of Åbo/Turku, participated as well. These towns linked the peasant producers of the region and the wider Baltic trading systems, based on the towns of the German Hansa. Stockholm and its hinterland had a special attraction for the Bothnian peasant traders. In addition to being the major international trading center of Sweden, it sat astride the entrance to Lake Mälar, which in turn provided access to the Swedish breadbasket and its important mining region, *Bergslagen*. This region offered the traders ready markets for their fish as well as access to producers of grain. Prodigious amounts of salted cod and Bothnian herring, the *strömming*, passed through the Stockholm customs station every fall, and while we do not know how many East Bothnian traders were content to sell their goods in Stockholm, many ventured into the Lake Mälar region. Here some spent the winter working in the region as hired hands, primarily as threshers, returning to their homes in the spring. They generally took their wages in cereals, which they traded for fish in their villages, completing the cycle on their next visit to the Mälar region.[12]

The merchants of Stockholm and the South-Western Finnish towns favored the extreme northern reaches of the region, and it was left to the peasants of the central and southern landscapes to carry their surpluses to market themselves. The coastal communities of Southern East Bothnia were among the most active in this trade and, as I have argued elsewhere, formed a distinct economic landscape, characterized by its reliance on trade and on its almost exclusive commercial links with Stockholm.[13]

The first six decades of the sixteenth century was by all accounts an era of economic and demographic expansion in Bothnia. In several of the more densely settled areas, such as Mustasaari and Vörå, subdivision of farms was already under way in the 1550s. It is likely that by then these parishes were no longer self-sufficient in cereals and that imports formed a key element in the provisioning of the population there.[14] As a consequence, reliance on non-agrarian activities was increasing. These, first and foremost fishing and trading, had always been central to the coastal economy, but with the growing population pressure they would have assumed increasing importance for the local economy. Since the principal export of Southern East Bothnia was salted fish, the need to import large quantities of salt provided an added impetus to trade.

The physical environment encouraged this diversity of economic activities and the flexibility that it offered the population. The coastal area of Southern East Bothnia forms a typical skerry coastline with a multitude of islets and coves girding the mainland. Off the parishes of Mustasaari and Vörå the skerries widen as the *Kvarken* sill creates a line of shoals and islets stretching westwards toward the Swedish coast. Due to the continuing uplift (ca. 85 cm per century in this area) and the very gradual slope of the land, the coastline changed constantly, moving the shore outward up to two km per century, creating new shallows and islands. Within the span of a few generations, reed-choked shallows in sheltered coves were transformed into meadows clustered with alders, which in turn would be converted into arable land through human agency. On exposed shorelines where silting was impeded by wave action, stunted alders gradually gave way to copses of coniferous trees. The result was a patchwork of fields and meadows nested between outcrops of rock and forested rocky moraines.[15] While beneficial to agriculture, the uplift created continuous problems for navigation and fishing, as coastal waterways closed and spawning grounds were destroyed, only to be reestablished further out to sea.

All farms were freehold, i.e., the owners disposed freely over their properties, but were required to pay rent, tithes and taxes to the crown. In 1561 these amounted to about 9 mk. (the price of a good live cow) per farm, varying somewhat according to size, the number of dependents, dairy cows and fishing rights, all of which were taxed.[16] The number of cottagers was small; those who were taxed made up less than 10% of the households and, given the very limited access to grazing and inshore fishing of the landless, there probably was no economic base for a much larger number. Some of them were possibly itinerant traders, but the bulk of the trade from the three parishes was undertaken by the peasant households themselves.

This, then, was the environment in which the population of coastal Southern East Bothnia made its living. Cereal cultivation, animal husbandry, fishing and sealing were the principal occupations. Household size was large, as one would expect in a multi-resource environment. About 1570, at the peak of the sixteenth century economic expansion, it averaged six to seven adults and teenagers in the densely inhabited southern parishes of Mustasaari and Vörå. In the more recently settled and less densely populated Pedersöre, the average was 3.7 per household. In overall population, the ratio between Mustasaari, Vörå and Pedersöre in this period was roughly 3:1:2, with the Pedersöre's population concentrated in the coastal zone.

After the generally favorable conditions in the first half of the sixteenth century, the Bothnian economy was subject to no fewer than three long-term negative developments in the period under review. The terms of exchange for Bothnian goods relative to imports of salt and cereals started deteriorating around the middle of the sixteenth century. This development was exacerbated by increasingly heavy taxation beginning in 1563, and finally, around 1570 the weather took a serious and lasting turn for the worse.

A major characteristic of the price inflation, which affected growing areas of Western Europe, was the relatively faster rise of prices for basic foodstuffs and commodities, such as cereals and salt – the very products that made up the bulk of Bothnian imports. The effect on prices in Bothnia was dramatic; the exchange value of the typical Bothnian surpluses of fish, butter and hides underwent a steep decline. By the decade of the 1590s prices for all these commodities, in relation to salt and cereals, had fallen to close to 50% of their value in the 1540s. Between them, salt and cereals made up about two thirds of all of Bothnia's imports, and given East Bothnia's heavy reliance on production of salted fish, the figures may have approached 75% for the three parishes under study.[17]

The effect of this decline in exchange value was compounded by war. From 1563, Sweden was at war for thirty-two years, first in the Nordic Seven Years'

War against Denmark, Lübeck and Poland (1563-70), subsequently against Russia; a war which with several truces lasted from 1570 to 1595. Extraordinary war taxation became an onerous and constant burden. From being negligible in the years leading up to 1563, it jumped for the remainder of the decade to an average of 41% of the land rent, tithes and other »regular« payments imposed on the East Bothnians. From 1571 to 1588, the average rose to 47% and soared to 123% for the period from 1589 to 1595, the year the peace treaty was signed with Russia. This latter figure even omits the extractions from quartering of soldiers, for which the peasants were rarely compensated. The amount of these extractions are unknown, but judging from the peasants' vehement complaints, they they must have been significant.[18] Since the bulk of the taxes were paid in kind, the combined effect was to reduce the amount of goods available for trade by the peasants.

The final blow to the economy was not man-made; in 1570 the climate became abruptly colder. A dendrochronological series from Torneträsk, in Northern Bothnia, shows that the distance between annual rings decreased from an average of ca. 0.8 mm for the century and half preceding 1570 to ca. 0.4 mm a few years later, and this reduced rate of growth persisted for at least a century.[19] Narrative sources confirm this development, reporting longer winters and increasing incidences of crop failures. The most immediate impact was on the lucrative spring seal hunt, which declined by 40% after 1570.[20] In the longer term, cereal cultivation suffered as marginal fields were abandoned and yields fell. The effect on animal husbandry was similarly negative. The period during which the animals could graze in the meadows may have been reduced by as much as one month, so additional winter fodder was needed to maintain the herds. Constant disputes in the *häradsting*, the local circuit courts, over ownership of hay from the common meadows suggest that increasing the supply of fodder was not possible. Fodder for the animals became a scarcity and fewer animals could be fed during the longer winters.

The combined impact of these three negative developments was to undermine the economy of East Bothnia. By 1580, close to 10% of the farms in the province were exempted from paying taxes and a further 3.3% from paying both rent and taxes; in 1590, these figures had grown to 13.5% and 9.4% respectively. The crown was also forced to reclassify farms into whole and half units in order to secure part of the fixed rent, *mantallet*, assessed on each farm; otherwise the growing number of marginal farms would have defaulted on this payment. By the year 1600, this classification rated farms from one to one-twelfth of a standard unit, resulting in a 9.5% reduction of the fixed rent from the 1570 base, above and beyond any exemptions.[21] The impact on trade was even more dramatic.

The long period of peace and economic expansion in the Swedish state system came to an end in 1563. Harvests continued to be abundant until the end of the 1560s, however, so there were probably few shortages of cereals before 1570. On the other hand, Danish blockades forced up the cost of salt until 1570. While trade to Stockholm was disrupted

Regional integration

Table 5.1: Trade in Bothnia around 1562
Comparisons between Southern East Bothnia and selected towns.

Commodity	Merchants in Stockholm	Merchants in Finnish towns	Peasant traders in Mustasaari	Peasant traders in Vörå	Peasant traders in Pedersöre
Salted fish	5079 mk.	36 mk.	2962 mk.	1403 mk.	1597 mk.
%	20.6%	0.3%	43.8%	59.4%	47.5%
Salmon	15305 mk.	6745 mk.	2059 mk.	416 mk.	580 mk.
%	62.1%	56.8%	30.5%	17.6%	17.2%
Dried fish	157 mk.	1508 mk.	529 mk.	218 mk.	209 mk.
%	0.6%	12.7%	7.8%	9.2%	6.2%
Butter	3624 mk.	1157 mk.	526 mk.	78 mk.	508 mk.
%	14.7%	9.8%	7.8%	3.3%	15.0%
Hides	490 mk.	604 mk.	682 mk.	247 mk.	483 mk.
%	2.0%	5.1%	10.1%	10.5%	14.3%
Seal oil	0	1779 mk.	0	0	0
%	0.0%	15.0%	0.0%	0.0%	0.0%
Total	24655 mk.	11829 mk.	6757 mk.	2333 mk.	3377 mk.
%	100%	100%	100.0%	100.0%	100.0%
Ship companies	33.25	56	16.75	6.25	7.75
Value/Ship Co.	742 mk.	211 mk.	403 mk.	373 mk.	433 mk.

Notes: Data for Stockholm and Mustasaari, Vörå and Pedersöre are averages for 1560-1562 and 1564, those for the finnish towns (Åbo/Turku, Rauma and Björneborg/Pori) are from 1562. The Stockholm data cover trade from all of Bothnia as well as occasional imports from the Gulf of Finland; salted fish includes »strömming« and cod.
Sources: Stockholm merchants and southern East Bothnia, Kammararkivet, Lokala Tullräkenskaper, vols. 307, 309, 310, & 311. Finnish Towns, FRA 4648, f.2-11.

during the later phases of the war, the data on the pre-war trade in table 5.1 above, giving averages from 1560-1564, may be regarded as representing the end of a period of prosperity, before the economic pressures intensified.

The trade of merchants from Stockholm and the towns of South-West Finland are included for comparison. They illustrate, *inter alia*, the fundamental difference between merchants and peasant traders. The former were resellers; they sought out areas, such as Northern Bothnia, that produced goods with the highest exchange value on their established markets – primarily the towns of the German Hansa. Salmon, dried pike and butter were popular commodities there, as was seal oil (rendered blubber) which was widely used in lamps, and for softening and waterproofing leather. Hides of domesticated animals also found ready markets. The »strömming«, a local herring, on the other hand, was rarely exported to the Hanseatic towns; the higher quality herring from the North Sea and the Sound were preferred, even though they cost between one-and-a half and twice as much as the »strömming«. In contrast to the Finnish towns, Stockholm also had an important domestic market in the Mälar region for salted fish, especially »strömming« and cod. This is the logic behind the East Bothnian peasant traders' preference for Stockholm over the towns of South-West Finland. The entire area, spanning from Southern Finland over the Åland archipelago to the Stockholm skerries, teemed with »strömming« and cod. Accordingly, merchants from South-West Finland had no need to purchase what the locals produced on their doorstep.

In contrast to the merchants, the peasant traders were largely limited to selling their domestic surpluses. These depended on local resources and on what the population found advantageous to extract from them. In the early 1560s, the peasant's goods were a fair reflection of the household production. They consisted of what was left over, once household needs had been satisfied and rents and taxes were paid. The only exception was salmon. Little salmon was caught in Mustasaari and Vörå, and the significant amount carried by the peasants to Stockholm came from Kemi, Io and Lochteå in Northern East Bothnia, where we find names of peasant traders from Southern East Bothnia in the records of local harbor fees. (This is one instance where we get a glimpse of the »lanthandlare«). Some salmon was caught in Pedersöre, but most came from the north. Otherwise, the commodities reflect the surplus-producing activities of the local peasant economy. Although the mix of commodities varies somewhat among the three parishes, it reveals roughly similar economic activities, i.e. fishing, animal husbandry and trading. The main difference is that, while the volumes from Mustasaari and Vörå reflect the approximate population ratio, i.e., 3:1, exports from Pedersöre are relatively lower, reflecting the declining involvement in the Stockholm trade further north in East Bothnia.

The combined value of the trade from the three parishes demonstrates its importance, not only to the local economy, but also in comparison with that of the town-based merchants – 12,500 mk., compared with close to 12,000 mk. for the Finnish towns and 24,700 mk. for Stockholm. The value per ship company, however, requires some comment. The number of peasant traders in a ship company ranged from one to more than twenty, with most lying between four and eight. So each trader brought an average of 60-70 mk. worth of goods to Stockholm.[22] The Stockholm merchants averaged somewhat more than two per ship company, so the average would be about 350 mk., while the Finnish merchants seem to have traded mostly as individuals, giving the individual merchant an average of about 200 mk. per annum.

The development for the next three decades from 1570 to about 1600 of the Stockholm trade from Mustasaari, Vörå and Pedersöre is outlined in the following tables. Four-year averages for 1569-72, 1579-82 and 1590-93 will be used to track the changes in volume and commodity mix.

The combined onslaught of declining prices, increasing taxation and deteriorating weather are plainly noticeable al-

Regional integration

Table 5.2: Trade from Mustasaari to Stockholm
Four-year averages at constant (1560) prices

Commodity	1560-62,64	1569-72	1579-82	1590-93
Butter	526 mk.	68 mk.	8 mk.	26 mk.
%	7.8%	2.6%	0.4%	0.7%
Salmon	2059 mk.	258 mk.	0 mk.	0 mk.
%	30.5%	9.9%	0.0%	0.0%
Strömming	2962 mk.	1947 mk.	1246 mk.	3279 mk.
%	43.8%	74.6%	67.0%	85.4%
Dried Fish	529 mk.	207 mk.	283 mk.	95 mk.
%	7.8%	7.9%	15.2%	2.5%
Hides	682 mk.	130 mk.	88 mk.	24 mk.
%	10.1%	5.0%	4.7%	0.6%
Hops	0 mk.	0 mk.	20 mk.	0 mk.
%	0.0%	0.0%	1.1%	0.0%
Tar	0 mk.	0 mk.	215 mk.	418 mk.
%	2.0%	0.0%	11.5%	10.9%
Total	6758 mk.	2610 mk.	1860 mk.	3842 mk.
%	100.0%	100.0%	100.0%	100.0%
Ship Companies	16.75	21.25	18.25	27.00
Value/Ship Co.	403 mk	123 mk.	102 mk.	142 mk.

Source: Kammararkivet, Lokala Tullräkenskaper, Vols. 307, 309, 310, 313, 314, 315, 321, 322, 324, 326, 346, 347, 352.

ready in the data for 1569-1572. Despite intensified effort – the average number of visits from Mustasaari to Stockholm increased by 31% – the total volume fell by 61%, mostly at the expense of salmon, butter and hides. This decline continued and by the 1580s the volume, measured in constant prices, had dropped by 72%. The drop was caused by the disappearance of salmon, the virtual disappearance of hides and butter, the rapid decline of the mainstay, »strömming«, and of dried fish. Clearly, heavy taxation had eaten into the local surpluses of foodstuffs and the traders had abandoned their trips to Northern East Bothnia in search of salmon. The number of dairy cattle was also declining, further reducing marketable surpluses of hides and butter (see table 5.5).

A resurgence in exports of »strömming« and the appearance and growing importance of a new commodity, tar, account for the partial recovery in the early 1590s. In this period, these two products accounted for 96% of all commodities from Mustasaari sold in Stockholm. Their lower value – a barrel of tar was worth about one-third of a barrel of »strömming«, one-sixth of a barrel of salmon and one-twelfth of a barrel of butter – accounted in some measure for

Table 5.3: Trade from Vörå to Stockholm
Four-year averages at constant (1560) prices

Commodity	1560-62, 64	1569-72	1579-82	1590-93
Butter	78 mk.	5 mk.	40 mk.	116 mk.
%	3.3%	1.1%	3.4%	4.8%
Salmon	416 mk.	0 mk.	0 mk.	0 mk.
%	17.6%	0.0%	0.0%	0.0%
Strömming	1403 mk.	401 mk.	428 mk.	1282 mk.
%	59.4%	84.3%	36.9%	52.8%
Dried Fish	218 mk.	47 mk.	18 mk.	6 mk.
%	9.2%	9.9%	1.6%	0.2%
Hides	247 mk.	23 mk.	0 mk.	20 mk.
%	10.5%	9.9%	0.0%	0.8%
Tar	0 mk.	0 mk.	675 mk.	1003 mk.
%	0.0%	0.0%	58.1%	41.3%
Total	2362 mk.	476 mk.	1161 mk.	2427 mk.
%	100.0%	100.0%	100.0%	100.0%
Ship Companies	6.25	4.00	9.25	11.50
Value/Ship Co.	378 mk.	119 mk.	126 mk.	211 mk.

Source: See table 5.2

the increasing number of vessels going to Stockholm every year. This trend, however, started before tar entered the Stockholm trade. We can only speculate what drove the larger number of skippers to venture to Stockholm despite the drop in volume. It is possible that they were seeking winter work in greater numbers in the Mälar region to compensate for their reduced income from trading. This would give an economic rationale for their going to Stockholm with drastically reduced cargoes. Similarly, the rising value of the cargoes in the 1590s would be explained by the fact that growing numbers were now finding winter work at home producing tar.

The development of Vörå's trade followed the same general pattern as that of Mustasaari, though the decline was steeper – a drop of no less than 80% – during the first decade. The decline was arrested earlier, however, already in the 1580s due to the rise in tar sales. The complete recovery of volume by the 1590s was due to the doubling of the volume of tar, and to a recovery of sales in »strömming« and butter, some of which may have come from the neighboring inland parish of Kyro.

While the trade data for Pedersöre follow a similar trend to that of the two other parishes, the mix of commodities retained more of the prewar pattern. Though the value of sales from animal husbandry (i.e., butter and hides) de-

Tabel 5.4: Trade from Pedersöre to Stockholm
Four-year averages at constant (1560) prices

Commodity	1560-62, 64	1569-72	1579-82	1590-93
Butter	508 mk.	274 mk.	136 mk.	186 mk.
%	15.1%	14.6%	9.3%	5.6%
Salmon	580 mk.	280 mk.	48 mk.	118 mk
%	17.2%	14.9%	3.2%	3.5%
Strömming	1597 mk.	876 mk.	755 mk.	2074 mk.
%	47.3%	46.6%	51.4%	62.2%
Dried Fish	209 mk.	235 mk.	36 mk.	63 mk.
%	6.2%	12.5%	2.5%	1.9%
Hides	483 mk.	216 mk.	24 mk.	179 mk.
%	14.3%	11.5%	1.6%	5.4%
Tar	0 mk.	0 mk.	470 mk.	715 mk.
%	0.0%	0.0%	32.0%	21.4%
Total	3359 mk.	1881 mk.	1469 mk.	3335 mk.
%	100.0%	100.0%	100.0%	100.0%
Ship Companies	7.75	8.75	13.75	16.75
Value/Ship Co.	433 mk.	215 mk.	107 mk.	199 mk.

Source: See table 5.2

clined by two thirds from the 1560s to the 1590s, it still represented about 10% of the total value, against 5.4% for Vörå and only 1.5% for Mustasaari. Again, the increase in sales of »strömming« and tar contributed to a recovery of the total value to close to prewar levels.

It is worth noting, however, that the recovery of the volume of trade was complete for the two northern parishes in constant monetary values only. By the 1590s the *exchange value* in terms of salt and cereals, the principal imports, was only 50% of that of the prewar decades. While these peasant societies had been able to compensate for increased taxation and deteriorating weather, they were powerless in the face of international price-movements.

While it is impossible to quantify the discrete effects of the three negative economic developments that beset the Bothnian region during the thirty years of our investigation, it is nevertheless possible to draw some qualitative conclusions from the above data on how each of these developments affected trade from the three parishes, and therefore on their influence on economic activity there.

The worsening terms of exchange for cereals should encourage an increase in local production, and there are indeed signs that this was attempted. In the densely settled south, where land was already scarce, efforts were frustrated by the deteriorating weather, while they met with some success in Pedersöre (see table 5.5). Given their lack of success, we may suppose that the population in the two southern parishes resorted to substituting fish for grain in their diet in order to maintain its calorific intake, thereby reducing the surplus available for sale. Increased taxation worked in the same direction, so it is not surprising that sales of fish to Stockholm fell dramatically for the first 20 years of our period. There was no substitute for salt, however, and the drop in the volume of »strömming« between 1569 and 1582 may have been brought about in part by the rising price of this import. Fishing was relatively unaffected by the weather, however, which may explain the subsequent resurgence of exports of »strömming«. Once other surpluses, such as butter and hides, had disappeared there was little, other than tar that the coastal populations had to sell.

The deteriorating weather affected animal husbandry, and the virtual disappearance of exports of butter and hides is also reflected in the number of taxed dairy cows, which declined significantly in the same period (table 5.5). Furthermore, it is likely that the weather was responsible, at least in part, for the decline in sales of dried fish, though there is no direct evidence of this. Narrative sources note that the weather not only turned colder, but that the cloud cover increased and that precipitation increased – conditions that would make dry-curing fish more difficult.

The most noticeable effect of the change in the climate on the economy, however, is the relative growth in the importance of economic activities that were the least affected by the weather, i.e., production of salted fish and tar. Thus, we observe the gradual conversion of a peasant economy based on trading its diversified surpluses into one concentrating on »strömming« and tar. The heavy taxation definitely played a role in this change as well, first and foremost because taxes siphoned off the foodstuffs, hides and skins that would otherwise have entered open trade, and secondly, because fishing was relatively lightly taxed and tar production not at all.

This transformation, which can be observed in all three parishes, took more than twenty years. It was hastened by a severe crisis in the trade: their combined exports fell by almost two thirds from an average of 12,500 mk. in the early 1560s to 4,500 mk. twenty years later. Tar from East Bothnia made its appearance in bulk in Stockholm only in 1578 when 1,200 barrels were registered in the rolls. Vörå, whose trade had dropped by almost 80% in the ten years from the four-year average in the early 1560s to that from around 1570, accounted for more than 40% of the volume in 1578. This parish was to continue to lead the landscape in tar production and in the subsequent recovery well into the first decades of the seventeenth century.[23]

Although there was a general recovery of trade from the three parishes it was not uniform. Mustasaari fared the worst, Vörå, with its significant tar production, managed to export slightly more in value in the early 1590s than thirty years earlier, while the volume of Pedersöre's exports were about the same and had re-

Regional integration

Table 5.5: Demography and cattle

Parish	Arable (Spl./farm) 1570	Change 1570-92 %	Dependents per farm 1570	Resource index (Spl./Dep)	Dairy cows per farm 1570	Change 1570-92 %
Mustasaari	12.8	- 9.7%	6.7	1.91	5.2	-32.7%
Vörå	20.8	- 4.8%	6.4	3.25	6.2	-29.5%
Pedersöre	14.4	+ 3.8%	3.7	3.89	6.5	-63.7%

Note: Spl.= Spannland, about 1/4 hectare. The »Resource Index« is the inverse of the population density. The much larger drop in the number of taxed dairy cows in Pedersöre (the last column) presents a problem, as it flies in the face of my assertion that this parish was the least affected by economic pressures. There is some evidence, however, that the peasants in this thinly populated area were more adept in hiding their cattle from the tax assessors.
Source: Maarbjerg: *Scandinavia in the European World-Economy ca. 1570-1625*, 1995.

tained more of their original mix. To find an explanation for these differences, we must consult the demographic data for the three parishes.

In East Bothnia, the area of a farm's arable land determined its rights to other key resources. Thus, grazing, meadows and reed marshes for winter fodder, as well as forests and inshore fishing were allocated in rough proportion to the arable land. Arable land is therefore a good measure of the total resources available to the individual peasant household. The »Resource Index« makes it clear that the pressure on resources in Mustasaari was much greater than in the two other parishes. This impression is strengthened further by the decline in arable land, which suggests that more marginal land had been taken under cultivation there than in the other parishes during the expansion up to 1570. By the same token, the net expansion of arable land in Pedersöre, though modest, was possible only because of its relatively low population density; i.e., there was still suitable land available for cultivation. Most likely, it was the greater general availability of free resources there which enabled the population to maintain an economy more closely resembling the prewar one.

The unequal distribution of resources may also explain why Vörå developed its tar industry so early, and increased production ahead of the two other parishes, despite its much smaller population. We know little about the ratios of usable timberland to the area of arable land in the three parishes. It seems safe to assume, however, that it was of the same magnitude in Vörå and Mustasaari, with their similar topography, and significantly larger in sparsely-populated Pedersöre. With its greater population density, most of Mustasaari's timber resources were probably already dedicated to traditional uses, such as construction, tools and heating.[24] With its low population density and many scattered settlements, Pedersöre was short of the concentrations of labor necessary for the collective effort that was required for large-scale production of tar. Vörå, on the other hand, with its large household size, appears to have had a favorable mix of labor, settlement density and sufficient timber resources.[25]

The patterns of trade of the three parishes studied here demonstrate the resilience of pre-modern peasant societies, especially those actively involved in trade. The high degree of self-sufficiency, which characterizes all such societies, clearly played a role in allowing the households time for the necessary readjustments to the significant economic and climatic changes which affected them in the period under review. Local substitution of foodstuffs, reallocation and intensification of labor, be it working in the Mälar region during the winters, seeking new fishing grounds or building up tar production, all illustrate the range of options open to the East Bothnian peasantry when confronted with economic crisis. Nevertheless, the study also underscores the limits to such a recovery; where resources were already under pressure, as in Mustasaari, the range of options was limited and recovery could only be partial.

After the year 1600 price pressures eased, and by 1620 the terms of exchange were approaching their 1540 levels as the inflationary pressures abated in the wider European economy.[26] War and taxation continued to be a permanent feature of the Swedish economy for the next century, however, as did change in weather (which we now refer to as the »Little Ice Age«) with its frequent crop failures.

Tar production proved to be the long-term salvation of the province overall and of the southern parishes in particular. Just when the East Bothnians most acutely needed a product to compensate for the taxes and weather that sapped their traditional trade, European demand for tar increased and supplies from the traditional supplier, Prussia, started to stagnate because of overexploitation of its forests.[27] In 1578 East Bothnians had sold 1,200 barrels of tar in Stockholm, virtually all from the three southern parishes. By 1600 this volume had grown to over 4,000 and in 1624 it was close to 9,000, peaking in 1648 at more than 41,000 barrels of tar and pitch.[28] The income from this production enabled the East Bothnian peasantry to mitigate the worst blows of Sweden's incessant warfare in the seventeenth century.[29]

Notes

1 An earlier version of this article was presented at the eighth conference of the Association of Historians of the Northern Seas, in Esbjerg in August 1997.

2 See Åke Sandström: *Mellan Torneå och Amsterdam, En undersökning av Stockholms roll som förmedlare av varor i regional- och utrikeshandel 1600-1650*, Stockholmsmonografier 102, Stockholm 1990, Part III: Regionalhandelen; John P. Maarbjerg: *Scandinavia in the European World-Economy ca. 1570-1625. Some local Evidence of Economic Integration*, New York 1995, pp. 167-176.

3 Nils Friberg: *Stockholm i det bottniska farvatten. Stockholms bottniska handelsfält under senmedeltiden och Gustav Vasa*, Stockholmsmonografier 58, Stockholm 1983; Sandström (see note 2).

4 Kammararkivet, Sandbergs Saml. Vol.QQ, f. 40ff.

5 Sandström (see note 2), p. 204.

6 Svenska Riksarkivet (RA), Lokala tullräkenskaper, vol. 415 I & II, 416. In 1624, with 57 vessels going to Stockholm from Southern East Bothnia, a total of 10 head of livestock were entered in the customs rolls. Feathers were a more common item, typically 1-2 barrels per vessel. They were, however, a low-value item – in 1559 the price in East Bothnia was 1 mk per barrel, or about half of that of a

Regional integration

barrel of tar; Finska Riksarkivet (FRA), 4606 f. 26v.
7 Friberg (see note 3), pp. 243, 253 and 258.
8 RA, Lokala tullräkenskaper 556-569; Finska cameralier 90: I-IV.
9 *Historia de Gentibus septentrionalibus* (Rome 1555, transl. Robert Gete et al., Uppsala 1909).
10 Gunvor Kerkkonen: Bondebefolkningens binäringer vid 1500-talets mitt, *Svenska Litteraturselskapet i Finland. Historiska och litteraturhistoriska studier nr. 37*, Helsingfors 1962.
11 Maarbjerg (see note 2), pp. 178-180. E.g., the wealthy Pedersöre trader Hans Fordel is listed among Stockholm merchants in the 1560 customs rolls (*Lokala tullräkenskaper*, vol. 307.)
12 B.V. Åkerblom: *Vörå Sockens Historia*, I, Åbo 1937, p. 383.
13 Maarbjerg (see note 2), p. 208.
14 Op. cit., p. 202.
15 Michael Jones: *Landhöjning, jordägoförhållanden och kulturlandskap i Maxmo*, Bidrag till Kännedom av Finlands Natur och Folk, utg. av Finska Vetenskaps-Societeten H. 135, Helsingfors 1987, p. 15.
16 FRA 4627, 4634 [prices], 4639-41.
17 Maarbjerg (see note 2), pp. 188-190 and 202.
18 These extractions led to a rebellion in the province in 1596, after which the records cease until about 1600.
19 T.S. Bartholin: Dendrochronology in Sweden, N. A. Mörner and W. Karlén (eds.): *Climatic Changes on a Yearly to Millenial Basis*, Dordrecht 1984, p. 262, fig. 2.
20 Roger Kvist: *Sälfangsten i Österbotten och Västerbotten 1551-1610*, Research report no. 3, Umeå University Center for Arctic Cultural Research 30, 1983.
21 1570: FRA 4713, f. 2v & FRA 4718, ff. 7 & 9; 1580: FRA 4757, ff. 3v, 17v & 33v; 1590; FRA 4789, ff. 2, 20 & 38v; 1600: FRA 4817, ff. 4 & 40-41v.
22 This figure seems quite high for a single household, and it is likely that there was some »engrossing« by the individuals who sent their goods to Stockholm, i.e., that they bought up the surpluses of their non-trading neighbors.
23 Ingmar Calonius: Orsakarne till städerna Nykarlebys, Jakobstads och Gamlakarlebys uppkomst, *Fennia*, 80 Nr. 2, 1956, p. 114.
24 50 medium-sized pine trees yielded about one barrel of tar, Nils Erik Villstrand: Med stor möde i en hop gropar i marken. Tjärbränning kring Bottniska viken under svensk stormaktstid, *Historisk Tidskrift för Finland*, 77, 1992, p. 45.
25 In the nineteenth century, when mass production techniques had been refined, it took eight to nine man-days to produce one barrel of tar. That it was significantly higher in the sixteenth century is confirmed by earlier but less reliable estimates of between 10 and 20 mandays per barrel (Villstrand, 1992, pp. 49-50). Thus, Vörå's modest production of about 500 barrels in 1578 would have absorbed between 5,000 and 10,000 man-days of labor, contributed by an unknown number of the ca. 290 households in the parish.
26 Maarbjerg (see note 2), p. 190
27 Villstrand 1992 (see note 24), pp. 40-41.
28 Sandström (see note 2), p. 248.
29 Nils Erik Villstrand: *Anpassning eller protest. Lokalsamhället inför utskrivningarna av fotfolk till den svenska krigsmakten 1620-1679*, Åbo 1992, pp. 228-240.

CHAPTER 6
Ploughing burghers and trading peasants

The meeting between the European urban economy and Sweden in the sixteenth and seventeenth centuries

By Åke Sandström

The Swedish economy in the sixteenth century was to a large extent self-sufficient.[1] Not so that no trade within the country or with other regions in Europe existed, but the overwhelming majority of the Swedes lived their lives with a very loose attachment to the market.[2]

When the Swedish rulers in the early modern period decided to let Sweden follow the course of the major European states with their growing central governments, the problems of revenue-raising within the existing kind of »primitive« economy became evident. Methods to obtain new incomes were demonstrated by the politics implemented by more developed European states like England, France and the German principalities, whose governments had for centuries been improving the techniques to increase taxes and other forms of revenue. But even if the prototypes of the more demanding tax-state could be easily studied abroad, this did not mean that the procedures of tax-construction and tax-harvesting were easily transferred to Swedish soil. The kingdom was characterized by a small population scattered over vast regions and by a low degree of urbanization. On an area bigger than France there lived just over one million Swedes and Finns – and the few towns held only four to five per cent of the total population.[3] When the Swedish government, despite these circumstances and difficulties, tried to follow the route blazed by other European states, the need to develop instruments more suitable for Swedish conditions soon became apparent.

One of the most urgent tasks for the Swedish Crown was to channel the existing uncontrolled or weakly controlled trade among the Swedish subjects to places under government supervision. Some of the methods to be used had to a large extent already been described in the Swedish law of towns (*stadslagen*) from the mid-fourteenth century, a code which in its turn was strongly influenced by the German town laws (*Stadtrechte*) of the twelfth and thirteenth centuries.[4] This code of law had formally been valid all the time since its publication, but the Crown lacked the resources and sometimes even the interest to see the law implemented in the economic field.

Although the general principles were drawn up in earlier codes of law, the form in which the Swedish market was to be organized in early modern times was a complex one. The framework of

Regional integration

Fig. 6.1: Important trade centres in Northern Europe in the sixteenth century.

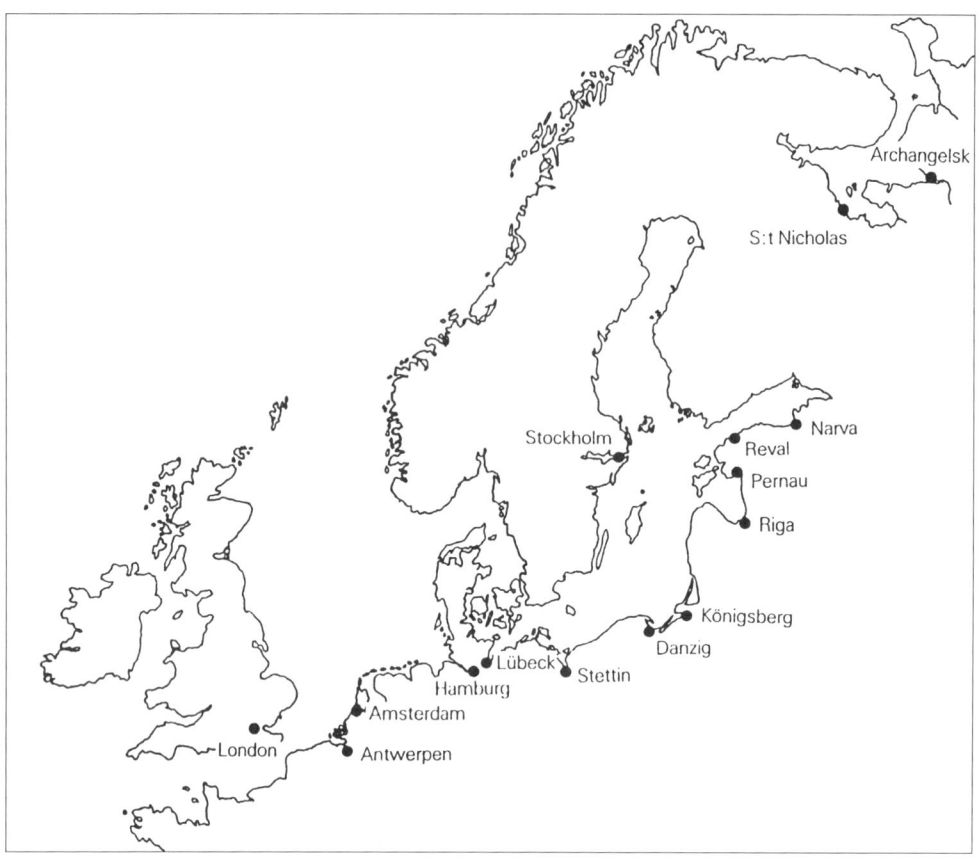

Source: Åke Sandström: *Mellan Torneå och Amsterdam*, 1990, p. 18.

laws designated to shape this market was only indistinctly formulated in the sixteenth century and more formally expressed during the first half of the seventeenth century.[5] The general principle of this legislation prescribed that the rural population were obliged to deliver their products to the uptowns (*uppstäder*), i.e. towns endowed with the right to act as middlemen between the countryside and the staple towns (*stapelstäder*) which had a monopoly on foreign trade. Thus, the domestic trade was constrained to a vertical relationship between the rural producers and the foreign consumers – and from the European producers to domestic consumers. One of the main aims of the Crown was to make taxation possible on all levels of this system.

Even if the main structure of this system followed a medieval formula, there were important differences in the way in which it was implemented in the sixteenth and seventeenth centuries. The early Vasas of the sixteenth century were often unrealistic in their assessments of the Crown's ability to enforce royal decrees on the Swedish market, as was their understanding of the nature of the Swedish economy. This economy can be viewed as a shortage economy

Ploughing burghers and trading peasants

Fig. 6.2: The principle of the Swedish »staple townsystem« regarding distribution and taxation of goods

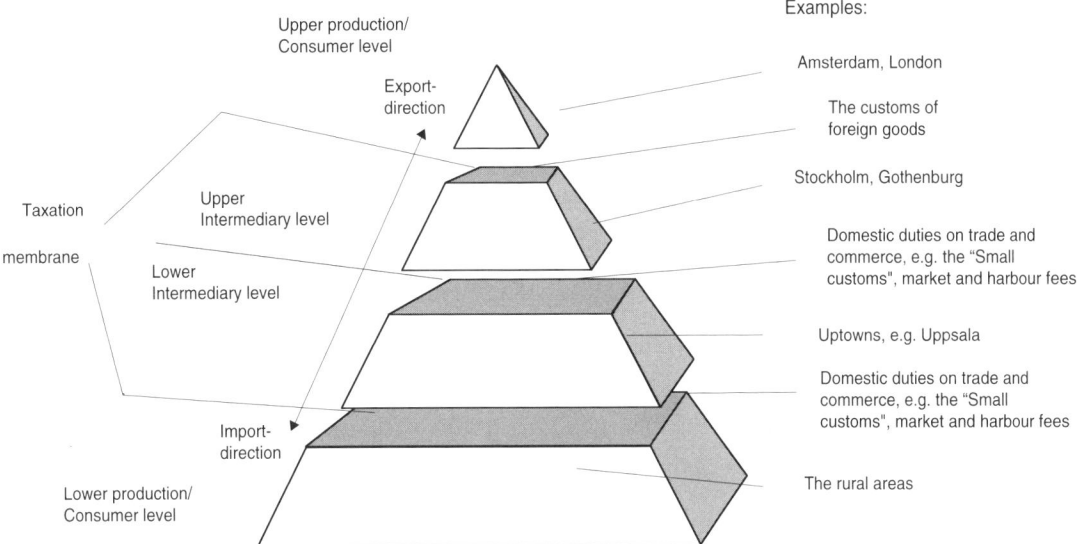

Source: Åke Sandström: *Plöjande borgare och handlande bönder*, 1996, p. 26.

with a scarcity both of goods and capital. Of course, this situation severely limited the Crown's freedom of action in economic policy. Despite this fact, large-scale projects with the aim of reforming the Swedish market were launched in the sixteenth century, as were laws aiming to regulate the trade, production and economic behaviour of the Swedes. Most of the time these economic plans were built upon the principle shown in fig. 6.2.

One of Gustav Vasa's favourite projects of the 1550s was designed to draw the trade from Russian- and German-controlled towns to the recently founded town of Helsinki. The goods gathered in Helsinki were to be transported across the Baltic, through the lake Mälaren west of Stockholm and further by an overland route to a small market settlement called Askersund in central Sweden. The king also hoped that this place would attract merchants and goods from the western parts of Sweden – which in their turn had contacts with the ports on the Atlantic coast.[6] This project failed – like most others of its sort – after leaving the Chancellor's office. The Swedish Crown did not as yet possess the means of power necessary to carry out far-reaching economic projects.

This pattern was to be changed during the reign of Gustavus Adolphus and his chancellor Axel Oxenstierna from the second decade of the seventeenth century. Now the line of action changed to the more pragmatic one to choose the means to promote a taxable market, and preferably a market that was growing as well. The government was willing to discuss methods and means to reach this goal, but not the goal itself.

There was certainly need for fresh income in the treasury. With the active Swedish foreign policy of the seventeenth century and the ambition of her leaders to place the country among the leading nations in Europe, the need for revenue was always present. In this field – the growth of the central state with its concomitant economic costs – Sweden did not only follow the European development; in relative numbers she probably exceeded many other nations.

The Crown faced several obstacles when trying to convert the poorly regulated Swedish market into a taxable shape, and far from all of them were to be overcome during the Vasa regime from the 1520s to the 1650s. Not only were the participants on all levels of the market unwilling to be brought to order: the personnel that the Crown had to depend upon to implement this order were often tempted to make personal profits or to help their neighbours in the local community close favourable deals. If they did not act in that way, and instead tried to do their jobs, e.g. by arresting people and goods in connection with illegal trade, it was highly probable that they would get into difficulties in their local communities. An eloquent example of this is provided by the Inspector of the Customs in the Finnish town of Vasa. He executed his work with such energy that he once, in 1646, took the priest to court accusing him of having sailed from the countryside to Stockholm with goods, which was against the law. The priest claimed – in front of the embarrassed members of court and parish – that he had undertaken the journey in order to buy medicine in Stockholm. The court found, on obscure grounds, that the priest had made his trip with the permission of the governor. The inspector continued to carry out his tasks in the same harsh manner, but the local community waited for an opportunity to strike back,

and it came in the winter of 1649. The protocol of the court shows a poorly camouflaged malicious pleasure in the fact that they were dealing with the child of the customs inspector, who was accused of having stolen hay out of a barn in the woods. This crime – which would normally have been considered a minor one – gave the court an opportunity to confiscate parts of the inspector's property.[7]

This example from Vasa gives an explanation of why so few crimes of trade were brought to court in the countryside, even in areas known to hold numerous peasant-traders. A bailiff who dragged neighbours to court for trading in the way they and other locals had done for generations was not likely to be popular. These difficulties with the Crown servants were about the same in the 1520s as in the 1650s.

Another area in which little happened despite the more intensive efforts of the government was the pedlars' trade. The costers of the Swedish towns were buying and selling almost anything on street corners and in alleys. Of course, these men and women were obstructing the efforts to create a better order in the Swedish market. Therefore it seems to be an inconsistency that the Crown in effect accepted this commerce. Instead of forbidding the activities of the costers, the Crown tried to fit those, often poor salesmen and -women into an order controlled by the authorities. A first attempt to permit and control the costers was made in 1603 in Stockholm. Instead of the usual prohibition of this activity, the town council issued an order allowing six persons to buy fresh fish in the Stockholm archipelago, bring it to town and sell it there.[8]

Twenty years later, the Crown made an attempt to regulate the business of the costers on a nation-wide scale. A statute was issued proclaiming that special houses should be built for the costers in every Swedish town. The buildings should have separate rooms for different categories of costers. The peasants of the hinterland were supposed to arrive with their products at these houses, where the costers could make their purchases and also sell their wares – with the exception of milk, egg, vegetables and sausages. The costers dealing in these products were instructed to take their goods to the main square of their town to sell it there. The importance of cleanliness and the prohibition against selling liquor were specially stressed. As for the question of how many costers each town should have, the Crown left that decision to the bailiffs and councils of the towns.[9]

The statute of 1623 was no success. There is nothing to indicate that the regulations were carried out. In 1635 another statute was published with almost the same content – and with the same lack of result.[10] The economic activities of the costers were beyond the reach of the Crown. The costers were not only an economic problem, but a social one as well: the alternative to the activity of those underprivileged people was an increased number of beggars in the streets. If the regulations were impossible to impose, the Crown had in practice little option but to allow the activity.

But the most serious problem was the unfavourable conditions for the establishment of an economic system based on the urban sector of the Swedish society, a society to a large extent rural in its nature. According to the view of the authorities, there should be a strict division of economic functions between the burghers of the towns and the people living in the rural areas. This division is illustrated in fig. 6.2. The peasants often lived very far from the nearest town, and could not depend upon it if any need for buying and selling should occur. And even if the distance did not pose any hindrance, the fact that the burghers of many Swedish small towns did not have the economic strength to attract domestic or foreign merchants often did. Therefore the rural population often acted as their own merchants, transporting as well as selling their goods in more distant towns – and not even necessarily Swedish ports. Against the law, peasant vessels sailed to German ports in the Southern and Eastern Baltic, trips that could sometimes cover more than 1,000 kilometres. Of course, this ability of the rural population did not make economic life easier for the burghers of the small towns. Without trade these burghers had to rely upon traditional agrarian labour, or – more accurately – they had to rely on a diversity of activities, including trade when the opportunity presented itself, but for most of the time they were busy cropping, fishing and herding cattle.[11]

Thus, the Swedish population of the time cannot be simply divided into burghers and peasants, at least not if their economic functions are considered. There was indeed no lack of burghers relying more on the soil than many peasants did, and on the other hand many peasants handled and traded goods by volumes that many small-town burghers only could dream about. In reality daily life of a majority of the burghers and the peasants alike was filled with a wide diversity of agrarian as well as, in the eyes of the Crown, urban occupations.

The implementation of the labour division between different towns and between towns and countryside in the staple town system would probably had been easier if the system had developed in answer to some needs of the participants in the market, which seldom happened.

From the second half of the seventeenth century the Crown struggled to get a firmer grip on domestic trade, while at the same time developing the taxation of it. The most far-reaching project was the foundation of the so-called »small customs« (*lilla tullen*) after an old continental model. In the small customs all »edible, wear- and tearable« goods brought to markets, market towns and other towns were subject to a customs fee of 1/32 of the value of the goods.[12] In order to implement this customs, it was decided that every town and market place in the country was to be surrounded with fences in which gates with custom controls were to be placed. This project would indeed have been worthy of the early Vasas. But the important difference from these earlier projects was that the Crown to a large extent persisted in implementing this new customs system, along with a fundamental reform of the customs on foreign trade as well, from the 1630s. This new duty on domestic trade caused a lot of anger among the subjects, and sometimes even riots. But still, the customs reform was accomplished, and fees on milk, bread, hay, shoes, pots etc. were collected until the beginning of the nineteenth century.

When transforming the Swedish market into a taxable shape, the Crown had to deal with four different groups of market participants: the rural population, the uptown burghers, the burghers of the staple towns and the foreign merchants. These groups formed a hierarchy where the peasants formed the base and the merchants of the foreign towns the apex, as shown in fig. 6.2. The attitude of the Crown toward each of these four groups varied considerably. The Crown's freedom of action was limited in the base because major interventions could harm production. A similar limitation was present at the top of the hierarchy: if the Crown for instance increased the customs duties on goods brought to Sweden, foreign ships were likely to reduce their number of visits, or they would completely avoid Swedish ports. This was probably the main reason behind the discrepancy between the harsh tone towards foreign merchants in Swedish laws on trade and the actual freedom of movement these merchants enjoyed in Sweden. Although forbidden in law, it was not unusual that foreign merchants attended domestic markets. Nor could the Crown force its policy very strongly on the burghers of the staple towns. With a weakened class of merchants in the main trading towns, there was an immediate risk that the trade would decrease, and with it the tax incomes of various sorts. Another risk was that foreigners, whom the Crown had even less chance of controlling, could gain control of the trade. Thus, the Crown's freedom of action was most significant towards the burghers and other inhabitants of the uptowns. This group was also considered the most expendable in the economic policy of the Crown. The

Crown was even willing to let the merchants of the staple towns visit the traditional markets held by the uptowns, where the uptown burghers used to trade with peasants, fishermen and miners as middlemen between them and the stapletowns. Rather than allow the common people of the countryside to trade in places beyond the control of the Crown, they were allowed to deal directly with the merchants of the staple towns. The burgher of an uptown could do nothing when the two parties between whom he was supposed to be the middleman, closed deals under his very eyes. How the problem appeared to the uptown-burghers was described in a complaint from the town of Västerås 100 km west of Stockholm to the chancellor in 1618: If they (the burghers of Västerås) got their hands on some iron and took it to Stockholm, the burghers of the staple town offered so little payment that it hardly covered their expences. The Stockholmer burgher knew that the burghers of the uptowns were forbidden to sell to any others. When the uptown burghers wanted to buy goods in Stockholm for their trade with the peasants, the Stockholmer demanded high prices and did not care if they bought or not, because he could sell directly to the peasants himself.[13]

The uptowns were the big losers of the tax-oriented staple town system of the seventeenth century. The merchants of the uptowns repeatedly asked for the privilege to ship their goods abroad themselves, but the Crown refused and even diminished their existing limited rights of foreign trade.

It is needless to say that the implementation of the staple town system presupposed the existence of towns. Hence, with the very low degree of urbanization in many regions, new towns had to be created. And this was done on a large scale, especially between the two last decades of the sixteenth century and the middle of the seventeenth century. During that time, about 40 new towns were established in Sweden and Finland. But the new towns were far from enough to solve all the problems following the staple town system. The newly founded towns were with few exceptions created as uptowns, i.e. towns with obligations to serve the staple towns with goods, and this fact brought about the troubles in the economic situation of the uptowns already mentioned.[14] In this situation markets and market towns were developed as substitutes for many existing but economically weak towns. The markets and market towns can in this perspective be viewed as temporary towns with visitors of better capacity to trade than the burghers of weak uptowns. On those markets the rural population were allowed to exchange their goods, often regardless of where they lived. Here they could sell their products to domestic and – although formally prohibited by the law – foreign merchants of better capital strength than »their own« burghers at home. The numerous markets and market towns are one of the more important characteristics of the Swedish version of the European urban economy.

The connection between the Swedish economy and the European urban economy was to be established between the Swedish staple towns and the emerging centres of the new European world economy on the Atlantic coast, which up to the mid-seventeenth century were, above all, the Dutch ports.[15]

Regional integration

The shift from the dependence on the older regional Hanseatic economy to the world economy under Dutch leadership is clearly detectable in the source material from the foreign customs in Stockholm. The Swedish capital accounted for approximately 60-85% of the nation's foreign trade during the first half of the seventeenth century and can thus be regarded as a reliable indicator of the national development.[16]

The Stockholm import figures should not lead to the conclusion that the trade with the old Hanseatic German ports was reduced. This was not the case. The trade with the medieval commercial giants of Lübeck and Danzig and other Hanseatic ports increased as well, but not at the same pace as foreign trade on the whole. Far from sharing in the so-called general crisis of the seventeenth century, the foreign trade of Stockholm rose between four and five times during the first half of the seventeenth century.

The diagram (fig. 6.3) could be used as an illustration of the Swedish participation in the process of integration on the new European market. Another, and in a way more eloquent sign of this development was the Dutch import of firewood from Stockholm's hinterland. The long-distance transport of this bulky cargo increased in the 1640s to such an extent that the prices of the important product rose substantially in the Swedish capital.[17] The authorities feared a shortage of firewood in the capital and therefore increased the customs duty several times. The integration of the European market had already progressed so much in the 1640s that firewood chopped in the forests and on the islands surrounding Stockholm helped to heat the houses of Amsterdam.

Fig. 6.3: The import to Stockholm 1600-1650 from Baltic (Goods from the east) and Atlantic (Goods from the west) ports according to the Stockholm customs journals (»Tolag«)

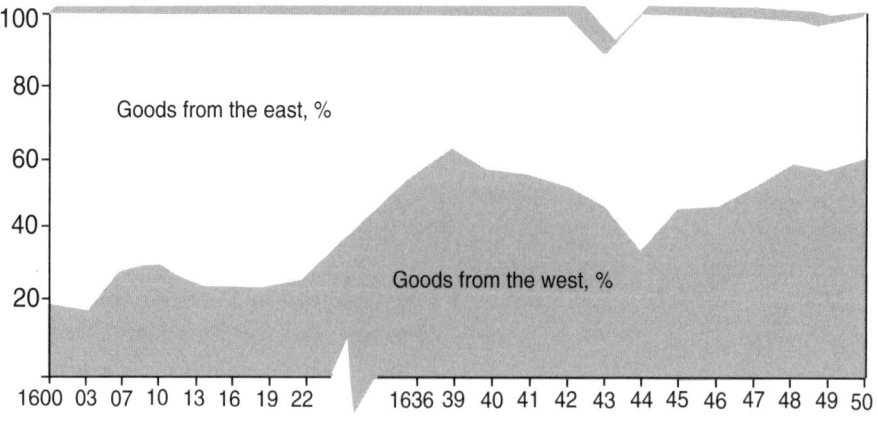

Note: The export figures follow approximately those for the imports. Departure ports have not been possible to determine during years not reaching 100% in the figure. The decline in 1644 is explained by the war between Sweden and Denmark, which severely disturbed the trade through the Sound.
Source: Åke Sandström: *Plöjande borgare och handlande bönder*, 1996, p. 184.

Ploughing burghers and trading peasants

Fig. 6.4: The registered volume of trade in Swedish silver thalers among the 100 most important importers and/or exporters in Stockholm 1650 according to the journals of the Stockholm »Tolag«

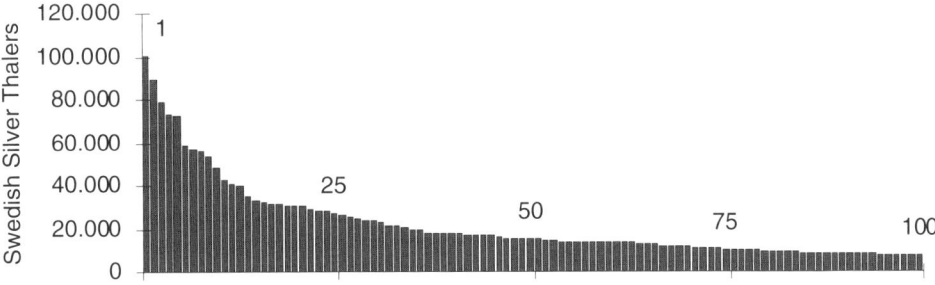

Source: Åke Sandström: *Plöjande borgare och handlande bönder*, 1996, p. 187.

Another question is which group of merchants in the Swedish staple towns was responsible for this connection to the new economic order in Europe. Even if the general view of the Swedish integration in Europe is that it took place on a broad front during the seventeenth century, it can be established through studies of the Swedish foreign trade towards the mid-seventeenth century, that this connection, when it came to the exchange of goods, took place with the help of the Crown itself and a very small number of financiers. A majority of the merchants of the Swedish staple towns continued to trade with the same German ports as their ancestors had done in the Middle Ages. How is it possible to come to this conclusion? From the town's own office of the Stockholm foreign customs, detailed journals of the foreign trade have been preserved. This income from foreign trade was donated to the capital by the Crown in the 1630s to finance the extensive reshaping of the streets, harbours and buildings of the medieval town. In these sources, the records of the Stockholm tolag (related to the German word Zuschlag, i.e. addition), which are kept in the City Ar-

Fig. 6.5: The registered volume of trade in Swedish silver thalers among the 962 importers and/or exporters in Stockholm placed after the top 100 traders 1650 according to the journals of the Stockholm »Tolag«.

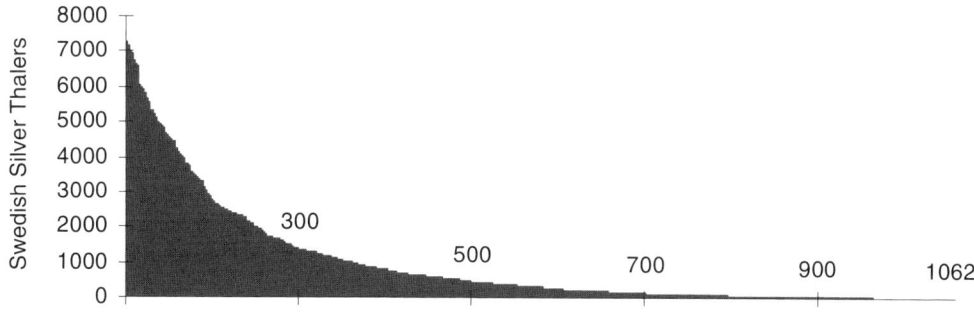

Source: Åke Sandström: *Plöjande borgere och handlande bönder*, 1996, p. 187.

103

chives of Stockholm, it is not only possible to find the quantities, origins and destinations of the goods. The books also reveal who answered for which parts of the cargoes and how much trade those persons had during the year. The books were used as tools for the taxation of the traders, hence the detailed records. This material, which is very suitable for socio-economic investigations of the early modern period, is surprisingly seldom used in the research. During the year 1650, well over one thousand importers and/or exporters were registered in the customs journals. In the diagrams (figs. 6.4 and 6.5) of the importers' and exporters' volume of trade in Stockholm, the Crown, the trading companies and those of the nobility who were liberated from taxes (at this time there was no general exemption from taxes for the Swedish nobility) are not included.

The question of the remaining 1,062 importers/exporters in Stockholm is simple: How was the volume of trade divided among the participants in the Stockholm foreign trade? The answer to this question could also be very brief: it was very unevenly divided. The result is shown in figs. 6.4 and 6.5. The first diagram presents the one hundred traders with the highest value of traded goods, and the other diagram shows the rest of the participants in the foreign trade. The conclusion is that a small élite dominated the foreign trade of Stockholm: less than 10% of the participators owned more than 70% of the volume. This minority was responsible for the connection of the Swedish market to the new European market. Of the »minor« merchants, only a small fraction traded with the Netherlands or England, the rest stuck to Baltic ports such as Lübeck, Danzig, Stralsund, Königsberg, Rostock and Greifswald.

During the first half of the seventeenth century firm ties had been created between the Swedish market and the European world economy with its bases in the urban commercial centres of the Atlantic coast. This process was accompanied by the struggle of the Crown to create such order on the Swedish market that made a more effective taxation possible. And order – or in any case better order – was brought to the unregulated economy of the country. The market was turned into a more taxable shape towards the mid-seventeenth century than it had been 50 or 150 years earlier. Of course the subjects still tried to smuggle, cheat and trade illegally, and the Swedish burghers continued ploughing and the peasants continued trading for a couple of centuries more. But by the mid-seventeenth century the Crown had a better grip on the domestic economy and larger revenues from it than ever before. The meeting between the European urban economy and Sweden in the sixteenth and seventeenth centuries did not mean that the Swedish Crown copied the more advanced system. It meant an adaptation of it to fit Swedish conditions, and it also involved a connection to the European urban system that still exists.

Notes

1 This article is based on my book: *Plöjande borgare och handlande bönder. Mötet mellan den europeiska urbana ekonomin och vasatidens Sverige*, Studier i stads- och kommunhistoria nr.

15, Stockholm 1996. The English title of this article is a direct translation of the Swedish title of the book.
2 For a general outlook over the economic history of Sweden Eli F. Heckschers work is still useful, e.g. *An Economic history of Sweden*, Cambridge, Mass: Harvard University Press 1954. For a more modern overview, see Lars Magnusson: *Sveriges ekonomiska historia*, Stockholm 1997.
3 Sven Lilja has carried through an enormous task by establishing the rate and pattern of urbanization in the early modern Sweden. See Sven Lilja: *Städernas folkmängd och tillväxt. Sverige (med Finland) ca. 1570-tal till 1810-tal*, Stads- och Kommunhistoriska Instituttet, Stockholm 1996, and: *Tjuvehål och stolta städer. Urbaniseringens kronologi och geografi i Sverige (med Finland) ca. 1570-tal till 1810-tal*, Stads- och kommunhistoriska institutet, Stockholm 2000. Database: *Urbanisering och urbana nätverk i Sverige (med Finland) ca 1570 till 1770*, Stads- och kommunhistoriska institutet, Stockholm 1994.
4 *Magnus Erikssons stadslag.* I nusvensk tolkning av Åke Holmbäck och Elias Wessén. Rättshistoriskt bibliotek, sjunde bandet, Lund 1966.
5 Robert Sandberg: *I slottets skugga. Stockholm och kronan 1599–1620*. Stockholmsmonografier vol. 105, Stockholm 1991, chapter 2 and 3; Åke Sandström: *Mellan Torneå och Amsterdam. En undersökning av Stockholms roll som förmedlare av varor i regional- och utrikeshandel.* Stockholmsmonografier vol. 102, Stockholm 1990, chapter II:1.
6 Eino E. Suolahti: Helsingfors under 1500- och 1600-talen, *Helsingfors stads historia*, 1, Helsingfors 1950, p. 134; Lars-Arne Norborg: Jönköping under medeltid och äldre vasatid, *Jönköpings stads historia*, Jönköping 1963, pp. 225–226; Sandström 1996 (see note 1), pp. 30-32.
7 Sandström 1996 (see note 1), pp. 87-88.
8 Folke Sleman och Göran Setterkrans (eds.): *Stockholms stads tänkeböcker från 1592*, Del 5: 1603–1604, Stockholm 1959, 8/12 1603, p. 162.
9 Carl-Fredrik Corin and Folke Sleman (eds.): *Privilegier, resolutioner och förordningar för Sveriges städer*, Part VI (1621–1632), Stockholm 1985, p. 180.
10 Magn Lagerström: *Stockholms stads ordinantier, påbud och publikationer...*, Stockholm 1731 (without pagination), Ordning och stadga, huruledes köphandeln och hantverken rätt delas 1635, paragraph XXXII.
11 Sandström 1996 (see note 1), chapter 2, Städernas försörjning.
12 K. Bodell: *Stad, bondebygd och bergslag vid mitten av 1600-talet. Varuutbytet i Örebro och dess omland enligt tullängdernas vittnesbörd*, Stockholm 1970, pp. 69–78.
13 Folke Sleman (ed.): *Privilegier, resolutioner och förordningar för Sveriges städer*, Part V (1611–1620), Stockholm 1964, pp. 258-259.
14 For a general outlook over the foundations of cities in early modern Sweden, see Birgitta Ericsson: De anlagda städerna i Sverige (ca. 1580–1800), *De anlagte steder på 1600– 1700 tallet. Det XVII nordiska historikermøte i Trondheim 1977 (Urbaniseringsprosessen i Norden, bd. 2)*, ed. Grethe Authén Blom, 1977.
15 The Dutch domination of the European economy is studied in Jan de Vries: *The Economy of Europe in an Age of Crisis, 1600–1750*, Cambridge 1976, and Immanuel Wallerstein: *The Modern World-System, II. Mercantilism and the Consolidation of the European World-Economy*, New York 1980.
16 Sandström 1990 (see note 5), chapter V.
17 Op. cit., pp. 367-369.

Chapter 7
Vestfold and Telemark
Two regions in South-Eastern Norway in the seventeenth and eighteenth centuries

By Øystein Rian

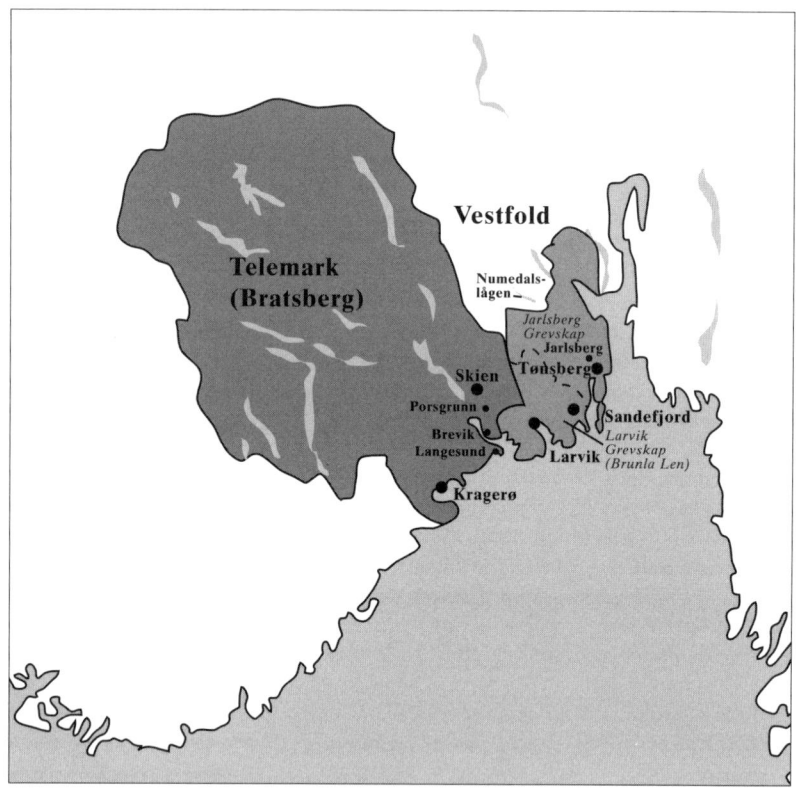

Fig. 7.1: Towns and counties in Vestfold and Telemark

Vestfold and Telemark are two neighbouring counties in South-Eastern Norway on the western side of the Oslo fjord. I have studied their development during parts of the early modern period, Vestfold from 1671 to 1821 and Telemark in the seventeenth century. The time span of the Vestfold history was decided by the urge to investigate how the region was affected by the status of its two counties, Larvik and Jarlsberg, enfeoffed to two counts who enjoyed extensive privileges as members of the highest order of nobility in the absolute monarchy of Denmark-Norway.[1] The aim of the Telemark-investigation was to give a

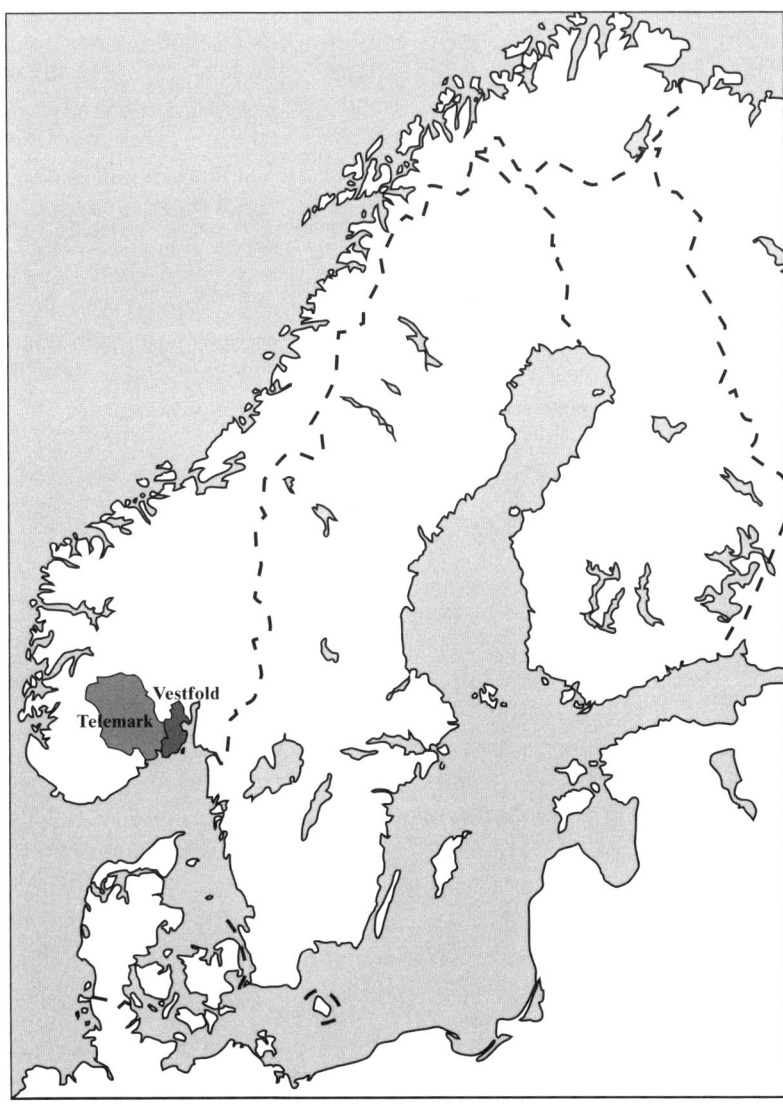

Fig. 7.2: The regions of Vestfold and Telemark

picture of the development of the state finances in a Norwegian region during a century when taxes were increased substantially – and to examine the connections between this financial development and growth in foreign trade.[2]

A striking diversity

The Norwegian regions show a striking diversity, especially when one compares districts in different provinces. But this has also been the case within each region, even quite small ones, as in the case of Vestfold, which comprises only

2,300 km², 1/140 of the whole country. These differences were caused by diverse geographical and topographical circumstances in interaction with specific historical developments. Both in Vestfold and Telemark, there was a marked contrast between the coastal and the inland areas. The former were more densely populated, and more intensively cultivated, all towns were located there, and they communicated easily with other coastal areas and with foreign ports. The interior was characterized by forests and mountains, especially in Telemark, an area seven times larger than Vestfold, covering more than 15 000 km². However, the more important agriculture was in the interior districts, the more similar local societies were to the coastal areas with regard to the structure and relations of the population – especially when communications with the coastal areas were good. The countryside in heavily forested and mountainous areas near the sea resembled the inland, as was the case in the northern parts of Vestfold.

There was a contrast between the tenant system in the coastal, agricultural areas and other districts, where the peasants themselves owned most of the land. This contrast was most obvious in Telemark, where the peasants in the coastal areas owned only between 10 and 20 per cent of the land, while peasants in many interior districts owned about 90 per cent of the land. In Vestfold the peasants in most of the coastal areas owned between 10 and 30 per cent of the land, compared to 50-60 per cent in other areas. There was an age-old tendency that the parishes where tenancy prevailed were also more heavily taxed than districts dominated by owner-occupiers, partly because land value was higher, and some important taxes were assessed in proportion to the land register rate. The people in the interior of Telemark traditionally did not pay as much in taxes as people in the more central districts elsewhere, and this had always been the case, since inland Telemark was integrated into the Norwegian realm – later than almost all other Norwegian districts – towards the end of the thirteenth century.

Southern Vestfold was one of the few Norwegian regions where the nobility still dominated society in the seventeenth century. The traditional basis of their position was the fertile agricultural land near the medieval city of Tønsberg, but from the sixteenth century forestry became more important, and the involvement of the nobility in this business was concentrated in Larvik, a new centre south of Tønsberg, situated at the mouth of two watercourses, Numedalslågen and Farris. Along the Farris River a series of sawmills were built, and this became the basis for an extensive trade in timber. It was the noble family of Jernskjegg, later Lange, which organized this trade, whose main feature was export of sawn boards to the markets in Western Europe, particularly to the Netherlands. As a result of this development, forest properties became much more valuable, and the Vestfold nobility bought up many farms from local peasants in Southern Vestfold.

It is interesting to note the modernizing role that the nobility played in organizing the timber trade as a large-scale business. This was, however, brought about by a combination of economic and political power in a way which was redolent of feudalism, indeed it should perhaps be called feudalism, and the system continued to be semi-feudal until the nineteenth century. For considerable periods, the head of family had the fief of Brunla *len* (county), which was the county where their sawmills were situated and where they acquired most of their land. This was in itself a highly profitable combination of business and official authority, and in the beginning of the seventeenth century, the Jernskjegg family was one of the richest noble families in Denmark-Norway. When a son-in-law moved to Denmark in the 1620s, he sold the estate to Gunde Lange, who had to finance the transaction by getting heavily into debt. His son Nils Lange suffered great losses when his castle Fritsø was destroyed in a natural disaster at a time when he had been made responsible for his irregular administration of the state finances at the Akershus castle in the 1640s. Nils Lange had been a commissary of finance under the auspices of the governor of Norway, Hannibal Sehested, who fell from the king's favour and was dismissed in 1651.

The counties of Larvik and Jarlsberg

Consequently the Lange family had to pawn its estates, and this paved the way for the governor of Norway, Ulrik Frederik Gyldenløve, who in 1671 became count and was given the fief of Brunla »len« as his county. He secured for himself the right to redeem the whole of the old Lange estate, and he was also given the right to buy all crown estates in the county, both land which the king had already sold to other buyers and land which was still owned by the king. In addition to these estates, Gyldenløve and his successor bought other farms in order to consolidate their property holdings. In this way they became the owners of 55 per cent of the land in the county of Larvik.

The rest of Vestfold, the county of Tønsberg, in 1673 became the county of Peder Schumacher Griffenfeld, the dominating minister in the early 1670s, until he fell from favour and was deprived of all his offices and his county in 1676. A new count, the German mercenary, General Gustav Wilhelm Wedel, was given the fief of the county under the name of Jarlsberg in 1683. The count acquired the right to buy all the crown land he wanted in Jarlsberg, but the share of land owned by the family there never exceeded 14 per cent of the total and was reduced to 4 per cent after 1750.

The contrast between the landownership of the two counts must be ascribed to structural differences. The Larvik estate was organized around two industrial conglomerates, the Fritsø sawmills and the Fritsø ironworks, both situated near Larvik. The tenant farmers were obliged to work in these industries, mostly for the ironworks, which needed vast amounts of charcoal, while most of the timber for the sawmills was bought along the upper reaches of the Numedalslågen river, from Sandsvær and Numedal, where the count of Larvik secured for himself the right of preemption of such timber as he required. In Larvik county a system of repartition was organized, whereby forced delivery of quotas of charcoal at fixed prices was imposed on the peasants. The county of Larvik produced a great surplus of about 20,000 *riksdaler* per year in the beginning of the eighteenth century, growing to more than 40,000 riksdaler at the end of that century.

In the county of Jarlsberg there was not a comparable core of industries, so the count's property consisted of scattered tenant farms, which gave him an income from rents. No large-scale farming was organized there either, but in the period of 1720-50 the count made an attempt at running a copperworks, but he failed and the king allowed him to sell most of his lands to pay the expenses he had incurred.

Peasant politicians and the power of the counts

There was a great contrast between the Larvik and the Jarlsberg systems, since the count became far more powerful in Larvik, while in Jarlsberg there were other important estate owners. The peasants in this county were able to acquire a growing proportion of land during the eighteenth century, when the other estate owners also sold off their land. At the end of the eighteenth century the Jarlsberg peasants owned more than 70 per cent of the land; they now constituted a strong farmer population, while the peasants in the county of Larvik owned just under 30 per cent of land in their county.

This difference made itself felt in the way in which the two counties were governed. The only factor they had in common was the fact that the two counts did not usually live there, but preferred to spend their time in the capital Copenhagen or in important positions elsewhere. In Jarlsberg there were a few officials, who were given a rather independent position by the count. Most of them were recruited from the élite families in Christiania (present-day Oslo), and they became more and more attentive to the wishes of the peasant population, all the more so because the towns in the area were not integrated into the county, so that the burghers had greater difficulties in getting support for their demands. According to the official system of trade, the towns had a privileged position in their respective hinterlands. Peasants were not allowed to sell their products directly to foreign skippers, who traditionally sailed to small harbours and avoided Norwegian merchants as middlemen. This trade continued, and the burghers failed to influence the count and his officials to stop it. Indeed all sorts of mercantilist regulations were sabotaged in Jarlsberg, and as a consequence the peasants got better prices for their products. Hence they gradually became more prosperous during the eighteenth century.

An important factor in this development was the ability of the peasants to organize themselves in political campaigns. The count and his officials were confronted with peasant campaigns when they tried to raise the rates and fees which all inhabitants in the counties had to pay. Peasant leaders travelled from parish to parish, especially in the last decades of the seventeenth century and the middle decades of the eighteenth, met the peasantry outside the churches and won their support in refusing to pay the new rates. They collected money for representatives who travelled to see high-ranking officials and the king with complaints about the rate increases, and they even brought the count to court to frustrate his attempts to maximize his income. The outcome was usually that some of the increases were carried through, while others were abandoned. After 1720, the counts of Jarlsberg earned about 6,000 riksdaler per year, not a very impressive income from a county with more than 20,000 inhabitants, but in combination with their salary as high officials (usually as officers or diplomats), they became quite rich. Their own county officials were also affluent – there seems to have been widespread corruption, which must have kept them in style, without being so extractive as to hamper economic development, which was clearly favourable in the second half of the eighteenth century, with a certain proto-industrial development, and above all a great breakthrough in shipping. This was clearly the greatest achievement of the Jarlsberg system, that peasant skippers were able to develop into successful shipowners, who at the end of the eighteenth century were beginning to carry on trade between foreign harbours, to a considerable extent in the Mediterranean, and even overseas to America.

In the county of Larvik the whole political and economic system was centered far more closely around the count and his activities. In spite of its being a highly profitable business, the count himself almost never lived in his county; he spent most of his time in Copenhagen as a member of the nobility for whom it was most natural to be at court and play a political role. Gyldenløve's son, Ferdinand Anton Danneskiold, count of Larvik from 1704 to 1754, was for many years the director of the Copenhagen West India company, which ran a slave trade from West Africa and a sugar trade from three West Indian islands. In person he thus represented the integration of his own business activities as a Norwegian count with the overseas activities of the great Copenhagen company. It is not surprising that the company became a major customer of the Fritsø ironworks. In fact, good connections were vital in securing orders for the ironworks, and no other ironworks' owners in Norway had such excellent connections as the count of Larvik, especially Gyldenløve, who was a prominent member of the royal family. Thus the count secured for himself a continual stream of orders from state agencies, and on very favourable terms; the military bought the greatest quantities, so it was fortunate for Gyldenløve that he was one of the highest ranking officers in Denmark-Norway. He was even able to intervene by ordering artillery officers not to be so strict in their control of the cannons delivered from Fritsø! The count-general does not seem to have been bothered by the fact that lax control posed a threat to the soldiers who were exposed to cannons, which not infrequently exploded, killing the men who operated them. The combination of political and economic power was not only a success as far as the count's income was concerned. It was also used to expand production, especially of iron. As a result, the Fritsø ironworks became by far the biggest producer of iron in Norway, and at the same time the sawmills operated with a secure supply of timber. The combined effects of these businesses were a strong demand for labour, and the population was growing rapidly, far more than elsewhere in Denmark-Norway up to 1720, after which growth in the Larvik region was no longer exceptional.

Regional integration

In the eighteenth century, the county of Larvik was one of the most prominent examples of absentee lordship in Norway. Remote owner- and leadership had been widespread in Norway in the sixteenth and seventeenth century, when the king was the dominating landowner, and the Danish nobility acquired a considerable share of noble estates in Norway. These Danes owned up to half of the 15 per cent of Norwegian land value that was owned by the nobility around the year 1600, i.e. 7-8 per cent. The Larvik system did not function as smoothly as its profitability might lead us to expect. The reason for this was that the lion's share of the cash paid for Fritsø deliveries was transferred from the customers directly to the count in Copenhagen, who spent it extravagantly without setting aside enough money for the operations in Larvik. As a result, the peasants and the workers were forced to accept delays, payment in iron and other measures. The absentee lordship also resulted in galloping corruption. The count appointed a growing corps of officials, who administered production and controlled the whole population in order to mobilize their efforts and ensure their compliance with all regulations and prohibitions. Among the latter, it was most important to force the peasants to utilise the forests entirely according to the needs of the Fritsø factories, and enforce the prohibition against selling unauthorised quantities of timber to Norwegian and foreign skippers and merchants. This system was maintained, but in combination with increasing bribery; the officials took money in return for granting dispensations from rules. In addition to this practice, they forcibly secured themselves higher salaries by borrowing the count's cash without paying it back. As a consequence the system became unbalanced in the years around 1770. Both count and officers had spent money beyond their means, while the population was deprived of freedom of action and independence. The count was declared incompetent, first in the 1770s, and then again later, when a new count had spent money even more wildly in the luxurious ways of the Copenhagen aristocracy, in the 1790s. The count's saga was brought to an end when the king bought the county of Larvik in 1805 for 920,000 riksdaler.

The history of the county of Larvik is a mixture of success and failure. The natural advantages of the district combined with a concentration of all types of power made it possible to continue the operation of this economic system, but in a way which finally made everyone a victim of aristocratic mercantilism, even the absentee count who lost his grip on reality and squandered his money. Luckily for him he had another county, the Danish island of Langeland, which the family was able to keep after the sale of Larvik. In Larvik town and the neighbouring Sandefjord, the burghers took advantage of the growing laxity and corruption by operating outside the system, especially in developing shipping on the basis of the fine milieu for this trade in Southern Vestfold. The shipping trade here was not as dynamic as in Jarlsberg, since the opportunities were not as free as they were there. On the other hand, one might say that it was a common feature of the Vestfold towns that they were prevented from dominating the economic life of their hinterlands, and consequently they had to fall back on the competence which they had inherited. Thus, shipping, which was originally a sort of compensation, at the end of our period became a great success in an age when other Europeans were busy waging war against each other.

The economic development of Norway in the seventeenth and eighteenth centuries is quite amazing. At the beginning of the 200-year period, more than 90 per cent of the population lived in the countryside as peasants, but it has been estimated that about 1/3 of the production was exported. There was an extensive import of grain, even a majority of the peasants themselves had to buy grain. This demonstrates that the peasants were not only agriculturalists, they combined agriculture with forestry, and in the western and northern parts of the country primarily with fishing. In the long run, the foreign trade paved the way for an urbanization, but only from the second half of the seventeenth century. In Vestfold, only 10 per cent of the population lived in densely populated areas in the 1660s, but this percentage increased to 15 in 1720 and 24 in 1801.

The new regional élite in Telemark

In Telemark, which I have studied with regard to the seventeenth century, urbanization started even earlier than in Vestfold. The breakthrough came in the second half of the century. This development must be seen in the light of the organization of external trade in large-scale operations under the leadership of a new regional élite. Telemark did not have the same tradition of nobility as Vestfold, so land holdings by the nobility constituted not more than one or two per cent of the registered land value in the whole county. The burghers in the town of Skien owned three or four times more than that in the 1640s, and their share was increasing. But as we have already pointed out, the peasants of the interior were the dominating landowners, some of them were in fact wealthy estate owners, while most peasants owned their own farms.

At the beginning of the seventeenth century, foreign trade was already a major factor in the economy of Telemark, and it was continuing to grow, for a long time mainly because the timber trade was expanding. From the 1620s a growing iron industry was established, and from the 1670s shipping became increasingly important. As a consequence of this development, urbanization in Telemark increased from 10 per cent about 1600 to 25 per cent as early as 1700, mainly concentrated in Skien and the new town of Kragerø, but also in smaller towns like Porsgrunn, Brevik and Langesund, to some degree even in production centres for timber and iron. The population of the county doubled in the seventeenth century, from c. 11,000 to c. 22,000. We can demonstrate the dynamism of the Telemark example by comparing it with Iceland. In c. 1600 the population of Telemark was 1/4 the size of the population of Iceland, in 1700 1/2, and in 1800 equal to the population of Iceland, c. 47,000.

In Telemark too, the nobility made its presence felt, especially as governors of the county, which at that time was called Bratsberg.[3] The Bratsberg governor administered the Crown's estates, the most important part of which was the sawmill industry. Telemark had many long watercourses and great forests, from where the timber could be transported downstream to Skien, or to Kragerø, and from the smaller watercourses to other harbours. More than half of the 100-150 sawmills were located on land owned partly or wholly by the Crown. Most of them were leased to private operators, burghers, officials and peasants. The governor and his bailiffs operated some of the biggest sawmills directly for the Crown, demanding free timber from the peasants or at least the right of preemption. This was done in an effort to make the Crown self-sufficient in its supply of strategic goods. It was not a success in the long run, being sabotaged both by the peasants and in fact also by the bailiffs who were lax in the enforcement of their demands, probably because they themselves were running competing sawmill businesses. Both they and their noble master were more positively interested in taxation, in which they were involved as a business: receiving goods from the peasants, selling them on the export markets, paying taxes on behalf of the peasants and putting the profit of the trade into their own coffers.

When the iron industry was launched on a larger scale in the 1620s by a group of non-noble owners, the noble governor of Bratsberg soon became so interested that he manipulated them out of business and secured the ownership for himself and his family in 1635. This inaugurated a period of 35 years when the nobility and foreign capitalists took the lead in the Norwegian mining industry, in Telemark represented by the noble families of Urne, Gedde and Ahnen and by the Dutch capitalists Gabriel and Selio Marselis. They were contemporaries of the Lange family i Vestfold, and one could say that after 1670 Gyldenløve prolonged this system in the county of Larvik. In Telemark the activity of the noblemen in the sawmill industry as governors, and in the iron industry as private owners, lasted only until the 1660s. From that time onwards, the clients of the nobility took the lead in the further development of large-scale business operations.

The clients started their careers as bailiffs, combining their authority as officials with their economic power as merchants in the »trade for taxes« system. The surplus from this tax trade must have been very great, for many of the bailiffs became very rich. But they usually quit their strenuous jobs after 5-8 years, continuing as merchants on a large scale, combined with some other official functions which their governors helped them obtain, as members of the magistrate of Skien, as presiding judge (*lagmann*), customs officer, etc. While the noble families who acquired the important office of governor of Bratsberg never settled in this region, their clients, many of them Danes like their masters, never moved from Norway, and with very few exceptions settled in Telemark. In this way a new élite was formed. The fathers were followed by their sons, daughters or sons-in-law, who expanded their businesses, and they, too, were often merchants in combination with official functions.

The new élite of merchant officials first secured for themselves control over the sawmill industry. The Crown had first, in 1616, tried to prohibit most of the sawmills which it leased to private men. Then, in 1618, it instead demanded far higher dues in combination with a system whereby people had to apply for new leases, a policy which favoured men with connections. Eventually, in the beginning of the 1660s, the Crown sold most of its property in Telemark, including all its sawmills, those which had been leased out as well as those which the governor and the bailiffs had run on behalf of the Crown. All the sawmills were first sold to Jørgen Bjelke, the last Bratsberg governor under the old regime. He did not keep them, but sold them to a large group of Skien merchant officials, with the presiding judge, Claus Andersen, as the leading organizer. He was a bailliff's son and a former bailiff himself. Claus Andersen was given the important and prestigious office of »lagmann« with the help of Catherina Sehested, the widow of his former master, Sivert Urne. His connection with this noble family went back at least to his father, Anders Mikkelsen, who in the 1620s had served as a bailiff under Sivert's older brother, Eiler Urne. Most of the crown lands in Telemark were first sold to Catherina Sehested, who employed Claus Andersen as administrator. In a short time they were transferred to Claus Andersen and the other merchant officials in the Skien élite. In this way they established themselves as great estate owners in the 1660s. Some years later men of the same background bought the ironworks from their noble owners, and even engaged in shipping from the 1670s. In this way some of them, especially Claus Andersen, presided over a conglomerate of properties and businesses.

In contrast to this development, the peasants and also smaller merchants were ousted from their active participation in foreign trade, mostly because the ownership and operation of sawmills was concentrated in a few hands. An additional reason was the steep increase in taxation, which made it far less profitable to run small businesses. The more effective customs service played a part in this, and finally it was a significant fact that the merchant officials controlled the regional state finances.

In 1632 the customs services in Norway were reformed. Up till then the state had not managed to increase its revenue from customs by nearly as much as was its aim, especially because the skippers were allowed to report the tonnage of their vessels without being controlled by customs officers. In most districts the bailiffs, or the constables as their deputies, collected the customs revenues, without having the capacity to do it thoroughly. But in 1632 the king decided that henceforth nobody should combine the functions of bailiff and customs officer. All over the country, including Telemark, new customs officials were appointed. At the same time, the navy was authorized to board merchant vessels and control their documents to see if the skippers had paid their duty for the whole cargo. In this way it was discovered that the ships in fact had three times greater capacity than the skippers had hitherto claimed. During the 1630s the customs rates on the export of timber were raised and in combination with a far more efficient control, the customs revenues in Telemark were nine times greater than in the second half of the 1620s, about 20,000 riksdaler per year in the middle of the seventeenth century. We do not know the exact value of the timber export either from Telemark, or from the whole of Norway, but in these decades the state probably took 20 per cent of the value in custom dues.

What was the effect of this steep escalation? From the 1620s the price of timber began to fall on the European markets. This meant that the customs duties could not be passed on to the customers. Instead we see from the sources that the peasants were complaining that they got less money for the timber they delivered to the merchants, and both they and the merchants agreed in blaming the increase in customs duties for this. However, it is interesting to observe that they were unable to prevent this development, and that they did not have a common interest in doing so either. The more efficient customs service functioned in a way that centralized the export trade, away from the small-scale transactions to the great enterprises run by merchant officials. They were able to find the necessary capital to pay the large sums in tollage, especially by borrowing from the treasuries which they controlled; this happened mostly by delaying their payment of taxes and tollage, so that they actually used public funds as working capital. As far as the peasants were concerned, this concealed both the fact that the customs revenues were a tax on them as producers, and that the big merchants with their official connections reaped benefits from the system. So it was logical that the merchants stopped complaining, while the peasants were unable to continue their campaign against the more efficient customs service.

The tug-of-war about the taxes

Then there was a longer-lasting tug-of-war about the direct taxes. The more the taxpayers realized that taxes were a sort of confiscation of their production, the more they reacted with obstruction and sabotage. The peasants were required to deliver some of the timber to the king's sawmills or to royal construction sites in Denmark without receiving payment for it. Up to the 1620s, this was an obligation solely on the districts near the coast, where the inhabitants were more used to paying taxes than the inland peasants. When the obligation was extended to the whole of Bratsberg county, the farmers of the interior organized a tax strike, and then their colleagues in the coastal districts refused to deliver timber, too. The governor and his bailiffs charged them with this disobedience, and peasants all over the county were sentenced for it, but the officials did not enforce the demands energetically, and after a conflict which lasted for over a decade, the king abolished the timber tax and renounced the arrears. The officials probably also disliked the timber tax, for it could easily harm their own interests: they were heavily involved in the trade and were not interested in competition with the state, which also threatened to compromise them in the eyes of the peasants, since the officials were the ones who had to enforce the demands.

The state also had great difficulties in collecting a tithe tax on the sawmills. This was being paid on a tiny fraction of the actual production, in fact on less than five per cent of the total production in the 1620s. Then the state enforced a steep tax increase by demanding a fixed sum for every sawmill. Together with higher prices for leases for sawmills on crown land, this succeeded in increasing revenue from this source in the 1630s and 40s and in this way eliminated many of the small sawmills run by peasants. But pressure from sawmill operators and owners continued to make itself felt, and from the 1650s they managed to force the rates down, something which particularly benefited the operators of the biggest sawmills, most of them run by officials or their close relatives.

The central authorities had greater success in raising the level of direct taxes levied on farms, but here as well, there were more difficulties in achieving this than in expanding the volume of customs revenues. The direct taxes were radically increased for a couple of years during the Kalmar war 1611-13. This was a considerable success for the authorities, probably because of the short time span and the pressure of war which motivated both the demand and the actual payment. The level of farm taxes was then gradually raised from the 1620s to the 1680s, so that during each war, the level of taxes was considerably higher than during the preceding war. In the following peacetime the level decreased, but was still much higher than before the previous war. Beneath the surface, however, the development was not nearly so smooth. Compared with the intentions of the government, there were serious difficulties in the inland districts in the 1620s and 30s, and in the 1660s a new assessment of the registered land value met with such widespread resistance both from the new Bratsberg élite and the peasants that the continued increase in taxation was undermined – a development which did not become evident in the first years, but which made itself felt from the 1690s (see below).

In the 1620s and 30s, there was a distinct difference in the efficiency of tax collection between the coastal and the inland districts. In the former region the bailiff succeeded in collecting nearly as much as was intended by the tax decrees from the king, while the revenue collected in the latter region was less than 2/3 of the amount intended. It is difficult to determine how much of this was owing to a partial tax strike and how much was the result of manipulation by the bailiff. It seems that it was a combination of these two factors which lay behind the deviation. It is also evident that the county governor did not coordinate the activity of his bailiffs in order to maximize tax collection, so the difference in counter pressure from the peasants determined the actual level of taxation.

This situation was changed when a new county governor was installed in 1640. His predecessor, Eiler Urne, had close ties with the district where he resided for 20 years until his death in 1640. The new governor, Ove Gedde, was more the government's man, and this became even more evident when the king's son-in-law, Hannibal Sehested, became *stattholder* (viceroy) of Norway in 1642. Both he and the county governor enforced a more aggressive form of tax collection, both during the war of 1643-45 and afterwards. The trend was the same in the 1650s, especially during the two wars with Charles X Gustavus in 1657-60. In this way, the tax level was raised in both bailiwicks, and considerably more in the interior of the county than in the coastland, so that the level of taxation became the same in the whole county. This was achieved by punishing tax evaders with heavy fines.

Up to this point the officials and the

merchants had been interested in enforcing the tax increases, for in that way they were able to increase their trade: The peasants had to sell more and more goods in order to pay their taxes; they delivered timber to the merchants, who paid the taxes for them. Both these transactions and the collection of customs duties gave the merchants great opportunities to increase their profits. But in the 1660s the situation was about to change. When, in 1660, the wars were temporarily over, the peasantry was complaining bitterly about the taxes and the way the arrears were collected. The merchants were not so dependent on the state any longer. They had established strong merchant houses, bought sawmills and considerable areas of crown land. They started becoming worried about the level of taxation, and that their district might have to carry a heavier burden than other districts.

This became evident when the government ordered a new assessment of the registered land value in the 1660s. Two commissions assessed the production potential in all parts of the Oldenburg monarchy, but with more success in Denmark than in Norway. In 1661, ten regional commissions were appointed to assist the national commission of Norway – in Bratsberg as in many other regions with former bailiffs, now leading merchants, as members. It is not easy to understand why the central authorities did not fear the consequences of relying on them for this work, but the government must have counted on their continued loyalty. Apparently, that was exactly what they delivered. They travelled throughout the county, in many places weathering stiff resistance from the peasants, some refusing to drive them, others refusing to come to the meetings and furnish information about their farms, others again turning up to protest vociferously, and so on. This time, too, the resistance was strongest in the interior, but everywhere the peasants tried to minimize the value of the properties they owned or leased. When reporting back to the king, the commissioners stressed the great difficulties they had in their work, but in fact they themselves acquiesced in the minimizing of the land value. Above all, this becomes evident when one considers the fact that they, as merchants, estate owners and former bailiffs, had excellent knowledge of the economic potential of the region, but they still chose to report with monotonous regularity that the forests were yielding little timber.

A second commission on land valuation in the second half of the 1660s did not achieve a more reliable result, and consequently the government failed to get an up-to-date assessment of the economic potential of the county. In spite of this, when taxes were increased for another 20 years, the bailiffs were more strictly controlled from above than before. Consequently, it was not as profitable as it had been to be a tax collector, because they lost the patronage of the county governor and instead were exposed to the critical scrutiny of the new *amtmann* (county governor, post-1660) and the revitalized *Rentekammer* (Treasury). The bailiffs had less time to devote to their accounting, and this proved devastating to the majority of them who left their offices with payment deficits. Still, trade for taxes played a considerable role in the tax collecting system, but the scope for expanding this system was less than before 1660. Therefore the authorities turned to military force to extract more money from the taxpayers' pockets. This was done with the help of military quarterage, officers and soldiers being stationed in the homes of the people who owed taxes – the mere threat of this squeezing most of the arrears out of the taxpayers. From the 1670s taxpayers who were not peasants had to pay far more than before. This was a new trend. Up to that time officials, merchants and estate owners were taxed lightly, partly intentionally, partly as a result of their efforts to evade taxes by using their regional influence. It was above all a far more efficient auditing in the Treasury that eliminated these advantages, but as a consequence, the accumulated arrears were so large that many of them had to be collected by military quarterage.

In this way, the taxation became increasingly unpopular in the élite, and from the end of the 1680s the tax escalation was stopped, and the direct taxes were lowered slightly. This did not mean that there were no people who could pay more taxes. Among the peasants there were many who were quite comfortable with the level of taxation at the end of the seventeeth century, especially those who had good forests and were selling a lot of timber. As a result of the pressure on the assessment commissions in the 1660s, the level of taxation in the interior of Telemark was 1/3 lower than in the districts near the coast, in spite of the fact that incomes were now higher in the interior. All this was the result of the failure of the assessment, which made it necessary to halt the tax increases when they hurt those who had the most unfavourable assessments of land value.

At the same time, the big merchants who owned most of the sawmills started smuggling out great quantities of sawn boards. The central authorities provoked them into doing this by introducing an upper limit to production in 1688, and the customs service was given the task of enforcing this maximum. It was illegal to export more than the maximum, and as a consequence the merchants smuggled out the excesses in collusion with the customs officers! It was a gigantic fraud amounting to some 60 per cent of that which was being paid for in customs duties. When this smuggling was discovered, which first happened in the district of Oslo in the beginning of the eighteenth century, so many prominent people were involved, and the uproar in the élite over the consequences of punishments was so intense, that the government was forced to pretend that it had stopped the smuggling without punishing the big merchants – in fact they continued this practice in the following years.

In the county of Bratsberg, there were two groups of winners at the end of the seventeenth century: the new élite and the peasants of the interior. The new élite had climbed up in symbiosis with the state, by controlling the tax escalation until the 1660s. They secured for themselves the lion's share of the great timber trade, especially the sawmills industry. From the 1670s they also owned and ran the ironworks which they succeeded in expanding. The state was the dominant customer, its demand for iron was steadily increasing because of the strong militarization under absolutism from 1660. This development was favourable for the whole county, since after 1670, most of the state revenue was spent in Telemark, instead of being transferred to Copenhagen, which was the case with over half of the Norwegian state revenue. So even though the common people of the coastal districts did not enjoy any higher standards of living, there were more jobs, and the population increased rapidly. This was also a consequence of the growth in the shipping industry, which developed from the 1670s. Shipping, too, was dominated by the big merchants. In addition, they were the owners of the former crown lands which had been sold in the 1660s and 70s. About 1680, the new Bratsberg élite owned some 35 per cent of the registered land value in the county. After that time, they started to sell, mostly to the peasants, whose share of the land reached bottom at 55 per cent, whereupon ownership by the peasants increased again in the following years, mostly in the interior.

Conclusion

The examples of Vestfold and Telemark show us that no single factor alone decided the development of these regions. This was quite typical of Norway in an age when social, economic and political conditions varied from region to region. The historical preconditions were important, most clearly in the distribution of land ownership. Natural preconditions decided whether the timber trade was concentrated in a few great harbours or spread between many small ports. Political factors were important in many ways, most significantly in the way aristocrats and other élite families were able to secure benefits for themselves. The combination of administrative and economic powers was typical of the age.

This enabled the entrepreneurs to build up conglomerates of business houses, and, thus, compensate for the lack of a strong traditional urban base in Norwegian trade.

Traditional social relations made themselves felt in Telemark, where the strong farming population with considerable success resisted new taxes which were imposed on them. Here one may clearly talk about different political cultures in the coast and the inland districts; the peasants near the coast were far less unruly than their inland colleagues. Whether this was the reason for their paying higher taxes or vice versa is difficult to tell – most probably the influence went both ways.

The new Bratsberg upper class however did not achieve such a dominant position as the count of Larvik. The élite control of the administrative apparatus of the county was weakened towards the end of the century, while the count of Larvik had full control, also of the judiciary. Only as far as the administrators of the county of Larvik modified the privileges by corruption, the population was able to exercise considerable influence on the way in which the system functioned by paying officials for making exceptions to the rules.

The peasants in the county of Jarlsberg were able to assert themselves in opposition to conflicting interests as a consequence of regional power relations which developed in the seventeenth and eighteenth century and not as a result of historical preconditions. They exercised a stronger influence with much more favourable results than the peasants in the county of Larvik, because the obstacles in the Jarlsberg system were much less formidable than in Larvik. In

Jarlsberg it was necessary to build alliances between different groups to win political victories. Often the peasants were on the winning side, but the results could also be compromises.

In Norway at large, peasant influence decreased considerably during the seventeenth century. This influence was again strengthened during the eighteenth century, but not as much as in the county of Jarlsberg, because the burghers could defend their trade privileges better in other regions, where there was a normal royal jurisdiction.

All the same, alliance-building was widespread everywhere, and peasants were often participants in those alliances. The most tangible result was the downward trend in the level of taxation in the second half of the eighteenth century – in the 1790s Norwegians paid only one quarter as much in taxes as the Danes in spite of the fact that Norway had almost as many inhabitants and probably just as strong an economy. The reason for this is not that the government in Copenhagen wanted to be kinder to the Norwegians than to the Danes, but that an alliance of officials, other élite groups and peasants in the Norwegian regions managed to resist the government's efforts to modernize taxation by counteracting inflation and reaping its share of the growth in production.[4]

Defeating the royal policy of taxation was a victory for the periphery in its tug-of-war with the centre, and this victory demonstrates that Norwegian districts have been far from powerless in earlier times.

Notes

1 Ø. Rian: *Vestfolds historie. Grevskapstiden 1671-1821*, Tønsberg 1980.
2 Ø. Rian: *Bratsberg på 1600-tallet. Stat og samfunn i symbiose og konflikt*, Oslo 1997.
3 It got its present name in 1918.
4 O.A. Johnsen: *Norges Historie*, vol.V, Kristiania 1914, pp.186-188.

CHAPTER 8
Population development and economic reorganization of Southern Helgeland, 1660-1700

By Ragnhild Høgsæt

The area treated here lies in the southern part of modern Nordland, and comprises eight quarters (*fjerdinger*) with outer borders lying close to 65 and 66 degrees North. »Quarters« were precursors of modern Norwegian local authority districts. The eight quarters treated here comprised most of the southern half of the bailiwick of Helgeland. The area was divided into two parishes (*prestegjeld*). The parish of Brønnøy consisted of the quarters of Bindalen, Sør-Sømn, Nord-Sømn, Velfjord and Vega. Bindalen lies outside the area treated here. The parish of Alstahaug consisted of the quarters of Tjøtta, Alstahaug, Vefsn, Herøy, Nesna and Rana, the last two also lying outside this area.

The area had the advantage of fairly secure grain crops in low-lying areas, and inland settlements in particular had abundant pastures. In coastal areas pastures were less abundant, but on the other hand inhabitants here had access to fishing. In the spawning season, shoals of Arctic cod arrive in the seas off Herøy and Vega, and in some periods cod fishing has been very good there. In other periods fishermen from Southern Helgeland have had to go north and join in the cod fishing off Lofoten, and some of them have sailed to Northern Helgeland, particularly to the fishing station of Træna. The important thing, however, is that fishing has been of crucial importance to the people of Helgeland as far back as it is possible to study this phenomenon.

It is usual to view the connection between population and preindustrial agrarian economy like this: When population increased, the supply of labour was good, and there was less land at the

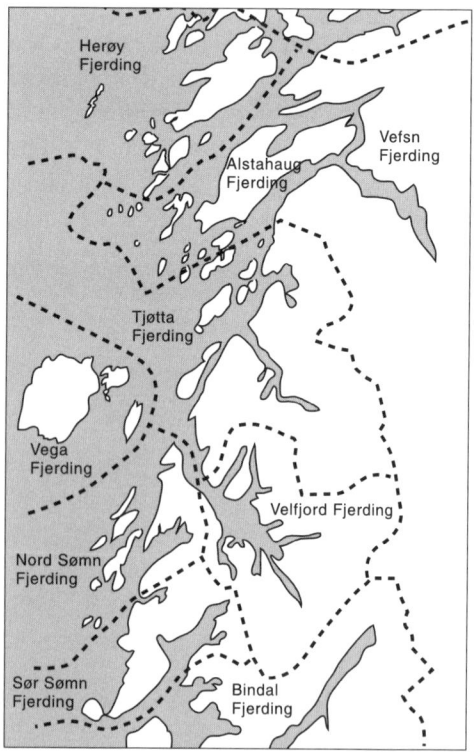

Fig. 8.1: The eight quarters of Southern Helgeland

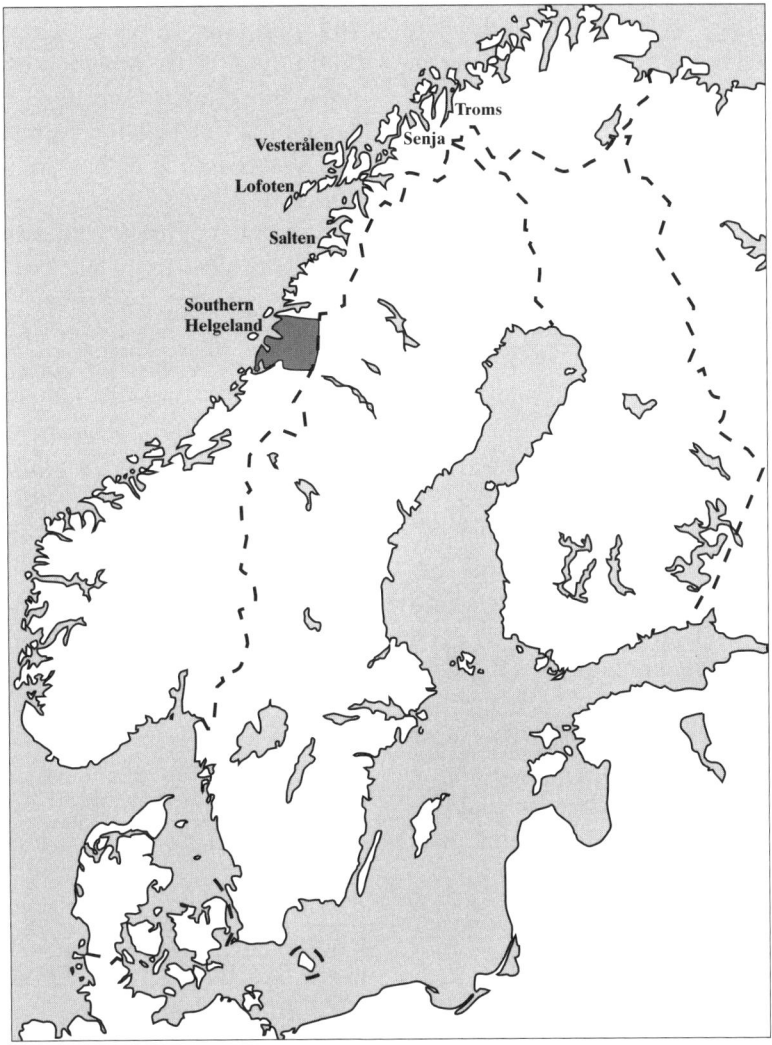

Fig. 8.2: Helgeland and its neighbouring regions in Northern Norway

disposal of every inhabitant. Thus, there was usually a transition from animal husbandry, which produces less food per acre, to arable cultivation, which produces more calories, but also requires a greater labour effort. And if population declined sufficiently, the process was reversed, and animal husbandry gained on arable cultivation.

However, in this area animal husbandry is probably more labour intensive than in the countries where this view had its origins. Close to the coast we can suppose that animals could fend for themselves in winter, but in inland areas this may have been difficult, even for seventeenth century farm animals. When snow lay a yard deep or more, even very hardy animals would have problems finding food, and in a biting

January frost, even sheep and goats might need barns to keep warm. A great deal of labour was probably necessary to house all the animals in winter. Gathering winter fodder must have been demanding. Hay had to be taken from outlying fields, entailing considerable work mowing and transporting it. Often, enough hay could not be made to provide fodder for the whole winter, and it had to be augmented by gathering moss (in coastal areas also seaweed and sea tangle) and by cutting and drying leaves which the animals could eat. Gathering additional fodder like leaves and moss also demanded a great deal of labour. Gathering winter fodder probably became more labour intensive the less land there was available for it, because even the least favourable sources of fodder had to be utilized. The demand for labour became even greater when most of the fodder had to come from outlying fields. Thus, animal husbandry could be very labour intensive in this area, particularly when it was necessary to make use of outlying fields and additional fodder like leaves and moss.

And the growing of grain gives such uncertain crops in the climate of Northern Norway, that it is risky to become too dependent on it. In the second half of the seventeenth century, this fact became so evident that peasants must have taken it into closer consideration when deciding what to produce.

The development of agricultural production

There were a number of harvest failures in Northern Norway from 1670 to 1700. One series of failures culminated in 1676, another in 1696. These harvest failures can be documented by tithe returns in church accounts from the deaneries of Helgeland, Salten, Lofoten and Vesterålen, and they are also mentioned in other sources.[1] If we take the great number of harvest failures for grain into consideration, late seventeenth century peasants must have seen it as sensible to rely more on animal husbandry, which was less prone to fail when summer weather remained cool and wet for weeks and weeks on end.

The development of grain cultivation can be followed through tithe returns. Grain tithes seem to have been collected according to the same rules all the time until about 1690. Around 1690 the »paupers' quarter« of the grain tithes was abolished, and this increased tithes from 7.5% to 10%.[2] Taking account of this increase, it is possible to use tithe returns to calculate the development of grain production from the peasant holdings of Helgeland all through the period of 1660-1700.

Tithe returns seem to indicate that grain production declined considerably in the South of Helgeland from 1660 to 1700. In the quarters lying in the parish of Brønnøy, the production of grain was close to 7 barrels on average from every peasant around 1660, but in 1700 it was no more than 3.51 barrels. In the parish of Alstahaug (the quarters of Tjøtta, Alstahaug, Vefsn and Herøy) the production of grain was reduced from 6 barrels on average from holdings around 1660 to 5 barrels in 1700. Production was better maintained in the parish of Alstahaug than in the parish of Brønnøy, but this was simply because the number of holdings increased in Alstahaug parish, while it decreased in Brønnøy.

Animal husbandry cannot be studied through tithe returns, which seem to give a misleading impression of the development of animal husbandry.[3] However, I have collected information about animal husbandry from the preliminary land register of 1723 and the land register of 1860, and I have compared this information with information on animal husbandry in the limited number of probate inventories from this area. There are around 50 such probate inventories which are dated from the 1690s. Almost all of them stem from the process of division of estates left by peasants, and we can compare the numbers of farm animals mentioned in the probate inventories with the number of farm animals mentioned in the preliminary land register.

My conclusions from this comparison are, first, that at the end of the seventeenth century the number of farm animals could still be increased. Secondly, probate inventories from the end of the seventeenth century seem to indicate that the number of farm animals was greater in the 1690s than what was stipulated as the norm for maximum numbers in the preliminary land register of 1723. The conclusion from this must be that Helgeland peasants had made great investments in animal husbandry at the end of the seventeenth century.

However, is it reasonable to say that they invested more heavily in animal husbandry around 1700 than they had done forty years before? There are some indirect arguments that such was the case. Regarding the state of the local economy at this time, there were no possibilities other than farming, and this mainly meant animal husbandry. Thus, animal husbandry expanded.

Cod fishing

We have several indications that the winter fishing of cod in Lofoten failed at the end of the seventeenth century. This meant that the settlements of Helgeland which were not situated close to the sea (in the area treated here, these are particularly settlements in the quarter of Vefsn) lost their most important source of income from fishing. They therefore had to rely more heavily on other sources of income. In the years immediately prior to 1660 fish catches were abundant. Peasants evidently got a considerable additional income by being fishermen in winter, when Arctic cod has its spawning season, and the need for adult men in farm work is least.

Participation in the cod fisheries can be studied in the registers of fish tithe payments, which have been preserved from the middle of the 1660s from the seasonal fisheries off Lofoten as well as Namdalen (in Northern Trøndelag, to the south of Southern Helgeland). Fish tithes were collected according to rules which make it possible to calculate the importance of fishing from fishing stations (*fiskevær*) within the quarters where the fishermen lived, and fishing from fishing stations in remote parishes like those in Lofoten or Namdalen. The king's fish tithe was always collected at the fishing station, but the part of the fish tithe which belonged to the vicar and the local church was divided into two parts, half of it being sent to the vicar and the church of the fisherman's home parish, the other half being kept by the vicar and the church of the fishing station. Thus, a comparison between the local fish tithe of the king and the local fish tithe of the churches and the

Regional integration

Table 8.1: Percentage of fish catches which derived from fishing outside Helgeland

Locality	Percent
Sør-Sømn	50%
Nord-Sømn	47%
Velfjord	63%
Vega	--
Tjøtta	88%
Alstahaug	63%
Vefsn	92%
Herøy	63%
All eight quarters	73%

Note: Calculations made from tithe returns reported in fief and church accounts AD 1612-1660 in »Lensregnskaper for Nordlandene«, Riksarkivet (The National Archives), Oslo

vicars makes it possible to calculate the importance of fishing on different parts of the coast. How dependent were the people of Helgeland on participating in cod fishing off Lofoten and Namdalen, and how far could they manage on the basis of the marine resources of Helgeland?

At the end of the 1650s, more than 70% of the fish tithes paid by inhabitants of this area derived from fishing off Lofoten and Namdalen. The percentage varied greatly, from nothing for the fishermen of Vega, to 92% for the fishermen coming from Vefsn. It can be no surprise that people from Vefsn had little opportunity to catch fish at home, Vefsn being largely an inland area. It is unexpected, however, that fishing far away from home was so important for several of the coast quarters (see table 8.1).

We understand the background for the differences between the Southern Helgeland quarters better if we turn

Table 8.2: Participants in seasonal cod fisheries in Lofoten and off the coast of Namdalen 1665/66 (average number per household)

Quarter	Lofoten	Namdalen	Total
Sør-Sømn	0.04	0.80	0.84
Nord-Sømn	0.02	0.62	0.64
Velfjord	--	--	--
Vega	0.14	0.03	0.17
Tjøtta	0.60	0.46	1.06
Alstahaug	0.32	--	0.32
Vefsn	0.98	--	0.98
Herøy	0.21	--	0.21

Source: Unpublished »Tiendemantal« from Lofoten 1664-1666 and Namdalen 1665/66, Lensregnskaper for Nordlandene og Trondhjems len, Riksarkivet, Oslo.

from the origins of fish catches to the frequency of participation in the cod fishing off Lofoten and Namdalen (see table 8.2). This survey gives a striking impression that the quarter of Tjøtta was a »border area« with considerable participation in the fisheries off Lofoten as well as Namdalen. The quarters lying in the parish of Brønnøy sent their seasonal fishermen only to the Namdalen fisheries, while the fishermen from the parish of Alstahaug (excepting Tjøtta, which was divided) caught their fish largely at Lofoten.

I have calculated the stockfish production of fishermen from the area treated here at between 12,200 and 17,100 våger (one våg is around 18.5 kilos), probably closer to the larger than to the smaller number. But during the following decades catches were reduced, and around 1700 the stockfish production of the inhabitants of Southern Helgeland was probably no greater than from 10,600 to 12,900 våger. In view of this development we can understand why people invested so heavily in animal husbandry, when grain growing appeared too risky from a climatic point of view. There was no viable alternative, and thus increased emphasis on animal husbandry seemed the only sensible alternative for the majority of peasants.

Table 8.3: Absolute numbers and index of holdings, 1665/66-1701

Quarter	Holdings		Index (1665=100)	
	1665/66	1701	1665	1701
Sør-Sømn	163	144	100	88
Nord-Sømn	88	91	100	103
Velfjord	138	132	100	96
Vega	82	86	100	105
(South	471	453	100	96)
Tjøtta	160	151	100	94*
Alstahaug	111	108	100	97
Vefsn	365	406	100	111
Herøy	90	83	100	92
(North	726	748	100	103)
Total	**1197**	**1201**	**100**	**103**

Note: * If we add 6 holdings (situated in Brastad, Myklebostad og Nordbostad) which are omitted from the tax register, we get an index of 95.
Sources: Male censuses 1665, 1666, and 1701. They are not published, but can be found in Riksarkivet, Oslo.

Stagnation in the number of peasant holdings

The increase in animal husbandry could only be possible if the number of holdings declined, so that more land became available for each of them. And if we count the number of holdings, we come to the conclusion that this is exactly what happened between 1665/66 and 1701 (table 8.3).

Helgeland was not the only area where the number of holdings was reduced at this time. The stagnation in the development of the number of peasant holdings in centrally situated settlements was already noticed in research many years ago, and it has been attributed to the level of annual land rents, which also served as a key to the assessment of annual taxes. Traditionally annual land rents were high on holdings which had already been cleared in the High Middle Ages. This also made for high entry fines and high taxes on these farms, so the crippling costs of running these holdings have been cited to explain why many of them became deserted in the seventeenth century.[4]

However, this explanation does not fit in with the development in the South of Helgeland. Peasant holdings in central and »expensive« areas here were indeed devoid of people, but they were still let and in productive use. Taxes were regularly paid on them – by the neighbouring peasants who had paid entry fines to be allowed to use the land. It therefore seems that the lack of resident peasants is not a sign that the cost of

Table 8.4: Replacement rate of tax-paying tenants per decade

Quarter	1670-1680	1680-1690	1690-1700
Sør-Sømn	39%	34%	30%
Nord-Sømn	46%	31%	30%
Velfjord	39%	23%	23%
Vega	39%	34%	14%
Tjøtta	33%	27%	28%
Alstahaug	36%	28%	34%
Vefsn	42%	32%	27%
Herøy	38%	32%	25%

Note: Replacement rate = the percentage of tenant names which were changed in the tax accounts in each of the three decades 1670-1700. A widow succeeding her deceased husband is not seen as a replacement, since her late husband's tenure would still be valid unless and until she remarried. Calculated on the basis of tax registers for »Den almindelige Landskat« (The General Land Tax), Riksarkivet, Oslo.

tenancy was too high, but rather a sign that peasants preferred to amalgamate holdings to raise their own incomes. Accordingly it is possible to regard the uninhabited holdings as a sign of more affluent rather than poorer peasants.

Because of the decline in the number of holdings, it became more difficult than before to find a peasant holding which was vacant. And the period of tenure lengthened, so vacancies became rarer, and the situation became all the more difficult for those looking for a holding which they could lease. If we take a look at how frequently tenants were replaced, we get a definite impression that becoming a tenant became more difficult at the end of the century (see table 8.4).

In general it seems that replacement of tenants was a process which slowed down. We cannot be sure why. Maybe tenants lived longer, or maybe the lack of alternatives made them stay longer in the same tenures instead of moving on. In any case it became more difficult for young people to find vacancies.

Cottagers

People who failed in their search for a vacant peasant holding, could try a less favourable solution to make a living for a family: they could live as cottagers. This social group was called *husmenn* in 1665, in 1701 they were called »husmenn« or *innerster*. An »innerst« was a man who rented housing space from other people, but just like »husmenn« they seem to be family men. (In the census of Southern Helgeland from 1701, they are frequently listed together with children). While the number of peasants was reduced in some quarters, the number of cottagers usually rose.

There seems to be some connection between the percentage of cottagers among the heads of households and the local average size of holdings, even though the customary arrangements from East Norway were practically unknown here. Those arrangements usually meant that cottagers paid for housing with a fixed amount of duty work for the farmer whose land they occupied. Thus, the need for labour has been seen as one of the reasons why farmers admitted cottagers to their land.

As far as I can see, there was a connection between the percentage of cottagers and the size of holdings even here, even though work duties for cottagers were not widespread. The most reasonable explanation seems to be that the opportunity of doing paid work for peasants was one of the conditions which enabled cottagers to make a living.

Table 8.5: The number of cottagers (*husmenn* and *innerster*) in Southern Helgeland 1665-1701

	Sør-Sømn	Nord-Sømn	Velfjord	Vega	Tjøtta	Alstahaug	Vefsn	Herøy	Total
ca. 1665	36	41	29	31	37-43	51-52	51	49-50	325-333
ca. 1701	43	52	25	35	61	67	90	63	436

Note: Numbers calculated from male censuses 1665/66 and 1701, Riksarkivet, Oslo.

Inherited right to lease – and trade in the right to take up leases

There were fewer holdings to let because some vacant holdings were snatched up by land-hungry neighbouring peasants, who already possessed an establishment which gave them a livelihood, but who wanted more land in order to acquire a better living. Accordingly it became more necessary than formerly to inherit the use of a tenancy. Being the heir of a tenant became a more and more valuable asset, and this can be studied through tax registers. I have done this in Nord-Sømn, where you can follow family relationships in the peasant community by studying the parish register of Brønnøy church from 1669.[5] The sons and sons-in-law of former (deceased) tenants dominated land tenure in Nord-Sømn almost completely. Immigrants had scant chances of acquiring land holdings at all, but may have had to search for an old childless tenant who might be paid to give up his holding in favour of the immigrant.

In the court register of Helgeland we find some information which can be interpreted as remnants of cases where tenants bought or sold their right to use tenant holdings – and this trade seems to have been carried on without regard to the property rights of the landowner. »Right of property« simply seems to have implied the right of entry fines and annual rents, while the »right of use« seems to have resided with and been inherited within the families of tenants.

In October 1696 Steffen Andersen sued Samuel Rasmussen Grøttem at the court of Sør-Sømn to reclaim a sum of 13 *riksdaler* which he had paid to Samuel to gain tenancy of a holding liable to an annual rent of 0.67 våg of stockfish. This land was part of the holding which Samuel rented from the land-owning estate of the late Jochum Irgens. The bailiff of the estate, Giert Lange, had refused to let this land to Steffen, so Steffen wanted his money back. The court judged that Samuel should refund the money, and asked no questions about how a tenant could demand a payment for recommending a new tenant to the bailiff of the landowner. It seems that the jury (*lagrettemenn*) found nothing irregular in this case, even though the sum of money was far greater than the legal entry fine for land liable to only 0.67 våg of stockfish in annual rent. This is only one of the cases where the court register seems to refer to examples of trade between peasants or would-be peasants in the right to use a peasant holding. And these are cases which are conspicuous contrasts to the lack of cases of breaches of the law regulating entry fines to 5 riksdaler for every våg of stockfish in annual rent.

Thus, inheriting the right to take up a lease became a valuable asset, and those who had no such inheritance were forced to find land which was not already claimed by a tenant. This was probably the reason why practically no quarters other than Vefsn had any increase in the number of holdings. Unlike the situation in other quarters, Vefsn had large areas which nobody leased and nobody used, and this made conditions for the farming of new land in remote settlements of Vefsn unique. However, not all of Vefsn was in this situation. Central settlements in Vefsn had a decline in the number of holdings, at the same time as peripheral settlements had a growth. This can have two different explanations. One is that peasants arranged marriages for their children in a way which concentrated inheritance of the right to lease on a limited number of families. The other possible explanation is that child mortality was higher in central than in peripheral settlements because infectious illnesses spread more easily in central settlements. Thus, the right to lease was inherited by fewer people in central than in peripheral settlements.

I am inclined to make a hypothesis that there is a connection between the development of the number of holdings and local population development. Tenants had great influence on the number of holdings. Land could not be leased anew as long as it was used by a tenant with a valid lease, so tenants who were still alive could stop the splitting of their holdings. Nor could they be forced to give them up as long as they complied with the legal terms of their lease. It also seems that it was usual for ageing peasants to appear before court, announcing that they would relinquish their lease – or a part of their holding – in favour of a named person (usually a son or son-in-law). Thus, it was possible for tenants to secure hereditary succession to the lease within their family. The arrangement was not without advantages for landowners either. They benefited by receiving a new entry fine even before the death of their former tenant, and they did not risk a depreciation of the holding by a long-lasting lease held by a tenant whose capacity for work was no longer satisfactory.

This development gave tenants who fulfilled their duties a very secure position, and in fact gave them the power to determine the number of holdings on the farms. And this had long-term consequences for the development of the agrarian society of Helgeland. It seems to me that the number of the surviving heirs of a peasant determined whether his holding was to be maintained, split up or amalgamated after his own death. If a peasant had more than one surviving child who needed a living, his holding would be split up to cater for their needs. If he had no surviving child, there was an opportunity for his neighbours to take over his land and amalgamate it with their own holdings. This would make for an amalgamation of holdings in central districts, where contacts with the world around were frequent, thus easing the spread of infectious diseases. We can therefore assume that child mortality was higher in central than in remoter districts, so a greater number of peasants in central districts would have few or no heirs alive at their own death.

There was a greater growth of population from 1660 to 1701 in the parish of Alstahaug than in the parish of Brønnøy.[6] A critical evaluation of the source material gives reason to suspect the census of 1665 of such great omissions that the apparent population growth in Brønnøy parish from 1665 to 1701 was probably not real, or else very small. This fact was reflected in the development of the number of holdings from 1665/66 to 1701 (see above).

Towards a stagnating population?

Around 1665/66 there were probably around 4,850 inhabitants in the quarters belonging to Alstahaug parish, and

Regional integration

Table 8.6: Reconstruction of population development 1665/66-1701

	1665/66	**1701**	**Change**
Sør-Sømn	1137*	922	-19%
Nord-Sømn	921*	811	-12%
Velfjord	1010*	869	-14%
Vega	731*	653	-11%
Sum South	3799	3255	-14%
Tjøtta	1193	1205	+1%
Alstahaug	861	968	+12%
Vefsn	2050	2917	+42%
Herøy	743	798	+7%
Sum North	4847	5888	+22%

Note: * The number is estimated. The census of 1666, which is most complete, has been preserved only from the parish of Alstahaug, and a comparison shows considerable omissions in the census of 1665. I started by making an estimation of population in 1665/66 for the quarters where both censuses have been preserved. Then I made an estimation of the population in the quarters lying in Brønnøy parish. I assumed that the numbers of people in the whole area treated here were distributed equally with the men who are named in the census of 1665, which is also preserved for the parish of Brønnøy.

around 3,800 inhabitants in the quarters belonging to Brønnøy parish.

In 1701 there were at least 3,355 inhabitants in the four quarters situated in Brønnøy parish, compared with 6,064 inhabitants in the four quarters belonging to the parish of Alstahaug. This development has been set out in table 8.6. These calculations show a considerable population decline in the south and a strikingly different development in the north, where population increased markedly.

Lower marriage rate?

When we try to evaluate the reason for this, it seems to be of some importance that the number of children was reduced in some of the quarters from 1666 to 1701. And if we take a look at the age of the large number of servants, we get the impression that the percentage of adult unmarried men increased very much from 1665/66 to 1701. If we make a survey of men from 30 to 39 years of age, we see that the percentage of these who still lived as servants or in the household of their parents increased very much from 1665/66 to 1701. This must be our conclusion when we regard the development in the number of men who headed their own households (table 8.7).

In 1665/66 nearly 80% of all men aged between 30 and 39 in the quarters of Tjøtta, Alstahaug and Vefsn lived as heads of their own households. In the quarter of Herøy, 60% of them did so. In

Table 8.7: Peasants and cottagers as percentages of all men 30-39 years of age 1665/66-1701

	1666	1701
Tjøtta	77-79%	50%
Vefsn	76-77%	56%
Alstahaug	78-80%	56%
Herøy	61%	60%

Note: Calculations from male censuses

1701 the percentage had fallen to less than 60% in Alstahaug and Vefsn, and had dropped to 50% in the quarter of Tjøtta. The situation in Herøy was almost unchanged.

The quarters lying in the parish of Brønnøy show a somewhat different picture. The percentage of men living in their own household in Velfjord and Vega in 1701 was approximately the same as it was in the quarters of Tjøtta, Alstahaug and Vefsn in 1665/66, close to 80%. Sør-Sømn and Nord-Sømn were in 1701 close to the level of Herøy in 1665/66 and 1701, with 60% of the men living as heads of their own households.

Accordingly, we have some reason to assume that the frequency of marriage declined in this area from the 1660s to the years immediately before 1701.

Declining birth rate?

If we accept the conclusion that the frequency of marriage declined from 1665/66 to 1701 we have reason to suspect that the birth rate also declined. This is a possibility which is very difficult to investigate owing to the quality of the male census of 1666, which seems to omit a considerable number of boys and younger men, judging from age proportions. But the census of Tjøtta seems less defective than the others, naming a large number of boys under one year of age. And in Tjøtta the number of young children declined considerably from 1666 to 1701 (see table 8.8).

If we take into consideration the number of men older than 20 years of age who seem to be omitted in the census of 1666, we must assume that there was no increase in the number of young boys and men in the quarter of Alstahaug, and in Tjøtta there was a considerable decline. The quality of the 1666 census from Vefsn and Herøy seems conspicuously poor, if we judge from the number of very young boys who are named. This leaves us with data from two quarters, one of them showing a great decline in the number of children, the other showing an increase which is so small that it probably only reflects incomplete lists of children in 1666.

If we take these facts into consideration, we must come to the conclusion that the birth rate had probably fallen a great deal, and that the population growth was tending towards stagnation at the end of the seventeenth century.

Regional integration

Table 8.8: The number of boys/men 1-19 years of age 1666-1701

	Boys under 20			Boys under 10		
	1666	*1701*	*Change*	*1666*	*1701*	*Change*
Tjøtta	239	233	-2%	134	112	-16%
Alstahaug	157	183	+17%	82	96	+17%
Vefsn	363	621	+71%	171	319	+87%
Herøy	131	165	+26%	58	87	+50%

Source: Male censuses 1666 and 1701, Riksarkivet, Oslo

Why and how the economy was reorganized

If we take into consideration the concurrent development of fishing, we can say that population was stabilizing, and that this was built on a reorganization of the local economy. At the end of the century, fishing was based on local natural resources more than had been the case around the middle of the century. Around 1660 the people of Southern Helgeland had produced around 70% of their stockfish by fishing off Lofoten and Namdalen. Around 1700 this relationship was radically changed, and only 54% of the stockfish produced by the people of this area was on the basis of fish caught in other areas.

There was also a change in where the fishermen of Southern Helgeland participated in seasonal cod fishing. Around 1660 the fisheries off Namdalen had very little participation by men coming from north of the quarter of Tjøtta, and most of the men of Tjøtta preferred to fish off Lofoten. But it seems that when cod fishing failed in the seas off Lofoten at the end of the century, even fishermen from the northern end of the area treated here preferred to sail to the Namdalen fisheries if they did not choose to stay near their own home. Shortly before 1700, a fisherman from outer Vefsn was prosecuted for being involved in a brawl at a fishing station off Namdalen (Gjeslingen). And the probate inventory of the decedent estate of Ravald Paulsen Skjeggenes in the quarter of Alstahaug of 1691 lists fish hanging to dry at Gjeslingen.

The result of this was a society with greater security of provisions. Peasants were well provided with hired labour, so they could put a great effort into the gathering of fodder before winter came. This situation became possible because a great number of people never got the opportunity to settle in their own homes, but had to spend life as the hired servants of strangers. They married late or not at all, and had very few children. These servants might regret that they were not allowed to clear a holding of their own in the outlying fields so that they could marry, but at least they did not experience children whom they were unable to feed. Clearing land in the outlying fields probably would not have given these families any secure living. Arable crops often would have failed on their high-lying land, while there was a strong likelihood that they could not afford animals which might have provided them with milk.

Economic modernization?

Was the society of Southern Helgeland in the late seventeenth century a »modern« society? I will define a »modern society« as a society governed by the principles of a market economy, where the value of money has a dominant position and governs decisions in economic life, where money circulates freely and is commonly available, and the exchange of goods with the outside world is a matter of course which is necessary for ordinary life in the community.

The use of money probably became more important in the seventeenth century. In 1626 cash money was so rarely used in the north of Helgeland, that the Danish vicar of Rødøy, Maurits Madssøn Rasch, could complain that this year things were »so frightfully expensive« in Bergen that you had to give 2 våger of stockfish for 1 riksdaler, and one barrel of flour cost 5 våger of stockfish.[7] It seems that the »frightful expenses« in modern parlance would be described as »frightfully low prices for stockfish«. We get the impression that the society of Northern Helgeland had a system of »merchandise money« (*varepengesystem*)[8] in 1626, so that low prices for stockfish would be naturally described as a situation with a high cost of living.

However, after 1660 it seems that money had much greater importance. We can probably find the reason for this in the system of taxation and land tenure. Formerly *leidang* had been the most important tax, and this was collected in kind. But during the first decades of the seventeenth century, the »leidang« lost its economic significance. The »extra tax«, later called »the general land tax« (*den almindelige landskat*) became the most important source of public income. This tax had to be paid in cash, and it amounted to a sum several times that of the »leidang«. Thus, taxpayers had more need of money. And they needed money not only to pay taxes.

Would-be tenants always had to pay entry fines in cash. In 1684 a law was promulgated which prohibited entry fines of more than 5 riksdaler for land worth 1 våg in annual rent. But a few years previously another law had decreed that annual rent should be paid with 1 riksdaler for every våg of »stockfish«, and triennial fines had been fixed at 0.5 riksdaler as early as in 1578, a rate which was confirmed by the Norwegian Law of King Christian IV (1604). This meant that the population of Helgeland not only needed money to pay their annual taxes, but they also had to pay more and more money for the use of their peasant holdings – they even needed money to pay rents. A hundred years earlier both rents and taxes had been paid in kind, but this was no longer accepted by landlords and public officials at the end of the seventeenth century. All the same we get a definite impression that there was little cash in circulation. There are 48 probate inventories of the decedent estates of peasants from this part of Helgeland in the time before

135

1700. Only 8 of them list cash money as part of the decedent estate. And when servants or foster-children demanded unpaid wages, they were always paid in kind (usually farm animals or clothes).

Thus, it seems that the breakthrough in the use of money consisted of its use as a standard of value. More than 80% of the 48 probate inventories list outstanding debts to persons living in the vicinity of the deceased person, and these debts are almost always assessed in money.

As regards debts to merchants and tradesmen, there is a marked difference between debts to urban merchants in Bergen and Trondheim and debts to local tradesmen (kremmere). Debts to urban merchants were usually reckoned in våger of stockfish, while debts to local tradesmen were usually reckoned in cash money. The reason for this was probably that urban merchants were usually stockfish exporters. Thus, it was very convenient for them to have their demands assessed in the traditional way, because it made it easier for them to demand payment in the kind of goods with which they supplied their foreign customers. On the other hand, local tradesmen were dependent on urban merchants to find a market for their stockfish. Their main income came from retail selling and buying in quantities which urban merchants may have regarded as too small for the amount of work involved. The goods of their trade were too varied and diversified to be fitted into a system of »merchandise money«. For how could they calculate a valid »merchandise price« for e.g. half a pound of nails, prunes, or raisins, and cast-iron kettles or different qualities of silk scarves?

We get a definite impression that money played a different role in different forms of economic transactions. Different kinds of economic transactions (buying, selling or payments of taxes or rents) and the payment of wages were carried out with different means of payment. Land rents were assessed in stockfish, but at the end of the seventeenth century they were paid with money. Servants had usually made agreements on money wages but they were nevertheless paid in kind.

We are tempted to ask whether the lack of money in probate inventories can be connected with the fact that demands for money to pay taxes to a distant government and to largely absentee landowners functioned as a kind of economic vacuum cleaner. This »cleaning« removed from the area all the money the inhabitants of Helgeland were able to provide. This seriously hampered local economic development and the exchange of goods between different settlements. If the inhabitants of Vega wanted to pay with a surplus of their coalfish when they wanted to buy grain from Sømna, the lack of cash possibly made it necessary for them to find Sømna peasants who both lacked coalfish and had a surplus of grain. This may have hampered the regional exchange of surplus goods.

Conclusions

Situations like this may have hindered the development of a market economy, where the maximum number of settlements could develop a system of regional self-sufficiency for Southern Helgeland, with optimal exploitation of local resources. If this was the case, royal need for maximum taxation may have undermined the possibility of economic development. In one sense we can say that this undermined an economic development which might have increased considerably the ability of the king's subjects to pay taxes.

However, it was hardly public demands for taxes which were the most important reason why the peasant communities of Southern Helgeland became an area of »zero growth« after 1660. It was rather the economic influence of peasants who were heads of households, and who were able to protect their economic position by preventing the erection of more holdings so that they themselves were able to increase animal husbandry. This development meant that the number of peasant holdings with a few exceptions (mainly in some distant settlements in Vefsn) stopped growing. Concurrently the catches in commercial fishing were reduced, and the stockfish production of the inhabitants of Helgeland was moved to fishing stations which were situated closer than Lofoten. It seems that fishing off Namdalen and within the bailiwick of Helgeland took over the place the Lofoten fisheries had occupied in 1660, maybe because the cod drifted towards the coast in a different pattern, and more of the fish turned up south of Lofoten.

At the same time the development of grain tithes seems to indicate that grain growing declined. And sources about the development of animal husbandry seem to indicate that this increased considerably. I have interpreted this as a sign that peasants staked a lot on the kinds of agriculture which were least vulnerable to climatic variations. This meant a greater emphasis on animal husbandry. With this trend it is easy to understand why peasants endeavoured to increase the extent of their lands. For an increase in animal husbandry presupposes that fodder is available, and fodder was easiest to acquire if the holding included large outlying fields. Thus, it became vital for peasants to prevent the clearing of new land and the building of new holdings.

On this background we can understand why it became more difficult than formerly to find a living as a peasant. It seems that young people had to be content to take work as servants or to spend a longer period at the home of their parents than had been usual around 1660. This meant that the age for entering into a first marriage increased, and it seems that there were comparatively fewer children in 1701 than immediately before 1666. Some youngsters may have reacted to impediments to marriage by trying to make a living as fishermen or day labourers, and the number of cottagers increased markedly from 1666 to 1701. But this was an insecure way of living, for it left them without provision when fishing failed. It also made them into a marginal group as regards food from agriculture, for when crops failed, peasants might have nothing to sell.

Thus, our main conclusion as regards the development of peasant communities in Southern Helgeland must be that the majority of the population, peasants, probably succeeded in securing a way of living, even though they were hit by a great number of crop failures. But one of the conditions for this was that the number of holdings did not grow. And the price for this had to be paid by the large number of young people who never succeeded in finding a peasant holding of their own, but in some cases managed to scrape together a living as cottagers. And it seems that this was not because it was impossible to increase the number of holdings, but because peasants resisted dividing agricultural resources between a number of families. Such a division might have been an impediment to peasants keeping the number of farm animals which gave them secure food provisions no matter how badly grain harvests failed.

Is it possible to characterize Southern Helgeland as a unified region, with clear connections within and to the outside world?

For the greater part of the population, the most important connections lay in the trade in stockfish with international markets. Stockfish was the commodity which was used to »buy« the money with which they paid an increasing amount of their goods, and their economic obligations to landowners as well as the king. The development of the production of stockfish was different from one quarter to another. This was due not only to the fact that they lay at different distances from the fishing banks, but also to the fact that the pattern in the drift of the shoals of arctic codfish towards the coast changed from decade to decade.

There were changes in the amounts of catches as well as prices, the ways credits worked and were given, and by whom they were given. The reasons for this could be found in international demand as well as the development of inland trade and the bourgeoisie. Traditionally the merchants of Bergen had controlled inland trade with fish as well as fish exports. In the last decades of the seventeenth century, however, the merchants of Trondheim gained an increasing part of the fish trade. They were able to compete more efficiently by seeking out the fishermen at the fish stations, as well as accepting to take the risk of losses during the transport from the fishing station to the place of export. For the former one hundred years the merchants of Bergen had let the fishermen take the risks of losses during transport. They had practically no competition, so they could sit quietly and leave transport of the fish to the fishermen and their cooperators, the owners of local community transport vessels (*jekter*). The merchants of Trondheim changed this situation in favour of the fishermen by collecting stockfish at the fishing stations. On the other hand their international trade connections were less developed. They were often unable to wait for payment from the fishermen who traded with them, and in situations of scarcity they were sometimes unsuccessful in acquiring grain.

Early in the period 1660-1700, the fisheries off Lofoten were very successful and they had great influence. Participation was greatest from Vefsn, where people anyhow had to sail a long distance to fish commercially. But even the men living on the coast of other quarters of Alstahaug parish frequently sailed to Lofoten to partake in the cod fisheries in winter. In the parish of Brønnøy, however, the men normally went south to Namdalen to participate in cod fisheries there. In this sense it can be said that the fishermen in the northern and the southern part of the area partook in different seasonal fisheries. Towards the end of the century, however, the fisheries of Lofoten failed almost completely. This changed the situation very much. Even the fishermen from the northern end of the area started to participate in the fisheries off Namdalen, or else they fished in the northern part of Helgeland (particularly in the sea of Træna). This may have changed the local economy of Vefsn towards a more uniform concentration on agriculture, because fishing was less accessible in this quarter than in the others.

For the area as a whole, it seems that stockfish production more than before became concentrated on local natural resources. It is probable that local production of stockfish in Helgeland was better maintained than the development of exports.

Notes

1 For instance they are mentioned in a petition for tax exemption sent by the presiding judge of Steigen. The petition was recommended by the district governor, Knud Gedde, who confirmed the economic problems of the district. The church accounts from all deaneries in Nordland can be found in the State Archive of Trondheim.

2 R. Høgsæt: Tienden som kilde til produksjonsutviklinga (The tithe as a source for production development), *Historisk Tidsskrift*, 1994, pp. 7-13.

3 Cf. note 2.

4 J. Sandnes: *Ødetid og gjenreisning* (Desertion and recultivation), Oslo-Bergen-Tromsø 1971, pp. 300, 319, 338ff.

5 R. Høgsæt: Their Ancestral Lands. Succession Rights of Norwegian Tenants in the 16th and 17th centuries, *Scandinavian Journal of History*, 1992, pp. 167-173.

6 A male census was taken in 1701 and this enumerates all males from the age of 1. In 1665 there was a census of all males from the age of 12, and in 1666 a census was taken of all male inhabitants. However, this last one is not preserved for Brønnøy parish.

7 M. M. Rasch: Dagbog fra Nordlandene 1581-1639, *Norske Magasin*, II, Christiania 1870.

8 K. Lunden: *Korn og kaup* (Grain and trade), Oslo 1978, pp. 27 ff.

CHAPTER 9
Fairs as periodical regional centres in Denmark, 1600-1900

By Ole Degn

Regional history

Until our time historians have often written history dealing with either rural or urban history, while relations between country and town have been rather neglected.[1] In recent decades, however, historians have become increasingly aware of the values of regional historical points of views.[2] A town is seen in connection with the surrounding area or maybe an area with several towns which are always placed in a hierarchy.[3] Here you have an opportunity to study the economic, social and demographic connections between the inhabitants and the economic life in a town and its surroundings. Structures and developments can be more easily detected and an area can be analysed, described and explained on the basis of e.g. Walter Christaller's central place theory from the 1930s.[4] The towns are seen in a hierarchy which forms centres in regions of varying size.

Chartered towns and annual fairs

Economic conditions until 1857 were regulated by legislation, which since the Middle Ages, with some exceptions, had given the chartered towns a monopoly of trade and crafts. This was based on a wish to encourage the wealth of citizens and society and thus the ability to pay taxes and duties, as well as a wish to ensure the country was supplied with the needed articles, first of all food.

In trade the citizens had a monopoly of buying and selling the products from the countryside, and foreign merchants were allowed to trade wholesale only with the peasants. Trade had to take place in the market place or at the annual fairs. The peasants were allowed to sell their products only in the market square, and in the market square, the citizens of the town had a monopoly to buy until 10 o'clock, after which trade was open to all.

The annual fairs

Until late in the nineteenth century the annual fairs were important elements in the economy as were the towns. At the annual fairs trade was fundamentally free. Here visitors, guests, i.e. citizens from other Danish as well as foreign chartered towns, could trade with peasants from the region, bypassing the local citizens. This was true not only of the annual fairs in the towns but also of annual fairs in the countryside. A few country fairs were large, but most were only of local importance. At a certain period the annual fairs in the countryside were regarded as being contrary to the legislation concerning the towns, and they were abolished by a statutory instrument in 1521. But in the long run, annual fairs near manors, parsonages, inns and villages could not be kept down.

The trade in everyday necessities in the form of exchange of articles between the population in the countryside and in the towns was handled in the market place – as well as in the merchant's houses. But for several reasons it was necessary to have larger trade places too: the annual fairs. This in spite of the fact that the merchants of the towns handled the trade with imported industrial products and raw materials while the tradesmen in many trades could supply customers with a wide range of manufactured goods. A low level of production, and combined with this a low level of consumption, made it necessary to concentrate trade. In a way which is now difficult to understand, the daily trade in the merchants' houses was at a low level. Even in a great merchant's house only a few customers were seen every day. Because of this, the supply often had to be restricted, and so there was a basis for the annual fairs, where sellers and buyers from a larger region could meet.

Because of this, annual fairs may be seen as centres of regions and we have reason to believe that analyses of the structure and development of these fairs as well as of the people attending them can throw light on important features of the regional historical process.

The economic legislation gave the towns a monopoly on commerce and crafts and this increased the importance of the annual fairs, because 80 per cent of the population lived in the countryside until the middle of the nineteenth century. Because of migration to the towns and the growth of the urban population in the second half of the nineteenth century, the relative share of the rural population fell, but in 1901 it was still 63 per cent.

The scene for the annual fairs in the town was in the square or in the old *algade* (Common Street), often with the involvement of the adjacent streets. Annual fairs could also be held in a place outside the town, especially annual fairs with horses and cattle. A fair with small wares could then be held at the same time in the town. The fairs in the countryside could be held in the village street or on a heath, like fairs near Ry, Hjørring and Hobro and the fair near Kliplev, where the whole area between this village and the old highway was considered to be a legal marketplace.[5]

That the annual fairs in former times played an essential role is seen already from the fact that the word »annual fair« (*marked*), together with the word »market days« (*torvedage*), has its own paragraph in the alphabetical index to the edition of royal rescripts, edited by the lawyer Laurids Fogtman at the beginning of the nineteenth century.[6] It is seen too from the extent of legislation and administrative provisions concerning annual fairs, where Fogtman's edition for the years 1660-1830 contains more than 400 rescripts etc.

The sources

The great importance of the annual fairs means that a comprehensive law material is available to examine their conditions. For the study of the importance of the annual fairs for regional history, six types of sources are available: customs accounts, bridge toll and harbour accounts (*bropenge- og havneregnskaber*), excise duty accounts (*konsumtionsregnskaber*), accounts of the city treasurer including stall-rent accounts (*stadepengeregnskaber*), excise duty accounts from the gates (*portbøger*) and ledgers with passports for travellers to the fairs (*markedspasprotokoller*).

The customs accounts are accounts from the collection of royal customs in the harbours or in the loading docks. They can be found in considerable numbers as supplements to the accounts from the counties before 1660.

The bridge toll and harbour accounts are accounts from the collecting of fees on articles, the money to be used for the maintenance of harbour bridges and harbours etc. The harbour was used for import as well as export and therefore the accounts can also give information about the area surrounding an annual fair, far inland, as will be seen in the following pages. These accounts are known from several chartered towns, possibly as supplements to the accounts of the city treasurer, as in the cases of Randers, Århus, Kolding, Ribe, Kerteminde and Kalundborg.

The excise duty accounts are accounts from the collection of the excise duties, introduced in 1657, and after a break, reintroduced in 1671. It was a duty collected when the peasants brought their agricultural products from the countryside to the towns, from 1688 also imposed on wine, brandy, salt and tobacco. The revenue entries from the different town gates where the excise duties were collected are summed up in the accounts. As the collection of excise duty for long periods was delegated to the councils of the towns, accounts of excise duties are found in long series in the Town Hall archives from Kalundborg, Skælskør and Fåborg and for some years from Odense, Århus and Ribe.[7] After 1789, when the delegation to private people or to the municipal corporation stopped, the accounts are found in the archives from the customs administrations, as those from Frederikshavn, Sæby, Skive, Skanderborg, Stubbekøbing and Stege.

The accounts from the city treasurer are in the form of an annual income listing the so-called stall-rent, i.e. the money collected as rents for a stall place at the fairs. As a supplement are often found specified accounts listing all the payers and their place of residence. The accounts from the city treasurer are found for some towns from the sixteenth century onwards, and from many towns from the seventeenth century and on. For the period 1772-1850 they are placed in the so-called checked accounts, kept from most of the chartered towns, as the accounts after the check in the Exchequer (*Rentekammeret*) were returned to the towns. For the period 1826-50 after being checked in the county administration they can be kept in the archives from the counties, if not returned to the towns.

The excise duty accounts from the gates are accounts from the collection of excise duties at the town gates. They are found in the customs archives for the period after 1789 and exist in long series from the towns Frederikshavn, Nibe, Stubbekøbing, for some years from Randers, Århus and Stege.

The ledgers with passports for travellers to the fairs contain information from the passports introduced in 1775 as part of a control system.[8] The trades people going to the fairs had to have such passports from the municipal corporations in the towns, or from a bailiff at a city court or a court in the countryside. The passports contained information about name, occupation, articles and the travelling route. Passports and ledgers or lists of passports are found in many Town Hall archives and the court archives, and lists are found in the archives from the Exchequer and the Department of Trade (*Kommercekollegiet*) in the Danish National Archives.

The importance of the annual fairs

In the evaluation of the importance of an annual fair as central place, several circumstances have to be taken into consideration. The number of visitors to the fair will be an indicator of the importance of the fair, just as the size of the geographical area from which the visitors came, sellers as well as buyers. The figures will be affected by the location of the fair, the market days, the time of the year and the number of days, how old the fair is, its traditions and its type.

Concerning the number of visitors at the different fairs, it is possible to get an impresssion of figures only for the trading people. In the harbour they paid bridge toll, and they can be found in the accounts of bridge toll and harbour fees. In the fair they rented places for their carriages, tables or stalls, and they can be found in the accounts of the city treasurer. After 1657 with a few interruptions they paid excise duties for several of their articles when they came to the town gate, and they can be found in the accounts of the excise duties. In a more indirect way, information can be found in the ledgers with passports for travellers to the fairs, which after 1775 were written as part of a control system where the municipal corporations issued passports to the trading people. It is a little difficult to get information about the individual fair as these ledgers in the individual towns registered people going to the different fairs – only occasionally those going to a certain fair. Besides the trading people of course, many others went to the fairs to buy, to look or to take part in the public entertainments. For these we can get no numbers.

The entries in the above mentioned accounts show that the number of people paying excise duty normally increased substantially in the days before and during the annual fairs. Already here the importance of the fairs is reflected. In the same way it can be seen that the number of merchants' customers also increased.[9]

The size of the surrounding area for the individual annual fair often appears indirectly from the statement of domicile for the trading people at the fair. Normally information about the domicile is given in the customs and excise duty accounts and the bridge toll accounts as well as in the stall-rent accounts. When the domiciles are marked on maps, the extent of the areas is revealed as shown by examples below.

The location of the annual fairs and the days of the fairs were published in the almanac from the University of Copenhagen from the end of the sixteenth century. More scattered information is also given in the letter books of the Royal Chancellery (*Danske Kancelli*). In the almanacs the development of the annual fairs can be followed in detail. The fairs are mentioned year after year for each of the provinces. From the years between the beginning of the seventeenth century and the end of the nineteenth century, about 250 fairgrounds are recorded. For some of the years the figures are given in table 9.1. From 57 fairgrounds with about 88 annual fairs in 1620, the figures increased to 69 fairgrounds with 138 annual fairs in 1674 (fig. 9.1) and to 182 fairgrounds with 681 annual fairs in 1860 (fig. 9.2).

Originally the annual fairs were mentioned in the calendar of the almanacs on the relevant dates. From the end of the seventeenth century things became easier for the travellers to the fairs: the annual fairs were listed in a special list at the end of the almanac, at first chronologically, from the year 1779 alphabetically.

The specification of the annual fairs in the almanacs is presumably accurate. Otherwise there would have been great problems at the time. This is indicated by an episode in connection with the almanac in 1787: because of a misprint it was stated for the town of Nakskov that fairs with horses would be held every Tuesday in Lent; it should have been Thursday, and the municipal corporation asked the government on which of the days it should be held. It had to be held on Thursday. Many people may have travelled in vain to the fair that year.

However, in addition to these annual fairs, apart from those omitted by mistakes, were an unknown number of illegal fairs. Maybe fairs which were abolished by the king, but yet held by the local population. Maybe fairs held by the population itself, like the people visiting the fair in Hjørring in the middle of the eighteenth century: coming there from the south on their way to the mill in Vrejlev, they held a fair with the sale of great quantities of brandy, so that this fair was called a »pig, cattle and brandy fair«.[10] This fact gives a certain unreliability to the numbers of the annual fairs. The figures have to be considered minimum figures. It is thought-provoking that in 1763 when the local population petitioned the king to have an annual fair legalized near the village of Lund a little east of Herning, one of the arguments mentioned was that a fair with horses, cattle and small wares had been held at this place on September 5th – for 43 years.

The location of the annual fairs (cf. fig. 9.1-9.2) shows that the islands in former times had relatively more annual fairs than Jutland. The growth in the number of fairgrounds from about 1800 was caused by the fact that Jutland got a large number of new (legal) fairgrounds. An important distinction between the annual fairs in former times was a consequence of a location either in a town or in the countryside. Rural fairs were prohibited in 1521 to give an advantage to the chartered towns. Yet, for example in 1620, there were two rural fairs, in Tommerup on Funen and in Kliplev in Schleswig. And in the course of time more and more rural fairs were allowed. In the long run, the fairs at the inns and manors and in the villages could not be kept down. In 1710 there were ten rural fairgrounds, in 1790 twenty and in 1860 about a hundred. The growth in the number of rural fairgrounds was caused

Fig. 9.1: Denmark's fairgrounds, annual fairs and chartered towns 1674

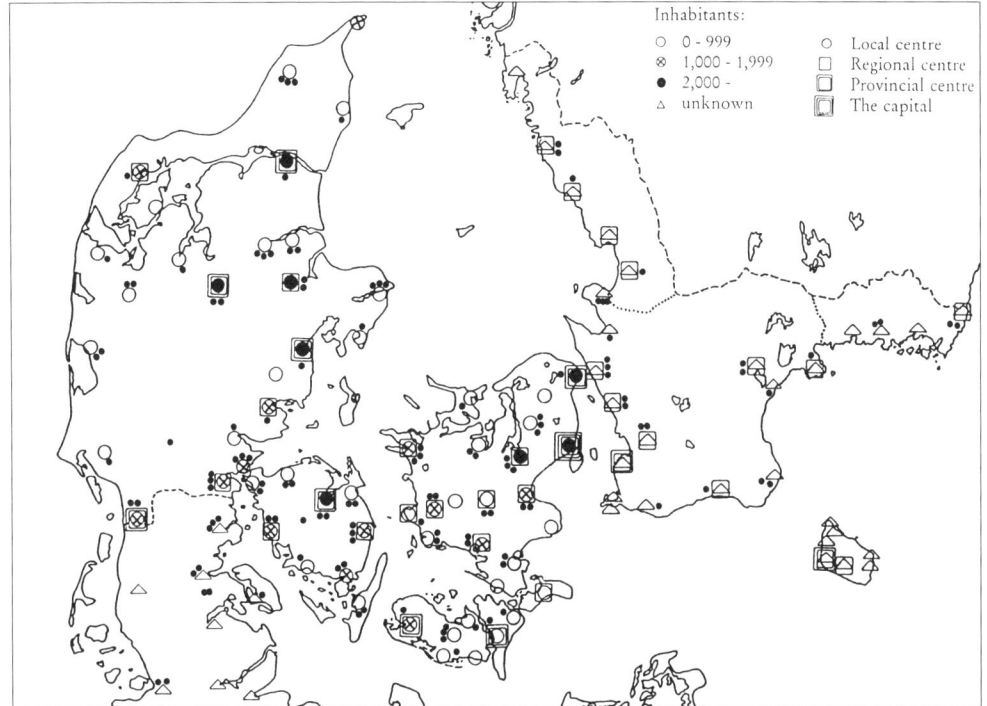

Note: Each of the dots marks one annual fair. The number of dots marks the number of annual fairs in the town concerned. The information about the towns in the regions east of Øresund is from the 1650s.

by development in North and South Jutland (Schleswig). Together they had, in 1790, 14 rural markets, in 1860 no less than 94. Presumably, the number of the annual fairs reflect the economic development and indicates a growth in agricultural production, trade and transport in Jutland, where the chartered towns, apart from East Jutland, were also more scattered than in the other Danish provinces.[11]

Unlike the fairs in the towns, the rural fairs did not have a natural location on a square or in the streets in a town which had maintained a position as an economic centre perhaps for centuries. The rural fairs were located in places which the new development gave a position as central places. Maybe it was on a bare field or on a heath, but in many cases it was a manor, a parsonage or an inn which became the physical setting for the fair. Particularly an inn was a practical background for a fair. In 1860, understandably, several fairs with a location at an inn are listed, like Flauenskjold Inn in Vendsyssel, Ans Inn and Knudstrup Inn south of Viborg, Vejlby Inn southeast of Randers, Ølstvad Inn and Ny Løgten Inn north of Århus and Tirstrup Inn in Djursland.

The age of the annual fairs is known in many cases, and fairs can be seen to have been held over centuries, even if

Regional integration

Fig. 9.2: Denmark's fairgrounds and annual fairs 1860

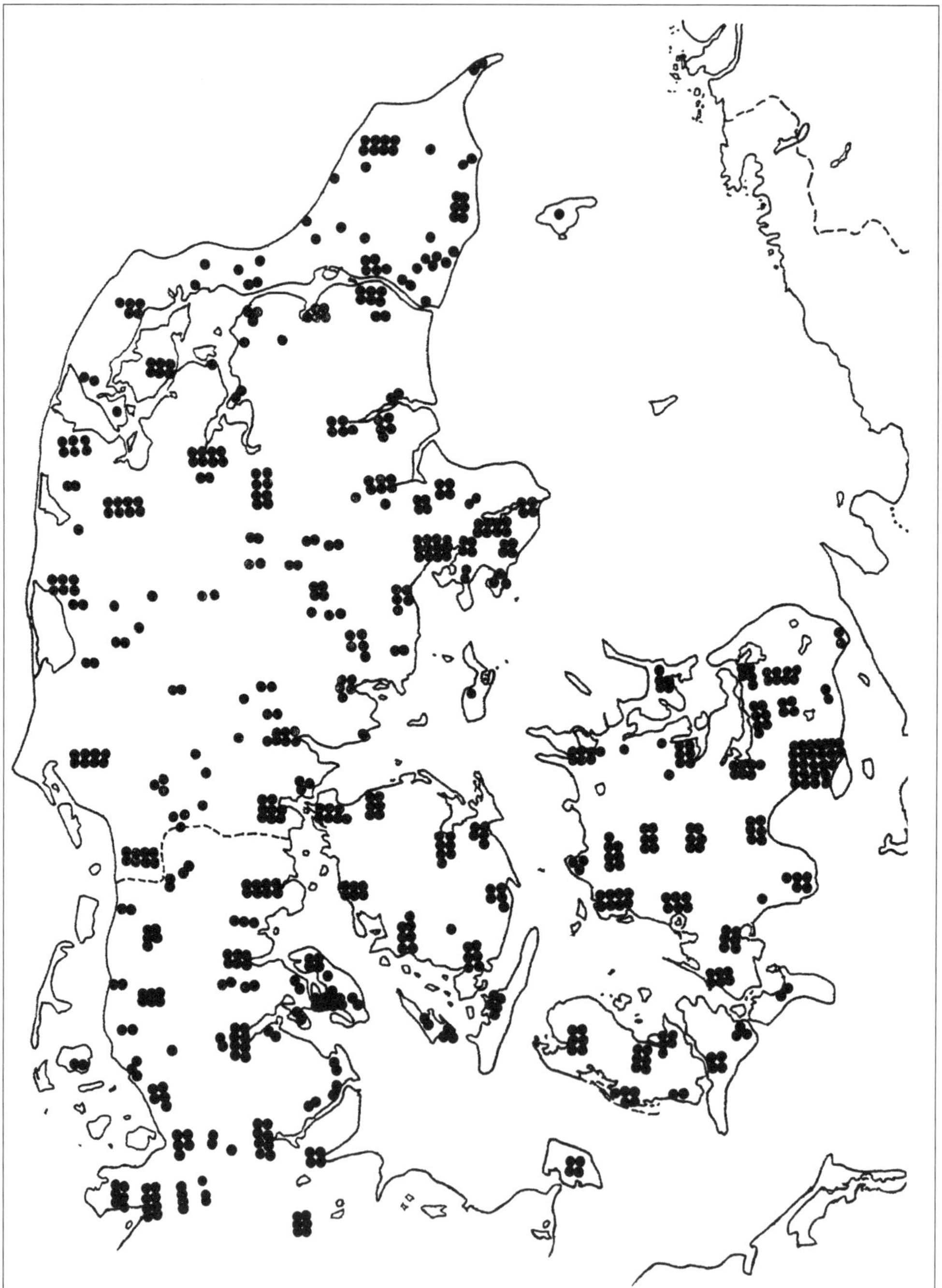

Note: Each of the dots marks one annual fair. The number of dots marks the number of annual fairs in the town concerned.

occasionally various changes and breaks can make it doubtful whether it is the same fair. Often, however, a surprising stability is seen. For centuries a fair could be held on exactly the same date. In 1622 King Christian IV found that in the town Lykkeby in Blekinge an annual fair was still held, in spite of the fact that in the year 1600 he had ordained that no trade and craft was allowed, in order to favour the new town Christianopel.

Obstinate adherence to traditions is also seen in the fact that even at the end of the eighteenth century annual fairs in several towns in Halland and Scania were held on exactly the same dates as in the years before these areas were made over to Sweden, more than a hundred years previously. Here even a change in nationality was without importance.

The great stability seen in connection with many fairs may mean that a fair reflected the economic forces in the region. If the same fair is followed through centuries, changes and developments in connection with it will demonstrate aspects of the economic development in the area.

With the growth in the number of annual fairs in the nineteenth century many fairs came into existence, which gradually developed in competition with others that had existed for centuries. If there was a need for the function of a new fair in the region, it could develop, but also fairs with a short existence were seen.

The days for the annual fairs were scattered over most of the year, but very unevenly. January and December had only a very few days with fairs, while March, June, September or October in the years under observation here dominated and had 20-25 per cent of the fairs in the year in question. Yet a development can be seen: in 1620 the month of June had most fairs, in 1656, 1674 and 1710, October and in 1790 and 1860, March. Presumably the shift from October to March was connected with a great increase in the number of fairs with cattle, and these were mainly held in Lent.[12]

From former times many fairs were held on certain days in the calendar, named after the old saints, like Saint John (Midsummer Day, June 24th), Oluf's Day (July 29th), Michaelmas Day (September 29th). Many fairs, too, had a medieval background in pilgrimage. Renowned fairs were the Midsummer Day fairs in Horsens, Ribe, Ringsted, Rudkøbing, Simmershavn, Stubbekøbing and Sølvesborg, and in the same way the Oluf's Day fairs and the Michaelmas Day fairs etc. were held in other towns. A fair, too, could be fixed in relation to one of the old ecclesiastical festivals, such as Easter and Whitsuntide, like the famous Whitsuntide fair in Aalborg. Here datings are even seen in Latin, like »Tuesday after lætare«, i.e. Tuesday after the fourth Sunday in Lent, »reminiscere«, i.e. the second Sunday in Lent or Wednesday after the first Sunday in Lent, and »trinitatis«, i.e. Trinity Sunday, the Sunday after Whit Sunday. In the eighteenth century, a long series of fairs was approved fixed to one or two of the days of the week in Lent and therefore held for six consecutive weeks.

In the seventeenth and eighteenth centuries some fairs were held on the same dates each year. Popular dates were not only the above-mentioned days, but also for example Bodolphi Day, Petrus and Paulus' Day, Bartholomew Day, Our Lady Day and Remigius' Day, June 17th,

Regional integration

Table 9.1: Fairgrounds (a) and annual fairs (b) in Denmark 1620, 1656, 1674, 1710, 1790 and 1860

Province	1620		1656		1674		1710		1790		1860	
	a	b	a	b	a	b	a	b	a	b	a	b
Zealand	14	25	13	25	13	39	18	92	20	81	26	164
Scania*	6	10	9	18	10	18	10	16	9	12		
Halland	2	3	3	4	3	4	4	7	4	7		
Blekinge			3	4	3	5	2	3				
Bornholm							1	1	1	1		
Møn							1	1	1	1	1	2
Lolland	2	3	4	6	4	6	6	13	6	11	5	24
Falster	2	2	2	3	2	2	2	2	2	3	2	7
Funen	7	9	9	12	9	17	9	22	9	27	8	43
Langeland	1	3	1	2	1	2	2	5	2	5	1	5
North Jutland	19	28	22	35	19	35	28	73	28	74	96	288
South Jutland or Schleswig	4	5	3	5	5	10	8	16	26	57	43	148
Total	57	88	69	114	69	138	91	251	108	279	182	681
Without Scania	49	75	54	88	53	111	75	225	95	260	182	681

*The fairs in the Scanian provinces are listed in the almanacs at least up to the end of the eighteenth century.
Source: The almanac of the University of Copenhagen, the stated years.

June 29th, August 24th, September 8th and October 1st respectively.[13] It is remarkable that the fairs held on a certain day were scattered over the provinces. It was the intention that travellers to the fairs should have the possibility of travelling from one fair to the next. In 1771 the tradesmen in Odense applied for a regulation of the fairs on Funen in such a way that there could be 6-8 days between each of them; people with much to buy or sell should have the opportunity of coming to all the fairs.

In the nineteenth century the days for the fairs seem to have been more scattered, but this too was necessary with the steep rise in the number of fairs. In addition a provison in the Danish Law (*Danske Lov*) from 1683 had cut down the number of possible fair days: it was stated that no fair was to be held on a Sunday or a holy day and this was soon extended to Saturdays and Mondays to safeguard the Sundays.

The date of the fairs on the calendar had a close connection with the range of articles and the alternation of the seasons. The fairs were held especially in March-April, in the days around Midsummer Day, in the last half of July and the first half of August and at the beginning of October. This was no accident. These were the Lent fairs, the summer fairs and the harvest fairs. The first period had the horse and cattle fairs, the last two periods were the harvest time and the slaughter time, when people prepared for the winter.

The number of days for a fair varied from one, the most usual, and up to 18, the number of days for Viborg's so-called *Snapsting* fair. Aalborg's Whitsuntide fair began on the first weekday after Whitsuntide and lasted that week and the next too. Viborg's two fairs lasted a fortnight each in 1710, Århus' Oluf's fair the same. Not many fairs, however, lasted even as long as ten days.

The days for the fairs were published in the almanacs from the end of the sixteenth century. The time for the opening of the fairs was also fixed. It could be at 10 or 11 o'clock in the morning, but in the nineteenth century more detailed indications of time were given. For the year 1860 for the fairs in Tønder it was fixed that the first fair began on May 30th at 4 o'clock in the afternoon and lasted until June 2nd at the same time. The last fair began on October 1st in the morning and lasted until October 4th in the evening. And two one-day fairs in August and September began the previous day in the afternoon. Time and days for a fair in a complicated way could also determine the character of the fair, as seen at Løgumkloster's spring fair in 1860. It lasted from 18th to 20th of April, and the first day had linen goods, wooden articles and pottery, while the selling of small wares was not begun until Wednesday in the afternoon, then Thursday was the main fair day and the fair ended on Friday afternoon at 4 o'clock.

It is difficult to decide whether the number of annual fairs at the different fairgrounds was important. On the face of it, it could be presumed that the existence of many fairs reflected considerable economic activity and strength, but there is no doubt that at times and in different parts of the country, the fairs were seen as a means to promote trade and industry in a locality. Therefore local people pressed the king to grant permission for more annual fairs. Especially the merchants were often interested in the fairs while the tradesmen could be reluctant because of the menacing increased competition from the tradesmen from other towns.[14]

That the connection between economic activity and the number of annual fairs could be inversely proportional can be seen from fig. 9.1, with the fairs in the year 1674. The signs for the chartered towns place them in the town hierarchy and it can be clearly seen that provincial centres like Elsinore (Helsingør), Nykøbing Falster, Nakskov, Odense, Aalborg and Århus had only a single fair, the only exceptions to this being Viborg and Ribe, with two annual fairs, perhaps because of decline. On the other hand small local centres like Holbæk, Skælskør, Bogense, Kerteminde and Ringkøbing had two fairs, Maribo, Hjørring and Grenå even three.

Already at the beginning of the seventeenth century precise regulations were made for the character of many fairs. There was a distinction between fairs with horses, with cattle, and with small wares and trade products such as linen and wooden products. In the nineteenth century there are several fairs with very restricted ranges of articles, such as geese (goose fairs), honey and fish products. While the animal and general fairs were found nearly all over the country, the restricted fairs were more special. A goose fair was found in Nykøbing Mors, a honey fair in Aalborg, a fish fair in Haderslev. At the fair near Christianshede southwest of Silkeborg, the sale of linen, knitwear, wooden products and garden products and at the fair at Knudstrup Inn south of Viborg, that of peasant small wares was allowed.

The miraculous spring fairs, like the fairs in Hjembæk near Kalundborg and in Mogenstrup and the Saint Søren's fair near Ry were named after the locality and a special funtion. These fairs had their roots back in the Middle Ages with pilgrimages and the use of miraculous water. These original activities were also the background for trade. The most colourful and, in connection with the chartered towns, the most interesting fairs were presumably the small wares fairs. Here there was trade in articles such as woollen cloth, linen, cotton or silk, fancy goods, articles of clothing, spices and articles for everyday use, for example of metal, leather and horn. Here since the Middle Ages there were also amusements and appearances and entertainment by performers and actors.[15] The small wares fairs, however, were abolished by law in 1873, in force from the end of 1882. Since then, mostly fairs with horses, cattle, sheeps and pigs were held.[16] The background for this was presumably the development in trade through shops and certain relaxations of restrictions for trade with the Trade Act of 1857 (*Næringsfrihedsloven*). At that time, however, references were also made to the fact that the small wares fairs were more and more popular entertainments rather than trade places.

When assessing a fair and its role in a region, it is of course important to consider its character and possible limitations in the selection of articles sold.

A special type of fairs were the servants' fairs held in the eighteenth and nineteenth centuries in several chartered towns, where they are known from Aalborg, Ringkøbing, Ribe, Kolding, Haderslev and Slagelse.[17] Here the employers and the servants met each other around Midsummer Day and at the quarter-days, the days on which servants used to change jobs, since 1770 on June 30th and December 31st. Agreements about service were made. Farmhands and servant girls who came from North Jutland let themselves be hired for meadow harvesting in Schleswig and the Ditmarshes. Particularly well known was the servants' fair held in Kolding in the street Rendebanen in connection with the Midsummer Day fair and a large Michaelmas Day fair. These fairs were also of importance regionally for large areas of the country, and for employment and the economy, they were of far-reaching importance.

The fairs as a starting point for regional historical studies

The value of the fairs as a basis for studies of several important conditions in the history of a region will here be illustrated by analysis of six fairs held at four fairgrounds, namely Ribe's Midsummer Day fair and Our Lady fair 1640, Århus' Oluf's fair 1696, Viborg's Snapsting fair 1774 and Hjørring's First fair and Last fair 1780. The source material is customs accounts and stall-rent accounts from the city treasurers' accounts.

The location of these fairs in a town on the west coast, a town on the east coast and two inland towns should demonstrate the possibilities in different types of fairs.

Ribe's Midsummer Day fair 1640 (fig. 9.3).
In the seventeenth century, Ribe had two fairs, the Midsummer Day fair and Our Lady fair in September. They can be followed in detail year after year from the beginning of the seventeenth century thanks to first, a series of bridge toll accounts, kept by the harbour treasurer, from 1639 in addition a series of so-called *Revier* duty accounts, then from 1672 the stall-rent accounts. The »Revier« duty was introduced by royal prescript in 1639 after the town had asked for a permission to collect a duty to be used for a planned dredging and regulation of the stream Ribe Å so that vessels could sail to the town. The duty was fixed at 1/2 rigsdaler (1 rigsdaler = 6 mark = 96 skilling) on every foreign craft (*skude*) and 1 mark on every boat and fishing boat, as well as 1 skilling on every rigsdaler value of articles imported or exported by foreigners and 1/3 skilling by natives, and to this came 6 skilling on every last [1 læst = 1.8 ton] exported by foreigners and 3 skilling by natives plus 1 skilling on every imported barrel of Frisian salt and 2 skilling on each exported horse.

Because of the position of Ribe near the frontier between North Jutland and the Duchy of Schleswig there seems to have been no problems determining the transport direction for the articles mentioned in the duty accounts. These accounts were kept at a place where the stream of south-bound Danish agricultural products like oxen, horses, grain, butter etc. and fish products like salted flatfish (*skuller*) and whiting met north-bound industrial products and raw materials like wine, cloth, spices, Frisian salt, hops, pottery etc.

In the days just before and during the Midsummer Day fair 1640, the accounts registered 270 people; these are, however, only a portion of the actual participants in the fair, as citizens from other Danish chartered towns were exempted from such a duty.[18] These visitors amounted to about a fourth of the total number of the duty-paying people that year.

Of the 270 people, 76 were from North Jutland, 171 from Southern Jutland or Schleswig. As domiciles, the Schleswig town of Flensburg dominated with 35, followed by another Schleswig town, Husum, with 16, Nordby on Fanø with 14, Sønderho and Sild (Sylt) each with 11, Haderslev and Langenhorn each with 9, Föhr with 7. Remarkable too is an area on the Limfjord at Oddesund, with 16 people from Nissum, Humlum and Venø. The payments on four crafts, seven smacks and 41 boats show that many came to the fair by sea, that is the many from Fanø, Mandø, Rømø, Sild and Föhr and from the coastal area between Ho in the north and Galmsbøl in the south.

The goods sold by the North Jutland visitors were agricultural products such

Regional integration

Fig. 9.3: Ribe's Midsummerday fair 1640: Duty tax paying guests

Note: Each of the dots marks one duty tax paying guest. The situation of Ribe is marked by an arrow.

as horses, fish such as eels, whitings and salted flatfish and wooden products such as boards, firewood and wheels. The goods bought were flax, hemp, salt and hops. The Schleswig visitors brought to the market fish and Frisian salt, especially from Galmsbøl, and bought horses. Merchants and tradesmen from some Schleswig chartered towns came to sell various articles, from Haderslev: hats, white bread and pots, from Flensburg: hats and stockings, tapes and woollen bands, copper and brass and pepper cakes, from Schleswig town: »marvellous articles« (*eventyrske varer*), from Husum: spices and pots, from Friedrichstadt: tobacco. From Garleben, 50 kilometres north of Magdeburg, several merchants came with hops.

The accounts show that during the days of the Midsummer Day fair duties were paid on 156,000 salted flatfish, 12,000 whitings, 19 wagon loads of eels, 18 barrels of rye, about 400 horses, 8,800 kg flax, 7 sacks of hops, a good 200 barrels of salt and a good 100 pairs of wheels, as well as other wooden products, small wares etc.

Ribe's Our Lady fair (September) 1640 (fig. 9.4)
As mentioned above, 270 duty-paying visitors came to the Midsummer Day fair in 1640 and paid »Revier« duties, and at the Our Lady fair the same year there were 98.[19] By comparison between the entries from the two fairs, it was found that 22 people visited both fairs, most of these from Flensburg, namely 10 people, but also several from Nordby on Fanø, Sønderho and Husum. Comparisons with accounts from other fairs would presumably make it possible to map patterns in this activity.

Of the 98 people, 26 were from North Jutland, and 68 from the province of Schleswig. As domiciles, Flensburg dominated with 36, then followed Galmsbøl and Risummohr with 9 each, Husum with 5. Payments from seven smacks and 41 boats show that many came to the fair by sea, in the same way as to the Midsummer Day fair.

The pattern in the buying and selling of the visitors was similar to that seen at the Midsummer Day fair, but no eels are mentioned, and horses, whiting and salted flatfish play a small role. On the other hand the quantities of flax, hemp and salt were much larger, 16,000 kg, 2,100 kg and nearly 900 barrels respectively. From Flensburg now, there were also hats and stockings.

The two fairs in Ribe are here described as examples of information on the basis of the »Revier« duty accounts, but they can be seen against a longer background in time. The figures from the stall-rent accounts are entered in the accounts from the city treasurer and have been summed up for the period 1560 to 1660. On the basis of these calculations, the two fairs in 1640 were just a faint shadow of the fairs in former times. If the index figures for the stall-rents from the two fairs in the 1560's are set at 100, then the figures for the 1640's were 23 and 6 respectively, after a gradual fall since the end of the sixteenth century. The fact probably reflects the decline of Ribe and also the economic decline after the war with the German emperor 1626-29.

Århus' Oluf's fair 1696 (fig. 9.5)
In the seventeenth century Århus had only one annual fair until 1685, the Oluf's fair, 29 July. That year it was moved to February 22nd, Saint Peter's Day, and at the same time they got a new

153

Regional integration

Fig. 9.4: Ribe's Our Lady fair September 1640: Duty tax paying guests

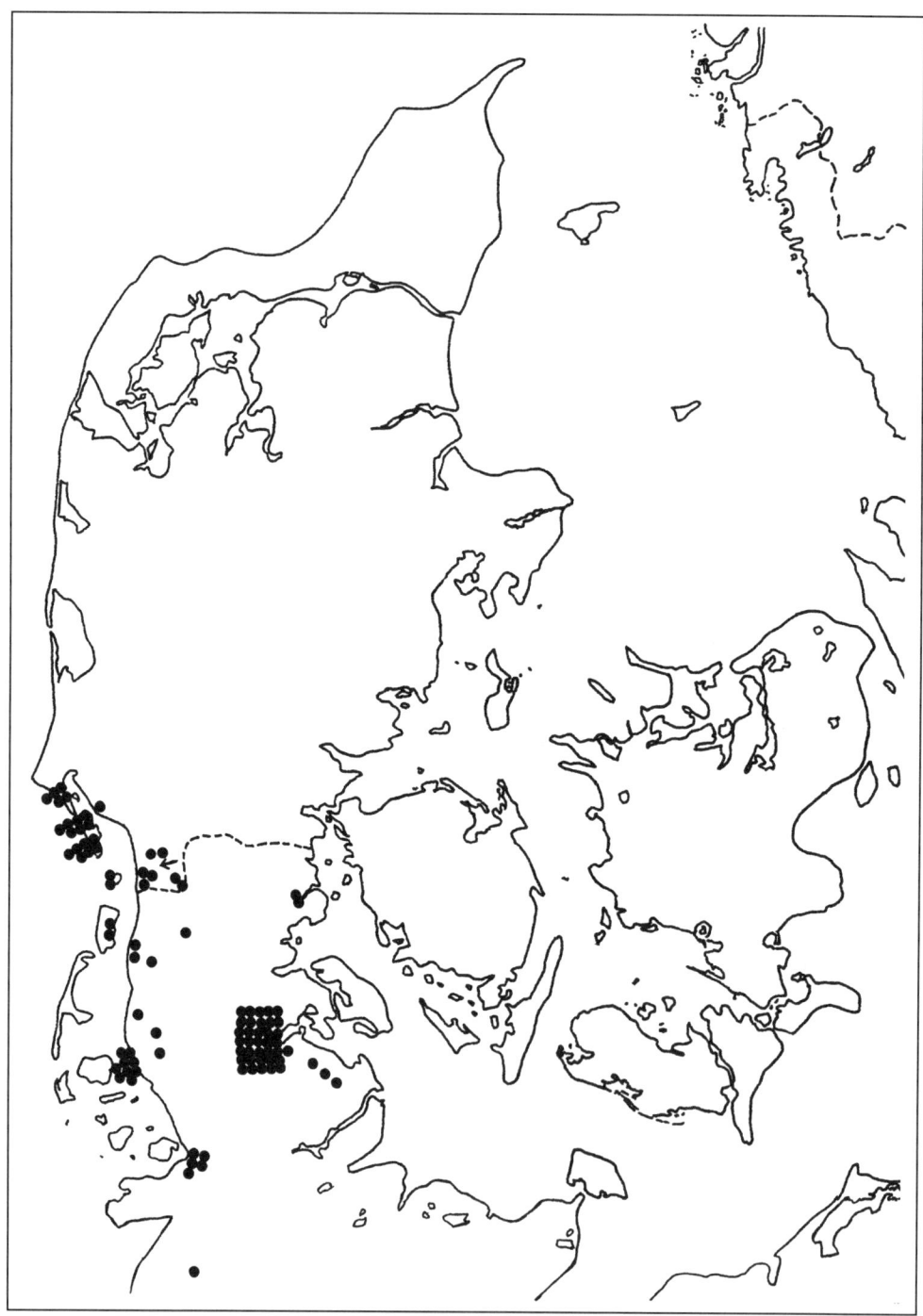

Note: Each of the dots marks one duty tax paying guest. The situation of Ribe is marked by an arrow.

Fairs as periodical regional centres in Denmark, 1600-1900

Fig. 9.5: Århus' Olufs fair 1696: Excise duty paying guests

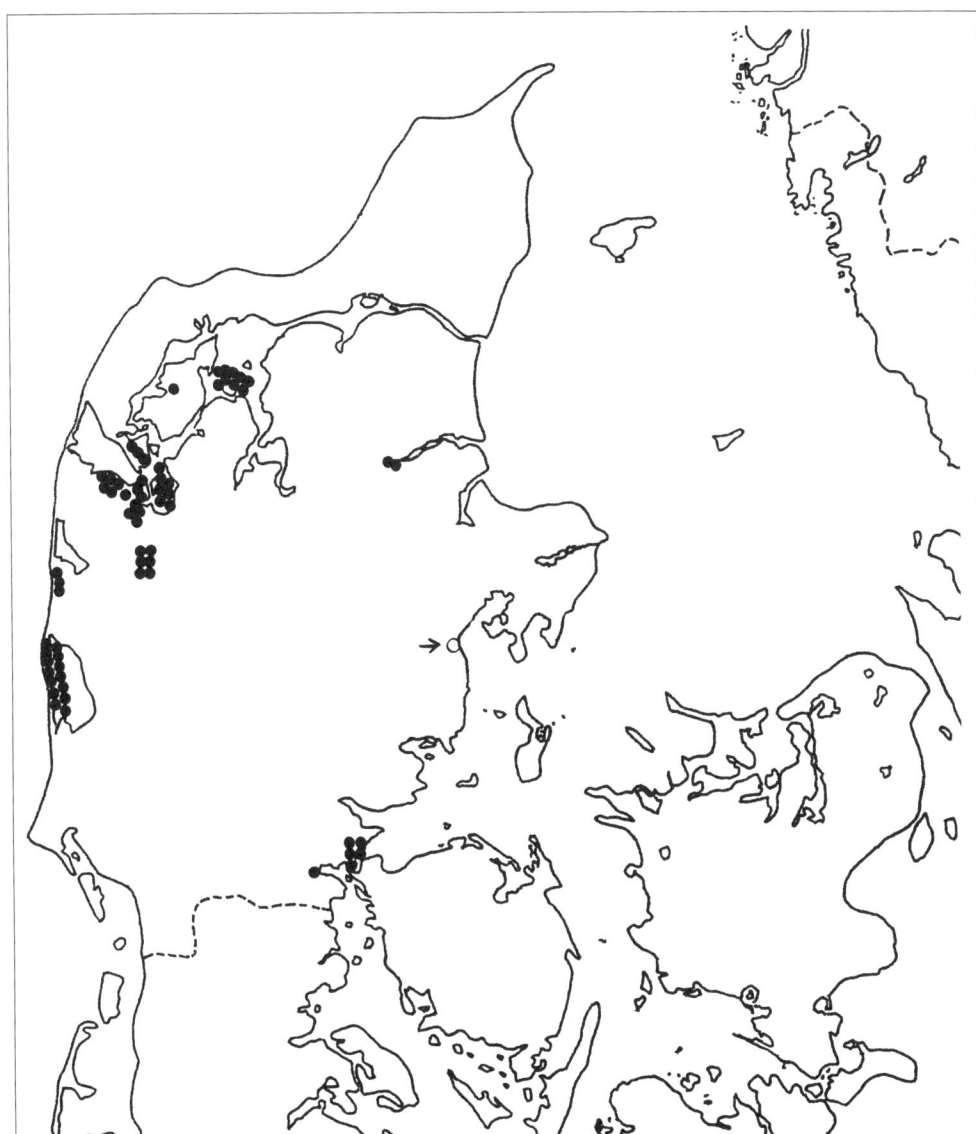

Note: Each of the dots marks one excise duty paying guest. The situation of Århus is marked by an arrow.

Regional integration

fair on October 12th, *Hvideras*, named after a criminal who, in the same year, was executed during the fair as entertainment for the visitors.

That the abolished Oluf's fair really was held in 1696 appears very clearly from the excise duty accounts for that year.[20] In the days 25th-29th of July many more people than usual paid the excise duty at the town gates. About 50 people carrying some special articles were entered by name and domicile so that it is possible to get an impression of the visitors. Here can be seen nearly 30 eel hawkers from Thyholm, Humlum, Venø and Fur (in the western Limfjord area), nearly in the same way as such people were seen in Ribe half a century earlier. In addition to these were 30 fish hawkers from Holmsland, Husby, Nissum, Holstebro and Hobro, 5 bakers from Fredericia and one baker from Kolding. The accounts show that these people brought 19,000 smoked eels, 38,000 whiting, nearly 2,000 flatfish and 3,000 stockfish to the fair. From other sources it is known that visitors came to the fairs by sea especially from Samsø with cabbage, wheels and firewood, others from Flensburg with hemp and *pryssing*, a special beer from the Prussian cities along the southern shore of the Baltic Sea, from Norway others with fish, skins, boards and laths.[21]

On the other hand, the two other fairs in the town played a small role. At the fair on February 20th there were three bakers from Fredericia, at the fair on October 12th, two bakers.

Viborg's Snapsting fair 1774 (fig. 9.6)
In the seventeenth century, the fairs in Viborg were held around 15th -16th January and around September 22nd, Saint Mouritii Day, but later the town was granted a third fair at the beginning of March. The first-mentioned fair was the famous old »Snapsting« fair, held shortly after New Year, simultaneously with the first meeting in the North Jutland court. It was also an important money market and was a time when payment fell due. It was held at the Old Square, the New Square and the Wheel Square, like the Mouritii fair. The horse fair that was held in the week prior to this fair, however, was held at Bispegårdstoft north of the town and was therefore also called Toft fair. In 1737 a fourth fair was granted at the beginning of November. In 1755 the fair in November was moved to October, simultaneously the fair in March stopped and the town got a new horse fair in February. From about 1700 the »Snapsting« fair was held in April, but in 1769 it was moved to June.[22]

For the »Snapsting« fair in 1774, information exists concerning the people who rented stalls for their articles, while the accounts unfortunately contain no information about the articles.[23] As can be seen on the map, the 38 stall-rent payers came from several of the North Jutland chartered towns, especially Horsens and Holstebro, and some Schleswig chartered towns, thus no fewer than 10 from Haderslev, and one from Svendborg on Funen. Among the trading people are mentioned 10 shopkeepers, 6 fancy goods traders and one porcelain trader, of tradesmen 2 bone turners, one bookbinder, one goldsmith, 2 braziers, 2 coppersmiths, one wigmaker, one rope maker and 4 saddlers.

Hjørring's First fair 1780 (fig. 9.7)
In Hjørring in the first half of the seventeenth century two fairs were held, on

July 10th the Canute fair (*Knudsmarked*), on Canute the King's Day, and on September 8th, Our Lady Day. To these from the middle of the century, a fair around 20th of October was added, replacing the Alhede fair, originally a cattle fair, but in the eighteenth century also a horse and small wares fair.

The Canute fair was also called the First fair. In 1780 it was held on 4th of July and just over 50 people came with their articles and rented stalls.[24] As can be seen on the figure, 3 came from Højen, 2 from Ajstrup, one from Hvorup, one from Sæby, 17 from Aalborg and 3 from Haderslev. Thus, the fair was much more local than those analysed above. With at least 17 people from Aalborg, of these 12 tradesmen, the fair in Hjørring functioned as a distant trade place for this town.

The presence of three merchants from Haderslev is interesting. Their domicile was more distant than any of the others, and they have also been considered a foreign element: in the accounts they are mentioned as »Holstein people«, in spite of the fact that they were from Schleswig. In a previous account their domiciles are mentioned, and one of them was among the 10 Haderslev shopkeepers participating in the fair in Viborg in 1774.

Of the stall-rent payers, no fewer than 19 were fishermen, three of them from Højen, 8 were merchants, 4 fancy goods sellers, one baker, one bone turner, one bookbinder, one saddler, one smith, 8 potters – with red pots, like the Jutland blackpots an important article for the fairs – and another 8 were tradesmen, as well as some other potters.

Hjørring's Last fair 1780
The same year the Last fair, held October 27th, had 53 visitors who rented stalls. Their domiciles were similar to those seen in the First fair, except that among the tradesmen were a hatter and a shoemaker.[25] In the time between these two fairs in 1780 a Middle fair was also held, but it was rather unimportant. Only three fishermen and a potter with red pots paid stall-rents, and it was expressly noticed that there were no Holstein people, tradesmen, fancy goods sellers or merchants.

Differences between the fairs

The description of the six fairs at four different fairgrounds has shown four fairs which were different in several ways. Particularly the differences in the size of the surrounding areas are obvious. Some fairs had a rather local character, with visitors just from the region. Other fairs had a surrounding area stretching beyond the province and maybe farther. On the basis of studies of a larger number of fairs it would perhaps be possible to see patterns and structures which again can throw light on different regions. Furthermore, it would be possible to characterize the regions through their position as domicile for travellers to the fairs, like the fish hawkers and the eel hawkers from the Struer region and the very mobile merchants from Haderslev.

The observed differences between the fairs, however, were caused not only by differences in time, location, surrounding area, character and date on the calendar. The differences also have their background in the type of source material. Customs accounts and bridge toll

Regional integration

Fig. 9.6: Viborg's Snapsting fair 1774: Stall renting guests

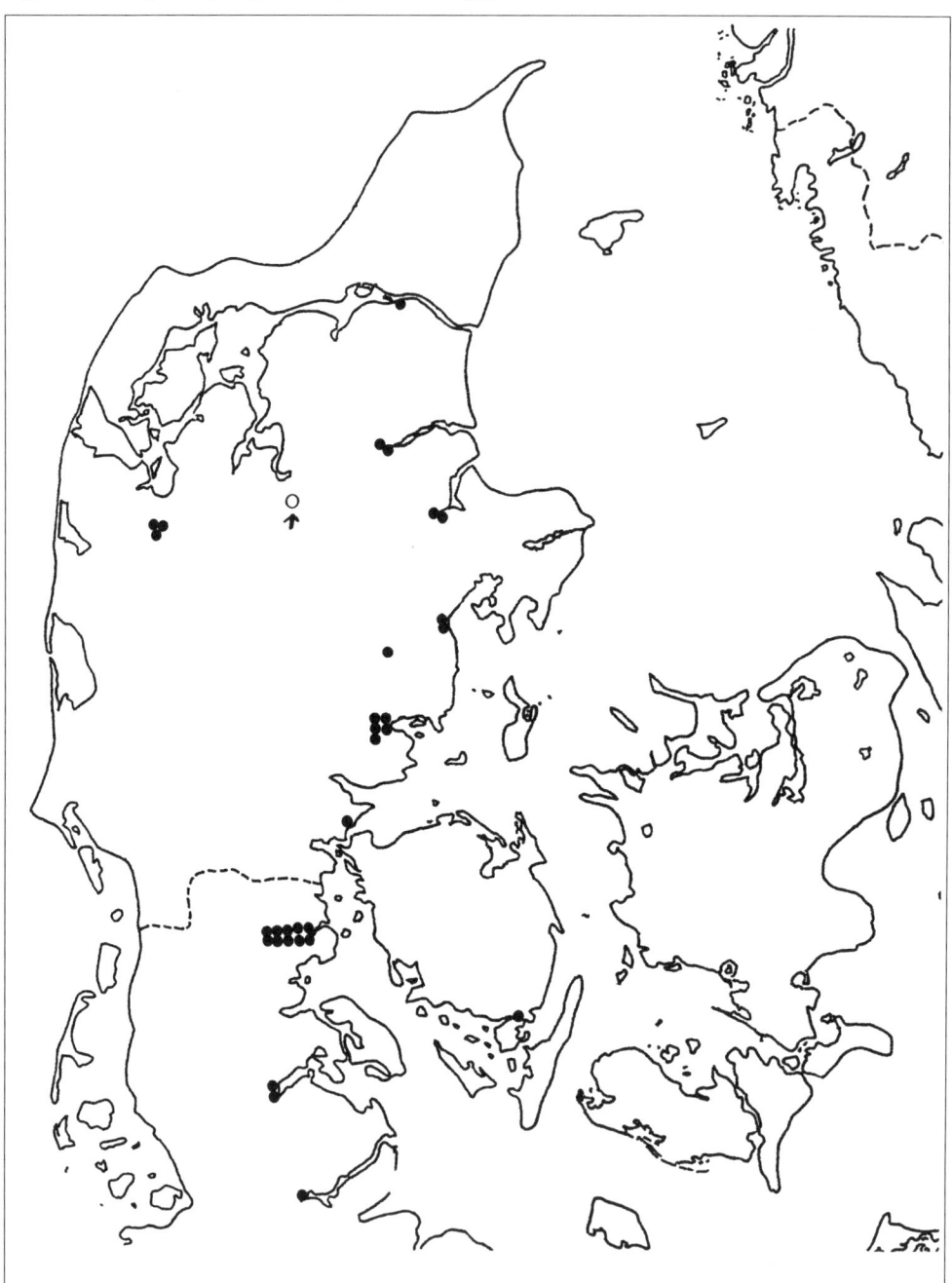

Note: Each of the dots marks one stall renting guest. The situation of Viborg is marked by an arrow.

Fairs as periodical regional centres in Denmark, 1600-1900

Fig. 9.7: Hjørring's First fair 1780: Stall renting guests

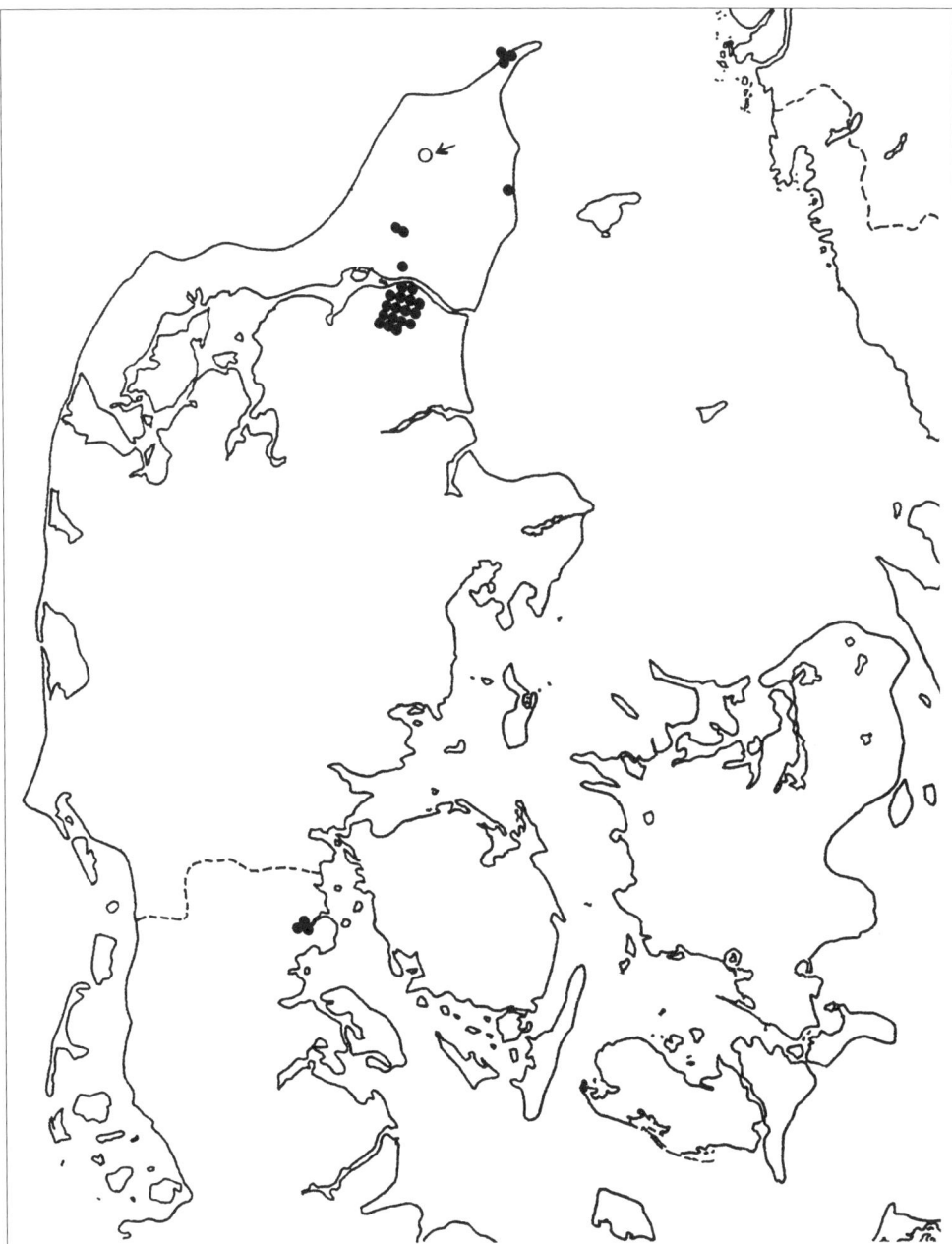

Note: Each of the dots marks one stall renting guest. The situation of Hjørring is marked by an arrow.

accounts list many more visitors to the fairs than the stall-rent accounts, which of course only list the people who rented stalls and paid for this. In the accounts from the »Revier« duty 1640, 270 and 98 duty-paying visitors respectively to the fairs are listed. The stall-rent accounts had entries corresponding only to 12 and 9 stall-rent payers respectively.[26] In addition to this, the customs duty accounts and the bridge toll accounts record goods transported for sale or for export. Of a different type again are the passport ledgers. If a certain fair is to be examined the information has often to be found in a number of archives from Town Halls and jurisdictions in the catchment area of the fair. Yet for some periods there are lists concerning the single fairs in the archives from the Exchequer and the Department of Trade.[27] In return they can give information about the travellers to the fairs as well as the articles they brought and so throw light on important elements in the history of a region.

Notes

1. The text traces some of the principal lines from an ongoing research into fairs and their economic importance in Denmark. Cf. too Ole Degn: Marked, *Dansk kulturhistorisk opslagsværk*, eds. Erik Alstrup and Poul Olsen, Århus 1991, pp. 611-13.
2. See Jørgen Mikkelsen: By – land – øvrighed. Studier i sjællandske købstæders økonomi og administration ca. 1740-1807 med særligt henblik på Korsør, Skælskør og Slagelse, 1995, pp. 11-85, Byen, oplandet og regionen – en forskningsoversigt (unpublished ph.d. thesis, Copenhagen University).
3. Ole Degn: *Rig og fattig i Ribe. Økonomiske og sociale forhold i Ribesamfundet 1560-1660*, 1-2, 1981. Börje Hanssen: *Österlen. Allmoge, köpstadfolk och kultursammanhang vid slutet av 1700-talet i sydöstra Skåne*, 1952, repr. 1977. Bjørn Poulsen: *Land – by – marked. To økonomiske landskaber i 1400-tallets Slesvig*, Flensborg 1988. Jørgen Mikkelsen (see note 2).
4. Walter Christaller: *Die zentralen Orte in Süddeutschland. Eine ökonomisch-geographische Untersuchung über die gesetzmässigkeit der Verbreitung und Entwicklung der Siedlungen mit städtischen Funktionen*, Jena 1933, cf. Ole Degn: *Urbanisering og industrialisering. En forskningsoversigt*, 1978, p. 98. Ole Degn: Small towns in Denmark in the sixteenth and seventeenth centuries, *Gründung und Bedeutung kleinerer Städte im nördlichen Europa der frühen Neuzeit*, eds. Antoni Maczak and Christopher Smout, Wiesbaden 1991, p. 151-69. The central place point of view is also used by Bjørn Poulsen: Løvinden og lokalcentrene. Den senmiddelalderlige sønderjyske bondes omverden, *Sønderjyske Årbøger*, 1989, pp. 102-11.
5. H.V. Gregersen: *Messe og marked. Det landskendte Kliplev marked*, 1955.
6. *Kortfattet repertorium over samtlige rescripter, resolutioner og collegialbreve i den Fogtmanske rescriptsamling*, ved C. Algreen-Ussing, 1-3, 1839: Markeder og torvedage, s. 594-606. The lawyer Laurids Fogtman (1748-1821) edited in 1806 part 1 of the principal work *Kongelige rescripter, resolutioner og collegialbreve for Danmark og Norge*, 1660 ff., and edited himself part 2-7, the last volume in 1812, whereupon it was continued by the above mentioned Algreen-Ussing.
7. Excise duty accounts: Kalundborg 1699-1746, Skælskør 1744-59, Fåborg 1713-91, Odense 1700, 1756-59, Århus 1694, 1696 and Ribe 1696-1700.
8. J.H. Schou: *Chronologisk fortegnelse over de kongelige forordninger og aabne Breve* 1670 ff., 1775.
9. Degn 1981 (see note 3), 1, pp. 146-47. Accounts of the same kind are known from other towns, see Ole Degn: Danske købmandsregnskaber fra tiden før 1700, *Erhvervshistorisk Årbog 1979*, 1980, pp. 7-40.
10. C. Klitgaard: *Hjørring bys historie indtil det 19. aarh. midte*, 1925, p. 158.
11. It is naturally difficult to discover to what ex-

tent the growth of the number of fairs in Jutland is caused by the fact that former illegal fairs were made legal.
12 Arguments for the increase in the number of cattle fairs without small articles fairs are not seen; the small articles fairs were not abolished until 1873, effective from 1882.
13 However, in 1620 for a few of the towns, September 29th, in 1656 in the same way, October 2nd.
14 Ole Degn: Borgernes by 1550-1720, Århus. Byens historie, 1, -1720, ed. Ib Gejl, 1996, pp. 304-06.
15 Bjørn Poulsen 1989 (see note 4), pp. 99-101.
16 Cf. law of May 23th 1873, the Trade Act (næringsloven) April 28th 1931 and Act of May 7th 1948 about fairs with horses and cattle.
17 On servants' fairs, see Kirsten Linde: »Afgået til Ribe marked for at søge tjeneste«, Hardsyssels Årbog 1996, pp. 61-76. Cf. Peter Henningsen's article in this volume.
18 »Revier« duty accounts 1640, the days June 20th-25th, Ribe Town archives, D 22-83, »Revier« duty accounts 1639-71, Landsarkivet for Nørrejylland (The Provincial Archive in Viborg).
19 »Revier« duty accounts 1640, the days September 5th-10th, cf. note 18.
20 Excise duty accounts 1696, the days July 25th-29th, D 2-87, Århus Town Hall archives, Landsarkivet for Nørrejylland.
21 Ole Degn 1996 (see note 14), p. 305.
22 Svend Aakjær (ed.): Viborg købstads historie, vol. 1, 1940, pp. 331, and vol. 2, 1940, pp. 543-54. On the Snapsting market, see too Hugo Matthiessen: Snapstinget, 1946.
23 The city treasurers' accounts 1774, supplement to the stall-rent accounts, D 33-648, Viborg Town Hall archives, revised accounts 1772-74, Landsarkivet for Nørrejylland.
24 The city treasurers' accounts, supplemented with the stall-rent accounts, D 10-225, Hjørring Town Hall accounts, the city treasurers' accounts 1772-80, Landsarkivet for Nørrejylland.
25 The city treasurers accounts 1780, supplemented with stall-rent accounts, see note 24.
26 The city treasurers' accounts, kept by Iver Nissen and Jens Jespersen respectively, 4.75 og 3.35 sletdaler respectively, as the rent of a stall at the square paid by a butterseller was 1.5 mk., D 22-335, Ribe rådstuearkiv, Landsarkivet for Nørrejylland.
27 See Jørgen Mikkelsen: Sjællandske markeder 1775-1800, Historie, 1994, p. 1-39. The Exchequer (Rentekammeret), the audit departments 1773-1840, 2435.25-26, lists of fairs 1776-99, Rigsarkivet (The National Archives).

CHAPTER 10
Merchant trade and fairs in Zealand, c. 1750-1810
A study in market economy

By Jørgen Mikkelsen

In his famous work about the world economy between 1400 and 1800, Fernand Braudel gives the following description of the Mediterranean economy: »The economy, all-invading, mingling together currencies and commodities, tended to promote unity of a kind in a world where everything else seemed to be conspiring to create clearly-distinguished blocs«.[1] The same can be said about Scandinavia in the early modern period. The nature of the economy with its tendency to cross frontiers causes problems in studying regional history. Often a diffuse demarcation of the region in question is all that can be achieved, and in many cases it is appropriate to divide the area into different zones, which are described and analyzed more or less intensively. Thus, one of the Nordic classics in this genre – *Österlen*, written by Börje Hanssen – takes its start in the town of Simrishamn and its immediate surroundings, but gradually all Scania – and to some degree all Sweden – is included in the description.[2]

This article, too, moves between several regional levels. After an introduction to some main features in Danish market town economy between 1500 and 1800, follows an account of merchant trade in the south-western part of Zealand in the second half of the eighteenth century and at the beginning of the nineteenth century. Here, I will present results from my investigation of whether each of the towns had well-defined trading hinterlands and whether the inhabitants in the rural parishes used merchants in more than one of the towns. In addition, I have examined the economic relations between the merchants and the wholesalers. The second part of the article is about the trade at the Zealand fairs. This description will primarily focus on the articles and the dealers. But I will also give an account of the opinions of the town authorities about the market trade and especially the question of starting up of new fairs. Finally there are some thoughts about the economic system on Zealand, compared with other parts of Denmark.

Danish market town economy in the early modern period

Unlike the other Nordic countries, a great number of towns were established in Denmark already in the Middle Ages. C. 60 of these were assigned market town privileges, which implied own jurisdiction, self-government (to some extent), and the right to engage in

Fig. 10.1: The Danish towns 1672 (for the regions east of Øresund: 1655)

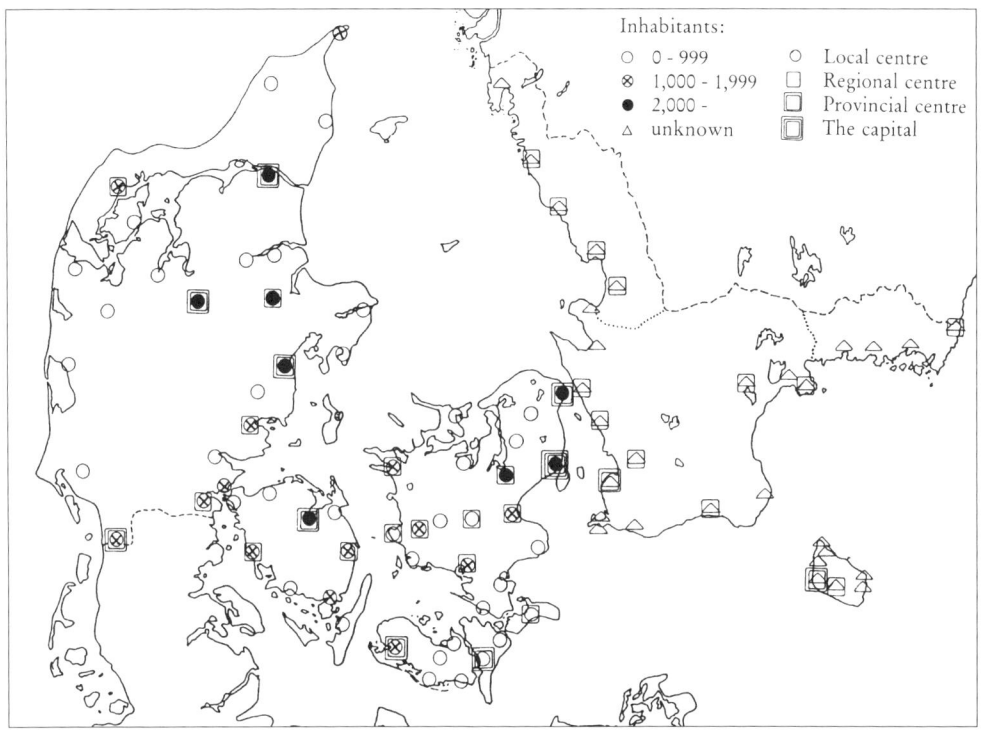

Source: Ole Degn: Small towns in Denmark .... (see note 4), p. 168.

trade, handicraft, shipping etc. The extensive town formation in this period meant that it was necessary to establish only a few new market towns between 1550 and 1850.

From a European point of view, the Danish towns were remarkably small.[3] At the census in 1801 – which is generally considered very reliable – about half the market towns had a population of less than 1,000, and indeed five towns had only 250-375 inhabitants. The three largest provincial towns, Odense, Aalborg and Elsinore (Helsingør), all had between 5,000 and 6,000 inhabitants. In comparison, 100,975 people lived in the capital, Copenhagen (København). This was more than the total population of all the market towns in the provinces.

Ole Degn has grouped the Danish towns on four levels: the capital, provincial centres, regional centres and local centres.[4] This categorization was made on the basis of population figures and different economic and administrative criteria such as customs receipts, average amount of property per taxpayer and the existence of county administration. According to Degn, the provincial and regional centres had more differentiated trade and could offer a wider assortment of articles and more credit possibilities than the local centres, so they attracted many customers from the hinterland of the small towns. Furthermore, the bigger towns had more social differentiation than the smaller ones. Ole Degn's stratification applies to the middle of the seventeenth century, but a similar picture would probably emerge if the model were used on the period around 1800.[5] Unlike many other countries, there were few changes in the Danish town hierarchy during the early modern period.[6]

Until the law about freedom of trade (1857), Danish legislation made a sharp distinction between town and rural occupations, but practice was otherwise. For instance there were – at least at the beginning of the nineteenth century – many more craftsmen in the rural areas than in the towns.[7] On the other hand, agriculture played an important role in many towns. A calculation about grain cultivation and consumption in the 18 market towns on the island of Zealand in 1771 shows that 8 of them could provide at least a third of their own requirements, and one town even had over-production. Conversely, 4 towns had a grain production of less than 5% of their needs.[8] The ownership of the land varied from town to town, but usually most of the agricultural land was divided between a large number of citizens, each having ownership of his part.

Trade in the market towns was not very specialized. Many craftsmen had more than one trade, and most of the merchants sold a wide assortment of articles: from iron and limestone to spices, textiles and sewing-needles. Many merchants also brewed beer and distilled spirits and served drinks to their customers. In 1775 the authorities in the market towns on Zealand were asked about a possible specialization of trading. A few mayors and town bailiffs were in sympathy with the proposal; they thought it would result in more skilled merchants. But most of the local authorities rejected the idea. The general opinion was that no merchant could get along by concentrating on certain products such as clothes or ironmongery. Sales were simply too small.[9]

The development of the Danish towns between 1500 and 1800 is roughly in accordance with Jan de Vries's description of Europe as a whole.[10] The sixteenth century and the first decades of the seventeenth were characterized by general population growth in the towns. After this there was a period of stagnation until the end of the eighteenth century. Between the censuses in 1672 and 1769, the recorded population of the market towns as a whole increased by just about 10%. In contrast, the population of Copenhagen doubled in the same period. At the end of the eighteenth century the conditions in the small towns improved. In the years from 1787 to 1801 alone, the population in the market towns as a whole increased by 17%.[11]

The demographic development in the towns must be seen in connection with the trend of prices. The towns had to take the surplus production from the countryside and supply it with manufactured goods. Therefore the towns were very dependent on the economic situation in the rural areas. Roughly speaking, more prosperity in the rural areas resulted in more demand for town products and – therefore – more prosperity in towns, too. While there were good trading conditions in the sixteenth and the beginning of the seventeenth century, the end of the seventeenth

Merchant trade and fairs in Zealand, c. 1750-1810

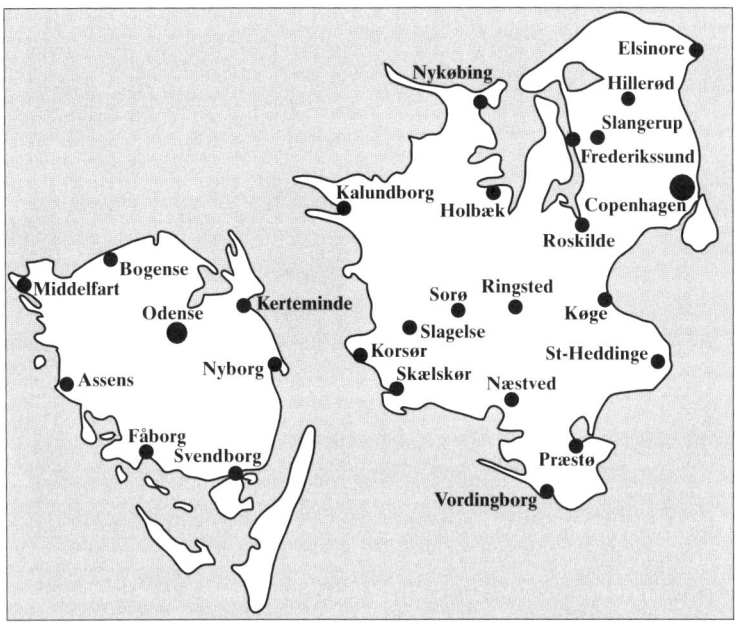

Fig. 10.2: The market towns in Zealand and Funen

century and the first half of the eighteenth was a period of recession with low prices. After 1750, corn prices rose sharply, although there were short setbacks in the 70s and 80s. Concomitantly, Denmark's corn production and export increased very rapidly: the total yield probably doubled between 1770 and 1800 and the export of corn products trebled – or more than that – during the eighteenth century.[12]

Another – often used – explanation of the stagnation of market towns during most of the eighteenth century is that the trade and customs policy greatly favoured business conditions in Copenhagen at the expense of the towns in the provinces. Some historians even talk about the capital's »cuckoo in the nest effect«.[13] There are, though, different opinions about the role of Copenhagen. Anders Monrad Møller has thus pointed out that the growth of the city resulted in a greatly increased demand for grain, meat, firewood etc., and this stimulated shipping in the market towns.[14]

In any case, a very clear example of *von Thünen zones*[15] can be observed on Zealand. In his description of the area surrounding Copenhagen c. 1700-1850, Holger Rasmussen has divided this area into three supply zones. The peasants who lived less than 10 km from Copenhagen brought milk and vegetables to the city and returned with mash, bran and manure. The farmers who lived at a distance of 10-20 km from the capital supplied it with hay, straw and – at the end of the period – potatoes. Farmers who lived beyond the 20 km »zone« mainly brought grain to the city. Rasmussen adds that local specialities could develop in each of the zones. He mentions the oatmeal production in Buddinge, the fishing in Skovshoved, the peat cutting in Sengeløse and Kirke

165

Værløse and the textile bleaching in Sørup; each of these villages is situated 10-20 km from Copenhagen.[16]

In a way, however, all parts of Zealand belonged to the catchment area of Copenhagen. Even peasants in Southern Zealand – more than 100 km from the city – sometimes went to Copenhagen in order to sell grain in the market square. Corn prices in the capital were usually much higher than in the provinces – because of the great demand – and of course the city had a much larger and more varied supply of goods, too. Some of the travelling peasants passed through many towns on their way to Copenhagen and the authorities in these towns often complained about the traffic. But the towns derived a certain advantage from the journeys. For instance the merchants in Køge (in Eastern Zealand) seem to have earned quite a lot by giving travelling peasants board and lodging.[17]

The peasants from South-Western Zealand could also go to Copenhagen for other purposes. The peasants on the estates of Gerdrup and Lyngbygaard (near Skælskør) had to do one Copenhagen trip each year – as a part of their corvée – and presumably similar rules have existed on many other estates. And probate cases from Slagelse and Korsør show that the merchants in the two towns very often used local peasants to freight merchandise from the capital. An example: From January to August 1786, the Slagelse merchant Jens Holm got 30 consignments from the Copenhagen firm Thomsen & Martensen. The trips were made by four peasants from the neighbourhood of Slagelse, and one of these was in Copenhagen nine times. It would be surprising, if the peasants did not use the Copenhagen trips to make private purchases and to sell their own products in the market square.

Moreover, the Zealand peasants had contact with the market of Copenhagen through the travelling hawkers, who were licensed to deal with certain articles. In 1721 the inhabitants in Valby village near Copenhagen were allowed to buy up poultry in all parts of Zealand in order to sell the products in Copenhagen. But according to a report from the merchants in Næstved (1747), the Valby dealers were not content with buying up poultry; they bought hides, old brass, copper, butter etc., too. And in a report from 1775, a merchant in Slangerup declared that the Valby dealers bought tobacco, indigo and »all sorts of textiles« from the manufacturers in Copenhagen in order to sell it to the North Zealand peasants.

Merchant trade in South-Western Zealand

At the census in 1801, Slagelse, Korsør and Skælskør had 1732, 1219 and 567 inhabitants, respectively. Korsør and Skælskør are maritime towns and Korsør in particular has had a strong maritime influence because of the ferry connection to Nyborg on the island of Funen. In spite of the difference in size, there was no significant difference in the number of traders in the three towns, but it is striking that all the largest merchants lived in Korsør. On the other hand, there were many more skilled and unskilled trades represented in Slagelse, and haulage business and farming also played important roles here. The *amtmand* (chief administrat-

Merchant trade and fairs in Zealand, c. 1750-1810

Fig. 10.3: South-Western Zealand 1772
Note: A section of a map of South-Western Zealand, made in 1772 by The Royal Danish Academy of Sciences and Letters (Videnskabernes Selskab). (Kort- og Matrikelstyrelsen)

ive official of the county) lived in Slagelse, while the *amtsforvalter* (county administrator), who was in charge of collecting taxes, lived in Korsør. Therefore it seems reasonable to consider Slagelse and Korsør as regional centres and Skælskør as a local centre.

South-Western Zealand is a suitable region to study the limits of trading hinterlands because of the short distance between the towns (15-20 km). To do this, I have investigated the debts of the rural population to the merchants. The sources are the merchants' account books (very few of these are preserved) and probate cases, which often have lists of debtors (these lists were produced by taking excerpts from account books).[18]

The study is by no means unproblematic. The account books do not cover cash payments, but only credit transactions. Moreover it is not certain that all the credit trade is entered, because most of the merchants probably recorded the daily credit in note books, and, at intervals, transferred the contents to the proper account books. But by then it was only relevant to record the debt that had not yet been paid. Likewise, the lists of debtors in the probate cases comprise only the customers who had not paid their debt at the time of the administration of the estate. Finally, it must be remarked that a list of debtors – in contrast to an account book – only tells us about the final result of a trade relation. It cannot be seen whether an entry covers one, two or perhaps more than a hundred purchases.

Despite the reservations, there are good reasons to use both account books and lists of debtors, but it is undeniably an advantage to have lists from many merchants at one's disposal. I have used data from about 30 merchants. Most of the lists contain from 30 to 300 names, but one list includes more than 1,500 customers.

The study shows that each of the three towns had its own hinterland. And there were remarkable differences in each of the towns between the clienteles of the individual merchants. Usually there was a clear connection between the address of the merchant and the geographical distribution of his customers. This can be seen most clearly in Skælskør. Thomas Bruun lived beside the harbour and the road to Stigsnæs (the area south of the town). Marking the addresses of his debtors on a map shows that disproportionately many of the customers lived either on Stigsnæs or on the island of Agersø (close by sea to Skælskør). In contrast, Carsten Meyer, who lived near the eastern gate, had a great many debtors in the villages east and northeast of Skælskør. Correspondingly, Peder Nold, whose premises were situated in the western part of the town, had rather many debtors in Boeslunde parish – between Skælskør and Korsør. These results are in accordance with several other Danish investigations about customer distribution,[19] and it seems to be a general feature that the country peasants mainly used merchants in the part of the town that was closest. The study of merchants in South-Western Zealand also shows, however, that family relations in some cases had an influence on the geographical distribution of the clientele.

However, there was also considerable overlapping between the hinterlands of Korsør, Skælskør and Slagelse. Each of the towns had an inner and an outer trading hinterland, but they could not even keep the close hinterland entirely to themselves. For instance, the estates south of Skælskør commonly let some of their peasants pass through Skælskør to sell grain from manorial dues to merchants in Korsør. Correspondingly, the large Korsør merchants were able to purchase grain from estates east of Slagelse. In the five years when the figures can be compared, about four times more grain was shipped from Korsør port than from Skælskør, and this should be seen in light of the fact that Korsør had a very small »core hinterland«. The merchants in Korsør must have been able to give a better price than their colleagues in Skælskør, and this is undoubtedly connected with lower freight charges, which again must be attributed to the much better harbour facilities in Korsør.[20] The Korsør merchants also seem to have had many more credit customers (i.e. customers who got credit from the merchant) in and around Slagelse, than the Slagelse merchants had in and around Korsør. The merchants in Korsør were probably able to sell goods more cheaply than the Slagelse merchants, because they did not have to include freight charges for road transport in the price.

In addition, an investigation was made of the extent to which the South-West Zealand rural population appear as credit customers with different merchants in the same town and with merchants in different towns. The investigation included 3,236 rural customers, who are named in the account books and debtor lists of 18 merchants. Of these, a total of 484 were found as customers with more than one merchant, and it can be seen that 249 got credit in more than one town (20 of them even got credit in all of the towns).[21] There are a lot of farmers and smallholders among the 484, and a few of these can be seen as credit customers with 5-6 merchants. The numbers are remarkably high when it is considered that we today know about only a very small fraction of the credit business of that time. In some cases, customers can have changed merchants in connection with bankruptcy or death, or because of dissatisfaction, but there are also clear examples that customers used several merchants at the same time. For instance a customer can have used a certain merchant for everyday trade, while he made sporadic purchases in other towns, when he was there to pay tax or other errands.

An examination of each account shows that the intensity of the trade relation between merchant and customer could vary a lot, and that a merchant could be used in various ways by different customers. This can be illustrated by some examples. In the years 1800-1803 the Rev. Chr. Dan in Gierslev village was a very frequent visitor in the shop of Jonas Lund in Slagelse. Among many other articles he bought fish, salt, tar, black silk, crockery, paper, wine and communion wafers. In return the vicar sold a part of his tithe grain to the merchant. This arrangement stopped in 1803. The following year Mr. Dan's credit purchases decreased to a minimum, and in 1806 they came to an end. Of course this does not rule out the possibility that the vicar can have been a »cash customer« in the following years, but it is most likely that he had found another merchant. The smith Andreas Birch in Slagelse, on the other hand, was faithful to Jonas Lund for more than

10 years, and over 25 deals are recorded in several years. But nearly all the purchases were of iron, nails and coal. Doctor Plum, too, was rather one-sided. During the 8 years when he was a credit customer with Jonas Lund, he certainly bought groceries, textiles, crockery and seed, but distilled spirits always played a crucial role in the deals. In the first half of 1801 the situation was quite extreme. In this period the doctor made 33 purchases, and altogether he bought c. 40 litres aquavit – and 6 litres vinegar, 6 kilograms green soap and 66 litres salt ... We must suppose that other needs were covered by other merchants!

While many townsmen had several pages in the account books, most of the peasant accounts are very meagre. Many of these consist of one small entry or a few entries at intervals of several years. The peasants must have largely managed by barter; only when it was not possible to balance the contributions from the merchant with those from the peasant, could the result be credit to the latter.[22] What we find in the account books, then, is the »tip of the iceberg« concerning merchant trade with peasant customers. The question is now: How big was the rest of the iceberg? Even if allowing credit was undoubtedly an important instrument in the competition between merchants, we may suppose that the merchants in general were cautious about doing so. Probably most of the merchants would hardly give credit to a customer unless he knew him fairly well and had confidence in his ability to pay.[23] This is presumably why far more farmers than smallholders are named in many merchants' account books and probate cases. So there is good reason to believe that the individual merchant had a more extensive network of customers – geographically as well as socially – than can be seen in the preserved material. And with that it seems very likely that many more customers than those we know of used more than one merchant.

Even the most copious probate case can only give a fragmentary picture of the merchant's network of contractors. In contrast, Jonas Lund's account books about dealings with wholesalers give a – presumably complete – picture of a medium-sized merchant's circle of suppliers. These two books mention a total of 52 suppliers, but only 12-20 a year. 15 of the contractors were from Copenhagen and 13 from Lübeck. The remainder came from a number of localities in Denmark, Norway, Schleswig-Holstein, Northern Germany and the Baltic area.

Jonas Lund had most commercial relations with the grocer Hans Fleischer Jonasen in Copenhagen. Jonasen was purveyor every year from 1795 to 1809, and some years Lund made more than 40 purchases. Lund bought c. 300 pounds of coffee several times a year. But Jonasen also furnished the Slagelse merchant with spices, groats, rum, communion wafers, medicine, tar, limestone, paper, green soap, thread and many other articles. Most interesting, however, are the many deals with books. Spelling books, textbooks, bibles, catechisms and almanacs can be seen rather often, and now and then there are also some new decrees. Finally there are a few unusual publications such as *The life of Bonaparte* (bought 25th February 1804).

However, some groceries are lacking in the supplies from Jonasen – tea, for instance. These requirements were met by other Copenhagen suppliers. One of them was agent Weissvoigt, who for many years also supplied Jonas Lund with flax, iron, limestone from Gotland, Finnish tar, pit coal and Norwegian salt. On the whole the same assortment is found in the accounts of several other Copenhagen wholesalers: Johan Bergskov, Tyge From, Suhr & Søn and Hans Wassard. From some of these firms Lund also occasionally bought groceries such as rice, raisins and lemons.

While Lund often bought flax, hemp and some other »heavy goods« from several suppliers at the same time, it is possible to point out – more or less – »sole contractors« for many other articles. Thus, a quite considerable part of Lunds supply of ironmongery came from Johan Henrik Putferken in Lübeck. Putferken is the only wholesaler, who is registered in all 21 years, and usually Lund made 3-5 purchases per annum. Nails and knives are found most often in the account books, but Lund bought sheet iron, scythes and scissors, too. Moreover, Putferken furnished him with silk, glasses, mouth organs, violins, salt and hops.

In contrast, Claus Wohlert in Altona supplied Jonas Lund with only one article: seeds. For about ten years Wohlert sold him seeds of clover, carrot, leek, bean, parsley etc.

While Wohlert was the only seller of his kind, Lund had three porcelain dealers. In each of the years 1789-94 he made one or two purchases at Hallesen in Rendsburg (in Holstein). The following five years he bought his porcelain from Joachim Fr. Levenhagen in Lübeck, and from 1800 to 1807 one annual purchase at Vorbes & Cordes in Lübeck is registered. A similar pattern applies to his tobacco trade. From 1790 to 1794 Lund made 3-5 purchases at Jørgen Henningsen in Flensburg. The following 12 years, Hans Chr. Henningsen in Flensburg was supplier, but some years Lund bought small quantities from D.B. Brandt in Lübeck, too. Finally, in 1807 and 1808 all the tobacco was bought from Fedder Feddersen in Flensburg.

Just like the ironmongery, the porcelain and the tobacco, most of the textiles in Jonas Lund's premises came from Schleswig-Holstein and Northern Germany. In 1795 87% of the textiles derived from here, in 1800 93% and in 1805 99%![24] But the Slagelse merchant spread his purchases: in all, he bought textiles from 17 firms, and 12 of these are registered only as textile dealers. In some years Lund got supplies from 8 wholesalers. Yet it seems that Lund used his wholesalers in different ways – in any case to a certain extent. For instance Hans Cort Göttig in Flensburg in some years was the only supplier of lace. However, Göttig also sold stockings, headscarfs and different fabrics – just like several other wholesalers. The most important supplier was Caplen & Ritter in Altona, which furnished Lund with a bigger quantity and broader assortment of textiles than any other dealer. After 1800, however, the trade with the Altona firm declined, and in 1805 it came to an end. After that Jonas Lund got most of his textiles from Nath & Groot in Lübeck.

Importation of the Norwegian products, train oil, herring, fresh and dried cod, salmon and mountain cranberry was characterized by »sole suppliers«. From 1789 to 94 Lund made 1-3 purchases per annum from Johan D. Schlømer. During the following 12 years, Peter Stamer was supplier, and in 1806 J. Rubach took over. All of these wholesalers lived in Bergen. Now and then some of the Copenhagen merchants supplied Lund with a little fish and train oil, too.

In the period 1800-08, Jonas Lund each year bought large quantities of bar iron and stoves at Næs ironworks near Arendal in Norway. In addition, he occasionally bought iron from wholesalers in Copenhagen and Lübeck.

There is an obvious parallel between Lund's contacts to the wholesalers and the relations between the South-Western Zealand merchants and their customers in the eighteenth century. Just as Lund spread his purchases over a number of suppliers (many of whom could have supplied him with more types of articles than they did), it can be shown that many customers – in the towns as well as the countryside – made use of more than one merchant at the same time. And just as Lund changed a number of his suppliers during the 21 years, his account book with customers shows many examples of intense trade relations which – suddenly or gradually – decreased or came to an end. This seems to show that the Zealand economy in the eighteenth century was more market-economy orientated than usually assumed: you made your purchases, where it was most worthwhile, quite simply!

The market trade

While the merchants' premises were local centres for exchange, the special market days were regional trade meetings. Most of the Danish market towns had at least one fair a year, and several of them had three or more. Normally a fair took one or two days, but the famous *Snapsting* in Viborg lasted at least 14 days. This market, however, was not only for the trading of goods, but also an arena for settling mortgage payments for all parts of Jutland. The smaller markets, too, had important additional functions. Many of the fairs were meeting places for relatives, who lived at a distance from each other. Likewise some markets were used by merchants and grain producers to make arrangements about grain supplies. And servants often used the fairs to find new jobs. Finally the attraction of the fun of the fair should not be ignored. The social functions undoubtedly kept alive more fairs than were necessary from an economic point of view.[25]

In 1775 it was prescribed that all tradesmen and craftsmen who wanted to go to another town to sell goods at a fair had to obtain a special passport. This paper had information about the name of the person, the nature and quantity of the articles, and the destination. When the seller came to the fair, he had to hand over the passport to the police. At the end of the year the authorities in each town were obliged to send lists to the central administration about the citizens who had got passports to fairs in other towns, and about sellers from outside who had visited the markets in the town. Only a small part of the lists is preserved, but it is enough to give a good impression of the trade at fairs at the end of the eighteenth century.

Some scholars have tried to make a connection between the number of trips

Merchant trade and fairs in Zealand, c. 1750-1810

Table 10.1: Visiting sellers at the fairs in each town 1785-91

Town	Number of fairs	Number of visiting sellers with passports	Number of towns	The towns from which there were most sellers	The trades with most visiting sellers
Frederikssund (1788)	3	172	9	Hillerød 43 Køge 41 Copenhagen 28 Holbæk 27 Roskilde 26	Shoemakers 58 Small traders 21 Hatters 18 Bakers 13 Saddlers 11
Elsinore (1785)	2	61	6	Copenhagen 43 Hillerød 13	Small traders 18 Shoemakers 15
Hillerød (1787)	3	234	14	Copenhagen 103 Roskilde 30 Elsinore 24 Køge 23 Holbæk 20	Small traders 69 Shoemakers 49 Ropemakers 21 Bakers 13 Skin dressers (tanners) 12
Holbæk (1787)	3	180	12	Køge 32 Ringsted 31 Kalundborg 24 Copenhagen 22 Roskilde 17	Shoemakers 68 Small traders 61 Goldsmiths 9
Kalundborg (1787)	2	127	16	Odense 29 Holbæk 19 Kerteminde 18 Korsør 12	Shoemakers 45 Small traders 26 Coopers 9
Korsør (1787)	1	40	8	Slagelse 11 Skælskør 7 Odense 6	Shoemakers 18 Small traders 3
Køge (1787)	2	194	16	Copenhagen 65 Næstved 32 Roskilde 23 Ringsted 19 Præstø 12	Small traders 49 Shoemakers 44 Skin dressers 17 Glovers 10
Nykøbing S. (1787)	2	78	9	Holbæk 48 Kalundborg 8 Roskilde 5	Shoemakers 24 Small traders 13 Skin dressers 12
Næstved (1787)	2	152	18	Ringsted 26 Køge 18 Copenhagen 16 Vordingborg 12 Præstø 12 Odense 12	Shoemakers 62 Small traders 26 Hatters 10
Præstø (1787)	3	165	14	Næstved 59 Køge 46 Vordingborg 36	Shoemakers 51 Small traders 34 Hatters 11
Ringsted (1788)	3	263	15	Køge 86 Næstved 56 Copenhagen 30 Holbæk 27 Slagelse 16	Shoemakers 74 Small traders 61 Skin dressers 24 Hatters 12 Bakers 12
Roskilde (1789)	3	317	14	Køge 89 Copenhagen 82 Holbæk 44 Ringsted 36 Næstved 16	Shoemakers 128 Small traders 67 Skin dressers 24 Hatters 16 Bakers 14
Skælskør (1788)	2	110	12	Næstved 26 Slagelse 25 Korsør 23	Shoemakers 31 Small traders 23 Skin dressers 9

Regional integration

				Næstved 43	
				Odense 32	Shoemakers 106
				Copenhagen 31	Small traders 63
				Korsør 30	Ropemakers 24
Slagelse				Kalundborg 27	Hatters 24
(1787)	2	322	19	Holbæk 27	Glovers 17
				Hillerød 43	
				Køge 19	Shoemakers 38
Slangerup				Copenhagen 14	Small traders 16
(1791)	4	102	8	Roskilde 14	Bakers 10
				Ringsted 26	
				Næstved 25	Small traders 47
				Copenhagen 21	Shoemakers 25
Sorø				Køge 20	Ropemakers 16
(1787)	2	158	14	Holbæk 18	Bakers 13
Store Heddinge				Køge 62	Shoemakers 36
(1788)	2	88	7	Copenhagen 10	Small traders 21
				Næstved 32	Small traders 28
Vordingborg				Præstø 19	Shoemakers 23
(1787)	2	88	13	Køge 8	Skin dressers 7

An example to guide the reader: Frederikssund had three fairs each year. The market list from 1788 is preserved. It shows that Frederikssund that year had 172 visiting sellers from 9 towns. 43 of these sellers lived in Hillerød, while 41 were from Køge, 28 from Copenhagen etc. 58 of the 172 visiting sellers in 1788 were shoemakers, while 21 were small traders, 18 hatters etc.
Sources: Rigsarkivet (The Danish National Archives), Rentekammeret 2435.25-26; Landsarkivet for Sjælland m.m. (The Provincial Archive of Zealand etc), Sjællands Stiftamt, Købstædernes markeder 1778-90, and: Skælskør byfoged, Markedspasprotokol 1775-1804.

to fairs and trading conditions. Thus, it has been maintained that market trade increased after 1790, when the peasants were better off and therefore able to buy more luxury articles than before.[26] However, caution must be exercised in drawing such conclusions. On going through the market lists, it is evident that the number of visiting market sellers (who were provided with passports) could vary a great deal from year to year. For instance there were 240 visiting sellers at the markets in Køge in 1784, but only 179 the next year. Presumably the weather conditions had some influence on the fluctuating number. Another factor is that it was rather common that a group of people from the same town went on market trips together. Some years, therefore, a town could be visited by many sellers from other towns, with which there was normally little contact.

If there is a positive correlation between the number of market trips and the total sales – and presumably this is the case – the Zealand provincial towns as a whole had a great trade balance deficit in the trade at fairs. Though a few towns had far more outgoing than incoming travellers. First and foremost the total deficit was due to the presence of sellers from Copenhagen and the island of Funen. Sellers from Copenhagen were found in nearly all of the Zealand towns, and they appeared in great numbers especially in Hillerød, Roskilde and Køge. But also rather distant towns such as Slagelse, Ringsted, Holbæk and Sorø had 20-30 Copenhagen sellers annually – at least in the late 1780s.

The sellers from Funen – of whom the great majority were shoe makers from Odense (the second largest town in Denmark) – preferred to go to Kalundborg and Slagelse, but some of them went all the way to Roskilde, Køge and Præstø.[27] On the other hand, practically no Zealanders went on a market trip to Funen. On the whole, Zealand sellers very infrequently went on market trade journeys outside their island – apart from the citizens in a few South Zealand towns, who were rather frequent visitors to the fair in Nykøbing and Stubbekøbing (on the island of Falster).

Table 10.1 shows that Roskilde, Ringsted and Slagelse were the Zealand towns that attracted most market sellers. In these towns more than 100 non-local sellers were present at nearly all fairs around 1790, and sometimes the number was more than 150. The three towns received each year sellers from at least 2/3 of the Zealand towns, but the same was true of many other larger and/or centrally situated towns.

At the other end of the scale we find Slangerup, which – in spite of 4 small wares markets – was only able to attract c. 80 out-of-town sellers a year. No doubt the low number ought to be seen in light of the fact that this part of Northern Zealand was very well-provided for fairs in the end of the eighteenth century. Thus, the neighbouring town, Frederikssund, had three fairs. Moreover the demand at each fair was presumably rather small because of the short distance to the capital with its abundant supplies. In this connection it is interesting to see that Slangerup was only able to attract sellers from a few and adjacent towns; in 1791, for instance, 42% of the sellers came from Hillerød.

A much more one-sided picture can be seen in Nykøbing Sjælland (Nykøbing S.), where 62% of the visiting sellers in 1787 came from Holbæk, and in Store Heddinge, where 70% were from Køge – in both cases the nearest (medium-sized) town. On the other hand Nykøbing and Store Heddinge had extremely low outward journey activity. For many years there were only two citizens in Store Heddinge who travelled to other towns, and usually they did not go any further than Køge and Roskilde.

Nykøbing and Store Heddinge were small towns with very modest commercial life. However, two of the larger or medium-sized towns – Elsinore and Korsør – had very little market trade with the other towns, too. Elsinore was visited almost only by citizens from Copenhagen and Hillerød, and Hillerød was also the absolutely dominating destination for the surprisingly few Elsinore citizens who went on a market trip. The citizens in Korsør had a rather »normal« journey activity, although the geographical radius was more limited than most of the other towns. Thus, 80% of the trips in 1788 were directed towards either Slagelse or Skælskør. However, it is astonishing that so few non-resident sellers appeared at the fair in Korsør. Most of the years, the number was c. 35-45, and even closely situated towns such as Kalundborg, Holbæk and Korsør were poorly represented.

It is natural to connect the small number of market visitors in Elsinore and Korsør with the fact that both of the towns had considerable shipping. Perhaps some sellers refrained from going to Elsinore and Korsør expecting that these towns were already so well-supplied that it would be difficult to sell their products. Many other circum-

Table 10.2: The market trips made by the Køge shoemaker Mathias Ritzau in 1788

Town	Date	Pairs of shoes	Pairs of boots
Store Heddinge	February 12th	50	10
Slangerup	March 18th	50	10
Hillerød	March 27th	50	6
Frederikssund	April 1st	50	10
Roskilde	April 22nd	150	10
Slangerup	April 29th	50	10
Slangerup	June 12th	50	10
Ringsted	June 19th	100	10
Præstø	June 24th	60	0
Hillerød	June 26th	60	0
Holbæk	July 1st	60	4
Sorø	July 15th	50	6
Roskilde	August 16th	100	30
Ringsted	September 23rd	50	30
Store Heddinge	September 30th	34	20
Holbæk	October 3rd	50	20
Præstø	October 13th	60	10
Roskilde	October 21st	30	30
Holbæk	November 11th	20	20
Ringsted	November 18th	20	20
Frederikssund	November 28th	30	30
Præstø	December 16th	30	30

Note: It can be seen that Ritzau brought many more shoes than boots to the spring and summer fairs, while he brought equal numbers of shoes and boots in the late autumn. Many other shoemakers acted in the same way, which undoubtedly reflects the seasonal variations in the purchasing patterns.
Source: Rigsarkivet (The Danish National Archives), Rentekammeret 2435.25.

stances, however, come into play. Thus, both of these towns – especially Elsinore – have a rather remote position seen from the point of view of most of the Zealand towns. A more indefinable – but presumably quite important – factor is tradition. If a fair had a reputation as a fine trading place and an important meeting place, this no doubt could be self-reinforcing.[28] In contrast, fairs with a bad reputation would have difficulty breaking the negative spiral. Then some fairs can have had small numbers of visitors, even if there was no obvious economic reason. Accordingly caution must be exercised in using market lists as indicators of town hierarchies – even if the relations between Holbæk and Nykøbing Sjælland and between Korsør and Store Heddinge tempt one to do so.

Fairs and distribution of goods

An examination of the market lists from the period 1775-1800 shows that the small pedlars were a very characteristic element in market life. Most of them had a varied assortment, but especially scarfs, caps, ribbons and buttons were offered in considerable quantity. Though a few sellers were very specialized. A hatter's widow from Næstved kept to selling doll's clothes, and at several fairs we find a picture seller from Roskilde and a barometer seller from Copenhagen. Only a few merchants sold articles at fairs in other towns, and these people brought just a few articles with them, typically flax and hops. The merchants in Korsør, however, frequently brought wooden articles, and the merchants in Næstved, Vordingborg and Præstø some years sold cloth at the fairs in the neighbouring towns.

More than 30 crafts are registered in the Zealand market lists from 1775-1800. In proportion to the total number of active craftsmen, hatters, glovemakers, bookbinders and goldsmiths were the most frequent sellers at market places, but also potters, ropemakers, saddlers, coppersmiths, spinning-wheel turners and bakers were very active. In absolute numbers, however, shoemakers predominated. Most of the towns had a considerable number of craftsmen in that trade, and in some places »overcrowding« was no doubt an important motive for many market journeys. This applies most strikingly to Køge. This town had 1,366 inhabitants according to the census in 1787; 37 of these were either shoemakers or shoemenders. In 1788 we find 26 shoemakers from Køge at the Zealand markets, and 14 of these made more than 10 journeys (some of them even 20-25).

Table 10.2 shows the market trips of one of the most active Køge shoemakers, Mathias Ritzau. As can be seen, the amount of the luggage varied. In particular it is notable that he brought an exceptional amount of footwear to the Easter and autumn fairs in Roskilde and to the June fair in Ringsted. Many other Køge shoemakers behaved in the same way. So, the total contribution from Køge to the Easter market in Roskilde was no less than 1,350 pair of shoes and 211 pair of boots. Of course the shoemakers from Roskilde and other towns marketed large amounts of footwear, too. Unfortunately we do not know how much was sold, but we can be sure that there was keen competition among the sellers!

Several scholars have been interested in the fairs as distribution links for the flow of goods. Börje Hanssen has classified the fairs in Scania. His study proves – among other things – that some of the fairs in the towns largely functioned as distributors of town products to the rural population, whereas the rural fairs had a more equal exchange of goods between the towns and the rural districts.[29] By means of the market lists

Regional integration

from Køge, Palle Ove Christiansen has tried to place this town in a trade network between supplier and purchaser towns. However, he treats the material inadequately by using the large number of market travellers from Næstved as an indication that Køge received much of its Lübeck goods via that town. For a close examination shows that only a few of the Næstved travellers to Køge were traders in ironmongery, textiles or fancy goods – the others were craftsmen.[30]

Nevertheless, the market lists give much interesting and droll information about the distribution channels for different goods. For instance it can be seen that traders from Copenhagen brought East Indian products (calico, linen etc.), woollen articles from the Faroe Islands and Iceland and gloves from Randers (one of the biggest towns in Jutland) to many out-of-the-way places in Zealand. Wooden shoes and black pots from Jutland are mentioned often, too. It is not surprising that some haulage contractors from Kalundborg in 1777 carried a great number of pots to Slagelse, Ringsted and Roskilde.[31] More remarkable is it that several Næstved citizens the same year had a rather big supply to Ringsted, and that people from Præstø provided Store Heddinge with these articles. In all these cases, however, it is a question of transport from a maritime town to the inner parts of Zealand.

»to the benefit of trade in the towns«

At the same time as the passports were introduced, the central authorities asked for proposals about »the most useful restriction« of the markets »to the benefit of trade in the towns«.[32]

The answers from the Zealand town authorities are exceptionally copious, and they show that the subject engaged the citizens. One of the most extensive letters was written by the municipal corporation in Køge, which pointed out that the craftsmen at the fairs got the necessary money to pay their taxes.[33] On the whole the fairs brought money into circulation and gave »many people of different business« the opportunity to earn money.[34] Admittedly, it was sometimes maintained that the earnings of a craftsman's journey could not offset the expenses for the rent of the cart. »But apart from the fact that such a complaint is seldom well-founded, it must indeed be ascribed to the injured party himself, because he either brings poor goods to markets or screws the prices up too high, and then he no doubt learns to remedy this another time, or else to stay at home, because it does not deserve belief that someone should perpetually travel to markets with a loss«. The corporation did not accept the argument that market trips delayed the work in the workshops either. For usually a craftsman let some of the servants stay at home, while he went to market.

But the fairs benefited the purchasers, too. They had the opportunity to get articles in one place, which they otherwise would have to find in several places, and at a higher price. The assertion that market goods were usually of low quality was rejected with a stolid argument: »But apart from the fact that it is generally possible to be careful, then so many years' experience must have taught people not to buy at markets if they have always been cheated«.

Finally the municipal corporation in Køge rejected the common moral objections in this way: »the lecher finds opportunity for lechery everywhere« and »an industrious and steady man ... probably does not drink more at market than at any other place«(!)

Some of the other town authorities also noticed the large sales of the craftsmen and the low prices, and the mayor of Næstved remarked that a restriction of the trade at fairs would undoubtedly result in increases in prices. The town bailiff in Vordingborg stated that the peasants for many years had used to buy most of their requirements at fairs, and that the craftsmen strove to finish a large quantity of products before the market days, because it was difficult to sell at other times. Likewise the town bailiff in Præstø remarked that the peasants often postponed their purchases of shoes and hides to the market days. He noted, too, that some peasants from Southern Zealand visited the markets in Ringsted and Roskilde, 40-50 km away. And he made the interesting remark that the touring market sellers often used the autumn markets to get cheap »winter provisions«. The statement illustrates that there were big local price differences.

Finally the business life in some small towns was so limited that it was necessary to hold fairs in order to give the local population access to special crafts. Nykøbing S., for example, had no goldsmith, coppersmith, turner, glovemaker, rope-maker, potter or hatter.

The municipal corporation in Elsinore was the only town authority that took a reserved attitude towards some market travellers from other towns. The corporation posed a question about Copenhagen traders' right to sell in Elsinore. Firstly the capital had no small wares market, where citizens in Elsinore and other provincial towns could sell their products. Secondly Copenhagen was visited by so many people from the rural districts that the traders in the capital had much more opportunity to sell their goods than their colleagues in the smaller towns. The municipal corporation does not mention that Elsinore – in contrast to so many of the other Zealand towns – could manage without supplies from non-resident market traders. Indeed, the Copenhagen sellers were presumably unwelcome rivals to the local tradesmen.

Market establishment and town conflicts

The Zealand town population was more frightened than damaged: the government abandoned the plans to restrict the market trade. On the contrary the number of fairs continued to grow, as it had done ever since c. 1600.[35] It is possible to follow this development very closely, since the establishment of a new fair required royal permission and such a licence demanded much preceding correspondence. When a Zealand town authority filed an application to the king, it was received by *Danske Kancelli* (the chancellery), which asked for a statement from *Sjællands Stiftamtmand* (the chief administrative officer of the diocese of Zealand), who supervised all towns in Zealand. He inquired from the authorities in the neighbouring towns to the petitioner. On the basis of these statements, he submitted his recommendation, and usually the chancellery

Regional integration

and the *Geheimestatsråd* (the kings council) complied with this.

On going through the Zealand market cases in the chancellery archives one gets the clear impression that many town authorities hoped that a new fair would act as a lever for the rest of the economy. Particularly towns in severe crisis had such a need. But the correspondence also shows that many mayors and town bailiffs kept an eye on the rights of the neighbouring towns. And obviously it was a widespread belief that progress in the nearest towns necessarily meant a decline in your own town.

The story about the conflict between Køge and Store Heddinge throws light on this matter. In 1776 the town bailiff in Store Heddinge applied for permission to arrange two small wares markets each year. He declared that the town ought to have the same privileges as other towns, when it paid the same duties. He asserted, too, that Køge had »absorbed all the sap of Stevns herred« and with that deprived the Store Heddinge citizens of their trade with the surrounding area (Store Heddinge is situated in the middle of this area).

The »stiftamtmand« sent the petition to the authorities in Næstved, Præstø and Køge. Only in Køge were there objections. The municipal authorities stated that a condition of arranging fairs was that the town in question had »supplies of real market products at low prices«. This, however, could hardly apply to Store Heddinge, which so greatly lacked merchants and craftsmen. And »because of its situation it cannot get merchandise at the same prices as other towns« (unlike most of the other Zealand towns, Store Heddinge is not situated by the sea). Until now the most important business of the town had been agriculture and distilling »by which it – rather than Køge – has absorbed the sap of Stevns herred in order to transform it into unhealthy liquids«. The municipal corporation in Køge had no doubt about the real purpose of the petition: the Store Heddinge citizens wanted to increase the sale of aquavit! In this connection it was remarked, too, that most of the petitioners were distillers. Finally the corporation noted that the Køge citizens had hardly any agriculture, so they were obliged to have trade and crafts. For that reason they were particularly vulnerable to new fairs in nearby towns like Store Heddinge(!).

After having obtained a new pronouncement from the town bailiff in Store Heddinge (he now declared that he would be satisfied with only one market a year), the »stiftamtmand« delivered his recommendation to the chancellery. He rejected the objections from Køge pointing out that Store Heddinge could never become a threat to Køge. Two months later the »Geheimestatsråd« gave its permission for an annual fair in Store Heddinge.

The next act of the drama took place in 1780. A number of craftsmen from Køge sent in a petition about a third small wares market in the town. Now it was town bailiff Holstein's turn to protest. He claimed that a new fair in Køge would be detrimental to Store Heddinge, and he added that Køge – with its shipping and trade – had many advantages over the small town in Stevns. The »stiftamtmand« once again was convinced by Mr. Holstein, and with that the matter was dropped. For, as usual, the chancellery complied with the recommendations of the »stiftamtmand«.

Now the Store Heddinge citizens had tasted blood. They revived their old wish for another fair. Among other things they asserted that it would »provide the town with more – and more skilful – craftsmen« (!). But in Køge the application aroused protest. Here it was pointed out,
- that Store Heddinge a few years before had got a dye-works that attracted peasants from all Stevns and
- that the distillers in Store Heddinge (because of the large grain production in the town and its situation in the middle af the fertile Stevns) were able to produce aquavit at a lower price than their colleagues in Køge, and that they used this advantage to sell aquavit to inns far outside the district that was the normal hinterland of Store Heddinge.

The »stiftamtmand« was not convinced. After weighing the different arguments he came to the conclusion that »it seems that it can serve to make a balance between the towns, if Store Heddinge is granted the other fair«. The »Geheimestatsråd« did so.

Seventeen years later, the Køge citizens at last succeeded in getting their third fair. As they wanted, it was in May. As the most important grounds, the citizens mentioned that in the spring there could be problems in procuring victuals in sufficient quantities. The mayor supplemented that at this time of year, it was necessary to buy provisions in the country and sometimes even in Copenhagen. Besides, he argued that an extra fair would help the craftsmen (carpenters, wheel-wrights, smiths etc.), for whom it was difficult or impossible to go to fairs in other towns. The new town bailiff in Store Heddinge had no particular remarks to this petition, and there were no objections on higher administrative levels, either.

Conclusion

This article has moved between two regional levels. »The small region« – South-Western Zealand – has proved to be a very suitable research object, when you want to analyze trade networks between merchants, wholesalers and customers. Local communities are too small and narrow to enable satisfactory mapping of such patterns. And on the national level, it would be an impossible task to make the necessary studies of details.

But »the small region« is difficult to delimit. The merchants were dependent on supplies from outside, and the peasants had economic contacts far outside the limits of the region – especially to Copenhagen. On the whole the capital left its mark very clearly on the economic development everywhere on Zealand.

Also when we deal with the trade at fairs, it is appropriate to treat Zealand as an entirety. For a large proportion of the Zealand towns had considerable market contact with most of the other towns on the island, whereas there was little contact with other parts of the country.

The studies of merchants' account books, market lists, reports from town authorities and other correspondence give the impression that the common perception of the Zealand economy in the eighteenth century ought to be revised. As recently as 1993, Peter Dragsbo characterized the economy in Eastern Denmark 1750-1850 as being marked by »a very well-established town-hinterland system«, »a sharp role-division between townspeople, nobility and peasants« and »a certain cultural differentiation between the classes«. In contrast he mentioned West Jutland with »an early market-orientation and an early abolition of the feudal ties«, »loose and shifting connections between town and country, with a lot of trading networks not including towns«, »a loose role-division, with e.g. trading peasants until the late 19. century« and »no sharp cultural differentations«.[36]

I do not contest that there were considerable differences between the economy in East and West Denmark. The mere fact that the closeness of the towns was much greater in Eastern Denmark indicates that the towns played a more important part in the economic cycle here. However, it is unlikely that the Zealand economy has been as closed as commonly assumed.

We have seen that Copenhagen attracted grain-selling peasants from all parts of Zealand, because the prices were much higher in the capital. Likewise the supply of manufactured goods was much greater in Copenhagen. Moreover some peasants were frequently in Copenhagen in their capacity of carriers. Furthermore, the Valby people and other dealers with specific privileges were intermediaries between the peasants and the capital. None of these trade activities involved the Zealand towns.

It has also been shown that there was a considerable overlapping of the hinterlands for the towns of Korsør, Skælskør and Slagelse. Thus, the merchants in Korsør attracted many customers from the »core hinterlands« of Slagelse and Skælskør; presumably the merchants in Korsør could offer a better price because of lower freight charges. It appears, too, that not only officials, but also craftsmen and peasants dealt with more than one merchant; some farmers and smallholders were even credit customers with 5-6 merchants. The peasant debt to the merchant was very small as a rule, so the peasant was by no means dependent on the individual merchant.[37] Moreover an analysis of Jonas Lund's account books show that at least this merchant had a very flexible purchase pattern: he spread his purchases over a great number of wholesalers, and he changed many of his suppliers during the 21 years it is possible to follow his activities.

Finally the market reports from 1775 show that a great deal of the consumption of the town and country population was bought at fairs, where the seller and the buyer usually did not know each other. Apparently commissioned work did not have great importance for the craftsmen. Furthermore, it appears that some peasants went to markets at a distance of 40-50 km from their home and that some market sellers used the autumn tour to buy cheap winter provisions. Finally the analysis of the cases of market establishment shows that petitions about new fairs were often received in a negative way by the authorities in the neighbouring towns, who feared the consequences for their own economic development.

To sum up: Market economy and competition were not – as often maintained – phenomena that appeared in the nineteenth century. On the contrary, they were basic conditions for the economic life in the eighteenth century. Transport costs, however, impeded the exchange of goods to a greater degree than afterwards. Naturally, traditional business connections existed in the eighteenth century, too, but that is also the case today.

Notes

1 Fernand Braudel: *The Perspective of the World (Civilization and Capitalism 15th – 18th Century, vol. III)*, London – Glasgow – Sydney – Auckland 1981-84, p. 22.
2 Börje Hanssen: *Österlen. Allmoge, köpstafolk och kultursammanhang vid slutet av 1700- talet i sydöstra Skåne*, Östervålla 1952 (repr. 1977).
3 On the size of European small towns, see: Peter Clark (ed.): *Small Towns in Early Modern Europe*, Cambridge 1995.
4 Ole Degn: Small towns in Denmark in the sixteenth and seventeenth centuries, *Gründung und Bedeutung kleinerer Städte im nördlichen Europa der frühen Neuzeit (Wolfenbütteler Forschungen, bd. 47)*, eds. Antoni Maczak and Christopher Smout, Wiesbaden 1991, p. 151-170. Degn has based his work on the central place theory, that was introduced by Walter Christaller in: *Die zentralen Orte in Süddeutschland: eine ökonomisch- geografische Untersuchung über die Gesetzmässigkeit der Verbreitung und Entwicklung der Siedlungen mit städtischen Funktionen*, Jena 1933 (repr. 1968).
5 Apart from the fact that the provinces east of Øresund were surrendered to Sweden in 1658.
6 On displacements in the town hierarchy in other Nordic countries, see: Sven Lilja: The Geography of Urbanization – Sweden and Finland, c. 1570-1770, *Scandinavian Economic History Review*, 1994, p. 235-256, Sven Lilja: Linköping i stort och litet perspektiv, *Det store i det små*, eds. Knud Prange et al., Copenhagen 1997, Sven Lilja: *Tjuvehål och stolta städer. Urbaniseringens kronologi och geografi i Sverige (med Finland) ca 1570-tal till 1810-tal*, Stockholm 2000, and Sven-Erik Åström: Anlagda städer och centralortssystemet i Finland 1550-1785, *De anlagte steder på 1600-1700 tallet. Det XVII. nordiske historikermøte Trondheim 1977 (Urbaniseringsprosessen i Norden, bd. 2)*, ed. Grethe Authén Blom, 1977, p. 134-181.
7 Sven Henningsen: *Studier over den økonomiske liberalismes gennembrud i Danmark. Landhaandværket*, 1944, p. 151.
8 Jørgen Mikkelsen: Korn, købmænd og kreditter. Om kornhandel og kornpriser i Sydvestsjælland ca. 1740-1847, *Fortid og Nutid*, vol. 40, 1993, p. 178-213 (especially p. 182f).
9 Jørgen Mikkelsen: »Handlingen i de smaae Kiøbstæder bestaaer i dend bahre Credit«. Økonomiske vilkår for de sjællandske købstæder i 1700-tallet – belyst gennem indberetninger, *Det store i det små* (see note 6), p. 138f.
10 Jan de Vries: *European Urbanization 1500-1800*, London 1984, p. 253ff.
11 Ole Degn: De nylagte byer og byudviklingen i Danmark 1600-1800, *De anlagte steder på 1600-1700 tallet* (see note 6), p. 11.
12 Erik Helmer Pedersen: Dansk landbrugsudvikling i det 18. århundrede. En oversigt, *Bol og by*, vol. 2.5, 1983, p. 53 and 64.
13 Ole Feldbæk: *Danmarks økonomiske historie 1500-1840*, Herning 1993, p. 130.
14 Anders Monrad Møller: *Fra galeoth til galease. Studier i de kongerigske provinsers søfart i det 18. århundrede*, Esbjerg 1981, p. 188.
15 The concept is named after the German economist Johann Heinrich von Thünen. In 1826 he advanced the theory that the distance from the growing district to the market is of vital importance for the use of the soil. Transport costs determine what it is reasonable to cultivate in each place. So if the differences in soil quality are ignored, the city will be surrounded by concentric production zones. Johann Heinrich von Thünen: *Der isolierte Staat in Beziehung auf Landwirtschaft und Nationalökonomie*, 1826. The theory has been tested on several Nordic cities, for instance Stockholm (Harald Gustafsson: Stad-om-land-perspektivet. En socken i Stockholmstrakten under förindustriel tid, (Svensk) *Historisk Tidsskrift*, 1990, p. 50-69) and Bergen (John Ragnar Myking: Byen og omlandet. Vestlandsk hushaldsøkonomi på 1600- og

1700-tallet, *Norsk bondeøkonomi 1650-1850*, eds. Anna Tranberg and Knut Sprauten, Oslo 1996, p. 97ff).

16 Holger Rasmussen: Københavnsbønder, *Historiske meddelelser om København. Årbog 1963*, Copenhagen 1963, p. 80ff.

17 Mikkelsen 1997 (see note 9).

18 Jørgen Mikkelsen: Købmandens kontaktflade – en regionalundersøgelse, *Erhvervshistorisk Årbog 1994*, Århus 1995, p. 106-145.

19 Per Boje: *Danske provinskøbmænds vareomsætning og kapitalforhold 1815-1847*, Århus 1977, p. 151f, Allan Frandsen: Bonden og købmanden, *Fortid og Nutid*, vol. 34, 1987, p. 5ff and Svend Larsen: *Studier over det fynske Rådsaristokrati i det 17de Århundrede*, vol. I, Odense 1965, p. 150.

20 Jørgen Mikkelsen: Søfart og havneadministration i Korsør og Skælskør ca. 1740-1800, *Årbog for Historisk Samfund for Sorø Amt 1995*, p. 7-52.

21 Of course there is an identification problem in studies like this. But the problem should not be exaggerated. Undoubtedly, the great majority of the debtors were heads of households (if not, there are formulations like 'in NN's service'). Even though most peasants had common names, there are rarely two heads of households with the same name in the same village at the same time. And if it did happen, the two persons will usually be called 'the old' and 'the young', respectively (such designations are found in several debtor lists).

22 Likewise the account book of Jonas Lund contains many examples that town dwellers paid their debts in the form of goods or services. In that way Lund got a great deal of shoemaker, turner, tailor, smith, bricklayer, carpenter and ropemaker work.

23 Andreas Jørgensen has published a secret contract from 1736 between all the merchants in Stege (a town on the island of Møn). The contract, which was found in the archive of the town bailiff, obviously aimed at reducing internal competition. Generally the merchants were not allowed to give credit of more than 2 rigsdaler to a person. If a peasant had sufficient security, however, he could receive more credit. And for the very prosperous farmers there was no limit on credit! The agreement also includes rules about maximum prices for grain from the peasants and selling prices for the most common goods that were sold to the rural population. (Borger og bonde på Møn i det 18. århundrede, *Arkiv*, vol. 1, 1966, p. 16-29)

24 The figures were calculated from the values of the textiles.

25 Jørgen Mikkelsen: Sjællandske markeder 1775-1800, *Historie*, vol. 2.19, 1994, p. 1-39 + 366-369.

26 Albert Thomsen: *Holbæk Købstads Historie*, Holbæk 1936-42 (repr. 1981), p. 469. Cf. Svend Larsen: Fynsk markedshandel, *Fynske minder 1960*, p. 70.

27 The craftsmen from Funen had a reputation for selling market articles at an extraordinarily low price. In a report from 1735 the municipal corporation of Slagelse asserted that the sellers from Funen »as good as give away their merchandise«, by which they allegedly not only prejudiced the Zealand craftsmen, but also ruined themselves. Rigsarkivet (Danish National Archives), Kommercekollegiet 1735-71, Dansk – norsk sekretariat, no. 28: Relationer over de danske stifters tilstand ..., 1735-36.

28 As late as about 1870 the fairs in Slagelse had such a reputation that they were able to attract buyers from a distance of 20-30 kilometres. (P. Arnskov: Slagelse Kram-markeder for 50 Aar siden, *Årbog for Historisk Samfund for Sorø Amt* 1917, p. 175)

29 Hanssen (see note 2), p. 209 and 256-258.

30 Palle Ove Christiansen: International Consumption Patterns in Peasant Households. A Danish Eighteenth-century Example, *Clashes of Cultures. Essays in Honour of Niels Steensgaard*, eds. Jens Chr. V. Johansen et. al., 1992, p. 293.

31 For many hundred years, there has been a ferry connection between Kalundborg and Århus (in Eastern Jutland).

32 The motive for this initiative was a wish to diminish the extensive, but illegal, pedlar activity in the country. The passport order had the same purpose. However, nothing indicates that the initiatives achieved the desired result.

33 In contrast to the trade on the merchants' premises, market trade was in cash. Cf. Hanssen (see note 2), p. 176 and 281ff.

34 The municipal corporations probably had the

beer sellers and the people, who let out rooms in mind. Such persons are mentioned explicitly in the report from Stege.
35 Cf. Ole Degns article in this volume.
36 Peter Dragsbo: Modern Times in West Jutland 1800-1920. A Periphery between Centres? *Facing the North Sea. West Jutland and the World. Proceedings of the Ribe conference, April 6 – 8, 1992 (Fiskeri- og Søfartsmuseets studieserie, nr. 2)*, eds. Mette Guldberg et al., 1993, p. 222ff. Dragsbo's article is based on studies by Ellen Damgaard, Esben Graugaard and Bjørn Poulsen. All of these have contributed to the conference report.
37 Danish research work mentions only a few examples of merchants having paid peasants' taxes.

CHAPTER 11
Making a regional system work

The Norway trade of Niels Hasselbalch and the other merchants of Randers, 1761-67

By Søren Bitsch Christensen

The main topic of this article is the actions of a Danish provincial merchant and his city colleagues within a very limited yet well integrated regional and economic system: from Jutland to Norway with grain and merchandise and back again with timber, fish and other necessities. Despite its modest distance, this was the most important trade route for Danish provincial towns until an opening towards the British and German markets was found in the 1790s and then again after the Napoleonic wars.[1]

During the second half of the eighteenth century, Danish international shipping became one of the largest and most important participants in international sea transport. At the end of the century, the Danish merchant fleet was a third of the size of the British fleet, half the size of the French fleet, and almost the same as the entire Dutch fleet.[2] Denmark took no part in international conflicts after 1720 which gave the country's shipping activities immense advantages.

The Danish government used these circumstances to consolidate the position of the capital of Copenhagen as the mercantile centre of the country by extending the city's role as the domicile for the overseas companies and in other ways granting it benefits, making it natural for international shipping to steer towards the port of Copenhagen.

However, it was not impossible for the Danish provincial merchant fleet to expand. From the mid-1740s until 1807 its tonnage doubled. Yet, all in all, the size of the provincial fleet amounted only to 20-25% of the size of the fleet of Copenhagen in the years 1782-1807.[3] During the last decades of the eighteenth century, provincial ships took part in the international freight transport between the Baltic and Western Europe and even to the Mediterranean. The number of services to the various ports was not impressive and Algerian passports were issued only to approximately 16 Danish provincial ships per year in the period 1749-1806.[4] Furthermore, the international mercantile shipping yielded only a poor return to the provincial towns, and it is a moot point whether the small Danish provincial towns actually had any real opportunity to obtain a reasonable return on the investments necessary to import goods directly from abroad.

The lucrative markets for the provincial trade were to be found within the national borders or very close by. For centuries the cattle and grain trades had been the Danish keys to open the door to the European market, even though the market share of the Danish cattle trade decreased considerably in the eighteenth century.[5] Grain had been a part of Danish exports since the late thirteenth century, when Danish merchants could be found in the Baltic and Flemish ports. It can be assumed that from a time around the High Middle Ages, Denmark had an annual export surplus of grain in normal years. However, direct export was broadly replaced by the buying up of grain by foreign agents on Danish ground. This development led to the confrontation between the Hanseatic and Dutch about the dominance of Danish trade; a battle which was won by the Netherlands in the sixteenth century.[6]

In times with great European demand, large amounts of Danish grain could be sold abroad. In the 1640s, 208,000-284,000 barrels of grain were exported every year.[7] However, Danish grain had only a marginal position on the West European market. Thus, the overall recession and the decrease in the grain prices from the mid-seventeenth century undermined the Danish export of grain, and in the places where it had previously been sold it was crowded out by Baltic grain, first and foremost, East Baltic grain. First the Dutch market was lost, then, after 1660, the markets in Saxony and Brandenburg, where Polish grain also became a competitor. Furthermore, it did not help the competitive position of Denmark that the quality of the Danish grain was questioned.[8]

From approximately 1650, Denmark reacted by reorienting her exports and making Norway her most important outlet. This was supported by a tariff and import policy from the latter half of the seventeenth century, which lasted until the so-called grain monopoly of 1735.[9] This monopoly consisted of a prohibition against foreign imports of grain to Denmark and the densely populated southern part of Norway and was in force until 1788. With time, however, numerous dispensations in years of need made inroads into it and it did not work efficiently throughout the whole period. Nevertheless, the monopoly had an impact. It stabilized Danish agricultural production and the economy of the Danish estates following the years of depression in the 1730s.[10] Norwegian iron, firewood and glass were given similar preferential treatment on the Danish market. In accordance with normal mercantilistic practice, the state intended to keep foreign products out.[11] Thus, even though the Danish grain trade was internationally marginal, it was a crucial tool in the internal economic policy of the state. With this grain trade policy, the provincial towns of Denmark and Norway were given the task of indemnifying themselves and the state; no regional trade patterns were to be formed that would burden the state's finances by the import from abroad of necessary building articles by Denmark or grain by Norway. The function of provincial trade was to stretch out a safety net to ensure the population's survival and ability to produce. Even when the provincial traders saw opportunities to take the plunge and engage in the international trade, they often had to draw back; speculation, for example in the international fluctuations of the grain trade market, was not tolerated. The most important objective of the provincial grain trade was to stay provincial.

Therefore, the mercantile cycle of the

Danish grain was simple. Grain was transported over short distances and was not subject to much speculation. The quantities in the grain trade were too small and the number of merchants and middle-men involved was too high for the grain trade to obtain any noteworthy concentration. And lacking concentration was crucial, since concentration – according to Fernand Braudel – was the determining factor in the superiority of overseas trade. Overseas trade is seen as the source of excess gain and trade expansion and as leading to trade capitalism and the international trade bourgeoisie.[12]

Braudel places the grain trade on all three levels of his schematic outline of the stages of capitalism. Being a product of self-sufficiency, grain belonged on the basic level of the multitudinous, autonomic and routine *material life*. Being a product traded in regular and transparent patterns, where seller and buyer were guided through common experience and both knew the course of barter, grain belonged on *the economic level*, typically seen in a market economy. Finally, grain could be exposed to a speculative trade in the shape of a capitalistic overseas trade, often in connection with the ever recurring famines. This is *the capitalistic practice*.[13]

Rarely did the Danish grain trade reach the third level. It was conducted within the second level with a few deliveries among the households on the first level. Nevertheless, it was the development of the grain trade which after about 1830 finally integrated Danish and international economy. With this perspective in mind, this article can be said to describe the situation prior to the decisive meeting between the traditional and the modern grain trade.

The merchant, the familiy and the town

The merchant Niels Severin Hasselbalch went bankrupt in 1800. Consequently, all his account books were confiscated. Fortunately for us, he had used a few pages of an old account book[14] as his ledger shortly before the bankruptcy and this book therefore was included in the confiscation. Had Niels Hasselbalch not provided proof of his days of glory in this way, he would only have left the impression of being a bankrupt. The book tells another story so we can start to look back in time with the knowledge that something interesting will appear.

Niels Hasselbalch was born in 1731 into a family of merchants.[15] After his marriage in 1770 – and long after the beginning of his career as an active merchant – Niels Hasselbalch obtained his trade license and citizenship as a merchant in Randers on 5 February 1772 and was put in charge of the town's postal service. This was a momentous date, because that same day his father renounced his citizenship and ended a business career that had made him one of the town's leading and richest merchants. Another member of the Hasselbalch family, Jacob, called »our dear brother« by Niels Hasselbalch, was a merchant in Randers. In 1767 Jacob was given a citizenship allowing him to »earn a living as a merchant and deal in grain, timber and other Norwegian goods, but only very little groceries«. At that time Jacob had been doing business with Niels Hasselbalch for several years.

The merchant's house was the family's most substantial asset. Niels Hasselbalch could not take over the house until 1769. Before, he had used a smaller merchant's house and a number of small houses and buildings estimated at half the value of his father's complete merchant's house. The family did not own a ship. However, they owned half of a so-called *kåg*, a small barge that could carry 250 barrels of grain.

A barge was necessary in order to conduct large-scale business from Randers. The city of Randers is situated where the river, Gudenåen, flows into the inlet of Randers and the barge service up the river is an old line of trade. Thus, the historical function of the town was to be a transshipping station between the river and the sea. However, reaching the sea through the inlet was not an easy task. Close to Randers the inlet was so muddy that the goods had to be loaded onto smaller boats or barges in the town and transported to the middle of the inlet to the ferry berth at Mellerup. From here the water was deep enough to sail with fully loaded ships.

Thus, geographical conditions made trade conditions difficult for the merchants of Randers. However, these conditions also worked in their favour; the land surrounding the town was good and fertile, and the town was a natural centre for an area with a large concentration of grain-growing estates. The market towns to the west and the north did not pose much competition. To the east, the market town of Grenaa presented more competition. It was well-situated for fishery and traffic from the capital of Copenhagen, but it was still just a small town with no more than 700 inhabitants. The only serious competition was to be found to the south in the larger market town of Aarhus. In 1769 Randers had 2,901 inhabitants while Aarhus had 3,837 inhabitants.

Niels Hasselbalch's ledger

The ledger used by Niels Hasselbalch shortly before his bankruptcy – making it possible for us to salvage his good name and reputation – was like a note book or a book about major transactions in the years from 1761 to 1767.

These transactions were primarily with Norway. »Til forhandling øster på Norge« (sent to be sold in eastern Norway) was the destination of a chain of goods, mainly consisting of grain and other foods, but also considerable quantities of cloth and distilled spirits. The book allows us to follow this chain from purchase to shipping, but seldom to the actual selling, since this task was often handed over to the shipmaster. On the other hand, the book also tells us what the return cargo consisted of. However, not much is found about the actual purchase in Norway.

The fact that the ledger was used only for notes and calculations unfortunately means that the transactions did not have to be presented as clearly as they would have been in an actual account book, serving as documentation for both creditor and debtor. The book was for personal use only and therefore not completely illustrative. Many times not all elements of a transactions were written down, a delivery of grain is, for instance, without indication of date and seller's name. Often conclusions can be arrived at by inference, especially from the surveys of the joint transactions with his brother Jacob.

Other times he shipped out grain and goods for other people with his own shipment. In certain cases it is difficult to separate this grain from the grain which he himself had actually bought

Table 11.1: Niels Hasselbalch's grain sale to Norway 1762-67 (barrels)

	1762	**1763**	**1764**	**1765**	**1766**	**1767**
Barley	144	174.5	354.5	254	433.5	297.5
Rye	43 (590)	135	199	48	0	175
Malt	251.5	416	970	693.5	430	568
Oats	(900)	35	0	210	63	0
Other sorts	0	18	12	3	17	0
Total	438.4 (1928.4)	778.5	1535.5	1208.5	943.5	1040.5
excl. malt	187 (1377)	362.5	565.5	515	513.5	472.5

from other merchants in town. Normally, some information can be found illustrating the right connection; from other notes it can be seen whether Hasselbalch had an outstanding account which could logically have been settled through the sale of goods.

In the following, references to the ledger are made by referring to the dates.[16]

Niels Hasselbalch's exports to Norway

The trade with Norway was the backbone of Hasselbalch's trading. An outline of his export to Norway is given in table 11.1.

From this it is seen that 1762 was apparently the year with the lowest export of grain to Norway. However, this is not true, because this year he also sold 590 barrels of rye to Norway as well as 900 barrels of oats to the royal agent Niels Ryberg who then sold the grain to the Danish army. This special export to Norway is not noted in the ledger and is therefore indicated in parenthesis.

There is no definite trend in the development. There is no expansion but the export fluctuates around 1,200 barrels yearly. The most important goods were, not surprisingly, malt, barley and rye. The export of malt was so substantial that without it the export would have decreased after 1764.

However, grain was not the only commodity exported by Niels Hasselbalch to Norway. In 1762 alone he shipped out distilled spirits, textile articles, linen, meat, butter, sheep's milk cheese, cow's milk cheese, wax and pork. How important were these goods compared to grain? From 1763 enough information about prices can be found to calculate the values. The result is shown in table 11.2.

This table underlines the importance of the grain. It found its way to Norway both as raw material and as distilled spirits. If the liquor trade is included, which Hasselbalch apparently conducted for others, the grain amounted to exactly 2/3 of the value of the total exports in

Table 11.2: Niels Hasselbalch's export to Norway 1763, according to his ledger (rigsdaler)

	His own sale	Co-sale with brother Jacob	Volume (appr.)	Percentage of total value
Grain	6332	0	778 barrels	37.2%
Salt	12	0	1 barrel	0.1%
Distilled spirits - his own sale	3721	0	8206 pot (1 pot = 0.968 litre)	21.9%
Distilled spirits - sale for others	1324	0	3661 pot	7.8%
Textile articles	812	0	-	4.8%
Linen	3632	268	11429 alen (1 alen = 62.8 cm)	23%
Cheese	18	0	112 pounds	0.1%
Pork, beef and mutton	848	0	6896 pounds	5%
Total	16699	268	-	99.9%

1763. It would have been desirable to have been able to make similar calculations for every year but the source material does not permit this. The number of estimated values would be too high. On the other hand, there is sufficient information about the quantity of exports in all the years. These calculations are shown in fig. 11.1.

One sees that the structure of Niels Hasselbalch's liquor trade changed. First, his own sale of distilled spirits practically vanished, second, the distilled spirits which he sold for others increased dramatically. It should be underlined, however, that very little is known about Hasselbalch's involvement in selling of other people's distilled spirits. It is possible, even quite conceivable, that he only transported their distilled spirits and that his own financial gain was a commission of some sort.

Trade in linen and textile articles such as gloves, sweaters, socks, mittens and wristlets is obvious as a characteristic but declining element of Hasselbalch's trade, just as trading in these products, widely produced as articles of domestic industry, was a general part of the provincial trade structure, particularly in Jutland.[17] It appears that Hasselbalch bought fabrics from the domestic industry and sent it to be bleached in a village near Randers.

Meat and butter also played a part in Hasselbalch's business. The purchase of these goods was quite systematic because the Hasselbalch brothers bought them from the surrounding estates, possibly in co-operation with their uncle. These goods were of no great importance in the total trade.

Regional integration

Fig. 11.1: Niels Hasselbalch's export to Norway 1762-67

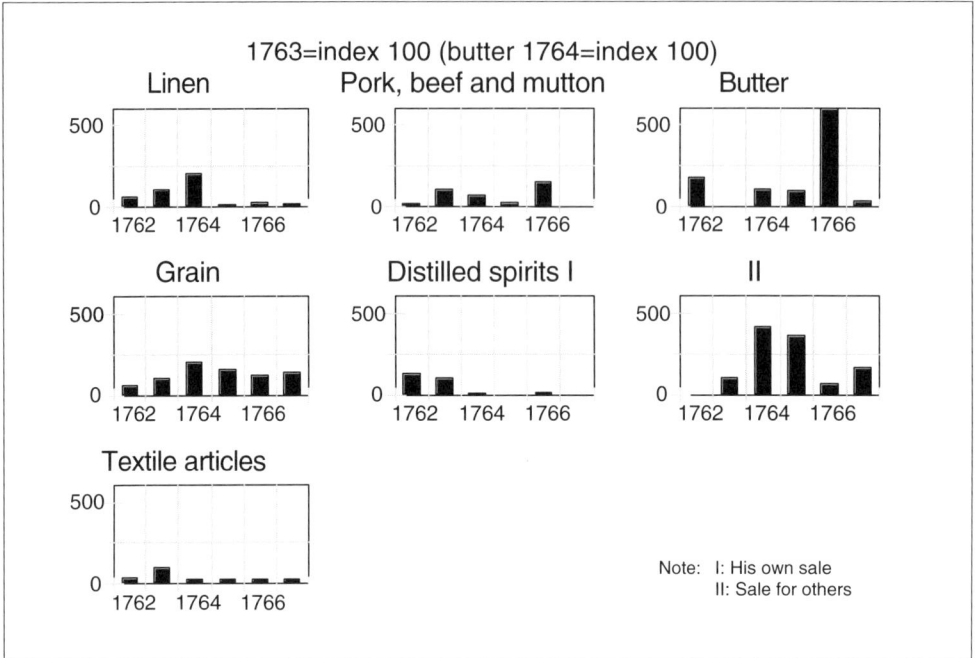

Grain trade and merchants in Randers, 1762

On the basis of this information – from a short period, as one should remember – a characterization of Niels Hasselbalch's business in Norway would be that it concentrated mainly on grain as the most important product, in the beginning of the period both as raw material and as distilled spirits. Later his own sale of distilled spirits ceased almost completely while he maintained a considerable export of other people's distilled spirits; a trade on which he was not likely to have made a large profit. Towards the end of the period a broad spectrum of activities, involving trade in fabrics as well as a small production of linen in a putting out system *in miniature* with sales to Norway was replaced by a more one-sided concentration on sale of grain to the Norwegian market. Niels Hasselbalch had become a grain dealer.

How typical was the business of Niels Hasselbalch compared to that of the other merchants of the town and how was it rooted regionally? Under normal circumstances no Danish source material can shed light on the complete grain trade of a market town, with regard to both purchasing and selling. However, the circumstances in 1762 were not normal.

When Charles Peter Ulrich, Duke of Holstein-Gottorp, had ascended the throne of Russia after the death of Tsaritsa Elizabeth I in 1762, one of the first things he did was to claim the former ducal parts of the Danish Duchy of Schleswig. A war seemed inevitable, and the two armies faced one another at Mecklenburg, but that same summer the war was called off by the deposition of the Tsar.

Prior to this, in the early months of spring, Denmark had mobilized her resources. First, the state had asked the estate owners what they would willingly sell to the royal granaries. As the replies were discouraging, compulsion had to be used. In a letter of 13 March the market town merchants were presented with the question of how much grain they had in stock, and furthermore how much they expected to receive according to contracts. In another letter of that same day the estate owners and clergymen were asked about their stocks of grain and about their estimated sale according to contracts. Furthermore, they had to give information about the persons to whom they had sold grain during the season.[18] A few weeks after the replies to these questions, all granaries on the estates and in the rectories as well as all merchants were subject to a control inspection by the state by the local magistrates. With this information in hand, the state now had a foundation for requisitioning against payment.

In principle, the control measure of the source material together with the replies required from both buyer and seller should have created the perfect representative material. However, no questions were asked about malt and barley as only rye and oats were necessary for the army; and even with this fine-meshed net, some information was lost.

By piecing together the information from the various documents, one finds information about a total of 9,999 barrels of grain in Randers. Not all of these had been bought, many merchants had home-grown grain from the town fields or from other kinds of field rights. No attempt is made to compensate for this fact.

Of those approximately 10,000 barrels of grain, 78% had been delivered to the merchants of Randers before early April. On the other hand, no less than 22% of the grain had not yet been delivered by the estates (the rectories had delivered all their grain) even though it had already been formally sold to the merchants.

A total of 59 businesses were investigated in Randers, and grain was confiscated for war purposes from 21 of them. 16 of the 21 persons on the list can be identified as merchants or rather grain dealers, partly deduced from their everyday trade activity, partly from the fact that they bought at least 100 barrels of grain. The remaining 5 can with some certainty be called »merchants of distilled spirits«. On average the 16 grain dealers had bought 562.9 barrels of rye and oats, the remaining 43 persons investigated had bought 23.4 barrels of rye and oats.

There is little information about where the large group of citizens who were not grain dealers got their grain. They must have got some of it from the town's grain dealers. For instance Niels Hasselbalch declared he had promised away part of 170 barrels of rye not yet received according to a contract. Other grain dealers probably did the same without finding it necessary to report this retail sale. One would imagine that smaller merchants would get grain by buying it directly from the peasants, however, there is very little evidence of this: One bought 36 barrels from peasants, another no more than 20 barrels. That is all. It is doubtful, however, whether buying from peasants was limit-

Regional integration

Fig. 11.2: Where grain was bought 1761/62 by the Randers merchants.

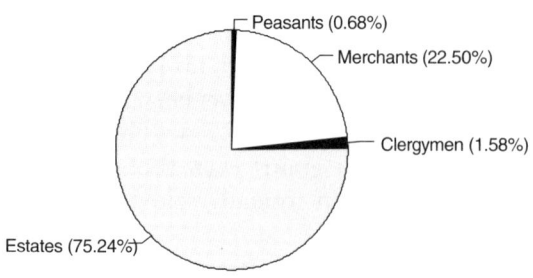

ed to this. The townspeople who did not trade in grain and had no share in the town fields could easily have got grain by buying at least some of it on the town market, to which the peasants must have delivered an unknown yet probably not very large quantity of grain.

The purchases of the grain dealers are much more illustrative. The distribution of the purchases is given in fig. 11.2.[19]

Taking into consideration the control measures in the source material, it is disappointing that we find information about where only the 5,579 barrels, the equivalent of 62% of the purchases of all the grain dealers, were bought.

Thus, identifying all the actual sellers is impossible. Some grain could have been in stock from the previous year or could have been grown by the merchants themselves. Furthermore, the peasants' share of the grain dealers' grain was most likely larger than the 1% indicated.

The catchment area of the Randers merchants' grain trade

The trade with the estates was predominant for the grain dealers proper. Twenty-one estates formed the supply network of the city which the 1762 material shows was the centre of a circle with a radius of about 20 km. The estates have been marked on fig. 11.3 as being either inside or outside the natural catchment area of Randers, defined as the area that is closer to Randers than to any other market town.

To a certain extent, Randers was able to overcome the rival merchants from the smaller market towns of Viborg and Mariager and gain control of the grain surplus of some of the estates within their natural catchment area. The major differentiation factor seems to have been access to navigable waters; Randers had access unlike Viborg and Mariager.[20] However, the merchants of Randers only went halfway to the more important harbour ports of Hobro and Grenaa. On the other hand they did not reach even halfway to Aarhus, while the merchants there apparently came more than halfway to Randers. None of the figures, however, show any major regional disruptions or dominance of one or a few market towns.

All in all this supply network gives evidence of the existence of a *predominantly non-hierarchical town or regional structure*. Within this structure, trade was conducted with the estates and organized according to a system of contracts, ensuring deliveries and possibly also fixed prices, even though there is no evidence of this. Thus 4,198 barrels of grain were sold by the estates to the grain dealers of Randers under condi-

Fig. 11.3: The catchment area of Randers, 1762

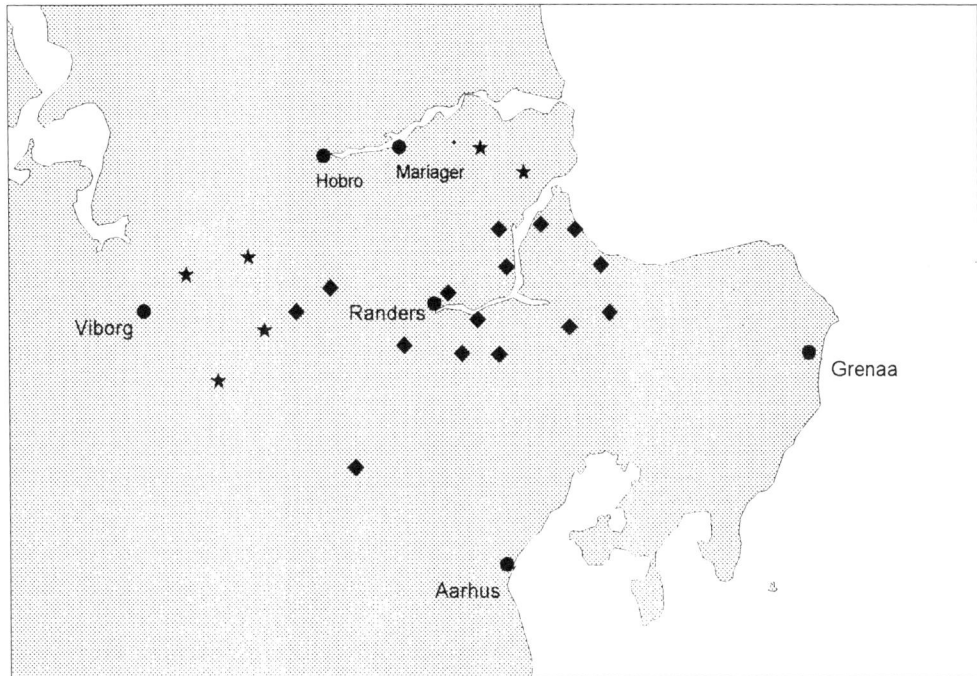

Note: Estates inside the natural hinterland of Randers are marked by sqares. Other estates are marked by stars.

tions which can hardly be characterized as being entirely market economic conditions. The price level played a part although not an essential one. Presumably, the price was elastic in relation to the harvest quantity rather than to its quality. A state influenced by the poor quality of Danish grain.

The question is whether the various merchants competed on prices to obtain contracts with the estates. There is no unambiguous answer to this question, but it is striking that most estates delivered grain to only one merchant. Two estates made deliveries to two merchants. In one of these cases, the two brothers Jens and Niels Rudolphsen Bay purchased grain from the Fussingø estate. Two other estates made deliveries to three merchants. Apparently, the other estates were satisfied with selling to one buyer, which does not indicate any real competition (although it cannot be ruled out that the estates invited other tenders).

Competition or the state of the market probably played a greater role in the grain trade between the merchants themselves. Three small grain dealers sold most of their grain to other grain dealers, while two large-scale dealers sold approximately half their grain to a fellow merchant in Randers. There are also numerous examples of grain, not yet delivered by the estates, being sold by one merchant to another. The driving force behind such deals and other larger deals between two merchants was, in the three most important cases, large deliveries abroad. Three grain dealers stood out among the others. One of them, Ditlev Kirketerp, stated that his 1,000 barrels of oats were to be paid for by Chr. A. Selpert, a merchant from Bremen. Presumably, this was a commission trade, financed from Bremen, which explains how he was able to buy 510 barrels of grain from other merchants. The other grain dealer, Jens Rudolphsen Bay, had bought 650 barrels of rye in total and 1,705 barrels of oats, the largest quantity in the town that spring. Of this, 405 barrels of oats were acquired by buying a smaller merchant's contract for the grain still on the estates Holbækgård and Estruplund. The purpose of this considerable purchase was to honour a contract with a merchant in Flensburg to deliver 2,000 barrels of oats before 16 April.

The third person was Niels Hasselbalch. Among other things he had bought a smaller grain dealer's contract for the delivery of 100 barrels of rye from the Demstrup estate, even though it was oats he stated to have sold to two men in Flensburg. All in all he was to have sold them 700 barrels of oats and in addition promised 170 barrels of rye to an unknown party. As previously mentioned, these plans were thwarted and he ended up selling 900 barrels of oats to the royal agent Niels Ryberg and 510 barrels to Norway.

The structure of the grain trade in Randers in the grain season of 1761/62 can be summarized as follows: The citizens were divided into three groups. There were those who did not sell grain and did not buy grain themselves by contacting the peasants. They got their grain from the town field, from the grain dealers proper and probably from the peasants' sale on the town market. The grain dealers proper were recognized by their activities searching out sources within the natural catchment area of Randers. The sellers were, most importantly, the estates, delivering according to already fixed contracts. The grain dealers were divided into two groups. The smaller group apparently aimed at selling to other merchants in town and thus conducted business with a certain speculative content. The other group were the export merchants, collecting grain to profit from it on markets abroad. A few acted on commission for foreign merchants or at least knowing they could sell it to certain buyers. It is striking that sale to Norway is never mentioned. This strengthens the impression that trade in Norway was not pre-arranged by buyer and seller. The grain was shipped to Norway and basically left in the hands of fate, in the confident expectation of the best possible outcome.

All in all, the structure of the grain trade was characterized by transparency and a low element of risk and may be described as *a contract economy*.

Niels Hasselbalch's grain purchases, 1762-67

Niels Hasselbalch's grain purchases in the years 1763-67 appear from his ledger, adding details to the overall picture, the pattern of which he generally followed. The additional information consists of terms of contract, price and payment and co-operation between the dealers. Hasselbalch's total grain purchases are given in fig. 11.4.

According to this information, Hasselbalch bought 6238.5 barrels of grain

Making a regional system work

during these 5 years. Of this, 45% was sold directly by the estates, 52% was bought from other merchants and 3% from others. The trade with the estates was the most stable one. The endeavours made to guard against non-deliveries and fluctuating prices, in other words the contract system, were conspicuous. In the cases where the date is indicated, it is clear that the contracts with the estates were made in the early months of winter and in February at the latest. At the time indicated, some of the estates would have finished threshing, others would not, but the overall estimate of the outcome of one's own harvest as well as that of others would be known, so deals could be made on that basis. However, deals were also made outside the contract system. These deals resembled what is normally understood as market sales, the unsolicited sale. The Østergård estate delivered 16 barrels of rye on 3 January 1766, and at an unknown time 31 barrels of rye were delivered from Vedø estate as well as 230 barrels of malt and oats from Kjellerup estate. However, these were the four estates, bound by contract, that kept coming back with new sales. By purchasing both by contract and on the market Hasselbalch brought the number of his contracts with estates up to a total of 10.

The trade with the estates was important because it was more affordable than trading with other merchants. Unfortunately, the source material concerning prices is not adequate. Despite much information very little concerns the two groups in the same year. It is implied, however, that Hasselbalch paid approximately 1 mark (i. e. 1/6 rigsdaler) more to the merchants. The low middleman's profit seems to indicate that the price was probably a sign of a balance of power advantageous to the estates.

There is one example of the estates being paid at the *Snapsting*[21] (with the

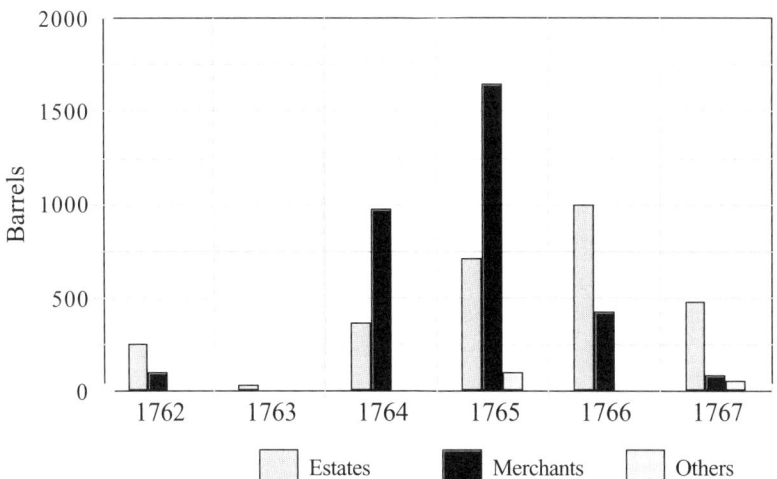

Fig. 11.4: The available data about Hasselbalch's grain purchase 1762-67

steward Thorn Thornsohn from the Hevringholm estate). But other than that it can be seen from the comments and accounts of the Hasselbalch brothers that they were usually paid when the grain had been delivered. This was only natural, because that was when it was known whether the estates were able to sell the agreed quantity after the threshing. An example of this can be found in the contract made on 5 December 1765 with the above-mentioned Thornsohn for 2-300 barrels of barley at 24 marks per barrel, 2-300 barrels of barley at 13 marks per barrel and 50-60 barrels of peas at 16 marks per barrel. In this case Thornsohn had problems with delivering the quantity agreed upon, he delivered only 190 barrels of rye, including deliveries from the Stenalt and Holbækgård estates. He must have bought these deliveries himself and sold them on to Hasselbalch. Of this rye, 158 barrels were sold to four local men. Three, if not all four of them were distillers. According to the information concerning prices the locals paid 4 rigsdaler and 1 mark, once again resulting in a middleman's profit of 1 mark a barrel.

The year before Hasselbalch had also sold grain from Thornsohn locally, once again primarily to distillers. Thus, he worked as a supplier for an important local production, and to complete the picture, it should be mentioned that the same people and many more shipped their distilled spirits to Norway together with Hasselbalch's shipments. The Hasselbalch grain trade was a pivotal point for his own business as well as essential for the distillers' business.

His grain trade activity was also a pivotal point for the local trade, because he bought considerable quantities from other merchants in town, not from the large-scale merchants, dominating the source material from 1762, but from smaller merchants who had a little grain in storage, while most of it had been sold locally. Compared with Hasselbalch, they were grain middlemen. More precisely, they were malt dealers. They seemed to have made their business on processing malt, sometimes even in considerable quantities. A distilled spirits dealer, who was otherwise rather ordinary, sold 400 barrels of malt according to contract and others sold 340 barrels of malt.

Hans Guldbrandsen, who occasionally worked as a shipmaster for Hasselbalch, is a fine example of this type of trader. With a trade license and citizenship from 1746 allowing him »to earn a living through retail business and on the sea as a shipmaster«, with a half share in a cutter 2 years later and with a house worth only 700 rigsdaler, he still worked as a grain dealer and processer of malt.[22]

On one occasion he bought 100 barrels of rye from Hasselbalch. Another one of these middlemen who had citizenship from 27 January 1751, giving him the right to do retail business, shipped considerable quantities of distilled spirits to Norway with Hasselbalch's shipment, in addition to delivering 300 barrels of malt to him. Another merchant can be found within this category, with a property estimated to be worth only 660 rigsdaler, but with no citizenship. He sold Hasselbalch 324 barrels of malt from 1763 to 1766, but also 54 barrels of barley and oats.

Hasselbalch also did business with the large-scale merchants. Three of these sold him 662 barrels of grain. But they were one-off situations, it is therefore most likely that he did business with these fellow merchants when he was given a favorable offer or the demand was large or acute.

It is not stated anywhere at what time of year these contracts with the grain middlemen were made. However, it can be concluded that they took place mainly in the late months of winter and early spring. This also corresponds with the fact that the middlemen had to settle their purchases first, which could very well have happened under the same conditions as Hasselbalch's trade with the estates. The estates were primarily paid when the quantity agreed upon had been delivered, whereas the merchants were often paid one part upon entering the contract and the rest later, often at the »Snapsting«. If the deal was made at the »Snapsting« which was apparently the case in 1764, the first half was paid then and the rest sometime during the summer. In any case, the merchants were always paid in part when the purchase was agreed upon and the rest of the payment could be made at the »Snapsting«, where Hasselbalch is only once seen to have paid for a deal with both another merchant and an estate.

The trade with the peasants and clergymen was minimal compared to the trade with the estates and the merchant trade. Two examples of this exist, the first of which is quite exceptional. On 10 June Hasselbalch's ship was loaded with grain from the clergyman in Voer, and more interestingly from the »Ørsted peasants«, two villages situated to the north of the Randers inlet between the town and Udbyhøj at the mouth of the inlet. Sixty barrels of rye and malt were bought from the clergyman and 43 barrels from the Ørsted peasants. The peasants actually received the best payment, 3 rigsdaler a barrel, which was a couple of skilling (1 skilling = 1/96 rigsdaler) more than the estates were paid that year. In 1767 an additional 51 barrels of barley from »village men« were noted, maybe this concerned the same Ørsted peasants. Furthermore, Hasselbalch expanded his aggressive activity by letting his uncle, Niels Skiøtt, operate as a buyer of grain on the nearby estates. Among other things Skiøtt was able to deliver no less than 140.5 barrels of malt in 1764 (origin unknown) and 160 barrels of oats, and 60 barrels of rye from the Stenalt estate in January of 1765.

The prices of Hasselbalch's deals were not seasonally fixed; they fluctuated from 1/2 to 1 mark. The source material makes it impossible to relate the fluctuations to the sellers, the season or the precise quantities. Many deals within the same season were concluded at identical prices. The fluctuations were larger between seasons. There was no unambiguous tendency but the prices rose, except the price of oats. The increase in price was most pronounced for a barrel of barley, 53% from 1764 to 1766.

Thus, Hasselbalch's trade pattern was not totally identical with the previously described general pattern of 1762. The biggest difference was his large purchase of grain from other merchants, which can be explained by the fact that this time the malt was included in the source material. It seems reasonable to conclude that this trade between merchants or between merchant and distiller/malt dealer is the closest one gets to market-economic conditions within the grain trade structure – even though an apparently fixed middleman's profit implies that custom also dominated here.

Regional integration

The advantages of trading with the estates also applied for Hasselbalch. It was safe and had a low element of risk. The willingness of the estates to enter into sales contracts early in the season proves that the same wish for security and stability was important in their calculations.

The element of competition must have been most profound when the merchants competed with each other for contracts with the estates. Hasselbalch's trade – which was gradually based more and more on grain dealing – was very much the same from one year to another, but there was still room for a more untraditional campaign to the village of Ørsted, its peasants and its clergyman.

Regional sales patterns

A single preserved customs account from Randers, 1767, provides us with further details of the regional connections within the grain trade of the town.[23] The total grain export was 36,058 barrels. In total, grain was being shipped 110 times by 54 shipmasters. Twenty-two of these were local, but to this number should be added 9 voyages by shipmasters from the island of Als, who were probably hired by merchants from Randers.

The local shipmasters and the hired Als shipmasters had a remarkable sailing pattern. No less than 94% of their grain was shipped to only three markets: the two Norwegian cities Drammen (72%) and Bergen (13%), and to Copenhagen (9%). The grain export from Randers had the same marketing structure as Aalborg's grain trade, but with an even more limited range of markets.

The trade between Randers and Drammen was so that one can speak of a virtual *regional integration* of the farming areas around Randers as suppliers, the Randers merchants as middlemen and Drammen as market. The cliché in the ledger of Hasselbalch, »sent to be sold in Eastern Norway«, covers a habitual reality.

This picture is strengthened when taking into account the activities of the Norwegian shipmasters operating from Randers, since 61% of their grain was also shipped to Drammen.

Other regional connections stand out. Shipmasters from Dragør – the most important harbour for cargo ships in Denmark – linked Randers even more closely to the district of Copenhagen. In 1767, they took 4,348 barrels or 71% of the town's outlet to the capital. Another – and a more surprising – regional band was a seemingly regular carrying trade with Elsinore. The town of the Sound Tolls had only a poor agricultural hinterland and was dependent on outside supplies. Thus, on twelve occasions shipmasters left Elsinore in ballast in small ships to buy grain in Randers, but in total they bought only 354 barrels. The distribution of the grain export from Randers is illustrated in fig. 11.5.

The grain trade of Niels Severin Hasselbalch seems to correspond to the general picture. The same applies to the other types of merchandise. The most important articles he sold were distilled spirits, pork, cheese, linen and other textile articles. Generally, the sales pattern of these articles looked like the one for grain, the greater part going to Norway, the lesser part to Copenhagen. For example, 44,408 pounds and 561 barrels of pork and meat was sent to Copenhagen and 115,422 pounds to Norway.

Fig. 11.5: Distribution of Randers' grain export 1767

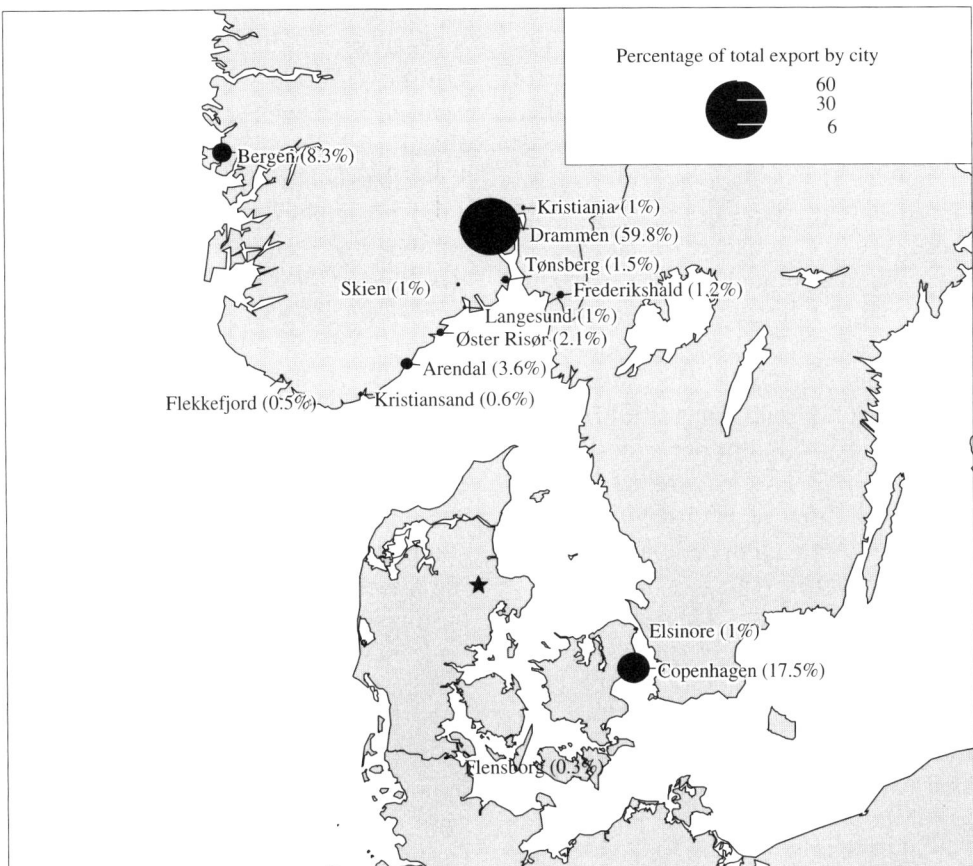

16,764 pounds of cheese went to Copenhagen, 24,390 pounds to Norway.

As a market, Copenhagen differed from Norway in the city's ability to buy more luxury goods such as powder of stag antlers and hides of hares and calves. Conversely, only Norway bought distilled spirits, in fact more than 142,000 litres. And linen and textile articles were sold not merely by Hasselbalch but also in large quantities by others of the town's merchants and shipmasters, amounting to 10,052 rigsdaler. Hats, gloves, homespun fabrics, linen, stockings and trousers – some, perhaps homemade, others from protoindustrial production – followed the grain to Norway creating further ties between the Jutland countryside and Southern Norway.

Although the figures are from one year only, the picture we get is of a stable and well-functioning trading network, integrating geographically separate regions.

The marketing in Norway

The customs accounts tell us nothing about the actual sale in Norway. Hasselbalch's ledger is far more informative.

Christen Drastrup was one of the small-scale merchants acting as middlemen for Hasselbalch. In addition Drastrup acted as another type of agent for Hasselbalch, he could basically be called a representative agent. He appears in Hasselbalch's ledger several times under wordings like the following from 27 April 1767: »discharged to shipmaster Hans Nielsen from Nøtterøy [Norway] to be sold by Christen Drastrup in Eastern Norway«. Twice he handles the goods sent out with the shipmaster Christoffer Ahlman and a third time he handles the goods sent out with the ship of Jens R. Bay. The customs account reveals that three of Hasselbalch's shipments went to Drammen and one to Kristiansand this year.

In all these cases Hasselbalch sent only a small quantity of goods with another merchant's cargo. Should Drastrup's role be understood in the sense that he was sent out by the town merchants to handle the shiploads, consisting of the goods from several merchants? Usually, Hasselbalch sent his goods with shipmaster Mogens Christensen, who also handled them in Norway. Other times Mogens Christensen, with citizenship from Christmas Eve 1760 allowing him to earn a living solely as a shipmaster, was sent out with another ship to trade the goods which Hasselbalch sent with it (e.g. 5 times in 1764).

The examples are numerous but it is sufficient to summarize that it was normal, in addition to the shipmaster, to send an agent with one's cargo to handle the goods in Norwegian ports. A trusted shipmaster could also perform the task – like Frederik Hansen, who among other things handled Hasselbalch's large shipments of gloves, linen and wool in the summer months of 1762. Is it indicative of the existence of a group of shipmasters and sailors who had experience in trade routines from the Norwegian ports and who also became grain dealers ashore, that Frederik Hansen also sold malt to Hasselbalch? In any case, on 4 April 1764 Frederik Hansen's citizenship was extended to include »grain dealing and handling of Norwegian goods but also the selling of small wares from an open shop«.

These conditions resembled those of the general pattern. It was quite common to bring shipments for others with one's own ship. Until some time after the mid-eighteenth century it was also common for the shipmasters to be sailing merchants taking care of their own businesses. Concerning the Norwegian trade, according to the Danish maritime historian Anders Monrad Møller, it was more likely that there were a domestic merchant and a sailing shipmaster than that the merchant and the shipmaster were one and the same person.[24] The reason was that the ships within this trade were the largest in domestic trade and the merchants had the largest businesses, which they could not well leave. Secondly, it was common for the merchants in the provinces to have started their career as shipmasters.[25]

Home from Norway

Apparently, Hasselbalch never accompanied his goods to Norway. It was difficult for him to leave the business at home. However, it can also be argued that his not being present at the sale of the grain or the purchase of the return cargo was more than anything a sign of a trade dominated by routines and few necessary calculations. As shown, Hasselbalch seemed to have a system for his purchases of grain and other goods. He co-operated with other merchants in joint shipments and perhaps bills of exchange, but he was not present in the situations where the system was to earn its keep. In any case he was not present in person. The maintenance of the system and the merchant's profit therefore rested on the predictability of the market and trust in the person who handled his goods.

He placed the sale of his exports to Norway and the purchase of the return cargoes in the hands of his shipmasters or the accompanying agents. Often he wrote down the instructions he gave them. An example of this is a trip from Randers on 14 June 1763 »to Eastern Norway« with Mogens Christensen as shipmaster. In this case the instructions were: »For return cargo must be bought 4 *skippund* (1 skippund = 159.6 kg), *Kræfting*, ironware, 3 form stoves of 1 skippund, 3 of 1½ skippund. A few quarter barrels of tar, must be a bargain. If he comes to the town of Drammen, 200 *bouteilles* (wine bottles) must be bought, 6 round vinegar carafes, 200 rigsdaler can be sent by post in *banco* notes.«

In an order from 6 June 1767 the shipmaster once again was told to go »to Eastern Norway«. This time the shipmaster had to remember to bring back: 2/4 barrels of English flour, 4 barrels of fresh caraway, ½ barrel of juniper berries, 1 pewter cabinet, 4 to 5 barrels of tar in *fjerdinger* (i.e. quarter barrels), 10 to 12 skippund of iron, 200 to 300 pieces of band iron. Hasselbalch notes that if the loading takes place in Oksefjorden, 20 to 24 skippund of iron should be bought. 300 to 400 rigsdaler could be sent by post as bills of exchange.

From a third trip starting on 30 March 1765 iron, *fyrvrag* (i.e. firewood), 200 rigsdaler worth of bills as well as 2-300 rigsdaler in bank notes should be brought home.

In these examples Hasselbalch intended to bring home a large part of the profit in cash or bills. Another possibility would have been to receive the dividend solely as goods, as in a trip »to Eastern Norway« where shipmaster Mogens Christensen was given the following instructions on 30 July 1765: »For return cargo is required boards from the town of Drammen or Kristiania. 2 small two-storey stoves, 2 larger ditto, cowberries, cloudberries, anchovies, 4 barrels of caraway, 1 barrel of English flour, 2 dozen bottles of English beer.«

Another trip was carried out under similar conditions in 1767 (no indication of date). In this case he required a return cargo of: 4 barrels of cod liver oil, 4 whole barrels of herring, 8 quarter barrels of herring, 5 barrels of cod in half barrels, 12 barrels of anchovies, 4 to 6 barrels of so-called *ravrekling* (dried halibut). The rest of the cargo should consist of fish.

Perhaps the most interesting thing in this connection is the role of the bills of exchange, the premise of the bill system being that a third party is involved in the transaction besides buyer and seller. Who was involved in Hasselbalch's transactions? Two small-scale Randers merchants appear. One of them is Anders Knudsen Mammen, the other one Christen Sparre. From another source we learn that they each held 1-2.5% of the town's timber stock, 2.5-5% of the

Regional integration

fish and 1-2.5% of its iron in 1761. Very little of their goods had been bought directly from or by way of Copenhagen.[26] In 1762 they held grain only for their own personal use. So it seems that they were small-scale merchants operating in Norway. Yet it was from them that Niels Hasselbalch in the autumn of 1765 sent a total of 620 rigsdaler to his brother Jacob, maybe with an additional 150 rigsdaler, but without any further information. Why were these payments made from two small-scale merchants to one large merchant?

The source material lets us down here, however, it implies that the Hasselbalch brothers could have received payment for their grain in Norway by receiving bills of exchange which the Norwegian buyer had drawn on Knudsen Mammen and Sparre who must have already accepted them. For the latter two the bills served as payment for goods they had bought in Norway. In this way Hasselbalch could get cash by contacting his local fellow merchants and the latter could get their fish, timber and iron from Norway by paying Hasselbalch. It was a system founded on trust – in the merchant world meaning credit. Actually, Hasselbalch gave credit by receiving bills in Norway instead of instant payment in cash. It was not until the return home that the cash flowed from the smaller local merchants. Obviously, the Norwegian merchant also gave credit – to Knudsen Mammen and Sparre – this way he himself got credit on the payment of the grain. In this way the Norwegian merchant sold his stock of timber, iron and fish on credit so that he did not receive cash payment until he sold the grain he had bought from Denmark.

If true, this connection explains the excellence of the joint efforts. The large-scale merchant Niels Hasselbalch could not dispense with the services of the small-scale merchants, unless he – and with him all other large merchants – was able to clear Norway of iron, fish and timber, so to speak. It was this trade which made it possible for the Norwegians to buy Danish grain. Can the cooperation between the, in principle, competing merchants about the export of distilled spirits and import of fish be seen in this light? In any case the practise of the merchants borrowing goods from each other and offering each other freight and storage was widespread.[27]

In addition to exporting a lot of distilled spirits for others, Hasselbalch in several cases also imported large quantities of fish for other merchants in Randers. On 9 July 1764 shipmaster Peder Sørensen returned from Norway with fish for 22 buyers. Among those were Niels Hasselbalch and the estates Stenalt and Støvringgård, while the rest were mainly large and small merchants. In all, fish worth 1,129 rigsdaler were imported with this shipment.

More important than the understanding of every step taken in these transactions is the realization that the exchange of Danish grain for Norwegian goods was not simply an exchange of goods or a barter. The profits from Norway were brought home both as goods and as bills/cash. Furthermore, the Danish-Norwegian exchange of goods was so complicated that it made room for a regional specialization of the business community.

The trade patterns of the merchants of Randers, 1735-1840

In the case of Niels Hasselbalch the Norwegian trade was the driving force – determining his actions in the regional economic system. How does this and the other conclusions fit into a larger context?

In 1735 all Danish market towns were questioned about their financial state. Just like the other replies, the reply from Randers[28] should be treated cautiously, it must have been very tempting to try to obtain special favours by revealing one's poor conditions.[29]

According to the reply from the town magistrate, its trade and business consisted of: 1) Malting and grain trade, 2) brewing and distilling, 3) trade in timber, iron, tar, fish, flax, hemp, ironmongery and other goods of a similar kind, 4) *delicatessen* trade, 5) trade in wine, 6) trade in small wares and condiments.

Furthermore, the reply stated that the principal trade was the grain trade, the malting was only of minor importance especially because of the low grain prices in Norway.

Distilling and brewing were of even less importance due to the fact that only 1/10 of the previous quantities were now sold to the villages. Item 3 was »mainly the ships' return cargo from Norway and the profit expected from that has so far been lost twice on the exported grain« (this was, however, an overstatement. The grain prices in Norway were 4% higher than in Denmark in the period 1711-1720 and 33% higher in 1731-1780).[30] In addition, the town imported a large part of its flax and hemp from Aalborg. The »delicatessen« trade also decreased, it was exported to Norway and Copenhagen but all in all it could only be called small shopkeeping. Generally, the magistrate of Randers found that: »the town in a few years has been so declining and set back so much that it cannot be considered half as important with regard to commerce and the assets of its people as it was 20 or 30 years ago«. The cause was both the growing problem with the silting up of the inlet, the difficult military billeting as well as the fact that the best men had died and their valuables scattered to the winds because of the division of joint estates.

As for the shipping, conditions were no better. It was mainly directed to Norway and Copenhagen and the Duchies. The trade with Norway was traditional: malt and rye, some smoked bacon and quite a lot of bad butter. In addition came frieze, cloth, gloves, stockings and other small wares which »mostly are being handled by the shipmaster and the men«. For return cargo came the usual goods. It is extraordinary that the trade in rye, oats and »delicatessen« was said to be larger to Copenhagen than to Norway.

This trade structure made room for six merchants and small shopkeepers »considered to be the principal ones« and eight more mediocre and less distinguished merchants and small shopkeepers, who could not do business without credit from outside (presumably the six first-mentioned could). As many as 50 small-scale merchants were left, supporting themselves by small-scale business, brewing and serving beer. To reach this number even the smallest firewood dealer must have been included.

The trade of Niels Hasselbalch 25-30 years later was founded on the same structures. It is striking that the sale of grain to Norway in 1735 was estimated to be lower than the sale to Copenhagen, but apart from that no other features can be characterized as striking. However, it is extraordinary that he included the trade in stockings, cloth and wool in his business, thus professionalizing this trade by taking it over from the shipmasters and crew.

The merchants in Randers were not organized in any actual guild, their only organization was a funeral guild from 1693, which in 1741 was allowed to elect a number of men commissioned to assist the town magistrate.[31] The funeral guild became a forum protecting the interests of the merchants, in 1758 leading to a temporary disruption when a new guild was founded, whose members were a number of mainly young, expanding merchants, among whom Niels Hasselbalch is found.

Could this strife also be an expression of a conflict between the expanding merchants of a new era and their older, maybe even stagnating colleagues? A new investigation has brought to light the changing number of merchants and their changing economic importance (table 11.3).[32]

These figures cannot be compared directly with the account from 1735; on the other hand – remembering the negative wording of the account which like the above-mentioned figures from 1682 should be seen in the light of a recent war situation – one can conclude that the merchant group of 1761 was experiencing growth. The growth was, however, merely a »catching-up« with the situation in 1640 when fewer merchants had formed just as large a part of the city's tax base. On the other hand, the merchant group in 1761 had drawn level with the situation in 1640 in relation to its internal distribution of the highest, middle and lowest taxpayers. For half the merchants in 1761, being a merchant meant an advance into the territory of the richest. However, the historian Rolf Engel concludes that the growth was relative because the total tax contribution of this group had decreased since 1682, and the apparent increase rested on the decline of the other occupational groups. This, however, does not alter the fact that the merchants constituting 1.5% of the town population in 1761 accounted for a larger proportion of the tax base than they did in 1640 when they constituted 1.7% of the population. The power of the merchants over the municipal government and the town's economy was unassailable.

Even in 1768 an account states that 38 out of 50 merchants conducted normal peasant trade as well as a complex business with grain, malt and similar heavy goods and textile products. Furthermore, 4-5 merchants equipped ships for Norway.[33] Thus, it was not a changed trade structure which caused the growth in the town's fleet up until that year (see below).

Later, the improved Danish business conditions also made themselves felt in Randers. The improvement was caused by international prosperity and the fact that Danish shipping utilized the country's neutrality. It is a well known fact that shortly before 1800 a number of ships from Randers were active in the Mediterranean and in overseas destinations with local merchants acting as shipping agents.[34]

The fleet's development illustrates the correctness of the statement that the relatively increasing importance of the

Table 11.3: The economic importance of the Randers merchants 1640-1761

Merchants and tradesmen	Total	Belonging to highest tax payers	Belonging to middle tax payers	Belonging to lowest tax payers	Merchants and tradesmen's proportion of the city's tax base. (In brackets the total town population)
1640	34	18	8	8	36% (2000)
1682	23	4	12	7	19%
1761	43	23	5	15	39% (2850)

merchants in the economy of the market towns in the years up to 1760 conceals the fact that their economic capacity declined in real terms, if the ships' carrying capacity is taken to reflect this. Table 11.4 also shows that the years around 1760 were a turning point. They were the last years of the recession and the first years of a recovery. The decade 1789-98 was the culmination of this development, suddenly interrupted by the naval war with Great Britain (1807-14) and consequently the many requisitions of ships. A new growth started with the so-called Grain Sales Period around 1840.

Thus, Randers followed the development of the national economy with regard to the turning points: the utilization of neutrality in the overseas trade, the setback of the war with Great Britain, followed by economic crisis and ending with the breakthrough of the Grain Sales Period. There were also purely local developments: from 1773 to 1800 considerable improvements were made in the navigation conditions in the Randers inlet.[35] The domestic trade structure remained unchanged. An account of foreign and non-local ships arriving in the port of Randers in 1779 shows that 17 ships arrived with timber and iron, as many as 14 arrived in ballast, 7 with salt, 5 with furniture, 3 with coals, bricks and fish. Twenty-one of the same non-local ships exported grain and »delicatessen«, 17 left in ballast, 11 with meat and bacon, only 5 with rye and 3 with distilled spirits.[36] It is remarkable that so many ships left in ballast, but according to the author who gives the information, it is just as extraordinary that the *Norwegian* timber ships did *not* sail home in ballast; the trade route Norway-Randers-Norway was institutionalized and apparently did not experience such a waste of capacity.

Concurrently with the exotic trade on the oceans and during the war with Great Britain, tradition and custom flourished. In his memoirs, the Secretary of the Royal Cabinet and topographic writer J.P. Trap described his childhood in Randers with his merchant father and maintained that the merchants' peasant trade was the foundation of the town economy. His father Niels Trap has been described as an enterprising young merchant who besides his peasant trade gained much from having letters of marque during the war with Great Britain.[37]

Niels Trap started out with a traditional business but with the help of a fi-

Table 11.4: The fleet of Randers 1720-1850

	Number of registered ships	Ship lasts (1 ship last=2600 kg)
1720	19	233.5
1725	16	163.5
1750	15	166.5
1760	14	146.5
1769	19	235
1789	27	481
1798	37	775
1810		c. 740
1820		c. 270
1830		c. 270
1840		c. 620
1850		c. 850

Note: The table is based on data from Ole Warthoe Hansen, Henrik Fode and Finn H. Lauridsen: *Søkøbstaden Randers*, p. 121 and 136. From 1672 to 1825 the tonnage of the Danish fleet was secretly reduced by 1/6 for competitive reasons.

nancial contact in Copenhagen he developed a business that tried to find new markets; he imported salt directly from France and presumably he established sales of agricultural produce on the markets in Northwestern Europe, still new to the provincial merchants. He drew bills of exchange worth thousands of rigsdaler on his connections in Hamburg and then used them to pay local business connections by means of his merchant in Copenhagen. His bankruptcy is another matter, which does not change the fact emphasized by the historian Per Boje that Trap was a personification of the development of the provincial merchants in the favourable years just after 1814, as they tried to gain ground as both exporters and importers on foreign markets besides Norway by moving their main business connections from Copenhagen to Hamburg. Here the merchants were able to grant them the necessary advances with which to buy agricultural produce. At the same time they gave them an opportunity to draw bills on them, in this way extending their credit in return for the Danish agricultural produce increasingly exported through this channel.[38]

Conclusion

Niels Hasselbalch was a merchant like many other provincial merchants in the eighteenth century. He followed the most basic mercantile route in the Danish-Norwegian economy. He purchased grain in the local economy, sold it in Norway and took in return timber, iron, fish and a few other goods that were sold locally. He made no attempt to reach the »capitalistic level« above what Braudel calls »the economic level«. The trade he took part in had been established through generations, its structure was regular with transparent transactions at all levels.

Does this do anything but refresh our memory of what we already knew; are the results in this article merely trivial?

First, a substantial result is the fact that trade connections between the estates around Randers and the merchants of the towns seem to have taken place within a *predominantly* non-hierarchical town structure. Was this a phenomenon only to be found in this corner of Jutland? The studies of Jørgen Mikkelsen point to the opposite. Mikkelsen talks about the market towns »to a large extent« operating in the same trade areas.[39] He has put forward a comprehensive material showing that out of 3,236 peasants, that were recorded as buying on credit from merchants in three Zealand market towns in the years 1750 to 1807, 484 can be found as customers of more than one merchant; 249 of these even in more than one market town. However, what conclusion to draw from this is open for debate. The numbers are high but, on the other side, they correspond to only 15 and 7.7%. And the grain trade seems to have been even less subject to competition between the market towns.

Second, the analysis has revealed that Randers had a limited role in what Poul Holm has called »the macro-region« of Jutland trade, the international trade between the North Sea and the Baltic Sea. In contrast to Aalborg, the »seascape« of Randers was narrow, limited to Southern Norway and Copenhagen. The trade between Randers and Southern Norway, especially Drammen, was so well-integrated that one can talk about a *micro-region* consisting of the estates within the catchment area of Randers, as producers, and the area around Drammen, as the market. With the actions of merchants like Hasselbalch providing the necessary connection in terms of trade and communication.

Third, this article has uncovered varied market-economic behaviour on »the economic level«. In addition to his grain sale, Hasselbalch organized the purchase of locally produced fabrics and other textile articles. The grain sale was, however, the central part of his business. There were three categories of grain dealers: Those who only used grain for distilling spirits, those who aimed at selling it to other merchants, and finally the actual merchants involved in grain dealing in order to sell grain on markets abroad.

A few looked further than Norway and among those were the few examples of a connection to an international, capitalistic grain market. These examples were sometimes an incentive to the entire system; middlemen were activated, grain was sold from merchant to merchant, even while it was still on the estates. However, the overall characteristic was caution. Agreements made a long time in advance lay behind many deals. A special feature was the widespread use of contracts between estates and merchants.

The picture of the Norwegian trade was also one of security and stability. It was almost without risk. Merchants could let their goods be transported together with the goods of other merchants and let them be handled by an agent or a trusted shipmaster. There was also co-operation concerning the return cargo. The market-economic competence that this demanded of the middlemen and shipmasters is worth mentioning once again.

For a long time the regional trade in Randers lived up to the mercantilist desire of the state to keep provincial trade provincial. Therefore – and because of unfavourable trade outlooks – there was no growth in the economy of Randers until about 1760/70. The growth came when the trade became international, while a generally positive trade outlook with increasing grain prices started in the second half of the eighteenth century. Having connections with business houses abroad and especially in Hamburg, Danish regional merchants were connected to the world market by the strong ties that linked the economies of Northern Germany and Britain. The regional merchants were not connected with goods of marginal importance to the regional economy such as most colonial products but rather with the agricultural produce essential to the regional economy. Essential to the producers and dealers, to agriculture and to the merchants.

Notes

1. Per Boje: *Danske provinskøbmænds vareomsætning og kapitalforhold 1815-1847*, Viborg 1977, p. 63. For background, see the article of Poul Holm in this volume and Søren Bitsch Christensen: Danmark og Europa 1200-1750. En oversigt over Danmarks integration og udstødning af den vesteuropæiske økonomi med særligt henblik på kornhandelen og 4 klassiske begrebspar (A survey of Denmark and Europe 1200-1750 with main emphasis on grain trade and estate structure), *Erhvervshistorisk Årbog* 1998-99, pp. 7-98.
2. Dan H. Andersen and Hans-Joachim Voth: Did Neutrality Pay? An Econometric Analysis of Danish Shipping to the Mediterranean, 1748-1790, *Folk og erhverv tilegnet Hans Chr. Johansen*, ed. Anders Monrad Møller, Viborg 1995, pp. 91-99.
3. Ole Feldbæk: *Danmarks historie, vol. 4, 1730-1814*, Gyldendals Danmarkshistorie, 1982, pp. 208ff. The term »provincial« does not include the two southern duchies (Schleswig-Holstein) or Norway.
4. Anders Monrad Møller: *Fra galeoth til galease. Studier i de kongerigske provinsers søfart i det 18. århundrede*, Esbjerg 1981, pp. 154ff. Algerian sea letters were required in order to sail beyond Cap Finisterre.
5. Erik Helmer Petersen: Dansk landbrugsudvikling i det 18. århundrede. En oversigt, *Bol og By. Landbohistorisk Tidsskrift*, 2., no 5, 1983, pp. 52ff.
6. Poul Enemark: Korn og kornhandel, column 147ff, *Kulturhistorisk Leksikon for Nordisk Middelalder*, IX, København 1964. Søren Bitsch Christensen (see note 1), pp. 15f, 33-44 (with references).
7. Gunnar Olsen: Danmarks kornavl og kornhandelspolitik i tiden 1610-1660, *Historisk Tidsskrift*, 10, vol. VI, 1942-44, p. 452.
8. Henrik Becker-Christensen: De danske købstæders økonomiske udvikling og regeringens erhvervspolitik 1660-1750, *Erhvervshistorisk Årbog* 1979, pp. 44 and 55.
9. Knud J.V. Jespersen: *Danmarks historie, vol. 4, 1648-1730*, Gyldendals Danmarkshistorie, 1989, pp. 95f.
10. Albert Olsen: *Danmark og Norge i det 18. Aarhundrede*, København 1936, p.16.

11 Dan Ch. Christensen: *Det moderne projekt. Teknik & Kultur i Danmark-Norge 1750 – (1814) – 1850*, Viborg 1996, pp. 63f.
12 Fernand Braudel: *The Wheels of Commerce. Civilization & Capitalism 15th-18th century*, vol. 2, Berkeley 1992, pp. 403-08.
13 Op. cit., pp. 455-457.
14 Erhvervsarkivet (The Danish National Business Archives), Niels Severin Hasselbalch, regnskabsbog 1761- 1800.
15 This passage is based on biographical data and information about trade topics in: Otto von Spreckelsen: *Viborg Bys Borgerbog*, Viborg 1955. Ole Warthoe-Hansen, Henrik Fode and Finn H. Lauridsen: *Søkøbstaden Randers. Flodhavn og købmandsby*, Randers 1980. The archives of Randers rådstue (Landsarkivet for Nørrejylland, The Provincial Archives, Viborg), D21, 313, »Borgerskabsprotokol« and 301, »Div. indkomne breve til magistraten vedr. indkvartering, magasinkorn etc.«, dossier A, and the archives of Randers købstad (same place) B50, 75, »Register til Randers bys skøde- og panteprotokoller 1736-82«.
16 From the above-mentioned conditions follows that some of the numerical data to be mentioned afterwards is only partially complete. Attention is drawn to the fact that the analysis of Hasselbalch's trade structure therefore may seem to be more solidly based than is actually the case. However, to account for the critical judgement of every piece of information I have thought would be too tiresome for the reader. However, each item of information used has been critically examined.
17 Becker-Christensen (see note 8), p. 81.
18 The archives of the *Rentekammer* (Rigsarkivet, The Danish National Archives) 2247.45, »Efterretninger om forråd af rug og havre i Jylland, indsendte i henh. til Rentekammerordre af 13. og 27. marts 1762«. The report was sent in by the *stiftamtmand* (regional governor) de Schouboe in Aarhus in his capacity as supreme local authority of the market towns of the diocese. The reply from Randers lies in the dossier with his report, sent to him by the *amtsforvalter* (an official of the county), see the archives of Randers Rådstue (Landsarkivet for Nørrejylland), D21, 301, »Div. indkomne breve til magistraten vedrørende indkvartering, magasinkorns udskibning og lignende 1716-61«, especially the dossier »Undersøgning og eftersynsforretning over det forråd af rug og havre som findes hos de handlende i Randers, og hvorpå er gjort beslag 31. marts 1762. Item beslag på skibe til transport etc. Endelig beslagenes ophævelse«. I am presently researching this material on a national basis and it forms a primary part of my Ph.D. thesis.
19 It should be remembered that some grain was traded more than once – including from one merchant to another – even before it was delivered from the estates. Hence, the numbers in the figure cannot be compared directly with the numbers just mentioned.
20 The town of Viborg was the size of Randers, but its grain trade could only supply the city itself. Since it was too far away from a proper harbour there was no larger business. See Svend Aakjær: *Viborg Købstads Historie III*, Viborg 1940. The other 3 towns mentioned here were rather small, having between 400 and 700 inhabitants except Aarhus with 3,800 inhabitants. Mariager did have water access, but was troubled by a poor harbour and a narrow inlet.
21 See the article by Ole Degn in this volume.
22 The archives of Randers rådstue, D21, 313, »Borgerskabsprotokol 1723-95« (29.12.1746), cf. »Alf. register over erhvervede og opsagte borgerskaber i Randers bys borgerskabsprotokol 1723-95«. The archives of Randers købstad, B50, 75, »Register til Randers bys skøde- og panteprotokoller 1736-66, 1766-82«, p. 42.
23 Rigsarkivet, Reviderede toldregnskaber, Randers, Antegnelser og ekstrakter 3, 1760-69.
24 Anders Monrad Møller (see note 4), pp. 183ff.
25 See for instance Aage Fasmer Blomberg: *Fåborg bys historie II 1750-1914*, Fåborg 1956, p. 89.
26 The archives of Randers rådstue, D21, 372, »Div. dokumenter vedr. undersøgelser af toldpligtige varer hos de handlende 1750-61«.
27 See the most recent study on this, Jørgen Mikkelsen: *Købmandens kontaktflade – en regionalundersøgelse*, Erhvervshistorisk Årbog 1994, pp. 128ff.
28 It was part of a survey done by the *General-Landets Økonomi- og Kommercekollegium* (i.e. the supreme state department for finance and commerce). Here I am using the published

Regional integration

version »Næringslivet i Randers for ca. 200 Aar siden. Relation af 1735 fra Randers Magistrat«, *Aarbog udgivet af Randers Amts Historiske Samfund 1918*, pp. 93-107.
29 Poul Enemark: *Erhverv i Århus 1735*, Aarhus 1963, pp. 11ff.
30 Albert Olsen (see note 10), p. 8. Add to this the calculation that the gross profit from the grain trade in the neighbouring town of Aarhus in the same year of 1735 was about 50%. There is no reason why it should have been much different in Randers, see Becker-Christensen (see note 8), p. 59.
31 N. Bay og L. Heerfordt: *Randers ældre Kjøbmands-Lüglaugs Historie fra 1693 til 1918*, Randers 1918, pp. 23f + additional pages.
32 Rolf Engel: *Randers Atlas 1500-1950*, *Scandinavian Atlas of Historic Towns 1500-1950*, vol. 10, ed. Ole Degn, 1999, p. 46. I wish to thank the author for letting me read the manuscript.
33 von Spreckelsen (see note 15), p. 251.
34 Anders Monrad Møller (see note 4), pp. 152, 156f and 179.
35 Ole Warthoe Hansen, Henrik Fode and Finn H. Lauridsen (see note 15), p. 15.
36 Op. cit., pp. 119f.
37 Per Boje: J.P. Traps erindringer om faderen, købmand Niels Trap, *Folk og erhverv tilegnet Hans Chr. Johansen*, ed. Anders Monrad Møller, Viborg 1995, pp. 151-170.
38 Op. cit., pp. 157f. The standard study remains Per Boje 1977 (see note 1), see pp. 122ff and 276ff.
39 Jørgen Mikkelsen 1994 (see note 27), pp. 121 and 139. Cf. his article in this volume.

CHAPTER 12
Aalborg as a regional centre, 1400-1814

By Poul Holm

This article examines the South Scandinavian seascape of the Kattegat, Skagerrak and the Limfjord from a regional historical perspective. Aalborg is viewed as the centre of the Limfjord, and as a component of a larger unit comprising those regions in Norway, Sweden and Denmark which border the Kattegat and the Skagerrak. This 'seascape' is seen as a micro-region within the international trade between the North Sea and the Baltic Sea. In the sixteenth century, Aalborg was a very active part of this macro-region. After the Swedish conquests on the east coast of the Kattegat in 1660, the Danish–Norwegian dual monarchy pursued a mercantilist policy which gave Aalborg and its trade a strategic role in the kingdom's trade. After the loss of Norway in 1814, however, Aalborg and the Limfjord became a remote corner within the much smaller Danish kingdom which reoriented its trade towards the west and thus assigned a much reduced role to Aalborg.

In the medieval and early modern periods, horses, fish and later cattle were sources of wealth in the Limfjord regions. The Fjord and the major rivers Rye Å and Lindenborg Å were protected waters providing easy transport to and from surrounding regions such as Thy, Mors, Salling, Hanherred, Vendsyssel and Himmerland. The easy voyage across the Kattegat linked the people from around the Fjord with Halland and Båhuslen, Halland then being part of Denmark and Båhuslen part of Norway. Aalborg was the main centre in this network of water-borne trade.

At its peak around 1600, Aalborg, the Limfjord and the Kattegat region were fully integrated into the economy of the North and Baltic Seas, that is, the exchange of raw materials from the Baltic for manufactured goods from the North Sea countries, especially the Netherlands. The area can be seen as a 'semi-periphery' between Amsterdam, the centre of the North Sea-Baltic Sea system, and the broader periphery, the Polish granary and the Baltic supplying tar and hemp.[1] The Limfjord products, salted herring and stable-fattened cattle, as well as shaped planks from Halland and Båhuslen, were value-added goods representing a higher input of labour than the cheap raw materials from the Baltic Sea. Around 1600, trade had also passed from the hands of German merchants, who had dominated trade during the Middle Ages, into the hands of local merchants. In other words, Aalborg's trading base in the Limfjord and the Kattegat was a well-defined and relatively wealthy micro-region within the North European trading system.

With the loss of Halland and Båhuslen to Sweden in the wars of 1644 and 1657-59, Aalborg lost an important

Regional integration

Fig. 12.1: The Kattegat-Skagerrak-region

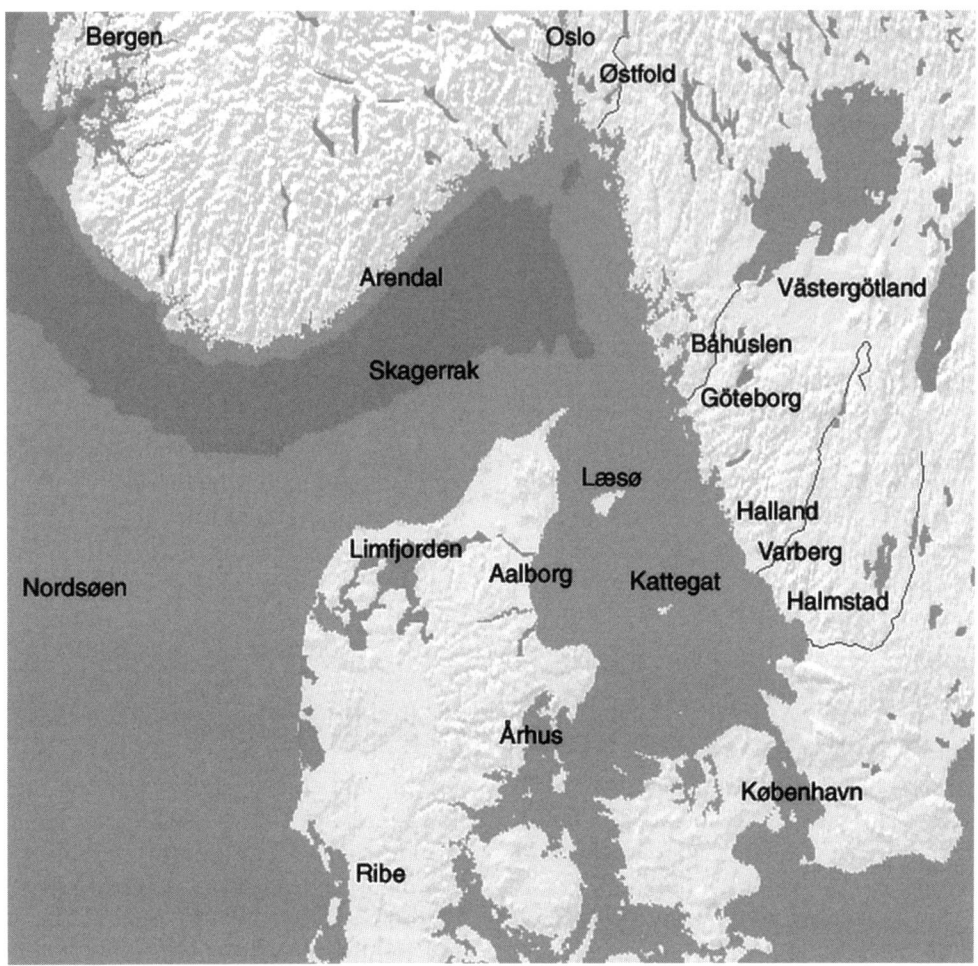

trading base. It nevertheless managed to retain its relative wealth throughout the eighteenth century while other Danish cities declined. Once again, it was the special geographic location of the Limfjord region within the broader area which set it apart. Thanks to the brief voyage to Norway across the Skagerrak, the rich estates around the Limfjord and the Aalborg merchants acquired a strategic role in the supply of food to other parts of the Danish-Norwegian dual monarchy. Aalborg became the trading centre for grain exports from Denmark to Norway, which was poor in food but rich in timber and iron. It was not until the nineteenth century that Aalborg became a peripheral trading centre within the Danish state. The prime factor which eroded Aalborg's trading position, and thus led to the decline of a regional dominance which had lasted since the late Middle Ages, was the loss of Norway in 1814, followed about 1840 by the opening of the western end of the Limfjord to ships entering the Fjord from the North Sea.

The fish trade in the late Middle Ages

In the late Middle Ages, Danish kings attempted, through regulation, to concentrate trade and industry in the towns. Exclusive trading zones were established around the towns of Jutland in the fourteenth century, restricting trading rights to burghers alone. Thus, in 1462, Aalborg was given a monopoly of trade within a zone extending four Danish miles or 28 kilometres outside the city.[2] The large estates around the Limfjord did, however, retain the right to trade independently. In the 1400s, the noble family Gyldenstjerne of Ågård in Hanherred supplemented their income from cattle farming and herring fishing in the Limfjord with timber imports from Norway[3], and the Gyldenstjernes became one of the richest and most powerful families of the period. There is no doubt that peasants also maintained a lively rural trade for a long period. However, the peasants of Central and Northern Jutland lost their right to engage independently in the cattle trade following their defeat in the religious and social unrest of 1534. The civil war left the peasants without leaders, partly through executions immediately following the end of the uprising, and partly in financial terms through fines imposed on the peasants and the revocation of freehold rights held by the rioting peasants. On the other hand, the peasants' defeat favoured the North Jutland nobility, which made full use of its privileges in the ever-increasing trade.[4] The landed estates in Hanherred appear to have profited even more than others because they were able to use the rich water meadows towards the Fjord for fattening cattle while also profiting from trade with Norway. Through several generations, the Griis family of Slettegård held positions as Danish navy officers as well as being merchants trading on Norway with their own ships.[5]

In the fifteenth century, the fishing industry on the Limfjord seems to have become ever more important alongside the big fishery in the Sound between the coasts of Scania and Zealand. Spring was the season for herring fishing on the Fjord and autumn in the Sound. The Fjord fishery thus filled a gap in the year for many merchants. Salt imports to the Scandinavian fishing industries were largely restricted to the Sound and the Limfjord. In other Scandinavian herring fishery centres, the herring appears to have been mainly wind-dried, despite the fact that this method is less well suited to the oily herring.[6] It is not known why the use of salt was not more widespread but concentrated in the Danish fishing industries, but it must be linked to the German merchants' dominant position in the salt trade and their similarly strong placing in the Danish herring trade. The Norwegian herring trade did not become of interest to German merchants until the second half of the sixteenth century, with the result that salted Limfjord herring was in demand everywhere in Northern Europe, although its quality was not as good as that of the Scanian herring.

In principle, the king had declared the Fjord free fishing waters in 1459 but special property rights developed based

Fig. 12.2: The region of Northern Jutland

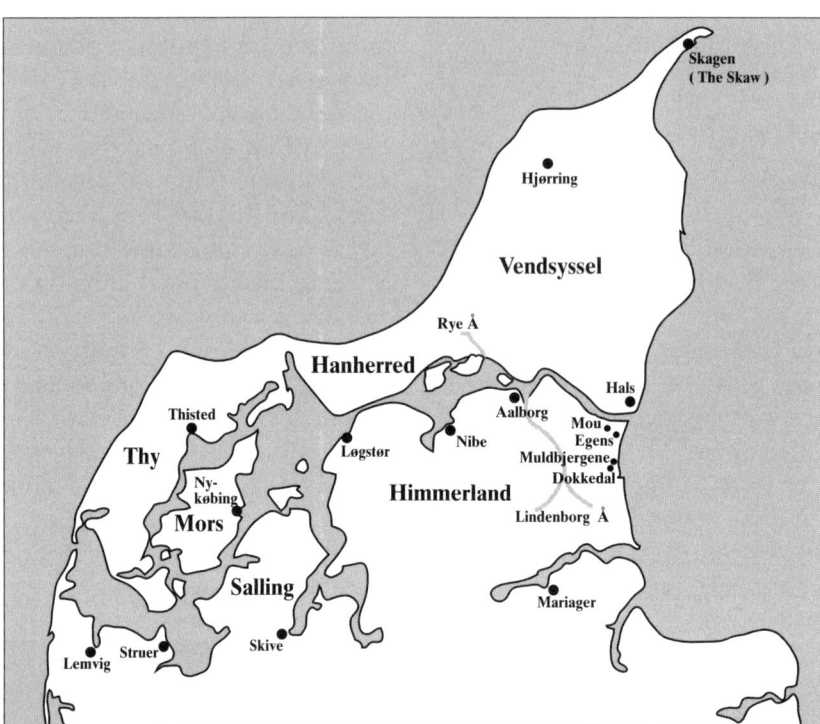

on the design of the fishing tools. The use of shore seine required access to good hauling sites, which had to be leased. Fixed gear such as traps and pound nets, which were the types most commonly used, led to the development of permanent user rights to the catching sites. These rights were mainly held by abbeys around the Fjord, which leased their right of use to peasant fishermen.[7] Towns such as Nibe and Løgstør owe their origins, at least in part, to the herring. Around 1500, new fishing hamlets arose along the Kattegat coast, namely Hals, Egense, Mou, Dokkedal and Muldbjergene. They attracted merchants from several East Jutland cities who came to trade. However, Aalborg succeeded in securing almost absolute control of the market, thanks to royal privileges.[8]

The export of herring was dominated by the salt merchants, i.e., the Lübeck merchants. Lists of members of Guds Legems Laug, the Corpus Christi Guild formed by Aalborg merchants, show that half its members were German in the period 1536-1575. In 1518, almost all the 2,600 barrels of herring exported were cleared through customs by German traders.[9] Exports may have been lower than normal that year. Accounts from the cities of Danzig and Lübeck show that the two cities each received 6-7,000 barrels of herring from Aalborg in other years. In comparison, Lübeck's total imports from all of Denmark in the 1490s were just over 14,000 barrels.[10] The figures indicate that at this low tide for the Sound fishery around 1500, fishing on the Limfjord may have been almost as important as that of the Sound. The increase in the number of fishing hamlets on the Limfjord during the sixteenth century also indicates a growth in fishing.[11]

The Hanseatic merchants distributed the Scania herring on the Western and Central European markets, while the Limfjord herring was sold mainly in the Baltic regions, Russia and on the domestic market. This difference was due to the high price of the Scania herring, which could only be maintained through quality labelling and stringent control of the salting. In 1509, a barrel from Scania cost 16 marks or the same as three oxen. The Limfjord herring was cheaper. The Scania herring was a full-fat autumn herring, which was considered the best product anywhere in Northern Europe. The price difference was due to the higher fat content of the autumn herring, but was also a result of the skilful marketing of their trademark product by the Hanseatic merchants. The sales patterns for herring from Scania and the Limfjord reflect differences in wealth between Western and Eastern Europe. The high prices exclude the possibility that barrel-salted herring may have been a staple food for ordinary people. Common people would only have been able to afford dry or perhaps lightly salted herring. The international fish trade was a highly specialised trade in luxury goods for the rich, especially for use in Lent.

The last quarter of the 1500s shows fewer German names on the register of members of the guild. During the same period, complaints appear from Aalborg merchants that German merchants obstructed their trade in Baltic harbours.[12] The Aalborg merchants were evidently taking over an increasing share of the trade, and therefore met with resistance in the German harbours.

The golden age of the city of Aalborg and the Limfjord estates, 1550-1650

After the mid-sixteenth century, Hanseatic dominance was replaced by a period of Dutch prominence. The decline in German financial power made room for the rise of local merchants, and in international trade there were many examples of fruitful collaboration between local merchants, landowners and Dutch merchant houses. Apart from fish, the trading goods were the traditional mainstay of trade, grain, timber and cattle.

As late as the mid-sixteenth century, trade was almost completely dominated by interests outside Scandinavia and increasingly from the Netherlands. Dutch ships took Norwegian timber and Danish grain to Amsterdam from where it was distributed as dictated by the market. Many Danish and even more Norwegian sailors sailed on Dutch vessels and learned navigation. Income in Norway was so dependent on Dutch ships that hunger broke out in Southern Norwegian cities when the ships stayed away in 1569 because of war.[13] The new element, however, was the growing Danish-Norwegian trade across the Kattegat and the Skagerrak. Although big landowners reaped immediate results, it was the cities which stood to gain most in the longer term from this major new development in trade. Trade in the Dual Monarchy's own resources, timber, grain and fish, created the basis of growth in shipping experienced by many towns

217

from the mid-sixteenth century. The government made it a strategic issue to make the country self-sufficient in timber and grain, thus providing the key factor in the development of Danish-Norwegian shipping for more than two hundred years.

Lübeck gradually lost its influence in the fish trade to merchants of Aalborg and Marstrand, on the neighbouring coast of Båhuslen. In a similar manner, the exchange of Danish grain for Norwegian timber led to the gradual erosion of Hanseatic dominance along the Norwegian coast. Dutch trade did not exert the same direct influence on local trade and often developed in a pattern of mutual advantage with Danish, Norwegian and Swedish merchants. The period of Dutch primacy in the world economy therefore coincided with a period of growing regional independence in Scandinavia.

The development of the Kattegat and Skagerrak sea trade

In the early sixteenth century, Danish waters were dominated by foreign ships. Some Danish merchants and noble families did, however, manage to compete successfully in international trade, and from the 1560s the Danish sea trade was in steady growth, benefiting both from the flourishing international market climate and from royal favours. The dual monarchy's breach with the Hanseatic powers was followed by the liberalization of trade and better law enforcement, an example being King Frederik the Second's Shipping Act of 1560. While Dutch merchants often stepped in where Hanseatic merchants had been forced out, the growth in demand in Amsterdam, the new Western European centre, meant that Dutch merchants needed Danish and Norwegian middlemen, who came to form the basis of a new merchant class. Local merchants were supplemented by immigrant Dutch merchants, fleeing religious persecution in their homeland. Many of these became naturalised citizens of Elsinore (Helsingør), Aalborg, Århus, Ribe and the Skaw (Skagen).[14]

The scene was thus set for accumulation of capital in Danish and Norwegian towns, which gradually developed their own trading routes. This liberalization was first felt in Danish cities, which acquired their own ships in the 1500s, while the Norwegian timber trade did not pass into Norwegian hands until after the mid-1600s.[15]

The development in shipping from the Skagerrak-Kattegat coasts through the Sound is reflected in the customs accounts for the Sound. In the mid-sixteenth century, the Swedish town of Lödöse, the precursor of Gothenburg (Göteborg), occupied a relatively strong position compared with the surrounding Danish-Norwegian harbours, but Båhuslen (Marstrand) and Northern Jutland (Aalborg) also had considerable trade. After 1590, Marstrand's and Lödöse's exports began to stagnate, while Aalborg continued its growth and became the clear leader in Danish shipping, followed by Varberg. The strength of Aalborg's position is indicated by the fact that it was the only harbour in Jutland capable of receiving ships greater than approximately 200 register tonnes. Aalborg had been sacked after 1534 as punishment for having been the centre of the North Jutland peasant riots, but at the end of the century it had risen to become the most important harbour outside the Sound.[16] Its registered ships were all engaged in south-going traffic either to ports along the Sound or the German cities on the Baltic. This information serves as historical evidence of a burgeoning sea trade in the Kattegat-Skagerrak region, but it cannot, of course, be used to determine whether this early trade was accompanied by an increase in trade within the region itself. We also have very little knowledge of what the ships carried in their hulls. To answer these questions, we must piece together a picture from other sources.

The herring fishery off Båhuslen

The Norwegian herring trade played a crucial role in the growth of Aalborg in the latter half of the sixteenth century. At regular intervals, rich hauls of herring could be taken along the Scandinavian coasts, when shoals of Atlantic or Baltic herring came close to the coast. In the years 1570-1590, Båhuslen experienced a herring boom with several hundred buyers on the coast every year. Thanks to accounts kept by the customs authorities of the Sound, we know that annually 40,000 to 70,000 barrels of herring passed south into the Baltic Sea through the Sound. Perhaps as many passed westwards into the North Sea. Indications are that this was where French and Spanish salt was first used in the conservation of fish in Norway on any major scale. The import of expensive foreign salt is a clear indication that merchants thought the Båhus herring valuable. However, the traditional method of drying the herring continued in use.[17]

In addition to foreign merchants, the fish trade also attracted Danish and Norwegian burghers and peasants in large numbers. Favours granted by the king appear to have had the effect of shifting part of the trade into Danish-Norwegian hands. A land register from 1589 shows that merchants from cities such as Fredrikstad, Aalborg, Flensburg, Sønderborg and Copenhagen owned several trading booths in the major fishing hamlets. Some booths were owned by local merchants from Marstrand, but merchants came from a string of cities around the Skagerrak and the Kattegat, including Oslo and Tønsberg in the north, Lödöse and Varberg in the east, and Elsinore, Kalundborg, Odense, Kerteminde and Skælskør in the south.[18] The fishermen were based in more or less permanent hamlets in the Båhuslen archipelago, and the work attracted thousands of inland peasants and labourers. Merchants from Denmark even brought their own fishermen.

Peasant traders from Båhuslen and Halland in Aalborg

The building boom in the period of brisk Danish economic growth c.1550-1620 provided work for numerous small peasant-skippers. The area around Viken, or the Oslo Fjord, was covered in forest, but as indicated by the Sound customs accounts, exports from this area only began in earnest after 1590. The race for timber first hit Båhuslen, where the forests were soon felled. Burghers and peasants from the region were under

219

royal orders to deliver each year's first shipment of timber to Copenhagen, where timber was always in short supply. The timber was also used in the construction of large castle projects, Elsinore (1540), Riberhus (1545), Aalborghus (1547), Koldinghus and Dronningborg (1551) and Kronborg (1580s). Frequent fires in the cities caused a steady demand for timber. When Nykøbing Mors in the Limfjord was razed by fire, new timber was bought in Båhuslen. Felling proceeded from the coast, which gradually assumed the treeless heath-covered profile which it retained well into the twentieth century. Around 1630, Båhuslen was considered to have been fully culled, and any timber exports still provided by the region came mainly from inland Sweden.[19]

The inner regions of Mid- and South Halland still held large forest resources by the mid-seventeenth century. Much timber was, however, also being taken from the border zone to Sweden, especially from Västergötland. Western Sweden was thus increasingly opening up towards the Danish-Norwegian coast.[20] Halland became a borderland between the Danish sea and the Swedish inland, and this was an advantage for the region's trade. The building craze led to a growth in the number of peasant traders to and from Northern Halland. In 1610-11 large quantities of lime were shipped from Mariager and Akershus for the construction of the fortification of Varberg.[21] Aalborg was not the primary destination for Halland trading vessels since Copenhagen must have been more important, but the accounts show a strong link, to which Halland contributed timber, rocks, horses and more, the ships probably returning with herring from the Limfjord in spring. The traffic increased in the 1580s, and during the 1600s boats from Båhuslen also began to arrive in Aalborg in increasing numbers. On the other hand, no Scanian traders appear in the accounts. They preferred the short-range trade across the Sound, mainly to Copenhagen.

Trade suffered heavily in the wars of the 1640-1650s, but Halland vessels called regularly at Aalborg as late as the early 1660s. These were medium-sized ships, the Halland vessels being slightly bigger than those from Båhuslen, averaging 28 as against 24 register tonnes. The size of the typical decked vessel for the Kattegat and Skagerrak traffic remained quite stable at this level until the middle of the nineteenth century. It was far bigger than the quite small open vessels of five-six register tonnes which dominated traffic across the Sound.

The trade from Northern Halland to Aalborg was dominated by certain parishes, especially Släp. The neighbouring parish of Onsala, on the other hand, which had even bigger ships and more men, sent only very few ships to Aalborg. Their ships were probably engaged in more distant trade.[22]

Aalborg as an international city

In the latter half of the sixteenth century, Aalborg rose to a position of power where the town may reasonably be seen as a regional centre for the Northern Kattegat and Skagerrak coasts. Merchants of the city were represented with booths everywhere from Båhuslen to Bergen. Aalborg controlled the big herring fishing industry in the Limfjord and held a major share of the Båhuslen fishery in the second half of the sixteenth century.[23] Together with the large fleet from the island of Læsø, the city's own merchant fleet took the timber transport between Norway and Denmark in hand. Aalborg's growth as documented in the customs accounts from the Sound gathered particular momentum after 1570, at the same time as the Båhuslen herring boom began.

After 1600, Aalborg became heavily involved in the Danish export of cattle. Thousands of oxen were fattened around the Limfjord and in Vendsyssel before being driven overland to markets in Holland and Germany. This trade generated great wealth in the city. When King Christian IV established three privileged wine and salt companies in Jutland in 1622, Ribe and Århus had to raise the required capital from a string of small investments made by the two cities and surrounding market towns. Each merchant contributed on average only 85 dalers. In contrast, more than two thirds of the capital of the Aalborg company was contributed by the city's own merchants, each making an investment of over 200 dalers.[24] Clearly, Aalborg was Denmark's second largest city at the time, not only in terms of population, but also in economic terms. The city's wealth had been founded on the Limfjord fishery. It increased significantly from earnings generated in the big Båhuslen fishing boom period 1570-1590, and after 1600 on new income from the cattle trade.

To this trade in the region's own products should be added the city's share in the transit traffic between Eastern and Western Europe. A small number of big merchants, among them Jens Bang, traded on Riga in flax and hemp and sent their own ships with timber from Norwegian harbours to Spain or Portugal. But most merchants were involved in the grain trade. They bought up grain partly locally, but mainly in Riga, Königsberg and Danzig, selling it to the Netherlands. Our knowledge of this trade is, unfortunately, scant and sparse. There are no customs accounts from Aalborg for this period, but future studies in foreign archives, not least in the newly opened Baltic archives, should throw light on the extent of this trade. It would nevertheless be reasonable to assume that Aalborg rose above its regional role between c. 1570 and 1660 to become a significant factor in the wider trade pattern of the North and Baltic Seas.

Sweden severs the links across the Kattegat

Just as close trade links began to encircle the Danish-Norwegian domestic waters, Sweden conquered the entire eastern coastline of the Kattegat and the Sound during the wars of the mid-1600s. The Swedish aim was to crush the Danish fleet's control of the Kattegat and to open the Swedish economy to the European market with exports of timber and iron from Western Sweden. In an attempt to establish a gateway to the North Sea, Lödöse and later Gothenburg were founded by the Swedish king as spearheads against the Danish-Norwegian maritime dominance. The Danish strategy was the exact opposite: to strengthen the economic importance of cities such as Aalborg and Varberg on either side of the Kattegat. King Christian

IV had built strong fortifications for the defence of Marstrand and Varberg. With the peace agreements following the wars of 1644-45 and 1657-58, the political map was completely changed and the Kattegat-Skagerrak was no longer a domestic Danish-Norwegian sea.

The Swedish historian Erik Grill has stressed that there were other than purely military reasons for this change in the political map of the Kattegat and the Skagerrak. His studies of customs accounts have shown that towns such as Varberg and Halmstad had catchment areas stretching far inland beyond the Swedish border. The annual market in Varberg was thus the meeting point not only for Danish fishermen, but also for peasants from Västergötland and overland traders from Borås. In return for fish and salt from the Skaw, Aalborg and Båhuslen, and salmon from the Ätran river at Falkenberg, the Västergötland and North Halland peasants sold butter. The Halland peasants sold homespun cloth to itinerant buyers from Borås and bought iron wares. Merchants in Varberg bought tar for export from Västergötland.[25] Large parts of the Swedish hinterland had thus turned their face towards the Kattegat coast. The question of who was to control this coast was therefore not only a military issue, but also very much an economic one. The alternative to a Swedish conquest would have been continued Danish economic infiltration deep into Swedish territory.

The loss of the Scania region was felt not only by the Danish state in general, but more particularly by Aalborg. The Swedish king pursued the same goal as the Danish king: the concentration of trade and shipping in the cities; and this policy was more easily enforced in the conquered regions. True, changing Swedish governors-general did realize that it would harm the peasant populations along the coast if their sea trade was hampered by restrictions, but Gothenburg claimed its full city privileges. From 1684, peasant coastal traders were only allowed to engage in domestic trade. For a brief period, they evaded this export ban by fetching timber from Østfold in Norway and continued their traditional trade on Denmark,[26] and their contacts with Denmark and Norway were never completely broken. They were allowed to fetch lime for public building projects from both Akershus and Aalborg, as was regularly documented throughout the eighteenth century,[27] and indeed we shall see below that the fish trade increased through the eighteenth century.

All in all, however, the east-west connection across the Kattegat had ceased by the end of the 1600s, reducing Aalborg's catchment area to Northern Jutland alone. Despite this setback, the city maintained its position as Denmark's second largest provincial harbour. It was saved by the fact that it was able to replace its international freight traffic with a crucial role as the central link in the sale of North Jutland grain to the Norwegian market.

Aalborg's safe position

The years around 1650-60 form a marked hiatus in the history of Aalborg. The Swedish occupational force in Aalborg in 1644 imposed heavy taxes on the biggest merchants. The merchants fell deeply into debts with the Hamburg merchants, and as direct trade of oxen between the landlords and foreign merchants increased, the city's cattle trade ceased. At the same time, Aalborg was being squeezed out of the grain trade in Danzig, and the city abandoned its trade with the Netherlands, its grain dealers turning instead to trade in Danish grain which was cheaper and of poorer quality, but which found a growing market in Norway after 1660. As a result of this restructuring, the biggest merchant houses disappeared and Aalborg's merchant fleet lost its pride, three vessels of more than 200 register tonnes each which had traded on the Mediterranean Sea. But despite the fact that the city was forced to abandon its international contacts, its medium-sized merchants managed well in the trade with Norway. It may not have yielded the highest of profits, but it was a safe and easy trade, and the city was ideally placed for it, enabling Aalborg to manage better than most Danish provincial towns after 1660.[28]

The basis of the city's power was its complete control of shipping in the Limfjord. Because the Fjord's western outlet had sanded up, all in- and outgoing traffic had to pass Aalborg and pay a duty there. This gave the city a firm grip on the entire Limfjord region, and the Aalborg merchants built up a finely meshed buying network reaching into all parts of the Fjord. Most of the transport from the west was carried out by local small traders with small flat-bottomed cogs capable of navigating the shallows around Løgstør. At the eastern end of the Fjord, Aalborg trading booths dominated the entire trade. The merchants erected booths along the river Rye Å, which was navigable far into Western Vendsyssel.[29] These outlying booths explain why coastal trade was of very modest scope along the Vendsyssel coastline in the seventeenth century.

Aalborg was the largest provincial city in Denmark. A census taken in 1672 shows that the city had over 4,000 inhabitants, a few hundred more than Elsinore and Odense. In North Jutland, the Skaw and Thisted came second with populations of c. 1,000. Hjørring and Sæby had 7-800 each. Most towns had suffered heavy decline caused by incessant war taxes and hostile occupations, but church registers show that Aalborg had a small but steady birth surplus throughout the seventeenth century.[30] Aalborg's relative strength can be seen in a series of comparable contemporary customs and tax figures.[31] The city's own fleet was considerable, but not unusually large compared to the size of the population. Throughout the eighteenth century it was the second largest provincial fleet, only surpassed by Århus and then later by Dragør.[32] The city's strength was first and foremost the fact that it was able to attract a very high turnover of trade. While 80% of the turnover of Århus harbour in 1733 was on its own ships, this only applied to 32% of Aalborg's; 25% was on Norwegian vessels and 16% on ships from Copenhagen. Swedish and other foreign vessels accounted for 8% each.[33] The city amassed a large fortune. Of the 2% war tax on wealth levied on cities, we see that Aalborg paid 13,823 *rigsdaler* in 1717, while Århus only paid 6,917 and Odense 4,441 rigsdaler.[34] The city possessed solid wealth, and while other cities declined heavily during the century, Aalborg stood its ground better than any other city. The basis for the city's wealth was its trade links across the Skagerrak

Regional integration

and with Lübeck. The herring trade had created the vast fortunes, while the grain trade provided their strong foundation. The grain was sold to Norway, while the herring went to Copenhagen and Lübeck.

Christian Magnus Olrik's prize-winning thesis from 1773 for the Royal Danish Agricultural Society on Aalborg's trade contains comprehensive customs accounts from the city. His work consists mainly of reprints of lists of goods, and on this basis it is possible to gain an insight into the city's exports. Northern Jutland's grain surplus was subject to considerable fluctuation, but the usual surplus appears to have been 30-50,000 barrels for export to Norway. In 1769, two-thirds of the exported grain went to cities in South-Eastern Norway, while 14% went to the Agder-Telemark towns of South-Western Norway and 20% to Bergen or Trondheim.

If grain production was unstable, the herring kept faith with no one. But when it came, it was the city's largest foreign export. Herring catches appear to have fluctuated between a low point of 5,000 barrels and a high point of 50,000 barrels per year. Trade was fairly equally divided between Danish and foreign destinations up to and including the 1750s.

When the herring trade declined in the middle of the century, the city compensated by establishing a number of major works, including a weaving mill, a tobacco factory, a hatter, a soapery and a sugar refinery, thus becoming the biggest industrial town outside Copenhagen. It might appear that Aalborg was moving away from its old trading basis. But not so: Norway was, as usual, the key market. This applied, for example, to the weaving mills, which consisted of cottage industries in the city's catchment area, where flax from the Baltic regions was turned into linen products intended mainly for Norway. Olrik's statistics show that after the loss of the herring trade, Aalborg more than ever gained its profits from its trade with Norway. On the other hand, the city had nothing to contribute to the export trade outside the Danish-Norwegian kingdom. Imports comprised mainly flax, hemp and small wares from the Baltics and salt from the Mediterranean. The modest trade with Sweden was predominantly carried out by Swedish vessels and was almost exclusively directed at Gothenburg; exports comprised mainly grain and wool while tar was almost the only import.[35] Thus, Aalborg had its sight set single-mindedly on its traditional role as the Danish connection to Norway.

The north coast

The coastal trade from the open beaches of Northern Jutland, i.e. Thisted and Hjørring customs districts, carried little weight on a national scale, but it was an important local factor. The main point of interest of the North Jutland coastal trade from a cultural-historical perspective is its strong element of 'traditional' peasant trading and its strong contacts to Southern Norway. Taking a broader view, we must not, however, forget that no matter how traditional it may seem, and however much its form may resemble the late-medieval rural trade from Halland and Nedenes, it was a product of the economic possibilities and options of its time. It arose in response to the struggle of the peasants in the seventeenth century to evade the control exerted by Aalborg over the Limfjord, which was only made possible by the need in Norway for cheap bread grain. To the peasants themselves, it was a late supplement to their old main occupation, the raising of cattle. Although cattle exports declined heavily during the eighteenth century, the domestic market for meat remained, and this was particularly important for the regions around the Limfjord. But to peasants whose main income derived from the production of grain, the Norwegian trade gained ever-increasing importance.

The Limfjord fishing industry, 1690-1808

The decline of the Båhuslen herring fishery after 1590 was followed almost immediately by an increase in the herring fishery in Western Norway but catches there were much smaller. While at its peak in 1585 Båhuslen had exported 70,000 barrels of herring east through the Sound, and an unknown number of barrels westwards, the exports from Western Norway reached a maximum of only 18,000 barrels in 1642.[36] In other words, the market had room for much more.

The Limfjord herring appear to have fluctuated in quantity in 15-20 year intervals during the seventeenth century. At first catches increased, but in the 1620s a decline set in, and in Nibe about 72 of the city's c. 200 houses stood empty. In the 1640s the good fishing returned, but around 1655 fishing was again very poor. The king's herring salter in Nibe had a monopoly on buying herring two days a week at market price. For the period of more than 55 years, for which figures have survived, he bought an average of 400 barrels of herring per year. This figure may presumably be multiplied by at least three to include trade on the remaining days, thus yielding a minimum turnover on the Nibe market of 1,200 barrels a year. Fluctuations were extreme. In some years at least 3,000 barrels were sold, in other years only 200. The long-term trend was, however, stable.[37] To these figures should be added catches from other sites such as Mou and Hals at the mouth of the Fjord, and the fishing hamlets around Aalborg, constituting a total export of perhaps about 60,000 barrels at its peak.

In contrast to Båhuslen, the Limfjord fisheries thus provided the basis for some exports throughout the seventeenth century. In 1652, Aalborg exported approximately 50,000 barrels of herring. In 1667, only 2,800 barrels were loaded onto ships for export from Aalborg, but after that, exports grew steadily from 8,000 to 14,000 barrels through the 1670s. More than half of these exports went to Norway.[38] From 1690, fishing enjoyed a genuine upturn, leading to exports of up to 30-40,000 barrels around the turn of the century.[39] A new period of wealth had arrived. It was marked by the fact that ownership of hauling sites in the Fjord passed from landowners to merchants in Aalborg and Nibe.[40] The Limfjord herring fishery was completely dominated by local merchants in the first half of the eighteenth century. Trade in Nibe grew after Nibe had gained independent export rights in 1699 and was granted full urban privileges in 1727,[41] but Aalborg continued, now as before, in control of the major share of the trading activities.

In 1706, 48% of the 53,000 barrels of salted Limfjord herring went to Danish cities, 9% to Norway and 43% abroad, undoubtedly mainly to Lübeck and Gothenburg. When the Swedish government later placed an import duty of 4 *riksdalar* per barrel on salted herring,[42] Swedish exports must have declined. The dried herring, almost 1,800 barrels, was almost all sold on the Danish market. On the other hand, fresh herring with a value of 153 riksdalar were almost all exported.[43] If the value is converted using more recent prices from Olrik's table, the 120 barrels of fresh herring comprised a decidedly modest share. Nevertheless, the buying up of fresh fish was a cause of dissatisfaction.

Buyers of the unprocessed herring came from Sweden, crossing the Kattegat loaded with ballast as early as March. Existing customs accounts for 1732-34 show that about 100 vessels arrived in Aalborg harbour each year from Southern Halland and Northern Scania in order to buy spring herring. Their purchases comprised 8-9% of the harbour's exports by tonnage. Calculated as numbers of arrivals, the Swedish traders were an even stronger presence. As they sailed in quite small vessels, every sixth boat entering the harbour was Swedish.[44] These buyers continued the pattern of trade across the Kattegat which was evident already in Aalborg's harbour accounts of 1574-1664. The only difference to the picture these two or three generations later was the fact that the Swedish traders no longer dealt in building materials such as timber and lime, but only in fish. This pattern of a regional herring trade across the Kattegat continued until far into the nineteenth century. It is interesting that the Swedes always bought the fresh non-processed herring, just as they did when buying haddock and plaice. The raw fish was the cheapest, and this was what could be sold on the Swedish market. As late as 1757, Swedish traders bought up about 50 barrels. The burghers of Aalborg and Nibe tried to enforce a ban on the export of fresh herring in order to force the Swedes to buy salted goods, but as Swedish fishing was growing at the time, the attempt only brought exports to a complete stop.[45]

Bohuslän's herring exports to Denmark

Fishermen of Båhuslen, which had now become the Swedish Bohuslän, began to take large quantities of herring in 1756 at the same time as bad years began both in Western Norway and the Limfjord. Because of poor fishing, the Aalborg merchants sold their boats and fishing rights to fishermen along the fjord. Trade across the Kattegat reached a peak in the 1790s, with the supply by the Bohuslän traders of fresh herring to Aalborg, the old herring city.[46]

The Danish government and the Aalborg merchants considered this trade a dangerous obstacle to any future progress for the Limfjord fisheries. An order was therefore issued in 1774 that salted and dried fish intended for Denmark must normally be bought in Norway.

The order appears to have had immediate effect, for Gothenburg's export records for 1776 show no exports to Denmark. The salted herring was sold first and foremost to England, Germany and Russia. However, the order had no effect on the trade in fresh fish. In 1778, Bohuslän's exports to Denmark and Norway were estimated at 30,000 barrels by the Swedish authorities.[47] This led to a request by the prefect of North Jutland for a general ban on the Swedish herring trade. The quantities entered in the customs accounts were not, however, substantial enough for the Chancellery to approve the request. The traffic was not stopped, therefore, until the Swedish king placed a ban on the export of fresh herring.[48]

The problems with the Swedish trade in fresh herring were identical to the problems Aalborg had experienced: the small traders in fish profited by it while the owners of large salting houses lost their supplies.

The war of 1808-1814

During the Napoleonic Wars, keeping up supplies to Norway became a critical issue. According to a British prisoner of war in Aalborg, more than half the ships leaving Aalborg for Norway in the winter of 1808-09 were captured in the Skagerrak and taken to Gothenburg.[49]

Following the British capture of the Danish naval fleet and the stationing of British men-of-war in the Skagerrak, supplies to Norway were under serious threat. In 1809, the Norwegian Provisioning Commission was established with its main seat in Aalborg, from where it was responsible for the coordination of the buying up and shipping of grain. The best option available to grain ships bound for Norway was to leave from the coast of North Jutland, where they had a chance of avoiding the British blockade and the Swedish privateers. But getting the supplies through was a problem. Famine broke out in Norway in the winter of 1809-10, costing some 7,000 lives.[50]

The war brought an end to 400 years of trade between Norway and Denmark, thus imposing an entirely new set of conditions on Aalborg's trade. Following the arrival of peace in 1815, an optimistic belief blossomed everywhere in Europe that the golden times of seafaring would return. The many ships lost during the war years were replaced by the purchase of used vessels or the building of new ones. For a couple of years, the need for reconstruction led to a growth in the international market, but then stagnation followed. One large merchant house after the other was forced to close, having committed themselves too heavily in their investments. The depression hit cities and rural districts throughout Scandinavia. Despite the fact that total tonnage only fell to the level of the relatively good years of the 1790s, the recession was felt much more keenly because it was accompanied by depreciations of assets and a seemingly endless string of bankruptcies.[51] The recession not only affected shipping, which had been accustomed to large fluctuations due to wartime conditions, but extended to the very foundation of trade as the demand for farm produce and timber fell and remained low throughout the 1820s.[52]

In the years 1815-1820, trade as a whole between Denmark and Norway declined. This was not directly due to the separation of the two states, but a result of the politics pursued by the defeated leaders. The Danish government decided to treat Norway as an unfavoured state, i.e. to add a 50% duty on imports from Norway. Norway reacted by prohibiting the import of Danish corn brandy. Brandy was the biggest industry of the Danish provincial towns, and the halving of production which was the direct consequence of the ban contributed to making the Danish agricultural crisis deep and long-lasting.[53] Nevertheless, the economic consequences of the splitting-up of the dual monarchy should not be overstated. As noted, grain exports to Norway had been around half a million barrels a year around 1780, and from 1820 until the mid-1800s the trade was again stable at an average of 580,000 barrels a year.[54]

The Danish provincial merchants who had controlled the trade from the Kattegat harbours to Norway were forced to their knees by the low prices of farm produce, especially grain. But despite the high customs duties that applied between Denmark and Norway, Norwegians had a relative advantage in being able to fetch meat, bacon and butter within such a short distance. The small-trader traffic between Nedenes and Northern Jutland which had started during the years of famine therefore continued to play an important part in trade between the two countries.

This did not, however, benefit employment in Northern Jutland. Local merchants were ruined by the duty levied on Norwegian timber, which destroyed their best trade. Aalborg's businessmen in particular had had their attention focused on Norway, and employment in Aalborg's industrial sector alone fell from 400 to 100 men between 1810 and 1835.[55]

North-Western Jutland turns to Britain

Thyland's small sea trade received a serious blow in the Napoleonic wars, but was on its way back when a natural catastrophe changed everything. In a storm in 1825, the North Sea broke through the isthmus Agger Tange, which had blocked the westernmost outlet from the Limfjord. The breach was gradually deepened and stabilised. After 1835, when larger vessels were able to navigate the Agger channel on a regular basis, the entire trading structure of North-Western Jutland was reorganized.[56] In one blow, the towns Lemvig, Thisted, Nykøbing Mors, Struer and Skive shed the fetters of the control which Aalborg had exerted on the Limfjord traffic. They also attracted the trade which had previously been the province of small craft operating from the open coast.

The West Limfjord towns suddenly found themselves well placed as protected harbours with direct access to the North Sea. In the harbour statistics of 1851, these cities already formed a distinct group in their strong orientation towards England. The shallow Løgstør Grunde still barred access to the eastern reaches of the Fjord for larger ships, but the channel Frederik den VII's Kanal, opened in 1861, allowed unimpeded passage for all ships. The Limfjord towns were thus set to enter the international trade between the North and Baltic Seas. The first coastal traders from Klitmøller moved to Thisted before 1840, and around 1850, the coastal trade from Thy and Vester Hanherred had already practically stopped.[57]

The early sea trade developed by the

Limfjord towns was based on the export of the region's own grain surplus to England, but gradually the vessels became a part of the international trade route pattern. Big merchants equipped schooners or brigs which took coal from England to Russia and the Mediterranean. Return goods were timber and grain from Russia and sulphur from Italy. Over a couple of decades, a prosperous seafaring culture developed in the formerly isolated and sleepy Limfjord towns. In 1860, Thisted was Jutland's fourth largest shipping centre with 65 vessels, surpassed only by Fanø, Aalborg and Århus.

The Limfjord region disintegrates

Aalborg had lost its strategic role in the Limfjord trade after the opening of Agger, and the declining trade with Norway had deprived the city of its most important market. Between 1840 and 1860, demographic growth in Aalborg was slower than for the other provincial towns in Denmark. The building of the railway line to Aalborg in 1869 and the dredging of Hals Barre at the eastern entry to the Limfjord in 1883-89 gave renewed vitality to the city and its harbour, but the city's position as the centre of North Jutland and the connecting link of the Danish-Norwegian dual monarchy was lost forever. Aalborg's infant steamship fleet became part of the Copenhagen-based DFDS shipping line in 1885.[58] Aalborg, on the other hand, saw renewed growth towards the close of the century, not in shipping, but in industry, establishing itself as a major provincial town with heavy industries whose capital and sea trade were dependent on Copenhagen. Aalborg's heyday as a regional centre for the Limfjord and indeed for the entire Kattegat-Skagerrak region had passed.

Notes

1 Poul Holm: *Kystfolk. Kontakter og sammenhænge over Kattegat og Skagerrak, ca. 1550-1914*, Esbjerg 1991. Poul Holm: Havskab og kystkultur, *Den jyske historiker*, vol. 68, pp. 37-50, 1995. Niels Steensgaard: Slotsholmen og verdenshavet. Kan adelsvældens og enevældens Danmark placeres i det kapitalistiske verdenssystem, *Søfart, Politik, Identitet – tilegnet Ole Feldbæk*, ed. Hans Jeppesen et. al., Viborg 1996, pp. 81-89.
2 *Danmarks Gamle Købstadslovgivning*, I-V, ed. Erik Kroman, Copenhagen 1951-61, p. 278.
3 Jørgen Würtz Sørensen: *Bondeoprør i Danmark 1438-1441*, Odense 1983.
4 Lars Tvede-Jensen: Clementsfejden. Det sidste regulære bondeoprør i Danmark, *Til kamp for friheden*, eds. Anders Bøgh, Jørgen Würtz Sørensen and Lars Tvede-Jensen, Aalborg 1988, pp. 232-50.
5 Kr. Andersen: Sandflugten, *Landet mod Nordvest. Thy og Vester Han Herred*, eds. C. Brunsgaard and Henry E. Pedersen, Copenhagen 1946.
6 *Kulturhistorisk Leksikon for Nordisk Middelalder*, 4, Copenhagen 1959, pp. 343-45, Emne: Fisketilvirkning. Knut Helle: *Norge blir en stat 1130-1319*, Oslo 1974, p. 170.
7 Holger Rasmussen: *Limfjordsfiskeriet før 1825. Sædvane og centraldirigering (Folkelivs studier 2)*, Copenhagen 1968.
8 Carl Klitgaard: *Aalborg Købmænd gennem 500 Aar*, Aalborg 1931, pp. 29-31.
9 Bjørn Poulsen: Fra middelalder til renæssance: Vækst og strukturændringer i søfarten på Aalborg 1518-1583, *Søfart, Politik, Identitet – tilegnet Ole Feldbæk* (see note 1), pp. 43-64.
10 D. Schäfer: *Das Buch des lübeckischen Vogts auf Schonen*, Halle 1887, pp. cxlii.
11 Hugo Matthiessen: *Middelalderlige Byer*, 1927, pp. 146ff.
12 E. Ladewig Petersen: *Dansk social historie*, III, Viborg 1980, pp. 203-05.

13 Albert Olsen: Handelen, *Holland-Danmark. Forbindelserne mellem de to Lande gennem Tiderne*, eds. K. Fabricius, L. L. Hammerich and V. Lorenzen, Copenhagen 1945, p. 166.
14 Louis Bobé: Personlige Forbindelser, *Holland-Danmark* (see note 13), pp. 360-370.
15 Albert Olsen: Almindelig Skibsfart og Søhandel i XVII-XIX Aarhundrede, *Danmarks Søfart og Søhandel*, I, ed. Bering Liisberg, Copenhagen 1919, pp. 326-328. Ståle Dyrvik et al.: *Norsk økonomisk historie 1500-1970*, Oslo 1979, p. 101.
16 Poul Holm 1991 (see note 1).
17 Lennart Dalén: *Den bohuslänska fiskelägesbygden*, Gothenburg 1941, pp. 85-86.
18 Johan Pettersson: *Den svenska skagerrakkustens fiskebebyggelse*, Lund 1953, pp. 115-16.
19 Åke Holmberg: Perioden 1550-1880, *Bohusläns historia*, ed. Erik Lönnroth, Gothenburg 1963, pp. 172-76.
20 Albert Sandklef: Hallands bönder, *Hallands historia*, eds. Curt Weibull et al., Halmstad 1954, pp. 568, 591-95.
21 Albert Sandklef: Halländsk sjöfart i danska arkiv, *Årbog 1966. Udgivet af Selskabet »Handels- og søfartsmuseets venner«*, p. 249. The customs accounts of Aalborg harbour for the period 1574-1665 give an impression of the extent of this trade, cf. Albert Sandklef: *Allmogesjöfart på Sveriges västkust 1575-1850*, Lund 1973, Appendix.
22 Albert Sandklef 1973 (see note 21), pp. 119-21, 210, 310-312, 329, 333.
23 P. C. Knudsen: *Aalborg By's Historie*, III, Aalborg 1933, p. 139. Claes Krantz: *På vestsiden af Kattegat*, Aalborg 1953.
24 Ole Degn: *Rig og fattig i Ribe*, II, Århus 1981, p. 117.
25 Erik Grill: Hallands städer, *Hallands historia*, I, eds. C. Weibull et al., Halmstad 1954, p. 734.
26 Ibid. Albert Sandklef 1973 (see note 21), p. 117.
27 Albert Sandklef 1973 (see note 21), pp. 335-38.
28 Gert Poulsen and Lars Tvede-Jensen: *Aalborg under krise og højkonjunktur fra 1534 til 1680 (Aalborgs historie, 2)*, Aalborg 1988, pp. 232-56.
29 Carl Klitgaard: En Fortids-Vandvej (Ryaa), *Jyske Samlinger*, 4.6, 1928-30, pp. 313ff.
30 Gert Poulsen (see note 28), p. 222.
31 See Henrik Becker-Christensen: *Protektionisme og reformer 1660-1814 (Dansk Toldhistorie, II)*, Copenhagen 1988, p. 386 (table 16).
32 Anders Monrad Møller: *Fra Galeoth til Galease*, Esbjerg 1981, fig. 6.
33 Op. cit., pp. 31-33.
34 C. Klitgaard 1931 (see note 8), p. 83.
35 Henning Bender: *Aalborgs industrielle udvikling 1735-1940*, Aalborg 1987.
36 Kåre Lunden: Fisket og norsk økonomi på 1500- og 1600-tallet, *Heimen*, 17, 1976, pp. 147-48.
37 Gert Poulsen (see note 28), pp. 248-49.
38 Op. cit., p. 251.
39 E. Ladewig Petersen (see note 12).
40 Holger Rasmussen (see note 7), pp. 312-17.
41 Carl Klitgaard 1931 (see note 8), pp. 81, 91-92.
42 C. M. Olrik: *Afhandling om Aalborgs Handel*, Copenhagen 1773, p. 156.
43 Op. cit., p. 237.
44 Anders Monrad Møller 1981 (see note 32), pp. 105, 116.
45 Carl Klitgaard 1931 (see note 8), Denmark, pp. 113-14.
46 Anders Monrad Møller 1981 (see note 32), p. 44.
47 Olof Hasslöf: *Svenska västkustfiskarna. Studier i en yrkesgrupps näringsliv och sociala kultur*, Gothenburg 1949, p. 170.
48 Johan Ludvig Lybecker: *Forsøg til nogle Betragtninger over Fiskene og Fiskerierne i Almindelighed, samt til en physisk – historisk – oeconomisk – og politisk Afhandling om Silde-Fiskerierne i Særdeleshed og fornemmelig det, som drives i Limfjorden, etc.*, Copenhagen 1792, p. 303.
49 Louis Bobé: En engelsk Krigsfanges Oplevelser i Jylland i Vinteren 1808 (Kaptajn James MacDonald), *Samlinger til jydsk Historie og Topografi*, 3:3:5, 1903, p. 400.
50 Florian Martensen-Larsen: *Korn til Norge*, Herning 1988, pp. 44-55.
51 Anders Monrad Møller: *Fra jagt til skonnert*, Copenhagen 1988. Ivan Lind: *Göteborgs handel och sjöfart 1637-1920*, Gothenburg 1923, p. 27. Frederik Scheel: Fra napoleonskrigene til navigasjonsaktens ophævelse, *Den norske sjøfarts Historie*, II:1, ed. Jac. S. Worm-Müller, Oslo 1935, pp. 111-12.
52 Ståle Dyrvik et al. (see note 15).
53 Gorm Kledal: Dansk-norsk samhandel ca. 1800-1830, med særligt henblik på virk-

ningerne af rigernes adskillelse, (unpublished thesis, History Dept., University of Copenhagen 1973), p. 82.
54 Per Boje: *Danske provinskøbmænds vareomsætning og kapitalforhold 1815-1847*, Århus 1977, p. 67.
55 Henning Bender (see note 35).
56 Finn H. Lauridsen: Da Lemvig fik toldstedret, *Her er det vi bor*, Lemvig 1974, pp. 9-21.
57 Alan Hjorth Rasmussen: *Skudefart og Limfjordshandel*, Esbjerg-Thisted 1974, pp. 24-26, 32-33.
58 Carl Klitgaard 1931 (see note 8), pp. 219, 233. Henning Bender (see note 35).

CHAPTER 13
Port towns, privileges, and changing fortunes
Mandal and its hinterland, c. 1650-1850[1]

By Finn-Einar Eliassen

Mandal, Norway's southernmost town, developed in the early modern period from a seasonal market-place in the sixteenth century, via the first permanent settlements clustered around three harbours at the mouth of a river in the seventeenth century, to a small town in the eighteenth century.[2] The Mandal river provided the vital connection between the market-place, and later the town, and a river valley, some 80 kilometres long. This is the Man*dal* (*dal* meaning valley) which gave its name to the river, and to the town at its mouth. It was also the natural hinterland which provided market and town with its main export articles: timber and timber products, the economic backbone of Mandal as a settlement and town. (Fig. 13.2).

Until the middle of the seventeenth century, there were no real towns on this south coast between Skien and Stavanger, and no fewer than five Danish and Norwegian towns acquired trading rights in Mandal: Landskrona, Helsingør, Skien, Tønsberg, and Christiania (present-day Oslo). The settlement at Mandal itself obtained limited trading rights in 1632 as a *ladested* (»lading-place«), that is, an export port, allowed to export timber products to foreign parts, but not allowed to import any foreign products at all, only grain from Denmark.[3]

In 1641, however, the town of Kristiansand was founded and given exclusive trading rights along the entire south coast of Norway, as well as in the corresponding inland region. All trade was to be centralized in Kristiansand, and all merchants were ordered to settle in the new privileged town, and conduct their trade from there.[4] Only three export ports were allowed to carry on their trade – Mandal was one of them – but only until the means had been found to direct their timber to Kristiansand as well. In the 1680s, even these three ports were formally abolished, and their merchants and shipmasters were to be resettled in Kristiansand – by force if necessary! This initiated a struggle between Kristiansand and its export ports which in Mandal's case was to last for almost a hundred years. The other export ports involved in this conflict were Arendal and Risør to the east of Kristiansand, and Flekkefjord to the west of Mandal. (See fig. 13.1).

There were two long periods of conflict between Mandal and Kristiansand, the first lasting from the 1670s through the 1690s, the second from the 1730s till the end of the 1770s. The struggle was at its most intense in the late 1680s and again in the 1750s, corresponding to critical periods in the his-

Fig. 13.1: South Coast towns in Norway, 1662-1801.

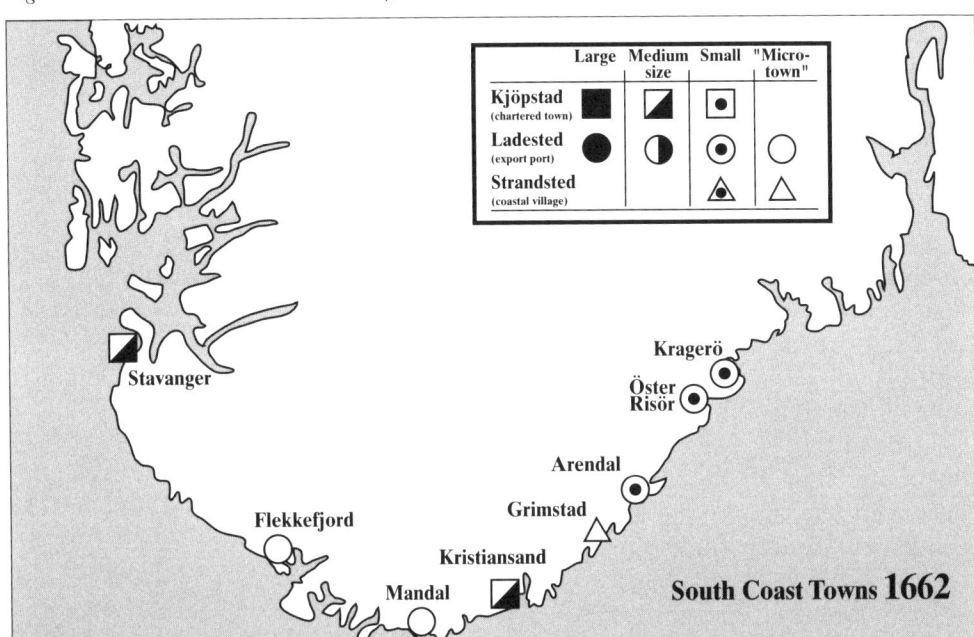

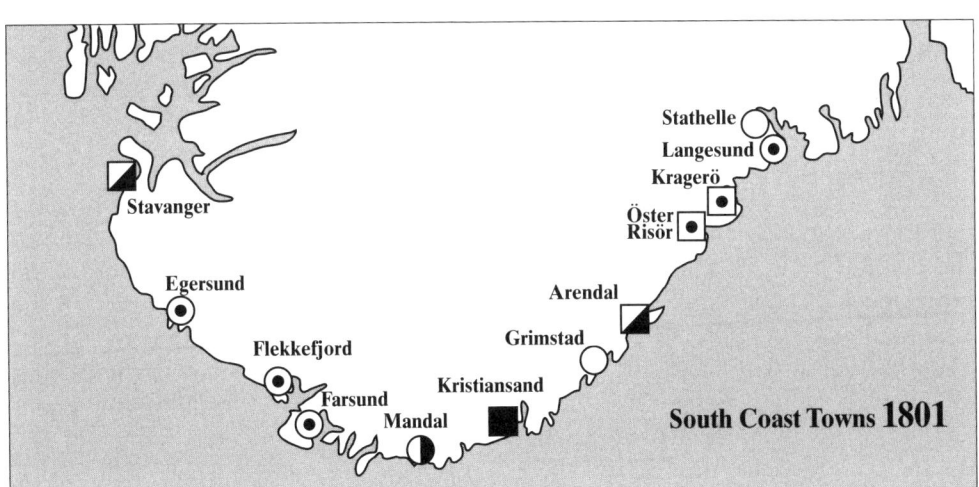

tory of Kristiansand. Through most of this conflict, Kristiansand had the support of both regional and state authorities, and the town itself was far greater than the small town of Mandal, as regards both population and wealth.[5] So how could Mandal hold out, without succumbing to its much more powerful neighbour?

Since it was Kristiansand's ambition to take over Mandal's trade, this would mean taking over Mandal's hinterland. So we shall start by examining that hinterland, and its relationship to Mandal town.

Mandal's hinterland

As we have seen, timber and timber products were Mandal's main export articles, and structural changes in the timber trade gave a crucial impetus to the development of the town, as distinct from a market-place. During the sixteenth century, the coastal forests, which had been the basis of the timber trade from the south coast of Norway, had been depleted, and in the seventeenth century, high-quality timber had to be obtained inland, and ever higher up in the valleys. The Mandal valley was the westernmost of the country's good timber districts, and by the mid-seventeenth century, the timber trade had reached the upper reaches of this valley, the great forests of Bjelland and Åseral (cf. fig. 13.2), which from then onwards were the main reservoir of timber for export from Mandal.

Originally, a great many farmers had been active in the timber trade on the south coast, working their own forests and selling timber directly to merchants and ship masters who came in the summer to trade in bays and inlets all along the coast. The market at Mandal had been especially important for such transactions, but there were several others along the coast, particularly to the east of Mandal. When timber had to be fetched further inland, and floated down the rivers to the coast, this had the effect of concentrating the trade at the mouths of the rivers, and also in the hands of a small group of merchants in each place. Even the most resourceful farmers were gradually driven out of the timber trade as it made ever greater demands on capital, transport, and organization.[6] Compared to visiting merchants from other

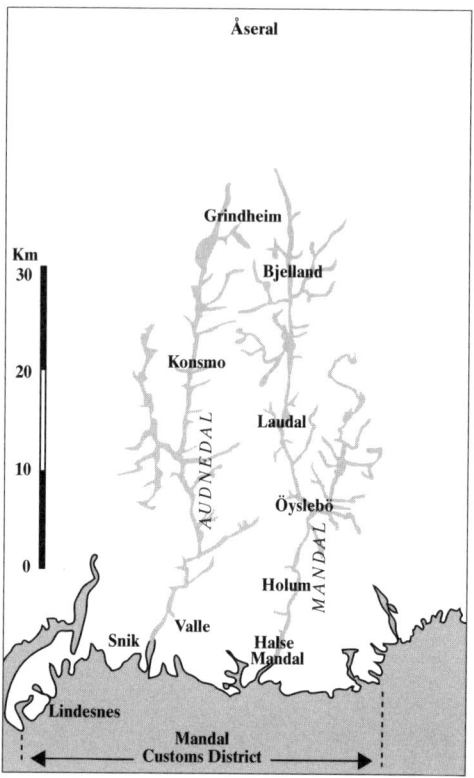

Fig. 13.2: Mandal town and its hinterland

Danish-Norwegian towns, or from other countries, the merchants of Mandal may have had less capital but more local knowledge, a wide net of contacts in the hinterland, and the enormous advantage of being on the spot, throughout the year, able to buy timber when prices were low, supervise the felling of the trees in the winter, when snow made transport to the riverside easy, and organize the floating of timber downstream with the floods of spring and early summer. They would also see to the storing of timber near the harbours, in preparation for the arrival of buyers and ships to carry the timber across the North Sea. As yet, Mandal had no merchant fleet of its own. This concentration of merchant middlemen at the mouth of the Mandal river, with no fewer than three good harbours – one of them in the river-mouth itself – and surrounded by craftsmen, innkeepers and customs officers as the trade increased, became the core of the export port and later the town of Mandal. From the middle decades of the seventeenth century it was a settlement with a couple of hundred inhabitants. Its hinterland stretched the length of the Mandal valley, and some kilometres along the coast on either side. As land transport was cumbersome, expensive and slow, and there were few roads, river and sea transport connected Mandal to its hinterland, and also served to limit it.

The timber trade was further developed towards the end of the seventeenth century. Sawmills were erected in the lower Mandal valley, where timber from Bjelland and Åseral was cut into planks and deals, which of course fetched a much higher price, thus increasing profits. From around 1690, Mandal merchants were able to export some of the timber products themselves, in their own ships. In the early eighteenth century several new sawmills were built by Mandal merchants and given privileges to cut for export. The town's leading family, the Nedenes family, based its considerable wealth on its dominant position in the timber trade, a position it was able to maintain through four generations, over more than a century. They entered into long-term contracts with farmers in Åseral for the delivery of timber, they organized the floating of timber downstream to the sawmills, the cutting of deals and planks, the transport of all timber and timber products to the har-

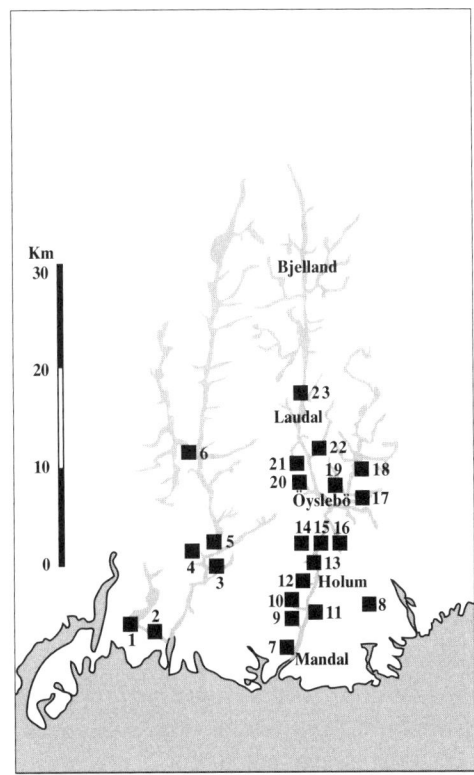

Fig. 13.3: Sawmills in the Audnedal and Mandal valleys, 1773

Note: No's 1, 2, 4, 5 and 6 (in the Audnedal) and 7, 10, 11, 12, 13, 14, 17, 18, 19, 20 and 21 (in the Mandal) were owned by Mandal merchants. Cf. fig. 13.2.

bour, and the export from Mandal, to a great extent on their own ships.[7]

The timber trade was based to a great extent on long-term credit, the merchants providing the forest-owning farmers with grain, iron, salt and other necesseties as advance payment on future deliveries of timber. The trade cycle was slow, it could easily take three or four years from the time the advance was given by the merchant, and a contract for the delivery of timber was set up, until he received payment from his customer in Amsterdam or Newcastle. But once set in motion, the cycle of credit, production and trade would run from year to year and over decades, providing the merchant with a steady and reliable supply of timber at agreed prices, and the farmer with foodstuffs and utensils which he needed. Even when times were bad, the merchant would take care to supply »his« farmer with grain and other necessities, to keep him alive and to secure future deliveries of timber when trade picked up. There was thus an element of reciprocity and »social security« in this system of credit and trade, even if the merchant always had the upper hand, and would normally be able to dictate the prices, both of merchandise and timber, to a farmer who was more or less constantly in debt. The forest itself would normally serve as security for the eventual settlement of the farmer's debt.[8]

The grain trade, based on imported grain from Denmark, was thus connected to the timber trade, but it was also a separate branch of trade for Mandal merchants. In the middle and upper reaches of the valleys of Mandal and Audnedal (see fig. 13.2), people were dependent on buying some of their grain in most years. In Åseral, the locally produced grain rarely lasted into the New Year. As a *ladested*, Mandal was the only legal port for the import of grain between Kristiansand and Stavanger, and in the eighteenth century between Kristiansand and Lindesnes (see fig. 13.1). Consequently, the hinterland for Mandal's grain trade was larger than for its timber trade, at least around 1700. Later, as we shall see, its timber trade expanded to take in the valley of Audnedal as well.

The third important product in Mandal's trade, salmon, represented only a small percentage of the towns exports. From the late seventeenth century, the Mandal merchants dominated this trade as well, buying fresh salmon from the landowners along the lower reaches of the Mandal river, who possessed the fishing rights, and organizing the salting, smoking, packing and export themselves. Some of the merchants even had fishing rights, as landowners near the river mouth.

Along the coast, the lobster trade was the most lucrative branch of the fisheries. This trade was monopolized by Dutch skippers from Zierikzee, but when the lobster trade was liberalized in 1721, Mandal merchants acquired a strong, perhaps even dominant, position in this trade as well. Their field of operation extended from Ny Hellesund in the east to Snik in the west, spanning the Mandal customs district.[9] (See fig. 13.2). Roughly the same area was covered by the Mandal ship salvage business, which developed into one of the town's main economic enterprises, dominated, like all branches of trade and shipping, by the Nedenes family.[10]

We see that Mandal's hinterland varied in extent and orientation, depending on the branch of trade and other enterprises, and also varying over time, generally growing with the growth of the town – or vice versa! The nearest parishes of Halse, Holum, and to some extent Valle in South Audnedal, from which a trip to Mandal and back could be made in one day, dominated the daily trade of the town. But the long-distance trade in timber, planks and deals, based on the credit trade with the upper Mandal valley, was the town's economic backbone. So all parts of the hinterland were important to the growth of the town, in different ways.

In the decades during and after the Great Northern War (1700-1720), Mandal grew into a real town, with some 4-500 inhabitants in the 1720s. This expansion was due to the economic activities described above, stimulated by the war and post-war booms in overseas trade and shipping, and fuelled by an influx of migrants, mainly from Mandal's closest hinterland – people who knew the town and often had friends and relatives there already.[11]

The period from the mid-1720s until the late 1740s was one of economic depression, especially in the timber trade. But with renewed expansion from around 1750, the timber merchants of Mandal extended their range of activity to include the Audnedal valley (cf. fig. 13.2). In accordance with the statutes, timber and deals from Audnedal had been exported through Mandal since the seventeenth century, but by local merchants from Naversund, Snik and Svinør, near the mouth of the river Audna. Now Mandal merchants built new, large sawmills in the lower Audnedal valley, they drew up timber contracts with forest-owning farmers in the upper reaches of that valley, too, and organized the transport and handling of timber, planks and deals from the forests to the export port, which was, of course, Mandal. At the same time, they intensified their activity in the Mandal valley, building new sawmills near the town and entering into (illegal) contracts for timber deliveries over periods of 40 and 50 years from Åseral farms. Mandal merchants had local agents in both valleys, who supervised the whole process from forest to harbour, making agreements with farmers and workers, to which end they were provided with beer for the workers and stronger drink for the farmers »according to their standing, ... especially for those who cut their planks well«![12]

The result of all this enterprise was that in the latter half of the eighteenth century, practically all the timber trade of the Mandal customs district was in the hands of Mandal merchants. But they were not without competition.

The conflict with Kristiansand

Even as the merchants of Mandal were extending their activities – and the town's hinterland – in the 1750s, Kristiansand merchants launched their fiercest attack on the small town. Once again, their aim was to take over Mandal's hinterland, and centralize the western region's trade in Kristiansand. A consortium of Kristiansand merchants acquired the customs farm of the whole southern coastline in 1749, retaining it for 27 years, largely as a means to curb Mandal's foreign trade, and that of its western neighbour, Flekkefjord. In the mid-1760s, one of Kristiansand's leading merchants, Jørgen Nilsen Moe, established his agent, Ingvald Andersen Morsøe, in the centre of Mandal town, in an attempt to outbid the Mandal merchants for the products from its hinterland, especially timber. Moe was indeed able to break into the Mandal timber trade, acquiring a sawmill in the Mandal valley, and even giving credit to some Mandal merchants to make them dependent on him. Moe also had agents further west along the coast, but »a substantial loss made him realize his mistake«, as a later observer put it, and in 1775 he went bankrupt. By then, Kristiansand's attempt to deal Mandal a fatal blow and take over its trade was already a lost cause, and in 1779, Mandal was awarded full privileges of foreign trade – the right to export and import all legal merchandise – which put it economically (but not politically or administratively) on a par with its large neighbour. In the following year, Flekkefjord obtained the same privileges. The eastern towns of Arendal and Risør had become fully privileged towns already in 1723.[13]

How can Mandal's victory over its far more wealthy and powerful neighbour be explained? There were obviously many reasons, but we shall focus on those which enabled Mandal to hold on to its hinterland, and even extend it, under fierce competition.

As we have seen, timber and timber products were the main export articles from Mandal, and it was also the timber trade, more than anything else, which served to define and structure Mandal's hinterland. One of the main objects of the Kristiansand merchants was therefore to take over Mandal's timber trade. But, evidently, this was easier said than done.

As a merchandise, timber was characterized by its low value in relation to its bulk and weight. Unless transport costs were kept to a minimum, they could easily raise the price of the timber to a prohibitive level. This was even more true in the valleys of Mandal and Audnedal, which were marginal forestry districts. Also, the timber products exported from Mandal were inferior to and therefore less valuable than products from the forests further east. Water transport – by river and by sea – was by far the cheapest mode of transport. Overland transport was expensive and cumbersome, and there were very few roads in Mandal's hinterland. So basically, transporting timber or timber products over long distances by land was uneconomical, and often impracticable. This made it practically impossible to redirect timber from the Mandal valley – let alone Audnedal – to Kristiansand, without losing money in the process. Only one road connected the middle reaches of the Mandal valley with Kristiansand, and it is significant that only there, at Mæsel, could Kristiansand merchants keep a sawmill for the export of deals from their own city. All other timber products from the Mandal valley, including deals and planks from all the other sawmills, were exported from Mandal town.[14]

Another option, which was practised for some years around 1750, was to direct all ships leaving Mandal with timber products via Kristiansand, so that formally, the export load was registered under that town, and the customs dues paid there. This reduced the extra transport costs, as compared to overland transport, but it was still a costly detour, adding to the sailing time and reducing the number of crossings a ship could make over the North Sea during a sailing season, and thus the profit margin of the trade. It was hardly a sensible practice in competition with other, more important timber-exporting towns further east!

In fact, Jørgen Nilsen Moe drew the only sensible conclusion when he established his agent in Mandal in 1764. Mandal's hinterland was so well protected by geographical barriers and the economics of the timber trade that the only way to take over Mandal's trade was by controlling the outlet in Mandal itself. But, as we have already seen, even this attempt failed, after a promising start. Knowing how the Mandal timber trade was organized and run, this should hardly surprise us. It required more than capital and commercial know-how to take over this complicated and well-organized system of trade, transport and credit. The heads of long-established merchant houses in Mandal had every advantage over the newcomer: local knowledge, local agents in the valleys, long-term credit relationships and timber contracts, and possession of the main facilities of the trade in the forms of sawmills, timber booms (where they could even obstruct the passage of timber belonging to a competitor!), and storage plots near the harbours. A newcomer, and only an agent at that, could not compete with the locals over the full range of trades and enterprises either, leaving him in a more vulnerable position than the leading local merchants who could spread their risks and be better able to bear periodic depressions in one or two trades.

Mandal's was not the only hinterland which seemed to have a kind of natural, geographical-economic protection against the intrusion of neighbouring towns and their merchants. Most Norwegian towns had a position similar to Mandal's, on a harbour, often at the mouth of river valley, which provided a naturally protected hinterland for timber and related trades. Occasionally, though, a town could break through such a barrier. Christiania managed to do this, drawing most of its timber for export from the valley of the river Glomma (Norway's longest river and main timber artery) by overland transport over some 20 kilometres. On a much smaller scale, the export ports of Son and Hølen south of Christiania, managed something similar. But in both of these cases, the terrain was much easier than around Mandal, and, in Christiania's case, its leading merchants were among the wealthiest in the country.[15]

In Mandal's hinterland, competing towns could only nibble at the edges, Kristiansand in the east and, at the very end of the eighteenth century, the new export port of Farsund in the west. But neither could make any great inroads into Mandal's trade. Farsund was much less of a threat than Kristiansand, not only because of its small size (about 500 inhabitants in 1801), but especially because it was based mainly on sea fisheries, its merchants never venturing seriously into the timber trade.[16]

More worrying to the merchants of Mandal was the competition they met from the inhabitants of the town's own hinterland.

Worlds apart?

There was a certain amount of antagonism between the farmers of the hinterland and the merchants of Mandal – especially over the provision of grain and other necessary commodities, which the merchants were using unashamedly to further their own interests, even in times of scarcity, keeping the prices high, and favouring farmers who had timber to sell. The traders of Mandal even refused to take part in public schemes for grain provision in years of crisis, unless they could make a handsome profit on it themselves. This provoked criticism not only from Mandal's hinterland, but also from government officials within the town itself.

All through the eighteenth century, Mandal merchants complained about farmers operating as tradesmen in the town's hinterland, dealing in imported goods, fish and animal products, and even timber. During the last third of the century, this competition increased, encouraged by a liberalization of the state's economic policies. Farmers were allowed to sell animal products to whom they chose, and people outside Mandal town, and outside the circle of burghers, were allowed to sell provisions to ships in the harbour of Snik west of Mandal. In addition to this legal trade, illegal commerce increased markedly towards the end of the century. There can be no doubt that the Mandal merchants kept the upper hand in their relationship with the farmers of the hinterland, but their position was being challenged. And the burghers' representative in Mandal had to spend an increasing amount of time investigating charges of illegal trading, and bringing charges against persons from the town's hinterland for such offences.

As part of Mandal's central position within its region, the town also functioned as an administrative centre for a variety of administrative districts, from the parish to the customs district and the *fogderi* – all of which carried the town's name. This gave the town and its inhabitants a leading role, not only politically, but even socially, within its region, and in relation to its hinterland. People had to come to Mandal from various parts of its hinterland, not only for commercial purposes, but also on public business, or even to attend the hospital for a venereal disease which was established there in the late 1770s. Conversely, both merchants and public officials from Mandal kept its region under close observation, making inspection tours and attending to private or public business, or both, as the case might be, strengthening Mandal's role as a centre to its hinterland in the process.

In the circumstances, it is not surprising that the ascendancy of Mandal town over its hinterland had a cultural aspect as well. It is obvious that townspeople, particularly the upper classes, but also further down the social scale, would feel culturally superior to the »rough farmers of the mountain districts« – which is how some of them characterized people living some 15 kilometres up the Mandal valley, at hardly more than 100 metres above sea level! Even though most of the inhabitants of Mandal had their roots in the countryside – either themselves or their forefathers having emigrated from Mandal's immediate hinterland – and maintained contacts with relatives and friends outside the town, there was a strong tendency for the townspeople to copy the material culture of the upper classes in the town, and for people in the hinterland to copy the townspeople's dress, furniture and name customs in their turn.[17] At the turn of the nineteenth century, there are clear indications that the majority of the inhabitants in the town of Mandal, which by then had some 1,600 inhabitants, regarded themselves as townspeople and distanced themselves from the rural district where they had their roots and relations.

Turning the tables

In 1807, Denmark/Norway was drawn into the Napoleonic wars, which were to affect the country, more or less directly, until 1814. The wars, accompanied by naval blockades and a halt to both the timber exports and the import of Danish grain, severely affected the economy of Mandal. Following an unprecedented boom in the pre-war years, to a great extent financed by large loans and foreign credit, the Mandal merchants found themselves unable to meet their obligations when the wars hit the town's foreign trade and its shipping. However, they had great hopes that peace would enable them to make good their losses and resume their dominance over Mandal's hinterland once again. But the war also had direct and indirect repercussions on the relationship between town and hinterland, almost reversing their previous roles.

In the first place, trade resumed after 1814, but only slowly, and it did not nearly reach the heights of the last pre-war years. Thus, most of the Mandal merchants found themselves in an even worse position after the war, when their creditors started to get restless, and it slowly became clear that many of them might never get their money at all. From 1815, Norwegian and foreign creditors descended on Mandal, demanding their money, and soon there was a veritable scramble of creditors trying to salvage at least some of their assets while there was still something to take.

This debt crisis was exacerbated by the financial policy of the Danish and, after the dissolution of the union in 1814, the Norwegian government. Two money reforms, in 1813 and 1816, led to the complete erosion of credit relations between Mandal and its hinterland. Especially the reform of 1813, which introduced a new currency, with different rates of exchange for different kinds of debts, hit the merchants of Mandal very hard indeed. Mortgage debts, which were precisely the sort of debts that many Mandal merchants owed, were subject to a progressive rate of exchange with age, which meant that such debts incurred before the outbreak of the war were increased by several hundred per cent in real terms. At the same time, the so-called »book debts«, which were not in the form of deeds of mortgage or similar documents, but were simple entries in a merchant's ledger, were converted at the current rate of exchange at the time of the reform, whatever their age. With the high inflation of the war years, the »book debts« – which were the kind of debts that people in Mandal's hinterland owed – would be reduced in real terms, while mortgage debts would be substantially increased. The combined effects of these principles were to throw the merchants of Mandal into a veritable debt crisis, while their debtors in the hinterlands were relieved of most of *their* debt burdens![18]

Although only some of the Mandal merchants had mortgage debts from the pre-war period, most of the others had incurred such debts during the first war years, in order to keep their business afloat. And, to make matters even worse when the day of reckoning came, most of the town's merchants had also stood security for each other's debts. Consequently, when the creditors called in their outstanding debts, this caused a »domino effect« among the merchants of Mandal: first, some minor figures gave up their estates, drawing others with them in the fall, and culminating with Mandal's leading merchants, Gjert Gjertsen Nedenes and Mathias Chr. Knutzen, going spectacularly bankrupt in 1822-23. Although some prudent merchants had managed to come through the crisis without fatal debts, and some of these were able to take over much of the trade from those who went bankrupt, the general effect was the collapse of the merchant élite of Mandal in the first post-war decade.

Farmers of the hinterland, on the other hand, were in a stronger position in the post-war period than before the war, especially in relation to the Mandal merchants. Although the farmers at first were hard hit by the blockade, and there was widespread scarcity of food and even starvation in the rural districts as well as in the town, the farmers were able to increase their production of grain and other foodstuffs by improved methods of cultivation and more intensive use of both soil and manpower. So the rural districts inland from Mandal came through the war years with a higher degree of self-sufficiency than before, and were thus less dependent on imports and on the Mandal merchants for their daily bread than they had been for more than a century. At the same time, the currency reforms, especially the one in 1813, as we have seen, served to liberate the farmers of the hinterland from the strong grip of the Mandal merchants. Most of them were able to pay their reduced debts, and were no longer obliged to provide timber for their creditors at buyer's prices. In fact, they were also less dependent on selling timber than they had been, being more self-sufficient. So they could afford to wait until prices were favourable, and sell to the highest bidder, playing off the merchants against each other. After 1814, some farmers even established themselves as middlemen in the timber trade, buying timber from other farmers, cutting it on their own sawmills, and selling the products to »someone or other«, mainly to Mandal merchants. In the 1820s, some farmer-merchants went even one step further, selling planks and deals to other privileged traders, outside Mandal. Farmers also took over many of the sawmills which had previously belonged to merchants who had now gone bankrupt. This happened especially in the Audnedal valley. But in both valleys, farmers claimed the right to organize the floating of timber downstream for direct sale to buyers from other Norwegian towns and districts outside Mandal. Their claims were supported by local and regional government officials.

This was a period when the ideas of economic liberalism were gaining ground in government policy and local administration, as expressed in substantial de-regulation in various economic fields. In 1818, farmers obtained almost full rights as far as the running of sawmills was concerned, and in the following years, the remaining restrictions were abolished. Furthermore, the local officials in Mandal knew of »no statute which could prohibit the farmers from selling their timber to whom they wished«.[19]

Even in years of depression in the timber trade, the forest-owning farmers of the Mandal and Audnedal valleys managed to make a small profit on the timber trade by keeping production down, to match demand and keep prices up. When the trade picked up again, the farmers could use their power as producers to press prices up – at least for a while – since they were not dependent on selling their timber at all costs. Increasingly, too, farmers cut their own timber into planks and deals with handsaws. Paradoxically, this increased their profit, and not only because planks and deals fetched much higher prices than uncut timber. Cutting by handsaw made more effective use of the timber, the handsaw cutting both more finely and with less waste than a sawmill. The higher-quality planks and deals also fetched better prices, and a handsaw was much cheaper and more versatile than a sawmill, which was dependent on a steady waterfall near a major river. In the 1830s and 1840s, great improvements in the road system of both valleys made it much easier than before to transport ready-cut planks and deals from almost any part of the two valleys to Mandal town, where they could be sold to »anyone« – that is, to the highest bidder.

During the first half of the eighteenth century, the roles of farmers and merchants in the timber trade of Mandal's hinterland were almost reversed. The farmers gained a much stronger and more independent position, and the Mandal merchants were reduced to a more passive role as middlemen and exporters, and were often bypassed by farmers in these roles as well, being forced to compete with buyers from abroad and from other Norwegian towns.

This turning of the tables in the economic field was accompanied, and even preceded, by a reversal of the political roles of town and hinterland. After the dissolution of the union with Denmark, and the passing of the Norwegian constitution in 1814, the new democratic political power was largely vested in the peasantry, both on a national and (from 1837) on a local level. The farmers made up the bulk of the electorate, and when they realized their potential power, they started to return their own representatives to the electoral assemblies and finally to the Norwegian parliament – the *Storting* – itself, in the 1820s. They gradually took over power in the elected assemblies, gaining control over budgets and legislation.[20] In Mandal, the merchants, and gradually even the government officials, lost their political power, and after 1815, no Mandal merchant was elected to the »Storting«. In the electoral assembly, the farmers' representatives decided who should be returned, and increasingly, they elected their own. Even though Mandal town gained local self-government in 1837, this served to isolate the town politically from its hinterland. In the »new Norway« which entered into a forced union with Sweden in the autumn of 1814, Mandal town could no longer dominate its hinterland either economically, politically, or, indeed, culturally. With political power and economic independence, the farming communities also found a cultural self-confidence which was partly fuelled by a contempt for the bourgeoisie, and for its urban culture.

Even so, the connections between the town and its hinterland were not severed, even when the rural districts gained local self-government separate from Mandal, and farmers could sell their timber and timber products to other than the merchants of Mandal. But the relationship between town and hinterland had changed in fundamental ways, becoming freer, more balanced, less predictable than it had been in the eighteenth century. Differences of interest had been revealed, conflicts had been brought to the surface, and the roles had changed. Around 1850, its hinterland was still of fundamental importance to the life and development of Mandal town – economically, demographically, socially, culturally, and even politically – but in different ways than before.

Town and hinterland

Looking at the changing relationship between Mandal and its hinterland in a wider perspective, there are some obvious conclusions to be drawn.

In the first place, a town's hinterland was defined and preserved by at least three sets of circumstances: geographical features, economic structures, and political decisions. Of these, the last mentioned seems to have been the least important, and, indeed, the consequences of political decisions in this field were often highly unpredictable. In Mandal's case, and very often in a country where distances and geographical features have played major parts in its history, geographical boundaries seem to have been of paramount importance in protecting the town's hinterland against intruding competitors on both sides, thus also preserving the town itself through periods of crisis. The stability of the hinterland, comprising first and foremost the Mandal valley, and secondarily – both in time and importance – the Audnedal valley, is a striking feature of the region through two centuries from the mid-seventeenth century until 1850, and after. But obviously, a hinterland without an economic structure binding it to its town is unimaginable, and we should draw the conclusion that it was the development of economic activities within a naturally demarcated and protected geographical framework that in fact created and defined Mandal's hinterland.

Secondly, it is slightly misleading to talk about a town's hinterland in the singular form. In reality, as we have seen, a town like Mandal would have a number of different hinterlands of different sizes and shapes, according to the trade or other activity in question. As the main export trade of Mandal, the timber trade and its related grain and commodity trades and credit relationships served to extend and shape the town's hinterland more than anything else. But we should not forget that if we turn to the fish trade, or the ship salvage business, we get hinterlands of different shapes and sizes. And, turning to the movement of people, both those seeking work and those who came to settle in Mandal (not necessarily the same people), we find a great degree of overlap with the commercial hinterland, but with a wider spread, and at the same time a stronger concentration in the parishes closest to the town. Cultural influences can be traced within the framework of both population movements and trade relations, and the administrative districts which centred on Mandal also largely corresponded to various definitions of its hinterland – at the same time also helping to define, extend and structure those hinterlands!

As we have seen, both commercial and administrative, and also demographic hinterlands could – and did –

change over time, both in extent and direction. And even the balance of power and dependence could change over time – normally only by degrees, but in extraordinary conditions, like those accompanying the 1807-14 wars, the changes could be dramatic.

Finally, both on the urban and the rural side of the equation, town-hinterland relationships had important social aspects as well. On the urban side, merchants, and to a lesser extent government officials, played the main parts, while some farmers were more strongly integrated into the regional trading network than others, as we have seen. On the other hand, the movement of people, and of cultural traits, often affected individuals and groups from various levels of the social spectrum, albeit not necessarily in the same way, or to the same degree.

Summing up, we should be cautious about simplistic models of towns and hinterlands, rather seeking to reconstruct as differentiated and sophisticated picture as possible. Nor will it suffice to base one's ideas of such a relationship on formal rights and privileges, or sweeping generalizations in official reports. What we need are detailed studies, based on as wide a range of sources as possible, and setting the town-hinterland relations within a broader context of economic, social, demographic and political conditions, both in town and countryside. It is a tall order and an ambitious undertaking, but only in this way can we, through »filters« of time, bias, and limited source material, get a glimpse of what the real relationships between a town and its hinterlands may have been like.

Notes

1 An earlier version of this article was presented to the 4th North Sea Conference, on »Maritime industries and public intervention«, in Stavanger in 1995. It has benefitted from the discussions there, especially from the points raised by the discussant, Sarah Palmer.

2 This article is based on my *Mandal bys historie* (History of the town of Mandal), vol.1 and 2, Mandal 1995, 1996. I have refrained from giving detailed references to primary source material material here, preferring to give more general information on the various kinds of sources which have been used, otherwise referring to my book, or to other printed works, where the specialist can find precise references.

3 There has been much confusion about the meaning of the term *ladested* among Norwegian historians, who have often taken it to imply a small town or at least a market settlement. Originally, however, it referred to a harbour without any permanent settlement being implied. Only in the mid-nineteenth century did it acquire the meaning *small town*, but already in the previous century, the term had gradually come to be used with this connotation. See my articles: Ladested, *Norsk Historisk Leksikon*, 2nd. ed., eds. S. Imsen and H. Winge, Oslo 1999, and: Ladested – fra havn til by (*Ladested* – from harbour to town), *Historisk Tidsskrift* (The (Norwegian) Historical Journal), forthcoming.

4 S. Steen: *Kristiansands historie 1641-1814* (History of Kristiansand, 1641-1814), Oslo 1941, especially pp. 52ff.

5 F.-E. Eliassen: *Mandal bys historie*, vol. 1 (see note 2), chapter 2 and 6. S. Steen (see note 4), pp. 148ff, 246ff and 324ff.

6 This development can be studied through a variety of sources providing various pieces of evidence, but above all through a couple of court cases, in 1625 and 1633, brought by farmers of the Mandal valley against merchants at the river mouth, accusing them of driving the farmers out of the timber trade.

7 The Nedenes family have not left behind any business or family archive, but their activities can be reconstructed in fairly great detail from port books, tax lists, court protocols, etc. The

Regional integration

family's leading figures were Tørres Christensen, around the turn of the eighteenth century, and his grandson and great-grandson, Frederik and Gjert Gjertsen, about a century later. On Tørres Christensen, see my biographical article in the *Norsk Biografisk Leksikon* (Norwegian Biographical Encyclopedia), 2nd ed. (forthcoming).

8   This system is well-known also from other towns, and from the fisheries as well as from the timber trade. (Cf. A. Nedkvitne: *Mens Bønderne seilte og Jægterne for. Nordnorsk og vestnorsk kystøkonomi 1500-1730* (While the peasants were sailing and the yachts were speeding. The coastal economy of Northern and Western Norway, 1500-1730), Bergen 1988, pp. 291-305.) These credit relationships can be reconstructed by using probate inventories, cf. my articles: By og omland på 1600- og 1700-tallet (Town and hinterland in the seventeenth and eighteenth centuries), *By og bygd, stad og omland* (Town and rural community, town and hinterland), eds. R. Fladby and H. Winge, Oslo 1981, pp. 122-138, and: Korn og kram, kapital og kreditt. Handelsvirksomhet i og omkring byer belyst ved skiftemateriale (Grain and merchandise, capital and credit. Trade in and around towns illuminated by evidence from inventories), *Skiftene som kilde – en artikkelsamling* (Inventories as historical sources – a collection of articles), ed. L. Marthinsen, Oslo 1996, especially pp. 72, 76ff. Unlike some other towns, Mandal's hinterland could not be reliably reconstructed on the basis of inventories, since the estates of many of the town's leading merchants were divided privately among the heirs, without an official inventory being made. Cf. the latter article, pp. 83-84.

9   Since the lobster fisheries and the lobster trade were subject to government regulation, a fair amount of documentary evidence is available, especially from the 1720s and 1730s.

10 Wreckage belonged to the king, so this enterprise, too, was subject to government supervision. However, the leading participants in the salvage business also doubled as official inspectors of wreckage and salvage, raising obvious questions about the information they give, but also providing interesting insights into their own thoughts about this business.

11 No census information is available from this period, but migration patterns can be reconstructed on the basis of naval rolls, tax lists, probate inventories, church registers, and law court protocols.

12 Port books, sawmill tax lists, law court protocols, and more general descriptions contained in official reports and in the protocols of special commissions provide much of the material for this paragraph, along with information gleaned from the documents relating to the conflict between Mandal and Kristiansand.

13 S. Steen (see note 4), pp. 324-332. M. Ringard: *Flekkefjords historie* (History of Flekkefjord), Flekkefjord 1942, p. 92.

14 Each sawmill that was privileged to cut planks and deals for export had both its legal production quantity and its export port defined in its letter of privilege. The port books contain information on the sawmill of origin for each batch of planks and deals, for control purposes.

15 F.-E. Eliassen: By og omland på 1600- og 1700-tallet (see note 8), pp. 128-133. K. Sprauten: *Oslo bys historie* (History of the town of Oslo), vol. 2, Oslo 1992, pp. 313-328.

16 O. A. Abrahamsen: *Farsund bys historie* (History of the town of Farsund), vol. 1, Farsund 1997.

17 Among the cultural traits whose dispersal can be followed along the lines indicated here are cotton textiles, coffee utensils, and double Christian names. See also F.-E. Eliassen: Zwischen Ausland und Umland. »Volkskultur« in den norwegischen Städten des 18. Jahrhunderts, *Städtische Volkskultur im 18. Jahrhundert*, ed. R.-E. Mohrmann, Münster 2000, pp. 65-80.

18 S. Dyrvik et al.: *Norsk økonomisk historie 1500-1970* (Economic History of Norway, 1500-1970), vol. 1, Bergen 1979, p. 222. K. Mykland: *Norges Historie* (History of Norway), vol. 9, Oslo 1978, pp. 235-237.

19 S. Dyrvik et al. (see note 18), pp. 227-229. The local conditions in Mandal's hinterland can be followed through complaints from the Mandal merchants to local and regional government officials, and their decisions in these cases.

20 F. Sejersted: *Norges Historie*, vol. 10, Oslo 1978, especially pp. 335ff.

CHAPTER 14
In the shadow of the town
Counter-culture and market economy in Northern and Middle Hordaland in the eighteenth century*

By Atle Døssland

The geographical framework of this article is the region of Northern and Middle Hordaland in the eighteenth century. This region was known as *Strilelandet*, the *Stril* country or *Strileland*, and it was the nearest hinterland of Bergen, which was still by far the largest town in Norway. The rural population of this region were known as *Strils*. I shall start by asking whether the »Strileland« had any distinguishing characteristics of culture or mentality at this time, and, if so, what conditions had formed these cultural traits among the »Strils«.

»Superstition« and conservatism in values

In 1787, Johannes Børilden of Lindås parish in Northern Hordaland accused his neighbour, Lars, of having visited a witch in Bergen. Allegedly, he had paid the woman to cause damage to Johannes, thereby causing his ruin. The local judge, however, held the view that accusations of witchcraft »must, in our enlightened age, be considered a consequence of ignorance and superstition«. Johannes therefore had to pay Lars 14 *riksdaler* in restitution, plus another 2 riksdaler to the poor of the parish. This case proves the existence in this area of a deep-rooted popular belief in sorcery and other supernatural powers.[1]

The episode was far from unique. Some years earlier, in 1769, a much more far-reaching case of witchcraft had wreaked havoc in a whole community a little further south in the region. Several farms in the centre of the island of Osterøy were badly affected by a form of cattle disease. Ole Kleiven, a man from a neighbouring community, was able to reveal, by mysterious means, that evil neighbours, identified by name, had cast a spell on the stricken cattle. For a handsome sum of money, he even offered to remove the spell himself. Thus, neighbour was pitted against neighbour, and accusations of spell-casting and other forms of witchcraft were rife. Not even the local *lensmann* (parish constable) dared to take issue with this belief in the supernatural.[2]

A century earlier, these incidents would no doubt have led to major witch-trials. By the late eighteenth century, however, local government officials like the judge, the bailiff and the county governor, under the influence of more modern ways of thinking, had distanced

247

Regional integration

Fig. 14.1: The county of Hordaland

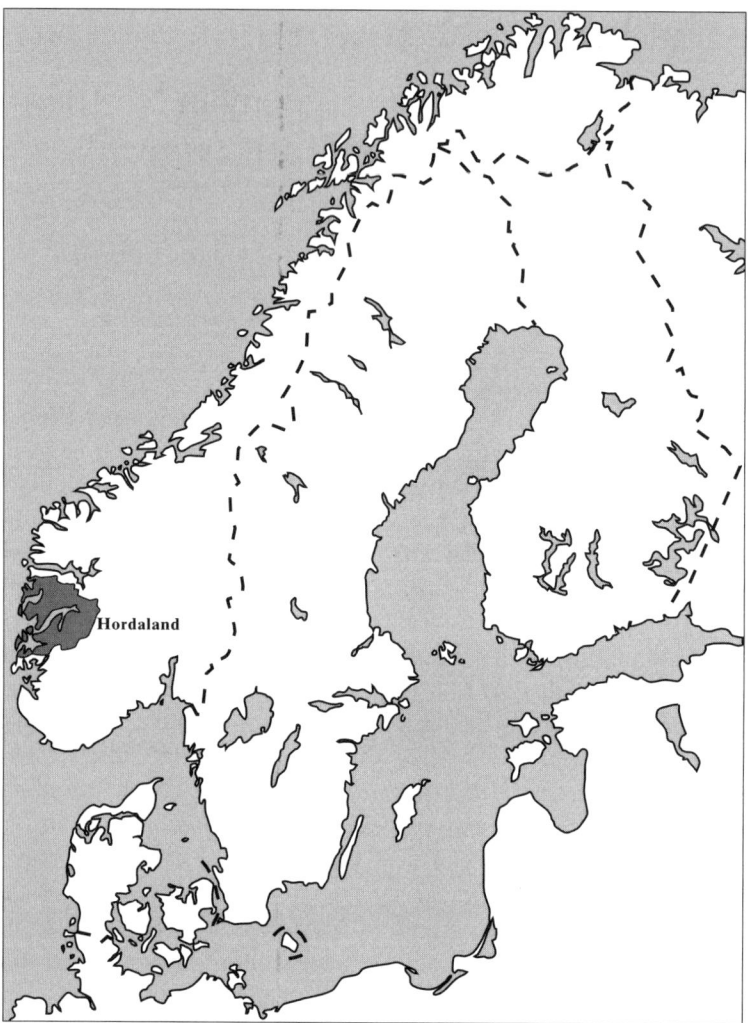

themselves from such ideas. The rural population, on the other hand, stuck to their pre-modern conceptions. We may be justified in saying that, in this matter, the »Strils« were lagging behind others in the civilizing process.

Long before this, clergymen and other government officials had been claiming that »Strils«, more than the rural population elsewhere, were subject to what was, in their eyes, superstition. In a description of rural life, written in 1723 by an anonymous person belonging to the »conditioned« or upper strata of society, a number of such traditions and beliefs are mentioned. »Still, there are some wise and enlightened children of God among the peasantry, who pay no heed to such fables«, the author reassures us.[3]

In the first half of the eighteenth century, a couple of clergymen from the

In the shadow of the town

Fig. 14.2: Bailiffs of Bergenhus county

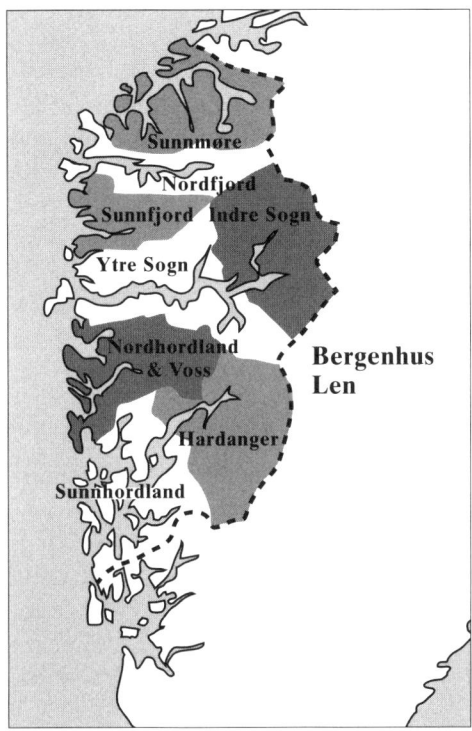

Fig. 14.3: Parishes in Hordaland, 1801

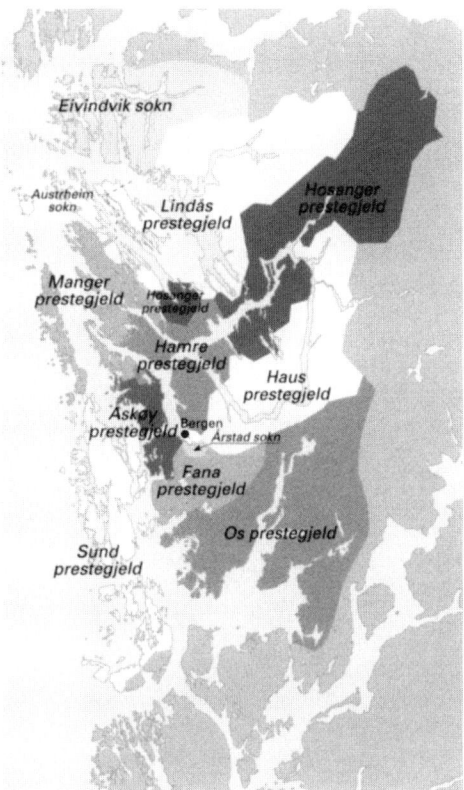

Source: Atle Døssland: *Frå 1650 til 1800*, Bergen 1998, p. 115. (John Ragnar Myking et al.: *Strilesoga. Nord- og Midhordland gjennom tidene*, vol. 3)

parish of Lindås directed strong attacks against so-called healing women or *signekoner*.[4] »It is truly sad to observe that superstitious beliefs and opinions, which have been dead for centuries in other places, should still be appearing like ghosts in this place«, a country doctor wrote in 1858. A colleague of his, Holm Holmsen, characterized the »Strils« of Middle Hordaland as unenlightened, superstitious people, in some ways lacking »a spirit of enterprise and a taste for culture and well-being, living in unclean, squalid, and mostly very poor conditions«. This is also the reason why the term »Stril« is used in a derogatory and contemptuous way, he adds. In his view, the wealth, skill and enlightenment of the local population increased with distance from Bergen, but decreased the closer one got to that city.[5]

By all accounts, opposition to parish schools was unusually strong in Northern and Middle Hordaland. Following a couple of abortive attempts in 1742, schools could not be established until 1748-50, long after the other deaneries in the diocese. Already in the late 1750s, the established school systems in several of the parishes seem to have disintegrated. In the parish of Lindås, for example, the teachers themselves had to go begging from one farm to another to get

249

Fig. 14.4: Skipreider, seventeenth century

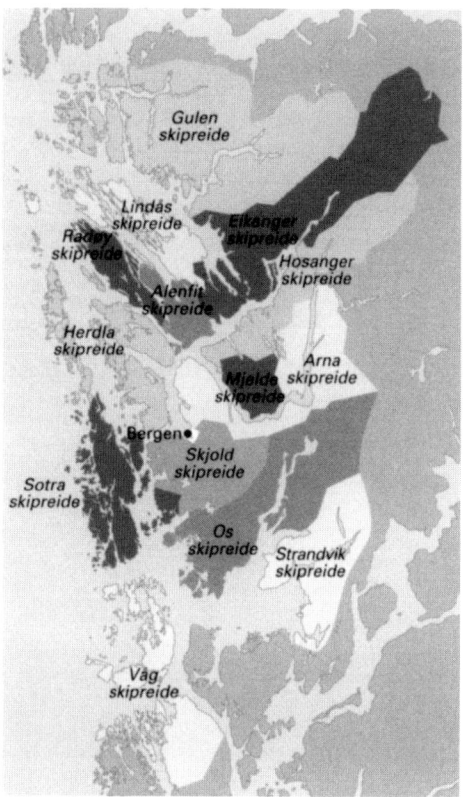

Note: Skipreider were the units of the medieval coastal defense system of Norway, surviving as later administrative units.
Source: Atle Døssland: *Frå 1650 til 1800*, Bergen 1998, p. 115. (John Ragnar Myking et al.: *Strilesoga. Nord- og Midhordland gjennom tidene*, vol. 3)

themselves wages comparable to those of simple farm hands.[6]

Even towards the end of the eighteenth century, reading and writing skills were claimed to be »a rarity in rural society«.[7] Admittedly, such statements by government officials are common, also in other parts of the country, but they were made more frequently and vehemently in the »Strileland« than elsewhere. Even a shrewd observer like the linguist and language reformer Ivar Aasen, himself of peasant stock from Sunnmøre, further north in Western Norway, gave a rather critical evaluation of the cultural level of the »Strils« in 1844, calling them »this stupid and half-wild people«. Later, however, he modified his verdict, concluding that the »Strils« were not »too bad, once one gets to know them well. (...) Their level of education is generally low, even if there is no lack of excellent brains, and all their ambitions seem to be directed towards subsistance and production«.[8]

Equally unanimous are the reports identifying an exceptionally strong conservatism in values in the region. »It is the view of the peasant here that the ways of his father, grandfather and great-grandfather and so on, will also serve him well, and he is convinced that his descendants will curse him for any changes he might make«, it was claimed in 1767. Similarly, in 1844 Ivar Aasen observed that the »Strils« were stubbornly clinging to the old and simple traditions of their ancestors.[9] We may be justified too in seeing the unusually sharp contrast between the urban dialect of Bergen and the rural dialect of the »Strileland« in the same perspective.[10]

There can be no doubt that the cases of witchcraft already referred to were most unusual in Norway at such a late date. Generally, reports about superstition, fatalism and conservatism were so frequent that it seems reasonable to assume that they were not unfounded, even if the strength of such beliefs and attitudes cannot be measured. One would expect a more modern mentality to have made inroads into the hinterland of what was by far the most populous town in the country. Towns are otherwise commonly assumed to have been the gateways of new ideas and attitudes in Norwegian society.

If this conservatism can be assumed to have been a characteristic of the »Strils«, we might equally well turn the argument around, interpreting these phenomena as evidence of the cultural self-awareness of the »Strils«, withstanding the pressures from the urban society, and sticking to their own independent »counter-culture« in opposition to the »civilizing« efforts of the regional élite. There is abundant evidence of the harassment suffered by »Strils« peddling their produce in Bergen. At home, they were often commandeered to convey members of the upper classes on their way to or from Bergen. The 1723 description mentioned above also records their ingrained distrust of strangers, often called *byfant* (urban rabble). We may see this counter-culture as a strategy for preserving the autonomy of the »Strils«.

An alternative interpretation could be to regard this as a consequence of material poverty – the »Strils« seeing themselves at the mercy of the elements, in an endless struggle for their daily bread, close to starvation level, lacking the surplus required for what we may term »cultural expression«. According to the view taken by the French *Annales* historian Robert Mandrou, speaking about the French peasantry of the sixteenth and seventeenth centuries, they were stuck in a pre-modern mentality.[11] We shall later see that both theories directly and indirectly concern the rural-urban relationship.

Counter-culture?

According to the first theory, the »Strils« did not lack »cultural expressions«. These were, however, of a traditional kind which were not appreciated by the urban and administrative élites. Accounts of weddings and other rural feasts bear witness to a remarkable flourishing of culture, expressing itself in a naive decorative art, folk literature, songs, and not least in music. Admittedly, the wedding tunes did not appeal to the taste of the local government officials. There was also a living tradition of religious folk literature in this period.[12]

However, the generally good-humoured author of the 1723 description also tells us that the »Stril« is »difficult and contrary« in all things and »will in no way adjust to the customs (*sermonie*) of others«. For instance, they would wear their own traditional dress, even though they were ridiculed for it in town. The peasants also flatly refused to employ the town musician Bonnü, who in the 1760s obtained a formal privilege for playing at weddings and similar events, in the countryside as well as in the town. They preferred to stick to their own fiddlers who were paid by each guest putting two or four *skilling* into the fiddle.[13]

Of all the phenomena listed above, the lack of a literary culture is the one which can be measured, albeit imperfectly. Those books that are listed in peasant inventories can at least give us an indication of the occurrence of books in private homes. (See table 14.1).[14]

This table gives an almost overwhelming confirmation of the statement quoted above. The »Strileland« had no part in the increase in the number of books to be found in rural homes which

Table 14.1: Proportion of peasant inventories containing books

District	1756-60	1806-10	1845
Northern and Middle Hordaland	6%	4%	18%
Southern Hordaland	8%	14%	
Voss	0%	46%	
Hardanger	12%	63%	
Outer Sogn	32%	52%	

Note: The 1845 figure refers to Northern Hordaland only.

seems to have been a feature of the neighbouring regions towards the end of the eighteenth century. Admittedly, the situation was not much better in its adjacent district to the south, Southern Hordaland. Nor does there seem to have been great differences between the various parts of Northern and Middle Hordaland in this respect. Scattered information from other, more distant parts of Western Norway also indicate a far greater occurence of books than what was common among the »Strils« at this time.[15]

We may ask if the peasants of the »Strileland« were not too ardent in their opposition to the authorities and their neighbours, so that they missed the opportunity of obtaining such qualifications as would have enabled them to play a part in public life towards the end of the eighteenth century. There may not have evolved a new peasant élite familiar with the language of power used among the ruling sections of society, similar to those we find within rural communities elsewhere in Norway. Indeed, did this result in the dialogue between peasant leaders and the rulers being broken?[16]

The facilities for such a dialogue had been better before the middle of the eighteenth century. The peasant élite dominated local court proceedings as *lagrettemenn* (formally lay judges, but dependent upon the judgements of the *sorenskriver* or royally appointed judge). The same persons were used actively as spokesmen of the local rural communities in various contexts. Their position was bolstered by the district bailiff (*foged*), who regularly and consciously picked the parish constables (»lensmenn«) from the same élite, using them as a buffer between himself and the rural communities. Only after 1746 was the rotation principle laid down in the law employed in the selection of »lagrettemenn«, with new appointments each year. This state of affairs was only slightly modified by the dominance of the old élite families in the newly established school and poor relief commissions, but these had, after all, only limited powers.[17] Economic, and probably also social inequalities among the peasants of the region also seem to have decreased towards the end of the century.

At the same time, few people attended the seasonal gatherings of the *ting*, the local meetings for administering justice, publicizing new statutes and legal documents, and collecting taxes. Only seven per cent of the peasants of Herdla attended the autumn »ting« of 1799, and the turnout was not much greater in Radøy and Hosanger. On the other hand, Alenfit and Eikanger show an attendance rate of more than 20 per cent, but in those districts, most of the inhabitants had a much shorter distance to travel to the »ting«. For the spring session of the »ting« in Lindås in 1805, only those persons attended who had legal cases before the court, and for the autumn session, only one in every five persons appeared. The bailiff was worried about the low turnout, which made it difficult for the government officials to become acquainted with the local population. In court cases that were even slightly complicated, advocates (known as *prokuratorer*) would regularly appear on behalf of the peasants, at least in the districts closest to the town. It seems that formal procedure was gaining ground in court cases, to the annoyance of the bailiff, who had to deal with all kinds of tricks invented by the »prokurators«. Only rarely would a peasant represent himself in a major case, he complained in 1798.[18]

This interrupted dialogue may have been a major cause of the famous *Strilekrig* (»the Stril war«), a widespread peasant revolt against an extraordinary tax which was held to be unfair, culminating in Bergen in 1765, and also of the strained relations between rulers and the ruled in the following decades. The »Stril«, who was formerly thought to be peaceful, amenable and obedient, was now considered unpredictable, choleric, bad-tempered and impudent.[19] On many subsequent occasions, the peasants mounted fierce opposition to and even sabotage against public duties, especially against compulsory roadworks. These public roads were often called *herremannsveier* (»gentlemen's roads«), of no practical use to the local community. At one such action, in 1794, the government officials were called »the king's thieves«, and someone shouted that things would not be put right until all government officials had been removed, as in France.[20]

Was it just by chance that the »Strileland« had practically no peasants among the first *ordførere* (elected heads of local democratic assemblies) following the reform of 1837, while regions with a strong literary culture, like Sunnmøre, Hardanger and Rogaland, also in Western Norway, had many peasant »ordførere«?

It is indeed possible that this »counter-culture« of the »Strils« may have been a barrier, not only to their adoption of a literary culture, but also to other aspects of what is often termed »the civilizing process«, headed by the upper strata of society.

However, leaving speculation aside, we shall now turn to the »misery theory«.

Poverty?

There is no shortage of descriptions of the poor living-conditions among the »Strils«. The dramatist and philosopher Ludvig Holberg in a much-quoted passage from 1737 wrote that although some members of the rural communities around Bergen might be living comfortably on their income from fishing, the majority were living in great poverty.

Their clothing was so bad that nowhere in the country were peasants looking more miserable, and »many a horse is as well-fed« as they were.[21] The royal commission which was set up to investigate »the Stril war« similarly characterized the region as an exceptionally poor one: »There is a general state of poverty and destitution among the peasants, and no prospect of any improvement«. Indeed, the administrative district of Northern Hordaland was the poorest in the whole country, and taxation proportionately higher than in other districts, according to the commission.[22] In our own times, many historians have found evidence to show that the »Strileland« must have been exceptionally poor.[23]

The materialistic and frugal attitude which is said to have been typical of the region, can also be seen as evidence of this. It has often been said that the »Stril« was exploited by the townspeople of Bergen, or that he was living in a backwater, a periphery exploited by the dominating centre. The statistics of agricultural production seem to confirm this picture. In 1723 and 1803, local food production could only provide two thirds of the calories needed by the population – 66.5% and 60% respectively, out of a normal requirement of 2600 kcal per person per day, according to my calculations. In this respect, the coastal areas were even worse off than the inland parishes.

The peasant inventories from the region give a more reliable indication of the material conditions. In September 1704, an inventory was made in the home of the widow Marte Monsdatter at Årås farm in Austrheim parish in Lindås, of the possessions left by her husband Anders Eriksen, who had died some time previously. Most of the things registered by the inventory commission were simple objects for everyday use, like an iron pot, a baking-plate, a scythe, a hoe, and an axe. In all, the value of the ironware was estimated at 2 riksdaler (rd). The wooden objects, worth 4 rd, included three chests, some barrels and vats, a cupboard and some plates. Equipment for sailing and fishing were more important: two boats and various fishing nets had a total value of nearly 6 rd. The cattle were even more valuable. Marte and Anders had owned nine dairy cows, five heifers, one bull and two calves, and also four sheep, four yearling lambs and one ram. The animals represented a total estimated value of almost 38 rd. The bedclothes and everyday clothes were worth less than 4 rd.

However, amidst all the evidence of a simple and frugal lifestyle, the men who made the inventory also found silver objects worth almost as much as the cattle, 32 riksdaler. One gilded silver belt alone matched the value of four good cows, two others were estimated at 9 and 6 rd respectively. There were also silver spoons, rings, and some smaller pieces of jewellery. A good copper kettle (5 rd) and some pewter plates and vases completed the list of goods, which were estimated at a total value of 92 riksdaler. The total debts, on the other hand, came to the amount of nearly 22 rd, including arrears of rent. Most of the debt, however, consisted of small amounts of money owed to neighbours and former servants. Only half a riksdaler was debt to a merchant.

The inventory from Årås was one of the wealthier in the region. The main basis of this wealth must have been cattle farming, but fishing probably also contributed to it. A fishing bay, Åråsvågen, belonged to the farm. An average inventory would contain total values of 77 rd in the early eighteenth century, and 119 rd around 1760. Even so, aspects of this inventory can be seen as characteristic of peasant inventories of this region in general. The objects bear witness to a frugal and modest way of life, with one exception, namely the silver. Large debts to merchants of Bergen, which might have been interpreted as evidence of exploitation, are conspicuously absent: debts to merchants amount to an average of 1.7 rd in the period 1702-08, only half of it to merchants in Bergen. Both at this time and around 1760, only a quarter of the inventories contained any debts to merchants at all.[24]

Additional evidence also indicates that the economic conditions in the »Strileland« were not exceptionally bad. The property tax lists of 1789 show the »Strils« being taxed on the basis of greater assets than people in the coastal regions further north, except Sogn.[25] And even if much of the population surplus of the »Strileland« was exported to Bergen, there was still at the same time an influx of immigrants to the region from other rural districts, especially from Sunnfjord and Voss. These immigrants must have found living conditions in the »Strileland« favourable compared to their home districts.

The greatest amounts of silver were found in the nearest hinterland of Bergen (cf. table 14.2). It seems reasonable to see this as evidence of a profitable trade with the town, at least from the adjacent parishes. But what could they sell?

Trade with Bergen

Although the agricultural production of the region, considered in isolation, fell far short of supplying the foodstuffs required to feed the population, a closer scrutiny of the data reveals one very significant fact: there was a very strong emphasis on cattle farming, which in 1723 provided more than 60 per cent of the total farm production as measured in calories, amounting to 1,050 kcal per person per day. This concentration on cattle probably resulted in a great surplus of cattle-based products, a supposition rendered all the more likely by the contemporary descriptions of the region, which are unanimous in describing a diet containing extremely small quantities of meat, butter and other animal products.

Such a production strategy may not seem entirely sensible, given the natural conditions of the region, with a shortage of pastureland. However, when we consider the proximity of the city of Bergen, where cattle products could be easily and profitably exchanged for grain, the situation becomes more understandable. In this way, and also by selling fresh fish, firewood, and other local products, the »Strils« would have found little difficulty in getting enough to eat. In 1757, the committee for poor relief defined the annual nutritional requirements of one of their clients, corresponding to 2,220 kcal per day, including only 500 kcal of cattle products and 250 kcal of fish, grain products making up the remainder. This corresponds very well with general descriptions of the regional diet, and quite well with similar evidence from Sunnmøre, further north on the western coast.[26]

Regional integration

Table 14.2: Silverware in inventories

District	Number of inventories	Average value of silver
Sotra	52	19.7 rd
Herdla	37	19.5 rd
Skjold	31	18.5 rd
Åsane in Arna	11	18.0 rd
Alenfit	21	17.4 rd
Mjelde	22	16.3 rd
Lindås	28	15.7 rd
Radøy	43	15.0 rd
Eikanger	25	13.2 rd
Hosanger	29	12.7 rd
Arna (without Åsane)	14	12.1 rd
Strandvik	35	10.3 rd
Os	39	6.5 rd
Gulen	41	4.7 rd
Våg	22	3.5 rd

Note: Districts of Northern and Middle Hordaland ranged according to the average amount of silver in peasant inventories, 1702-60.

Thus, we find that central parts of the regional economy were market-oriented. Woodland (for firewood) could be turned into capital far more easily than in districts further from Bergen, and for people living on or near the coast, fresh and live fish were the most important products for the great consumer market in the city.

Within the »Strileland«, it is possible to see different outer boundaries of economic regions, based on the production and sale of various products. For instance, it is possible to trace a boundary for the delivery of fresh milk to Bergen, quite close to that city, a more distant border for sour milk, and one even further away, for the supply of fresh meat to the regional capital. This state of affairs is clearly reflected in the distribution of dairy cattle and young animals (for slaughter) in the 1723 *matrikkel* (evaluation of farms). Farms close to the town had higher numbers of dairy cattle, while there were greater stocks of young cattle in districts further away. For firewood as well as for cattle products, there was an outer boundary for individual transport in small boats. An illustration of this is provided by a detailed registration of boats along the Osterfjord, made in 1806. Near the mouth of the *fjord*, and thus closest to the town, nearly every farm had a small boat for transporting firewood, known as *brennebåt* (»firewood boat«). Further in along the »fjord«, these »brennebåter« were bigger, often of a type known as *åttring* (built for four pairs of oars), but these were not found on all farms. At the bottom of the »fjord«, some farms had small yachts (*jekter*), which were also, presumably, mainly used for transporting firewood. Thus, the further one lived from the town, the less frequent the voyages to Bergen became, but also the larger the vessels and the greater the quantities of firewood per voyage.[27]

In the fish trade, we can identify an inner boundary for the transport of live fish to the town in so-called »fishchests«, which were towed behind rowing-boats, involving very hard work for the oarsmen. Further away from the town, along the coast, we find the outer acceptable limit for the transport of dead fish to be sold as »fresh« in Bergen. Urban demand and prices made it desirable for the »sea Strils« to extend these boundaries as far as possible.

Sounds and fjords leading to Bergen seemed custom-made for individual loads in small boats, especially north of Bergen. Overland transport of milk and firewood was much more cumbersome, and practicable only from the nearest districts, Fana and Åsane, home of the »land Strils«.

We can safely assume that the »Strils« living closest to Bergen engaged in extensive trade with the townspeople, dealing in cash rather than being tied to specific merchants through debt. But it was a vulnerable trade, especially because of the fluctuating grain prices. Fish were also unreliable creatures, making catches uncertain.

In such an economy, silverware could function as a crucial reserve of hard currency, providing security and stability.[28] The inventories show, however, that silverware was distributed very unevenly among the »Strils«. Other evidence confirms this unequal distribution of wealth, for instance the funerary expenses which were deducted from the assets in the inventories.

But although the »Stril« often appeared to be shabby and destitute, not least in an urban environment, we see that he would often have hidden assets. The author of *Saa Maata* (1723) must have noticed this, writing that the »Stril« is clever at »saving, hiding, and complaining«.

Ivar Aasen observed the same phenomenon more than a century later, describing the houses of the »Strils« as small and poor, but going on to explain that this was largely due to old traditions. Many of the inhabitants were quite wealthy, according to Aasen, but preferred to keep their assets in cash or real estate, rather than spending them on ornaments or luxury goods.[29] So the myths of the poor and badly exploited »Stril« are not confirmed by this evidence.

Regional integration

Centre and periphery

We seem to be left with the impression that the late development of a modern and rational culture and mentality among the »Strils« was due less to poverty than to an exceptionally strong counter-culture, which caused them to lag behind others in the civilizing process. However, we may have to qualify this statement somewhat. In spite of Ivar Aasen's view, the level of material wealth in the region seems to have been somewhat reduced towards the end of the eighteenth century, partly due to a reduction in fish catches, partly because of increasing competition in the urban market from producers in more remote areas. At the same time, farmers living close to the town were being squeezed ever harder by greedy landowners, who were collecting take-over fees from new tenants amounting to many times the legal maximum. Some of them changed their strategy to lease out farms to caretakers for a limited number of years, in return for exorbitant fees. A number of tenant farmers were forced to buy their farms at quite high prices.[30]

For a period after the Napoleonic Wars, the »Strils« were unable to export significant proportions of their surplus population to Bergen, leading to an unprecedented increase in population. A shortage of outfield pasture made it difficult to increase the number of cattle to any significant extent, greatly reducing the surplus of production per peasant household, and forcing the »Strils« to meet the increasing local demand for food by turning to labour-intensive arable farming. As far as can be measured by the presence of silverware in peasant households, production surplus was decreasing, and debts were increasing. On the other hand, a rising number of »Strils« were becoming owners of the land they were farming, but land ownership cannot be taken *ipso facto* as evidence of surplus and wealth. (See table 14.3).[31]

Although there are, as we have seen, many reasons to assume that the nineteenth-century »Stril« was less well-off than his eighteenth-century counterpart, we can still argue that any regional, archaic characteristics of the »Stril« mentality were mainly due to exceptionally strong elements of »counter-culture« and neighbourly opposition. The

Table 14.3: Average gross assets, debts, real estate, silverware, and cash in peasant inventories from Northern and Middle Hordaland, 1702-1848, in »cow equivalents«

Period	Gross assets	Debts	Real estate	Silverware	Cash
1702-08	27.7	4.0	4.4	3.9	0.4
1756-60	41.6	6.8	7.1	5.7	2.1
1806-08	35.0	7.9	11.9	2.1	1.2
1841-48	47.6	17.4	23.4	1.1	0.5

Note: 1.0 »cow equivalent« represents the average value of one cow in the relevant period.

role of poverty may have been to provide an additional set of breakes on the modernization process at a later stage. Such a counter-culture seems to have been stronger in the »Strileland« than in the hinterlands of other Norwegian towns, possibly due to the fact that Bergen was by far the most populous town in the country. At the same time, the urban culture of Bergen had for many centuries been under stronger foreign influences than any other town in Norway; it was an international, indeed a cosmopolitan city. The Bergen historian Anders Bjarne Fossen thinks that the exceptionally deep cultural conflict between Bergen and its hinterland stemmed at least partly from the fact that the merchants of the city got their main goods of trade, not from the town's nearest hinterland, but from much farther afield, mainly from Sunnmøre and Northern Norway – a unique situation for a Norwegian town. The »Strils« mainly delivered goods for ordinary consumption by the inhabitants of the town. The merchants of Bergen had no strategic trading interests of trade in the »Strileland«, and a correspondingly low opinion of the population of the region.[32]

The close ties to the town, and the common experiences of the »Strils« visiting Bergen, combined to create not only a counter-culture, but also a common sense of identity and an image of themselves, transgressing the purely local. This must also have had consequences for the dimensions of the »Stril war« and later actions.

This counter-culture also antedates the conflicts between centre and periphery which were a central feature on a national level in the late nineteenth century. At that time, improved communications, mass media, and not least a more general integration of the peasant economy in the market had led to a closer contact between rural society in all parts of the country and a dominating urban and élite culture. In Stein Rokkan's words, »the awakening local communities mounted a defence against the influence of an alien and internationally oriented urban culture«.[33]

* Translated by Finn-Einar Eliassen.

Notes

1 Statsarkivet i Bergen (Bergen State Archives) (SAB), Tingbok (court protocol) Nordhordland, 47, fol. 196a-197b.
2 A. Døssland: Trolldomsmakt på Osterøy 1769 (Witchcraft at Osterøy, 1769), *Frå Fjon til Fusa* (Local history society yearbook), 1993, pp. 23-33.
3 »Saa Maata« (»Roughly so«), 1723. Printed with an index and commentaries by Brynjulv Alver, *Frå Fjon til Fusa*, 1972, pp. 39-40.
4 T.W. Angell: Beskrivelse over Lindaas Præste-Gjeld (Description of Lindås parish) (1753), *Nordhordland og Midthordland Sogelag, Aarsskrift* (Local history society yearbook), 1927.
5 M. Krohn (country doctor in Lindås and Manger): Om folkets standpunkt (On the opinion of the people), lecture given to the Health Commission (*Sundhedskommissionen*), 1858. Transcription by the Institute of Social Medicine, University of Bergen, accessible on the Internet
(http://www.uib.no/isf/hist/krohn.htm).
E. Haarstad: Distriktslæge Holmsen om tilhøve i Midhordaland 1854 (Country doctor Holmsen on conditions in Mid-Hordaland, 1854), *Frå Fjon til Fusa*, 1954, pp. 86-87.
6 SAB, Biskopen i Bergen (The Bishop of Bergen), Skulefundasar og Indberetningar om skular frå Nordhordland og Voss (School foundations and school reports from Northern Hordaland and Voss), 1762- 1815.

7 SAB, Stiftamtmannen i Bergen (The regional governor in Bergen), Brev frå futen i Nordhordland og Voss (Letters from the bailiff of Northern Hordaland and Voss), 15.12.1758.
8 R. Djupedal: Ivar Aasen på Strilelandet (Ivar Aasen in the »Strileland«), Frå Fjon til Fusa, 1965, pp. 18, 34.
9 SAB, Stiftamtmannen i Bergen, Brev frå futen i Nordhordland og Voss, 27.7.1767. Djupedal 1965 (see note 8), p. 34.
10 See for instance O. Hetlevik: Eit stykke strilelandssoge (A piece of »Strileland history«), Frå Fjon til Fusa, 1957, p. 49.
11 See for instance A. Nedkvitne: Annalesskolen – en tradisjon i oppløsning? (The Annales school – the dissolution of a tradition?), Historisk Tidsskrift (The Historical Journal of Norway), 3, 1996, pp. 361-369.
12 See »Saa Maata« (see note 3) and »Anmærkning over Nordhordlehns Skikke« (A note on traditional customs in Northern Hordaland), after a manuscript in The Royal Danish Library, Copenhagen, Thottske Samling, c. 1750, transcription in Riksarkivet (The Norwegian National Archives), Oslo; printed in Nordhordland og Midthordland Sogelag, Aarsskrift, III, 1920, pp. 5-15. See also J.S. Welhaven: Billeder fra Bergens-Kysten (Pictures from the coast around Bergen), 1842, and O. Hanssen: Litt om religiøs folkedikting i Nordhordland (Notes on religious folk literature in Northern Hordaland), Frå Fjon til Fusa, 1954, pp. 58-62.
13 SAB, Stiftamtmannen i Bergen, Brev frå futen i Nordhordland og Voss, 5.9.1766.
14 The table is based on a random selection of inventories from Northern and Middle Hordaland: 231 inventories from 1756-60, 192 from 1806-08, and 150 from 1845. From the other districts, samples of 30-40 inventories were taken from each period.
15 In the three fogderier (local administrative districts, each headed by a bailiff) of Møre and Romsdal (the northernmost region of Western Norway), there were books in 15-45% of all (not only peasant) inventories, already c. 1760, rising above 30% in all three districts by 1800. At Jæren, south of Stavanger, there were books in between a quarter and a third of all inventories in the 1760s, and in about half the inventories in the 1780s. J. Fet: Lesande bønder. Litterær kultur i norske allmugesamfunn før 1840 (Reading peasants. Literary culture among the common people in Norway before 1840), Oslo 1995, pp. 106, 122-124. A. Døssland: Med lengt mot havet. Fylkeshistorie for Møre og Romsdal 1671-1835 (With a longing for the sea. County history of Møre and Romsdal, 1671-1835), Oslo 1990, p. 290. B. Lindanger: Soga om Sola og Madla (The history of Sola and Madla), Sola 1980, pp. 443ff. B. Lindanger: Randaberg. Kultursoge til 1945 (Social and cultural history of Randaberg until 1945), Randaberg 1988, p. 274.
16 Cf. E. Sandmo: Saker og ting (Cases and things), Arr, 2, 1995, p. 33.
17 J.R. Myking: Lagrettemenn og bygdeelite ca. 1650-1750. Eit eksempel frå Nordhordland (Lay judges and rural élite, c. 1650-1750. An example from Northern Hordaland), Heimen (The Home, journal of Norwegian local history), 3, 1996, pp. 179-188.
18 The information on »ting« participation from SAB, Tingbok Nordhordland, 49, and SAB, Stiftamtmannen i Bergen, Brev frå futen i Nordhordland og Voss, 26.1.1805. On the advocates: Brev frå futen i Nordhordland og Voss, 19.12.1798.
19 Angell 1753 (see note 4), p. 41. SAB, Stiftamtmannen i Bergen, Brev frå futen i Nordhordland og Voss, 29.6.1782.
20 H. Nilsen: Oppløp i Midhordlandsbygdene i 1794 (A revolt in the rural communities of Mid-Hordaland, 1794), Frå Fjon til Fusa, 1968, pp. 11-31. J.R. Myking: Fana bygdebok (Parish history of Fana), vol. 2, Bønder nær byen (Peasants close to the town) 1665-1865, Bergen 1990, pp. 258-263. Cf. SAB, Stiftamtmannen i Bergen, Brev frå futen i Nordhordland og Voss, 20.6.1785, 15.3.1788. Brev frå futen i Sunnhordland (Letters from the bailiff of Southern Hordaland), 5.3.1802.
21 L. Holberg: Den berømmelige Norske Handels-Stad Bergens Beskrivelse (Description of the famous Norwegian trading town Bergen), 1737, New edition, Bergen 1920.
22 Efterretning om Opløbet i Bergen 1765 i Anledning af Extraskatten (Information on the revolt in Bergen in 1765 against the extra tax), Saga, 1820, p. 493.
23 See for instance S. Dyrvik: Folkevekst og bondesamfunn (Population growth and peasant

society), *Kulturhistorisk vegbok for Hordaland* (Road book of cultural history of Hordaland), Bergen 1993, p. 46.

24 This is confirmed by A. Nedkvitne: *Mens Bønderne seilte og Jægterne for* (While the peasants were sailing and the yachts were speeding), Oslo 1988, p. 538.

25 S.J. Kalvatn: Formuesskatten 1789 – kort presentasjon og studie av ein landsdel (The tax on assets, 1789 – a short presentation and a regional study), *Heimen*, 2, 1996, pp. 111-124.

26 SAB, Overfattigkommisjonen (The supervisory commission for poor relief), pk. 97. Cf. A. Døssland: Sunnmørsk jordbruksøkonomi på 1700-tallet (The agricultural economy of Sunnmøre in the eighteenth century), *Heimen*, 1, 1983, pp. 30-31. In 1723, cattle production in Northern and Middle Hordaland amounted to 1054 kcal per person per day, falling to 905 in 1803, i.e. probably twice as much as they were consuming themselves. A usual combination of cattle products, if sold at normal prices, would give three times as many calories if exchanged for grain. Even more favorable exchange rates could be obtained for milk and fresh meat, which were the main trade products for the »Strils« to take to Bergen, because of the short distance. These calculations are based on extensive research and processing of the data contained in a property register of 1723, and a tax assessment of real estate of 1803, both in Riksarkivet in Oslo. These data have been adjusted after a critical evaluation of the sources. The calorie calculations have been made according to a model constructed by Kåre Lunden in his article: Poteta og den raske folkeveksten i Noreg frå 1815 (The potato and the rapid population growth in Norway after 1815), *Historisk Tidsskrift*, 1975, pp. 275-315, but some of Lunden's factors of calculation have been revised.

27 SAB, Båtlister (Lists of boats), 1806. See also J.R. Myking: Byen og omlandet. Vestlandsk hushaldsøkonomi på 1600- og 1700-talet (The town and its hinterland. Household economy in Western Norway in the seventeenth and eighteenth centuries), *Norsk bondeøkonomi 1650-1850* (Norwegian peasant economy, 1650-1850), eds. A. Tranberg and K. Sprauten, Oslo 1996, pp. 96-116.

28 I have registered a total of 454 peasant inventories from Northern and Middle Hordaland, concentrating on the periods 1702-08 and 1756-60. The inflation rate was insignificant in this period. In Northern Hordaland (minus Gulen), silver amounted to an average of 13.3 riksdaler (rd) in the first period and 19.9 rd in the second, corresponding to more than 20% of the movable goods in each instance. The neighbouring districts show the following pattern: Sunnhordland (Southern Hordaland) (1702-08): 7.8 rd/10% of the movables; (1756-1760): 8.2 rd/5%, Outer Sogn (c. 1760): 12 rd/8%, Voss (c. 1760): 6.3 rd/4.8%, Hardanger (c. 1760): 23.5 rd/13%. Scattered examples from other parts of Norway: Sunnmøre (1720-49): 1.9 rd/3.3% (all inventories, not only from peasants), Romsdal (early eighteenth century): 1.9 rd, Fosen (Trøndelag) (1711-35): 9.4 rd/6%, Lower Telemark (South-Eastern Norway) (early eighteenth century): 3.5 rd, Upper Telemark (1720-49): 17.9 rd/8.7%. In Gaular (Sunnfjord, western Norway), a sample of 48 inventories from 1781-90 shows only small amounts of silver, never more than 5 rd. At the end of the seventeenth century, a selection of inventories which is probably representative contains silver worth 14 rd on average. A.K. Engevik: Bonde og embetsmann (Peasants and government officials), unpublished thesis, University of Bergen, 1975. T. Buggeland: Den sal. mands efterladenschab i løst og fast (The movables and immovables of the deceased), unpublished thesis, University of Bergen, 1969. R.T. Hovde: En overmaade slet huusholdning (An extremely poor household), unpublished thesis, University of Trondheim, 1994. Fet 1995 (see note 15), p. 118. Lindanger 1980 (see note 15), pp. 544ff. The sample from Gaular was made by Anders Timberlid, and those from Sunnhordland, Hardanger, Voss, and Outer Sogn c. 1760 by the author.

29 »Saa Maata« (see note 3), p. 35. Djupedal 1965 (see note 8), p. 34.

30 A. Døssland: *Strilesoga. Nord- og Midhordland gjennom tidene* (The history of the »Strils«. Northern and Middle Hordaland through the ages), vol. 3, Bergen 1998, ch. 12 and 13.

31 The table is based on a random sample of 223 complete peasant inventories from 1702-08,

231 from 1756-60, 192 from 1806-08, and 150 from 1841-48. The average price of a cow was: 1702-08: 2.76 riksdaler, 1756-60: 2.87 rd, 1806-08: 6.63 rd, 1841-48: 6.32 *speciedaler*.

32 A.B. Fossen: Byen og Strilelandet (The town and the »Strileland«), *Kulturhistorisk vegbok for Hordaland* (see note 23), p. 74.

33 S. Rokkan: *Stat, nasjon, klasse* (State, nation, class), Oslo 1987, p. 70.

CHAPTER 15
Civilizing the wilderness
The social and agricultural transformation of West Jutland, 1750-1850

By Peter Henningsen

The inhabitants of the peninsula of Jutland have always been regarded in a special manner by the inhabitants of the East Danish islands. According to the common stereotypes, Jutlanders are not like other Danes – they are thought to be more efficient, more frugal and more hard-working than others, and the »classic« Jutlander is supposed to be self-confident, brave-hearted and tenacious, always doing whatever he believes is good, laws and prohibitions of the government notwithstanding. This image prevails not only among East Danes. The Jutlanders themselves approve of the image and time after time one can hear Jutlanders refer to this image as a fact: Yes, we Jutlanders are different: we are better and smarter than you East Danes and deep in our hearts we despise you a little for your laziness and inefficiency!

The inhabitants of Jutland dislike being ruled from a distant government in Copenhagen and always insist that they are better off on their own. This is even more true for the inhabitants of West Jutland. Somehow they seem to be even more stout-hearted and self-willed than other Jutlanders. The »cradle« of Jutland's identity and self-perception was certainly centered in this part of the country and modern Jutland has been sustained from here for many years.

So much for stereotypes and prejudices – but why has this image become so dominant and from where does it originate? How was it created? Did the Jutlanders make it themselves, or was it the Danish islanders who created this image?

It is not at all simple to give a clear and satisfactory answer to this question. I will, however, attempt to do so in very general terms by looking at West Jutland in comparison with the east of Denmark. My article will concentrate on the eighteenth and nineteenth centuries as this was the period when the region was transformed from a huge wasteland and turned into fertile and well-cultivated plots of arable land. These two centuries are a phase of transition in the West Jutland social and agricultural system. The source material for this period is abundant because of the interest in this transition from all over the kingdom of Denmark.

Before proceeding any further, I will clarify what is actually meant by the term »West Jutland«: from the German border to the Limfjord (*Limfjorden*), the Jutland peninsula is divided by a ridge, separating east from west. The southern

Regional integration

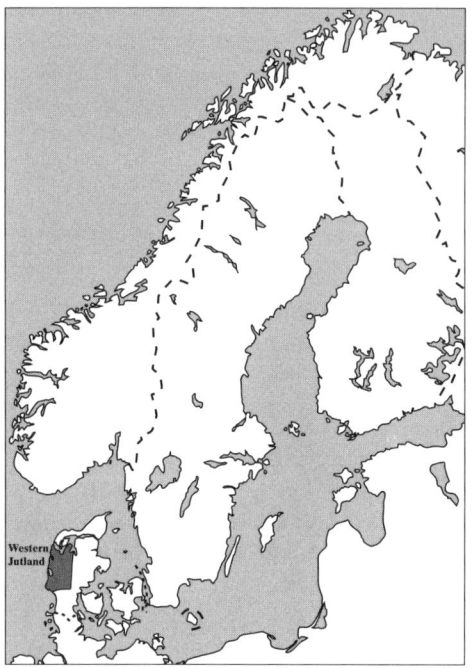

Fig. 15.1: The region of West Jutland

The social structure of West Jutland

East Denmark – that is East Jutland, Funen, Zealand and the smaller Danish islands – was in the eighteenth century characterized by a traditional manorial system. Land and villages belonged to a number of small and large estates owned by the nobility and well-off burghers, and the peasants were mainly tenants who, because of their contracts with the estate, were obliged to pay annual contributions and do corvée on the fields of the estate. The soil was fertile and suitable for crops. So the ordinary Danish farmer cultivated his land with barley, oats and, on a smaller scale, wheat.

In comparison with East Denmark, West Jutland was very different: West Jutland was dominated by vast moors and the soil was not as fertile as in the east of the country. The population was very sparse and lived in small, widely scattered villages. There were hardly any large estates in the region, and even small estates were few in number. Because of the poor agricultural soil, the nobility did not want to invest in West Jutland, and the fact that the region was far from the capital of Copenhagen did not increase their interest in it.

In the latter part of the eighteenth century, a great number of the small West Jutland estates were parcelled out and sold to the tenants. This meant that the region was more or less »cleansed« of noblemen and manorial estates by 1800.[1] In short, the inhabitants of West Jutland were not used to being subject to nobility or government officials, as they were mainly freeholders living far away from the administrative centres of East Denmark. They were accustomed to

limit of West Jutland is not, however, the German border. Rather it is the small river, *Kongeåen*, which in earlier times divided Jutland from the Duchy of Schleswig. So West Jutland is the area west of the Jutland ridge lying between the Kongeå and the Limfjord. The Jutland ridge, however, is not merely a natural border, it is also a cultural border. The dialects spoken west of the ridge are more or less the same and their patois is distinct from dialects spoken east of the ridge. In addition, the whole area west of the ridge has a quite different past from the eastern part. From time immemorial, the west had been covered in heather with few settlements and almost no manors and big estates at all, whereas the east was characterized by fertile farmland, many settlements and numerous big estates owned by the nobility.

manage everything on their own in the manner of their own choosing.

As the villages of West Jutland were very small – usually from 3 to 15 holdings – the farmers were not accustomed to any form of extensive village community unlike their East Danish counterparts, and many farms did not even belong to a village. Rather, they were situated by themselves on the moor with no neighbours at all, and accordingly they did not belong to any sort of community whatsoever.

Jurisdiction and administration in West Jutland

It was not merely on the surface that the social system of West Jutland differed from the manorial system of East Denmark. From a centralistic and governmental point of view, the region was incalculable and difficult to survey. So it was no easy task for the West Jutland *amtmænd* (county governors) to control their districts.

In the more »civilized« parts of East Denmark, the monarch and his government could rely on the secular and clerical institutions of the country to support them in their exercise of power. The traditional manorial system, headed by a lord who organized the collection of taxes among his tenants, carried out sentences, ensured that royal orders were obeyed, taxes paid and so on, was an efficient instrument of discipline for the absolutist regime, as were the »amtmænd« and the *stiftamtmænd* (regional governors). The local vicars also played a dominant role in their parishes. They were often the sole representative of the king in the community and accordingly

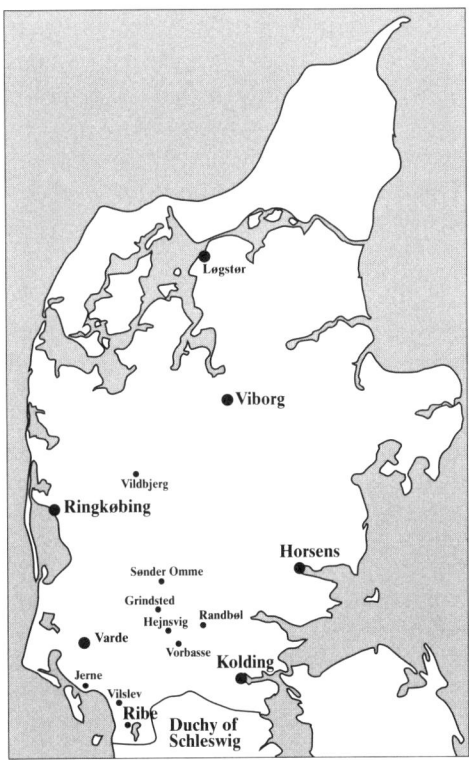

Fig. 15.2: Some of the market towns and villages in Nørrejylland (Jutland north of Kongeåen) in the eighteenth and nineteenth centuries

they carried out secular as well as religious tasks.[2] Those institutions were the only guarantors that society functioned according to the wishes of the monarch.

The situation in West Jutland was different. The principles of administration were the same, but their implementation was rendered almost impossible because of the great distances and the lack of estates. The vast counties and dioceses were sparsely populated and the small number of minor estates made the region hard to control. Even the parishes covered a large area and the West Jutland vicar could not count on seeing his whole community at church every Sunday.

The major problem was the lack of estates. The estates symbolized the well-integrated jurisdictional units of the kingdom, and the scarcity of estates in West Jutland meant that the interests of the king could not be looked after by estate holders in this part of the country. This task was carried out by the »amtmænd«, but because of the vast areas they had to cover, it was virtually impossible for them to do it. The »amtmand« of Koldinghus county for example had his residence in the East Jutland town of Kolding and even if he could possibly control the five closest East Jutland districts, he would never be able to survey the remaining three West Jutland districts in the heather-covered wilderness.[3] However, it was not the »amtmand« alone who had difficulties contacting the peasants of his districts. The peasants for their part had just as much trouble contacting him and the local district courts. The West Jutland jurisdictions covered vast areas of land and the West Jutland peasant appeared in the local court only on very rare occasions, unless he lived close to the place where the court was held.

The royal laws were read aloud by the judge at the local court or by the vicar in the church during the sermon, but as West Jutland peasants usually had a long way to travel to each of these institutions, they were not likely to get as much royal information as they were supposed to. The West Jutland peasants were totally dependent on oral information and hearsay to get news from the government and if the communication failed, as was very likely to happen, they did not get any information at all. Thus, the laws had little if any effect in the remote western areas of Denmark.

Lago Matthias Wedel, the author of a description of travels in Jutland, described the county of Ringkøbing at the turn of the eighteenth century, as »lawless«, and professor Engelstoft, who visited Jutland in the same period, agreed: the estate owners cheated their tenants and negotiated for clerical benefices. Even the vicars were corrupt and so were the »amtmænd« who were not averse to gold. In the district of Slet almost all vicars and peasants distilled spirits. However, they did not get fined since they bribed the local administrators at Løgstør.[4]

Another Engelstoft, who travelled the moors of West Jutland in 1830, commented upon this matter in his travel account, writing: »It is strange how little the royal laws are respected in the western part of Jutland – it is a total anarchy«.[5]

This statement was also appropriate regarding the extensive smuggling of goods and bullocks across the small river, Kongeåen, which divided Jutland from the Duchy of Schleswig. Huge herds of bullocks bound for the market places in Schleswig and Holstein were illegally transported across this stream at night by Jutland peasants: In 1773, for example, a bullock trader from the village of Seest was arrested for having smuggled a herd of 222 bullocks across the Kongeå and had to pay a fine of 325 *rigsdaler*, which was a considerable amount for an ordinary man.[6]

The customs officers at the border between Jutland and the Duchy of Schleswig had a hard time catching bullock traders and preventing smuggling, and it was, indeed, an almost impossible task. In

Fig. 15.3: The jurisdictions (herreder) in Nørrejylland in the nineteenth century

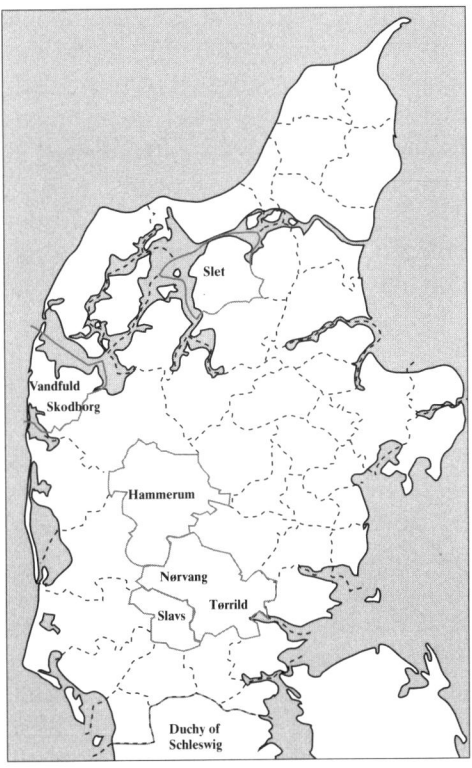

1788 it was claimed that the customs officers risked serious injuries if they interfered with the smugglers. It was even claimed that no officer had ever done so without suffering severe injuries to his health or paying with his life![7] In 1701 a customs officer complained to the authorities that smuggling would continue even if the border were guarded by 100 men and 10 gallows were placed beside them.[8] The »stiftamtmand« of Ribe diocese likewise claimed, in 1739, that the bullock traders often gathered 20-40 men who crossed the border armed with rifles with no chance at all for the customs officers to interfere with their business.[9] So the West Jutland bullock traders, who were often peasants from the vast moors, were not easy to cope with. They did whatever they pleased, no matter what measures were taken by the authorities.

The stubborn peasants on the moors posed a major problem for the tax collectors, too. The peasants frequently did not want to pay their taxes, and it was almost impossible to make them do so since they lived so far away from the towns. In the eighteenth century, it was very common for the government to farm out the taxes to private individuals, often by public auction. In 1746 the tradesman Andreas Flensborg from the East Jutland town of Horsens, who was farming the royal taxes in some West Jutland parishes in the county of Ribe, complained to the »amtmand« that he could not make the peasants pay their taxes. He asked the »amtmand« for military assistance to help him to collect the money, but the request was denied and Flensborg was told that he would have to take the peasants to court to get his tax money![10]

In the wilderness

The »amtmænd« and their officers had a very weak position in West Jutland. Implementing the laws of the king was a difficult and thankless task. If the »amtmand« wanted to make sure that the laws were actually being upheld, he had to travel the moors himself, something no one would do voluntarily in the eighteenth century. The moors were perceived as wild and impassable tracts of land with numerous dangers around every corner. Thus, the traveller was exposed to the dangers of being attacked by stray wolves, gypsies (the so-called *tatere*) and highwaymen. For instance when the government wanted to establish a commission to survey the land of the vast moor Alheden in 1757, the county governors had great difficulties finding anyone who was willing to carry out the work. The appointed persons complained as if they were being sent away to darkest Africa: where were they supposed to find food and accommodation in the gloomy wilderness? They would have to bring their own food and tents if they were to avoid a miserable death.[11]

The vast Alheden was said to be so beset by wolves that the local peasants had to carry home their dead sheep by the dozen, and the wolves were even said to congregate in such vast and bloodthirsty numbers that travellers feared for their lives.[12] When the winter was colder than usual, even the citizens of the town of Varde (Ribe county) were said to be afraid of the wolves straying around outside the town in their hunt for food.[13] This was why the authorities offered rewards to those who brought dead wolves to the local courts, where they were put in gallows specially made for the purpose.[14]

In short, there were plenty of good reasons not to travel the Jutland moors in the eighteenth century. The royal officers preferred to stay at home in their civilized towns and let the population on the moors take care of themselves.

In the eastern parts of Denmark, the government had a very efficient instrument in the village schools, as the rural youngsters were obliged to learn suitable behavior towards the king and his officers and obedience to God. After 1739-40 there were schools in every village in East Jutland and the islands, but there were few schools on the moors as the villages were so far from each other and were so small that they could not support a teacher on their own. Accordingly these small villages kept an ambulating teacher, who was often a pupil at a grammar-school in a nearby town.[15] This young teacher then walked from village to village and taught the village children in his spare time. As these villages had no schoolrooms, the classes were held on the farms, and the local peasants had to accommodate and feed the teacher.

Because of these circumstances the skills and willingness of the teacher were not always the best, and the teaching of the village children suffered accordingly. Thus, the royal exhortations did not have the same power on the moors and did not influence the West Jutlanders as much as in the eastern parts of the country.[16] Regarding schools, too, the West Jutlanders had to manage on their own.[17]

The mobility of the rural population

As for the village schools, the notorious law prohibiting the free movement of male peasants (*stavnsbånd*) did not seem to have any great impact in the West Jutland countryside.[18] As there were very few estates in the region, there were no lords from whom to ask permission to leave home, at least no noblemen, as was common elsewhere in the country. On the other hand, there were many tenants on the moors, but instead of being subject to a landlord, they were subject to the vicars, who often owned several holdings, or to some wealthy farmers who, like the vicars, had more than one farm in their possession. The vicar in the parish of Jerne, for example, accumulated large tracts of land and by the time of his death in 1747 owned no less than 900 *tønder hartkorn*[19] of tenant property throughout the county of Ribe.[20] In 1785 it was recorded that the vicar Christopher Sølling in the parish of Grindsted (Ribe county) also owned tenant property, though he did not own as much as the Jerne vicar: Sølling had three farms in as many villages in the parish.[21]

The peasants who were actually subject to a noble landlord usually lived far away from the manor, as the land of the estates was widely dispersed. So the landlord could not watch his tenants on the moors and the tenants could often run away from home without being seen by anyone. When that occurred, an announcement about the missing tenants was made at the local court and at the regional court in Viborg on three successive court days. Even in the local church, the vicar was obliged to make an announcement about the runaway tenants from the pulpit.

Estate owners both in East and West Jutland complained that their servants and farmhands ran away to the Duchies of Schleswig and Holstein. There was a particularly great need for female servants, who were not covered by the law prohibiting free movement. In 1768, the lord of the Engelsholm estate argued that women should be subject to the prohibition of movement law as well as the males, because the girls were running away all the time. Every year women from the district went in large numbers to Schleswig and Holstein, where wages were far better, with the result that those left behind demanded better pay or they would run away, too! Accordingly, the Jutland landowners time after time complained that wages were rising because of their proximity to Schleswig.[22]

In 1735 the »amtmand« of Riberhus county (called Ribe county after 1794) reported, that many young men disappeared along with the females to the Duchies every year, and some young men even went to sea on ships going to the Netherlands and to England. Apparently they never returned. Even youngsters under the age of fourteen, who were not yet subject to the law prohibiting free movement, seized the chance to run away before they reached the prescribed age. For instance, a former »amtmand« said that two boys had run away from the Visselbjerg estate, six from the Nielsbygård estate, eight from the Sønderskov estate, seven from the Estrup estate and seven from the estate of Hundsbæk.[23]

There seems to have been quite a lot of traffic of young men choosing to get away before they were subject to the prohibition of movement law, appointed to take over a tenant-holding or enlisted in the army by the estate owner who, under the law, had the sole right to do so. Accordingly, the estate owners complained that it was almost impossible to get a young male peasant to take over a tenant farm, as there were none to choose from – they were all gone to the Duchies.[24] Even if these statements were greatly exaggerated, there is no doubt that West Jutland youngsters did indeed disappear in large numbers throughout this period, as the living conditions of servants and farmhands were far better elsewhere – especially in the south, in Schleswig.

The law on prohibition of free movement did not restrict the mobility of the West Jutlanders at all, in the way it certainly did for those on the Danish islands. From time immemorial the West Jutlanders had been used to leaving the infertile moorlands in their search for a better life, since agriculture on the moors could not ensure a livelihood for new generations. The vicar in the parish of Sønder Omme (Ribe county) thus reported in 1690 that the population of his parish was very unstable, the youngsters often leaving in the winter to work on Funen, Zealand or Lolland, returning home in the spring when there was work available.[25] The West Jutland peasants did not yet consider cultivating the moors, because this idea was too foreign to their traditional way of thinking. Consequently, new holdings could not be established on the moors.[26]

Another reason for the great mobility of the rural population of West Jutland was the »servants' markets« that took place annually in the Jutland towns. Every autumn the Jutland farmhands and servants from the county of Ribe gathered in the East Jutland town of Kolding. Here they were engaged by East Jutland farmers as threshers, cattlemen, milkmaids or spinners during the winter. At midsummer a similar market was held in the town of Ribe, where the servants could get employment by the farmers in the marchlands of Schleswig and Holstein, who needed assistance in harvesting their hay and crops. There was a strong competition between the farmers at these markets because everybody wanted the best-suited men and women, and there were many visiting farmers from Funen, East Jutland and the Duchies. The farmers from the Duchies usually picked the strongest and best servants, as they could afford to pay better wages. Even the board and lodging provided by the farmers in the Duchies was better than the farmhands were accustomed to in Denmark.[27]

The West Jutland towns of Varde and Ringkøbing had similar markets at midsummer. Here farm-hands were hired for the summer by East Jutland farmers who even brought them back and forth! However, most of these markets came to an end in the beginning of the nineteenth century since the West Jutland peasants could no longer compete with the farmers from the east and from the Duchies. Accordingly the youngsters went directly to Schleswig and East Jutland instead.[28]

The itinerant merchants and hawkers from the Duchies, who often came to West Jutland to sell their products, also from time to time tried to convince the young Jutlanders to come home with them, since the inhabitants of the Duchies were said to prefer the Jutlanders to their own young people.[29] The Jutland servants were highly praised for their willingness to work, their soberness and frugality, and accordingly they were in great demand among the farmers. »They are all well known in the east of Jutland and in Funen for their threshing skills«, reported professor Begtrup in 1808.[30]

The stubborn West Jutland peasant

The common perception in the eastern parts of Denmark, and particularly in the capital Copenhagen, was that the peasants on the moors of West Jutland were poor and miserable people compared with the farmers on Funen and Zealand. Agricultural observers and agronomists focused on the low »hartkorn« figures on the moors, that is the low tax assessment of the moorlands, using the same »hartkorn« as a basis for their observations. Thus, they did not see that the West Jutland farmers did not make their living solely by growing crops, but were engaged in more profitable businesses. The observers were acquainted with those other occupations of the farmers, but they did not consider them important. Moreover, the West Jutland peasants were not obliged to pay tax on their other occupations as tax was mainly paid on land according to the »hartkorn« assessment, and so the other sources of income became even more profitable. As the farmers and smallholders only paid taxes according to their low »hartkorn« estimates, the observers had little idea of their real income, and so the peasants seemed to be poor and miserable.

Because of their other occupations, the peasants of the Hammerum district (Viborg county) were not interested in an extension of their agricultural fields. On the contrary, they would be more pleased if they had less! They would much rather spend their time knitting wool stockings, either for sale in the town markets or to the itinerant peddlers. A knitting peasant, with only a low »hartkorn« assessment (1-2 tønder), earned at least twice as much as a peasant who did not do any knitting but had three times as much »hartkorn«.[31] An increase in the »hartkorn« estimate would probably result in the knitting peasant being forced to abandon his prosperous – and tax-free – knitting and spend more time cultivating his tax-burdened land!

The same relationship between other sources of income and the traditional principal occupation of farming existed throughout the moorlands. The peasants in the parish of Sønder Omme (Ribe county), like the peasants from Hammerum, were not interested in the cultivation of the moors or in growing more crops on their sandy soil than they already did. Unlike Hammerum, the parish was not the centre of a big wool-knitting proto-industry. Instead the locals used the moors for grazing their bullocks, cows and sheep and for many other profitable purposes. Hence the peasants did not want the areas cultivated and least of all by foreigners from South Germany (Pfalz-Hessen) who were actually colonizing the region around 1760. In 1758 this parish was visited by two governmental commissioners, who had the task of checking the quality of the soil – that is, to see if the soil was suitable for agriculture and thus suitable for establishing German colonist villages. The owner of the small estate of Juellingsholm ordered some of his tenants to show the honorable gentlemen the area, but instead of leading the commissioners to the good moors and sandless fields, they showed them only bogs, marshes and other swampy areas, emphasizing that the hunting was very good. Accordingly, the commissioners forgot all about colonies and agriculture and spent the whole day hunting and shooting various sorts of birds!

The vicar of the parish, who was advocating the cultivation of land, had to admit, regretfully, that the locals did not want to relinquish their moors, which the vicar could not understand, since the peasants did not seem to get any pleasure from the wilderness other than »driving their animals across the land two or three times a year«.[32]

Johan Arnt Dyssel, who travelled the moors of Jutland in the middle of the eighteenth century, compared the local peasants with »the dog in the fable, guarding a haystack from which it never ate a single straw itself«: The peasants »would scream and yell in grief if even a single dwelling was built on a stretch of land that they never saw or utilized themselves«.[33]

Evidently, there was a lack of understanding between the educated agricultural observers of the time and the West Jutland peasants about whether the moors should be cultivated or not. The two groups actually inhabited two quite different perceptual worlds. The well-intentioned experts and vicars were convinced that the traditional East Danish agricultural system centred on growing crops was far better and more profitable than the West Jutland animal husbandry and the numerous subsidiary occupations of the population, such as knitting wool stockings, making black pots of clay, preparation of coal etc. It is true that breeding and selling bullocks were prohibited for ordinary peasants, but they did it nevertheless, smuggling the animals across the Kongeå by night or by selling the bullocks to itinerant merchants, who offered a better price than the tradesmen in the towns.[34] The attitude of the well-intentioned observers was simply that the peasants ought to look after the soil and nothing else. As the well-known Jutland vicar and poet, Steen Steensen Blicher, put it in 1839, »travelling and peddling is not the destiny of the peasant«.[35]

However, the breeding and selling of bullocks were part of the »black« or unofficial economy that was not registered anywhere, and hence tax-free! After 1788, when the ban on breeding and selling bullocks was lifted, the export of bullocks increased, and around 1830 it was said about the peasants of Ribe county, that »animal husbandry is regarded as the main occupation everywhere and the selling of grain only as a secondary occupation«. Some local observers even said that the limited cultivation of grain would have been even smaller had it not been for the fact that it provided fodder for the bullocks and cows.[36]

The peasants on the moorlands did not want to change this state of affairs just because some well-intentioned agronomists and observers told them to do so.[37] As the situation was, they were already very successful doing their jobs in the usual way, and the fact that they did not have to pay taxes on their work no doubt gave them a greater incentive to do so. They had many good reasons for sticking to the old order of things.

Apparently, the agronomists did not understand this point of view. On the contrary, they thought that the obstinacy of the West Jutland peasants was due to a stubborn conservatism, laziness and downright stupidity. In their opinion, the secondary occupations served no useful purpose since they exhausted the peasant and distracted him from his really important task of cultivating the moorlands and growing grain.

In the middle of the eighteenth century, the vicar in the parish of Vorbasse (Ribe county) claimed that the local peasants tired their poor horses far too much by using them in the summer to go to market places peddling their homemade handicraft and the famous black pots, homemade ceramics, which were in great demand at that time. At the same time they neglected their »summer duty« back on the farm. The farmers in Vorbasse cultivated their land very badly, being lazy and succumbing to depraved comfort.[38] In 1766 the vicar in Vildbjerg (Ringkøbing county) reported to the bishop in Ribe that »the squeamish smallholder prefers to sit indoors by the hot stove doing his knitting instead of doing outside work that will make him sweaty and tired«. Because of this easy way of life, the Vildbjerg people became so unaccustomed to outdoor life that when they happened to go out, they immediately caught all sorts of horrible diseases.[39] Another observer of life on the moors similarly complained in 1759 that »it is easier for the peasants to sit indoors, earning their living with their hands instead of working the fields, where they have to suffer from cold and heat. That is why the peasants are only mediocre farmers and do not worry a bit about their crops as long as they can get the necessary grain«.[40]

According to the well-meaning and progressive vicars and agronomists, the peasants should be forced to go out of their houses even if they could earn a living doing what they had always done.[41] From an agronomic point of view – and particularly from a fiscal one – the critics were right. But so were the peasants, when they rejected the hard work in the fields as being unnecessary. »The aim of the peasant was to produce whatever was most profitable«, as the Norwegian historian Stein Tveite puts it in regard to Norwegian peasants. This was just as true for the peasants of West Jutland.[42]

The »stiftamtmand« in the diocese of Ribe claimed in 1735 that the peasants, all things considered, were not total strangers to the idea of cultivating the moors, but as the newly cultivated land would be burdened with new taxes, they withheld their efforts. He believed that the solution had to be found in tax reductions or in exemption from taxes for a certain length of time.[43] More than a hundred years later, in 1852, the agricultural observer S. A. Fjelstrup likewise claimed that fear of new taxes had caused the withdrawal of »thousands of acres of land from cultivation in generally favourable periods«.[44]

Economic conditions of the West Jutland peasantry

Numerous writings and reports from the eighteenth century emphasized that the peasants on the Jutland moors were poor and impoverished people. For instance, in 1768 the vicar of Grindsted parish (County of Ribe) claimed that his parishioners were »mainly poverty-stricken and suffering«. In the parish of Hejnsvig (County of Ribe), it was said that »the poor people in the parish are numerous«. However, none of these accounts tell us by what standards they were poor. Were they poor compared with peasants from other parts of the country or was it in comparison with the vicar himself? Most Danish historians have trusted these gloomy accounts and thus believed that the peasants on the moors were poorer and worse off than their counterparts in East Jutland and on the islands. The question is: do the sources really support this assumption, or have the historians just been hoodwinked by the low level of tax assessment in West Jutland? Have they fallen into the »hartkorn trap« just like the agronomists of the eighteenth century?

Many historians seem to overlook the fact that the agricultural activity of the seventeenth and eighteenth century peasants was not one of specialization. On the contrary, the peasants were engaged in all sorts of different activities to secure their subsistence, and most of these activities have not left any traces in the historical records. The Swedish ethnologist Orvar Löfgren emphasizes this clearly in his essay from 1980 on Scandinavian peasants: »For a long time specialization was a far less secure economic strategy than a complex pattern of subsistence activities. Many of these economic activities belonged to a »hidden economy« which cannot be studied in conventional historical records, an economy which gave Scandinavian peasants more room to manoeuvre and perhaps a better economic position than many of the agrarian peasants on the continental plains«.[45]

The sources of the period usually emphazise that peasants are poor people, no matter what part of eighteenth century Denmark one is investigating, particularly when the peasants themselves have been quoted in the sources. It is always »we poor impoverished men« and so forth. No peasant ever called himself prosperous and fortunate, even if he really was. He was far too afraid of being burdened with higher taxes if he revealed his true wealth to the official administrators. Furthermore, it is common knowledge that the first half of the eighteenth century was a difficult time for Danish agriculture, and nearly all tenants were in arrears with the royal taxes and their annual contributions to the landlords. So the question that should be posed is whether this generally poor Danish peasant and the poor peasant of West Jutland are two of the same kind? Did the West Jutland peasants really suffer as much hardship as they told the officials and were they, in fact, worse off than other Danish peasants? The claimed poverty of the West Jutlanders (or any other Danish peasant for that matter) might not be taken so much for granted after all!

A freeholder from the southern part of West Jutland for example, who beyond any doubt was relatively wealthy, nevertheless complained about his great poverty in 1743: »My place is bad and sandy. Usually I cannot grow enough barley to feed my household. The farm has been given a higher »hartkorn« assessment than it is really worth, and if I have to pay taxes along with tenants and freeholders, my small children and I myself will be so impoverished that eventually I will not even be able to pay the same as a tenant. In great humility I therefore beg that the fine gentlemen will pity me poor fellow and prevent me from sinking into deep poverty«.[46]

In fact, there is no reason to believe that the farmers on the moorlands were worse off than other Danish farmers at the time. Whereas the East Danish farmers had to pay taxes on their whole income (the land), the West Jutlanders profited from a »black« economy and paid their taxes only on a small area of arable soil. In a periodical from 1798, an anonymous writer says that the condition of the West Jutland farmer is quite good. Actually there were a number of wealthy and distinguished farmers even in the most heather-covered areas of the region, wealth generated by their animal husbandry and their many »subsidiary« activities.[47] The owner of Nørholm manor near the town of Varde, A. C. Teilmann, shared the same opinion. He did not pay any attention to the perpetual complaints and continual grumbling of his peasants about the high wages demanded by farmhands and servants. He argued that the high wages corresponded to the proportional distribution of wealth among his tenants and the freeholders of the area: »It is always a sign of good times that the farmhands get good pay. This shows that the farmers' income is so much the better. That is the surplus from farming«.[48]

The argument of the nobleman is really quite logical: if the servants demanded so much in pay that the farmers could not afford it, then they would have had to go without! Thus, the conclusion is that the eighteenth century farmers on the Jutland moors were actually capable of paying high wages to the young farmhands and milkmaids. There is really no way they could have been as impoverished as they have been depicted in the numerous myths (often initiated by the farmers themselves, hoping to avoid a higher tax assessment in this way). A brother of A. C. Teilmann, T. R. Teilmann, who owned an estate close to the present town of Esbjerg, also claimed that his tenants were well off since they had a reasonable income and suffered no hardship.[49] On the other hand, an estate owner would normally say things like that, so we cannot fully trust him either!

The vicar in the parish of Vilslev (County of Ribe) reported to the bishop in 1766 that the peasants had become more prosperous over the last 30 years, due to the long period of peace and because they had been spared any crop failures. Moreover the peasants were now working harder to expand the area of arable soil, and they were improving their farming by making their land the main source of income. Accordingly the animal plague which affected the parish in the years 1745, 1748 and 1750, killing more than a thousand bullocks and cows, and impoverishing most farmers, was no longer affecting the parishioners who were now living in better conditions than ever before.[50]

Lago Matthias Wedel, who travelled the moors in the years between 1799 and 1804, wrote in his account of his travels that the local peasants of the Skodborg and Vandfuld districts (Ringkøbing county) were not perturbed when the writer talked about the enclosure movement on Zealand, since they managed their own farming well without any enclosure at all, and »their grain, cattle, horses, sheep, meadows, farms, sittingrooms, chambers, outhouses, conditions, wealth, knowledge and so forth certainly exceed what we find among our farmers in Zealand«.[51]

The agronomist Gregers Begtrup, who described the agricultural condition of Jutland around the turn of the nineteenth century, writes that the peasants on the moors in the county of Ribe could not exactly be described as wealthy, but they still managed far better than one would imagine – and not only that: »The prosperity among the peasants in the west is far greater than in many a place in the more fertile parts of Denmark, irrespective of how bad and sandy their arable land seems to be. The

Regional integration

farmers have fine houses, often made of bricks, fine furniture, good livestock and most people only have a very small mortgage on their freehold«.[52] In the moorlands of Vejle county, and particularly in the sandy districts of Nørvang and Tørrild, Begtrup reports that »due to the thrift of the farmers and their long-standing ownership of their freeholdings, even the bad parts of the districts are characterized by more wealth and better fortune than one would imagine«.[53]

Of the parishes of Vorbasse and Hejnsvig in the county of Ribe, it was said in 1819 that the conditions of the peasants there, too, were quite good: »Most peasants have only a very low »hartkorn« assessment and, according to that, only reasonable taxes to pay«. Because of the great distances to the towns, the farmers in Vorbasse and Hejnsvig were spared many burdens, which other farmers in better areas had to bear. Even in the case of the duty to supply forage when the army was passing by, they did not have to deliver cartloads of hay and straw as peasants did elsewhere. The vicar of the two parishes even relates that many a farmer among his parishioners had fortunes of several thousands rigsdaler. The farmers, particularly, had profited from the Napoleonic wars as the prices of barley, wool, butter, honey and bullocks increased dramatically.[54] However, a short decline followed the end of the wars, because England, which was the best market, imposed a ban on the import of foreign grain in 1819. The amount of grain available in Denmark increased rapidly and the prices subsequently fell at the same speed. Many Danish farmers were thus unable to sell their produce, and the tenants had difficulties paying royal taxes and contributions to the landlords, while the freeholders could not pay their mortgages.[55] This problem did not hit West Jutland quite as badly as Eastern Denmark, because animal husbandry rather than grain production was the main element of the economy in Western Denmark. So keeping cattle and bullocks as well as growing grain for the needs of the household proved to be a better business than just growing grain.

The probate inventories (*skiftebreve*) of peasants' estates in West Jutland testify to the good conditions of the farmers, too. A scrutiny of the estates in the district of Slavs (county of Ribe), which was moorland of the worst possible quality with regard to tax assessment, confirms that the farmers in this area were far from being poor. This study consists of peasant estates from six parishes of South-Western Jutland in the period 1750-1830. Of 163 peasant estates from freeholders, 118 left surplus capital to the heirs, while the remainder left a deficit. Of 39 peasant estates from tenants (mainly German colonists on the moor of Randbøl, who settled there in the years between 1760 and 1765), 22 left surplus capital while the remainder showed a deficit. Thus, it seems that the tenants were not as well consolidated as the freeholders. However, it is surprising that so many deceased peasants' estates show a surplus.

If we look at the amount of money that was left for the heirs, the picture becomes even clearer: 3 estates were recorded as having a surplus of more than 2000 rigsdaler when debts had been paid and 6 estates showed a surplus of between 1000 and 2000 rigsdaler, 14 between 500 and 1000 rigsdaler, 7 between

400 and 500 rigsdaler, 8 between 300 and 400 rigsdaler, 12 between 200 and 300 rigsdaler, 28 between 100 and 200 rigsdaler, and finally 62 estates left less than 100 rigsdaler to the heirs. This is quite a lot of money compared with the tenants of Eastern Denmark, who very rarely left more than a single farthing to the heirs.

Some studies of similar peasants' estates from the islands of Funen and Zealand from about the same period show that Zealand peasants were worse off than the West Jutlanders mentioned above. The peasants from Funen do not seem to have been either worse nor better off. Actually, it seems that the claimed poverty of West Jutland peasants is but a myth.[56] In any case it shows the importance of scrutinizing traditional myths and the need for more inquiries into West Jutland social and agricultural history. Is this picture of prosperous farmers from the South-Western part of the Jutland moors valid for all parts of the region or just for some areas? This is not the place for further investigation of this matter,[57] but the question is important with regard to the perception of West Jutland as poor and impoverished that has been handed down through the generations.

In modern times, West Jutland's identity and self-perception have been nourished on this belief, claiming that West Jutlanders have made their current prosperity from nothing – only by their own hard work cultivating the vast moors. Meanwhile, other Danish peasants were sitting in their living-rooms in cosy idleness! This picture may not be true. As this study shows, many West Jutland farmers were well off even before the cultivation of the moors started in the nineteenth century. Many West Jutland peasants had accumulated quite a tidy fortune by cattle- and bullock-dealing, cheating the authorities of customs and avoiding the payment of taxes.

The enlightenment and the perception of the peasantry

The people of the enlightenment perceived West Jutland as a poor and backward region, whose inhabitants were old-fashioned and stubborn. One certainly could not expect any sort of modernization of culture or cultivation of moorland on their part: they had to be taught what was good for them.

Agricultural observers, agronomists and those generally interested in the enlightenment of the common people, particularly of the peasants, took a great interest in the West Jutland question. The vast moors had but a small population and the same was true regarding the number and size of settlements. Compared with the »normal« Denmark, east of the Jutland ridge, West Jutland was a no man's land. West Jutland was always measured in terms of traditional conditions of life in Zealand and the other East Danish islands. The authors of travel accounts from the region were almost always people who lived in the capital Copenhagen, and their writings were meant for the public in the capital. The Danish islands always represented the point of departure for these travel accounts, and Zealand was the norm regarding society, people and the countryside.[58]

If the West Jutland moorlands were cultivated into fields of grain, housing thousands of new families, then the state would be able to extract taxes from the newly cultivated land and thereby improve state finances. Moreover, the increased population in West Jutland would contribute to the defence of the country by forming new units in a larger, powerful national army. Furthermore, »civilized culture« would have a chance to penetrate the area, securing new strongholds for the state enabling the government to control and direct the hitherto autonomous West Jutlanders and turn them into »normal« Danish peasants! This was as great and meaningful a task for the learned people of the Enlightenment as it was for the king and the government.

Strengthening the economy of the country was one of the most important issues in the Danish agricultural debate in the latter part of the eighteenth century. The concern for the formerly neglected West Jutland was suddenly very great, as the country was in need of new sources of income. The moors had to be utilized as quickly as possible by means of planned colonization (South German colonists) and cultivation of the wilderness.

A great number of ideas and opinions about this matter were aired in periodicals, books and other publications. However, not only the Jutland moors were being intensively discussed, the whole state of Danish agriculture and technology was exposed to scrutiny. Reforms of the traditional agricultural system of tenants, village communities, unenclosed land, corvée, plus improved ploughs and other measures were considered necessary if the Danish peasants were to have better living conditions and more general knowledge of the world outside the village. In the eighteenth century most people outside the farming community regarded peasants as somewhat stupid creatures. They were considered foolish, lazy, stubborn and disobedient to the authorities. They did not know what was in their own interest, and if some estate owner tried to carry out some progressive changes on his estate, they always objected, referring to the life of their ancestors and to the ancient traditions of the village community, which were held in very high esteem. Everything that was of great age – originating from »time immemorial« – was good and not to be changed. The culture of the peasantry was based on the centuries-old experience that changes usually appeared in the form of famine, war and disasters, and so they would have no part in any great changes at all. One never knew what the consequences could be for the sorely tried peasant!

On the other hand, it would be wrong to claim that the peasants were content with their conditions. But instead of looking forward to new golden ages, they were inclined to look back to a distant, mythological past. They imagined this past to be a happy time when all peasants were free-born men who did not have to suffer any noblemen or estate owners, since such people did not exist. According to this mythology, the peasantry had been held in high esteem by other members of society. They had had plenty of cattle and land and there were no taxes. It was this primeval condition that peasants longed for and talked about when changes were on the agenda and, oddly enough, these myths also nourished the French physiocratic thinking in the latter part of the eighteenth century. The physiocrats, too,

Civilizing the wilderness

Fig. 15.4: A part of West Jutland 1806

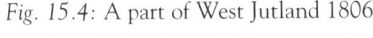

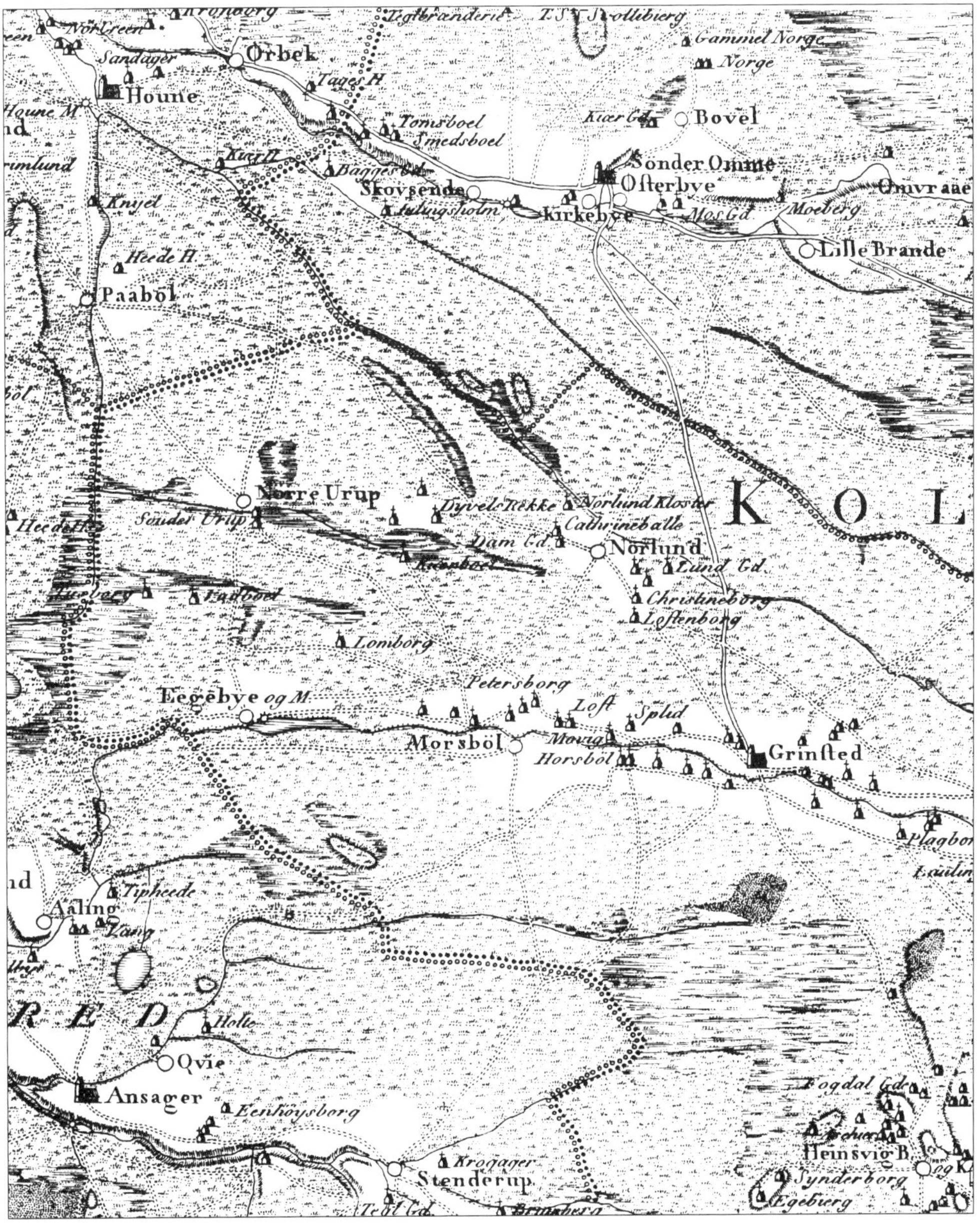

Note: A section of a map of Western Jutland (Lundenæs county etc.), made in 1806 by The Royal Danish Academy of Sciences and Letters (Videnskabernes Selskab). (Kort- og Matrikelstyrelsen) The landscape was characterized by vast moors. Only along the rivers were there some cultivated tracts. The section includes inter alia the villages Sønder Omme, Grindsted (Grinsted) and Hejnsvig (Heinsvig).

believed in the golden past of the peasantry and put all their efforts into restoring this mythological past by means of their writings. In this way, the myths of the peasantry became part of the political and agricultural ideas in the late eighteenth century, endowing the peasantry with a conservatism and sluggishness which still forms part of the stereotype.[59]

Because of their particular stubbornness and stout-heartedness, the West Jutland peasants were regarded by most progressive reformers as the poorest and most foolish of all Danish peasants.[60] The common expression »The dark Jutland« was thus not merely a description of the dark heather in winter, it also referred to the mental faculties of the West Jutland peasantry. However, the primary enemy was the heather and not the local peasant. The heather embodied the dark Jutland, in a manner of speaking, and accordingly it was seen as a nuisance that had to be uprooted if the region were to prosper.

The West Jutland campaign

Changes really did occur, in spite of stubborn peasants and rigid traditions. One of the main causes of change was the enclosure movement which, despite some opposition, began to make an impact on the moorlands in the years around 1770. As already mentioned, most West Jutland farmers objected to this great project since they did not see how it could benefit them. The West Jutlanders did not concentrate on grain production and accordingly, their arable fields, which were worked in common, were few in number, so they considered enclosure as a matter of interest only to the islanders of Eastern Denmark. The West Jutlanders managed quite well in their small communities and so they rejected the whole idea.

However, the problem in West Jutland was that no one knew which part of the moor belonged to whom and therefore no one could sell part of their moorland lots even if they were freeholders owning their own fields. The hidden agenda behind the enclosure movement in West Jutland was the project of selling unused parts of the moor, which could only be done if everybody knew exactly which parts belonged to whom.

It was mainly due to the activity of the local vicars that the enclosure movement gradually got started. In the parish of Grindsted (Ribe county) for instance, the vicar Christopher Sølling demanded enclosure in 1769 even though the villagers offered him money to withdraw his claim. After the enclosure, the expected sale of the most miserable parts of the moor soon followed. During the enclosure process, many peasants had been given lots on the moor, which were so devastated by peat-digging, sand drift, and fires that they were of no agricultural use. At the same time, demand for land, even moorland, increased rapidly among the growing population of the nineteenth century peasantry.

Nobody had ever been concerned with the cultivation of moorland to any great extent, but that changed as new generations grew up. Consequently, the purchase of small lots on the moors began, and cultivation soon followed. The farmers who were selling the lots did not care for cultivating the land themselves; they would much rather continue their animal husbandry and let the youngsters do the hard work of transforming the wilderness into arable soil.

The demand for moorland to cultivate was not caused by the increased population alone. The newly acquired knowledge of the beneficial uses of marl also played a part, since the cultivation of the poor lots would not have been possible without it. The small lots were also fairly cheap and consequently there was no scarcity of people with a burning desire to get a start in life this way.

The sales began gradually in the 1780s and continued into the next century, increasing rapidly. Even the law of 1819, which (due to the influence of Malthus) prohibited the selling of lots that were too small, did not represent an obstacle, as the farmers, instead of selling the lots, leased out the land as small holdings. It was primarily in the years after 1860 that the sales really took off. It took a very long time to open the eyes of the peasantry and make them realize how powerful and useful marl really was, as many peasants had had bad experiences with marl, using it as, or instead of, manure. But as knowledge of marl and its proper use spread, the trade in land, and its cultivation, increased rapidly. The formation of The Danish Moor Company (*Det danske Hedeselskab*) in 1866 naturally contributed to the advancement of this development.

During the nineteenth century the West Jutland landscape changed totally. The vast moors gave way to cultivated fields of grain, bogs were drained and laid out as fields, swampy meadows were transformed by the same means into fertile fields of grass. The population grew, as did the villages, and numerous small farms were built. After 1860, plantations of coniferous trees and hedges were created, and gradually the wilderness was transformed into an agricultural landscape of almost East Danish appearance – except for the lack of hills!

The role of The Danish Moor Company in this great process of change can hardly be exaggerated. The company provided the farmers with expertise and professional help in their struggle against the wilderness, and the manifold activities of the company meant that the moorlands were cultivated at a speed no one had ever imagined. West Jutland served as a magnet for young, enterprising people. As already mentioned, the prices of the lots were very reasonable, and successful cultivation depended only on the skills and initiative of the newcomer. If the newcomer was a hard working man he was almost bound to be successful. In many ways, conditions in nineteenth-century West Jutland resembled contemporary conditions on the vast American prairies in the Midwest: one could go to America in search of happiness and wealth, or one could go to West Jutland »breaking up« the moors. The opportunities were endless.[61]

Thus, a new way of life and a new sort of mentality were introduced into West Jutland. The stubbornness and conservatism of the traditional West Jutland peasantry gave way to a new enterprising spirit, represented partly by the newcomers and partly by the new generations in the old settlements. It was a somewhat self-righteous mentality, asserting the superiority of hard working West Jutlanders over the lazy East Danish peasants, who were allegedly living a comfortable life in idleness.

In earlier days, the Danish peasantry had measured their quality of life in terms of spare time, happy occasions and idleness by the hot stove. Now the hard-working peasant type was made the ideal, and idleness was banned as something almost sinful. In the new generations this newly gained self-confidence and self-righteousness among West Jutland peasants gained acceptance all over the country, and the Jutlanders became the image of an ideal peasantry. This image still exists among the modern West Jutlanders, who tend to regard the East Danes with a slight contempt.

Even modern East Danes believe that West Jutlanders are more enterprising and hard-working than themselves. The Westerners are praised for their honesty and industry, and it is somehow a recommendation to be a (West)Jutlander when one is applying for a job in the capital. The West Jutland image nourishes a modern Danish mythology, containing a picture of West Jutland as being the only place where old Danish virtues are still alive – virtues that probably never existed in real life!

Along with the rapid vanishing of the Jutland moors, a traditional way of life among the Jutland peasantry vanished as well. Not only was the traditional animal husbandry gradually giving way to grain fields and the cultivation of potatoes, by which a centuries-old agricultural system in the region was abandoned. The West Jutlanders were also being socially integrated with the inhabitants of the Danish islands in terms of administration and – especially – in terms of taxpaying. The region became more and more »civilized«, easier to govern and control, which had actually been the hidden agenda behind the cultivation. The desires of the eighteenth-century agronomists and agricultural observers had been fulfilled. The wilderness did not exist any longer. But something remained: the West Jutlanders' desire for autonomy and their antipathy to East Danish aspirations on their behalf.

Life in the periphery

Within the Danish Kingdom, West Jutland has a social and economic history that differs considerably from that of East Jutland and the Eastern Danish islands. But if one looks at the conglomerate kingdom of Denmark in the years before 1814, the region was not quite on its own regarding natural conditions and social organization.[62] West Jutland actually bears a great resemblance to similar fringe areas of Norway regarding social organization, agricultural systems, economic life and distance from administrative centres.[63] In most parts of Norway, too, the peasantry were beyond the reach of the administrators in Copenhagen, vast areas of land were left uncultivated, and the peasantry made their living from various subsidiary jobs. Like the West Jutlanders, the population of the Norwegian fringe areas were freeholders and very hostile to governmental control. There are many resemblances between the West Jutlanders and the Norwegian peasantry in the eighteenth century, as portrayed by the Norwegian historian Ståle Dyrvik. Both West Jutland and the outskirts of Norway were peripheries somewhat beyond control, and consequently, stout-heartedness and self-reliance flourished in the peasantry. The peasants were accustomed to managing everything on their own and did not like any interference from governmental administrators. As was the case in West Jutland, it is likely that the secondary occupations in Norway were not so much secondary occupations as main occupations. Agriculture may well have been their true secondary occupation. In a work from 1996, the historians Anna Tranberg and Knut Sprauten claim that in early modern Norway, the secondary occupations »were sometimes able to supply the farmer with a better income than agriculture and animal husbandry«.[64] So who decides which occupation is primary and which secondary?

Talking about the history of mentalities, it would be quite interesting to scrutinize the similarities between West Jutland and the fringe areas of Norway: Is it justifiable to compare the two regions in this matter? If so, how important were these mentalities in the development of the areas in the following century? And is the comparison of West Jutland with the American Midwest a reasonable one?

It is intriguing to find that anachronistic beliefs and images – sometimes of ancient origin and sometimes probably false – still circulate in modern society. West Jutland nowadays is apparently like any other part of the country, but not quite; the West Jutlanders have not yet given in. Something that is foreign to Eastern Danes is still lurking in the dark colour of the heather that remains – and that something is the stuff from which myths and legends are made.

Notes

1. F. Jerk: Ringkøbing amts herregårde gennem godsslagtningens tidehverv, *Hardsyssels Årbog* 1958. P. Henningsen: *Hedens Hemmeligheder. Livsvilkår i Vestjylland 1750-1900*, Viborg 1995, pp. 241ff.
2. In the West Jutland parish of Grindsted (county of Ribe) the local vicar in the eighteenth century sometimes carried out the management of deceased peasants' estates on behalf of the »amtmand«, who lived far away either in Kolding or in Fredericia.
3. The »amtmand« Hans de Hoffmann, in the latter part of the eighteenth century, had his residence in Fredericia.
4. S. B. Frandsen: *Opdagelsen af Jylland. Den regionale dimension i Danmarkshistorien 1814-64*, Oxford 1996, pp. 83, 85f.
5. C. Th. Engelstofts rejseoptegnelser fra 1830, *Samlinger til jysk historie og topografi*, 4 rk. 2 bd., 1914-16, p. 401.
6. P. Eliassen: *Historiske strejftog i Kolding og omegn*, Kolding 1923, p. 229. A farm-hand earned approximately 10 rdlr. a year in the latter part of the eighteenth century.
7. H. Matthiessen: *Den sorte jyde*, Copenhagen 1939, p. 162f.
8. P. Eliassen: *Kongeåen eller den gamle grænse*, vol. 1, Kolding 1925, p. 37.
9. Rigsarkivet (The Danish National Archives), Kommercekollegiet 1735-71, Dansk-norske sekretariat nr. 15, 1739-40, 1759 Forestillinger med og uden kgl. resolution (Ribe stift).
10. Landsarkivet for Nørrejylland (The Provincial Archives, Viborg), B 6 C Koldinghus amts arkiv no. 185, 1746 Restanceliste for familie- og folkeskat.
11. Jeppe Aakjær: Den jydske hede før kolonisationen, *Samlinger til jysk historie og topografi*, 3 rk. 4 bd. 1904-05, p. 354.
12. Søren Thestrup: Forslag om hederne i Nørrejylland til ager og eng at optage, *Danmarks og Norges oeconomiske Magazin*, vol. 3, 1759, p. 99f.
13. Rigsarkivet (The Danish National Archives), Danske Kancelli D 102b, Efterretninger om købstæderne og amterne, indsendt i henhold til oversekretærens skrivelse af 6.4.1743.
14. Rigsarkivet (The Danish National Archives), Rentekammeret 2245.128, 1731-32 Eksaminationsforretning over klager fra nogle bønder i Koldinghus Rytterdistrikt.
15. The ambulating teachers were also known in other parts of the country.

16 As regards religious education the pupils on the moors did not apparently suffer any lack of teaching. According to the bishop of Ribe diocese, Hans Adolph Brorson, the youngsters in his diocese seemed to know their catechism quite well in the years between 1742 and 1763. L. J. Koch (ed.): *H. A. Brorson – visitatsberetninger og breve*, Copenhagen 1960, p. 1ff.
17 Peter Henningsen 1995 (see note 1), p. 67f.
18 The law prohibiting free movement for male peasants between 14 and 40 years was introduced in 1733 and abolished in 1788. Under this law, a male peasant could not leave his place of birth without asking permission of the owner of the estate.
19 *Tønder hartkorn* was a Danish unit of land valuation which directly translated would be something like »barrels of hard grain«. It was a measurement for tax assessment: when a man had, say, 5 tønder hartkorn of land, he might own approximately 7.5 acres of land. The survey in hartkorn alluded only to the fertility of the arable soil. Therefore the hartkorn was higher in East Jutland and the Danish islands than in West Jutland, where the fertility of the soil was poor. One tønde hartkorn could be anything between 1.5 and 18 acres of land depending on the area. So a hartkorn survey is an expression of the quality of the arable soil, assessed for tax purposes.
20 Jørgen Dieckmann Rasmussen: *Stavnsbånd og Vestjylland. Blev bonden fri?*, Ribe 1988, p. 20.
21 »Specifikation over Hosbondere og Fæstebøndere i Grindsted sogn«. In: Landsarkivet for Nørrejylland, B 6 C Koldinghus amts arkiv, no. 207, Kopi af Amtets Herregaardes og Bønders Beskrivelse 1785.
22 Johan Hvidtfeldt: Stavnsbåndet, dets forudsætninger og virkninger, *Vejle Amts Årbog 1938*, p. 24f.
23 Jørgen Dieckmann Rasmussen (see note 20), p. 23.
24 K. C. Rockstroh: *Udviklingen af den nationale hær i Danmark i det 17. og 18. årh.*, vol. 3, Copenhagen 1926, p. 129f.
25 I. Karstoft: *Fra det nedlagte gamle Sønder Omme-Hoven pastorat*, Kolding 1948, p. 19.
26 Peter Henningsen 1995 (see note 1), p. 105ff.
27 Carl Dalgas: *Bidrag til kundskab om de danske provindsers nærværende tilstand i oekonomisk henseende, Vejle amt*, Copenhagen 1826, p. 202.
28 J. C. Hald: *Bidrag til kundskab om de danske provindsers nærværende tilstand i oekonomisk henseende, Ringkøbing amt*, Copenhagen 1833, p. 250.
29 Cf. note 22.
30 Gregers Begtrup: *Beskrivelse af Agerdyrkningens Tilstand i Nørrejylland*, vol. 1, Copenhagen 1808, p. 63.
31 Hans de Hoffman: Om Hederne i Jylland, *Oeconomisk Journal*, vol. 3, January 1758, p. 49.
32 Landsarkivet for Nørrejylland, C 4 Ribe Bispearkiv: no. 774, 1766-68 Præsteindberetninger til biskop J. Bloch (Report to the bishop of Ribe: February 3rd 1766).
33 Johan Arnt Dyssel: *Forsøg til en indenlands Reise forfattet 1763*, Copenhagen 1774, p. 13.
34 Søren Alkærsig: Om dansk Studehandel i det 18. årh., *Samlinger til jysk Historie og Topografi*, 3 rk. vol. 3, 1901-03; Søren Alkærsig: En smuglerhistorie fra 1729, *Fra Ribe amt 1905*; P. Eliassen: Studehandlere, *Vejle Amts Årbog 1919*; Esben Graugaard: Vestjysk studehandel som binæringsvej, *Bol og By 1990:2*; Johannes Møllgaard: Det »mørke« Jylland og »verdensmarkedet«, *Folk og Kultur 1988*.
35 Steen Steensen Blicher: *Bidrag til Kundskab om de danske Provindsers nærværende Tilstand i oekonomisk Henseende, Viborg amt*, Copenhagen 1839, p. 201.
36 Carl Dalgas: *Bidrag til Kundskab om de danske Provindsers nærværende Tilstand i oekonomisk Henseende, Ribe amt*, Copenhagen 1830, p. 216f.
37 In fact there is nothing unusual about the intensive cattle raising in West Jutland. The peninsula belongs to the Atlantic coastal belts of Europe. These coastal terrains were generally too moist for the cultivation of grain, and this meant that pasturage and cattle-raising had prevailed in these areas since the High Middle Ages. The other main zones could be distinguished as the interior terrain and the mountainous terrain. The interior terrain in the German lowlands and Eastern Europe for its part was simply vast tracts of cultivable land. Werner Rösener: *The peasantry of Europe*, Oxford 1995, p. 47.

38 Uddrag af et 150-aarigt Haandskrift om den jydske Hede ved sognepræst John M. Møller i Kærum, *Fra Ribe amt 1909*, p. 27.
39 Søren Toftgaard Poulsen: »En rig fader, men en fattig søn« – mergling gennem 200 år i Ringkøbing amt, *Arv og eje 1988*, p. 200.
40 Hugo Matthiessen: *Den sorte jyde*, Copenhagen 1939, p. 127f.
41 This was no doubt a result of the mercantilistic way of thinking that dominated in Denmark in this period. According to the doctrines of mercantilism, workers and peasants should be forced to do whatever the paternalistic elite found was good for the country. Obviously they did not take into account that ordinary people did not have any incentives to work for the good of the country instead of working solely for their own benefit. This conflict between elite and people is brilliantly described in: Dan Ch. Christensen: *Det moderne projekt. Teknik og kultur i Danmark-Norge 1750-(1814)-1850*, 1996.
42 Anna Tranberg and Knut Sprauten (eds.): *Norsk bondeøkonomi 1650-1850*, 1996, p. 10.
43 Hugo Matthiessen 1939 (see note 40), p. 100f.
44 S. A. Fjelstrup: Om de jydske Heder og deres opdyrkning, *Tidsskrift for Landoeconomi*, ny række vol. 13, 1852, p. 69.
45 Orvar Löfgren: Historical perspectives on Scandinavian peasantries, *Annual Review of Anthropology*, vol. 9, 1980, p. 211.
46 Jens Abildtrup: Selvejerbønderne i Bøvling og Lundenæs amter 1743. *Festskrift tilegnet Carl Klitgaard, Samlinger til jysk Historie og Topografi*, 5 rk. vol. 4, 1938, p. 110.
47 *Tilskueren for landvæsenet*, vol. 2, Copenhagen 1798, p. 31.
48 Rigsarkivet, Rentekammeret 432.44, Indkomne Betænkninger over Spørgsmaal til Landvæsenets Forbedring i Henhold til Cirkulære af 30.4.1768.
49 Kaptajn T. R. Teilmann's account in: Bondestandens Kaar i det sydlige Jylland i Midten af det attende Aarhundrede meddelt af dr. O. Nielsen, *Aarbog for dansk Kulturhistorie 1894*, p. 31.
50 Pastor Knud Lang's account in: Bondestandens Kaar … (see note 49), p. 35f.
51 Quoted from: S. B. Frandsen (see note 4), p. 83.
52 Gregers Begtrup (see note 30), p. 56.
53 Op. cit., p. 247.
54 P. N. Frost: *Statistisk-oeconomisk Beskrivelse over Vaarbasse og Heinsvig sogne i Slaugs Herred, Ribe amt*, Borris 1819, p. 43.
55 Carl Dalgas 1830 (see note 36), p. 196f.
56 Peter Henningsen: Bølgende agre af gyldent korn. Kornavlsideologien i dansk landbrugs historie. *1066 – Tidsskrift for historisk forskning*, no. 4, 1995, p. 4ff.
57 For more information about this investigation: Peter Henningsen 1995 (see note 1), p. 108ff.
58 S. B. Frandsen (see note 4), p. 79ff.
59 Peter Henningsen 1995 (see note 1), p. 71ff, 77ff. For more detailed information on the Danish physiocrats, see Dan Ch. Christensen (see note 41), pp. 66-80, 555-608.
60 Still, many observers believed the West Jutlanders to be the most clever and skilful, as their conditions of life were far better than elsewhere and as their mentality was not as humble as was normal at the time. So the Danish physiocrats held the West Jutlanders in very high esteem. Peter Henningsen 1995 (see note 1), p. 71ff.
61 Peter Henningsen 1995 (see note 1), p. 248ff.
62 Before 1814 the conglomerate state of Denmark consisted of the two kingdoms, Denmark and Norway, the Duchies of Schleswig and Holstein, Greenland, Iceland, The Faroe Islands and a number of colonies in Asia and the West Indies. In 1814 Norway gained independence but soon after, the Kingdom was annexed by Sweden. In 1864 the Duchies were lost in the war against Prussia, and the colonies were gradually sold off.
63 See for example Ståle Dyrvik: *Den lange fredstiden 1720-1784, Norges Historie*, vol. 8, ed. Knut Mykland, Oslo 1978, p. 44-186.
64 Anna Tranberg and Knut Sprauten (see note 42), p. 11.

List of contributors

Peter Aronsson, professor, fil.dr.
Växjö Universitet, S-351 95 Växjö, Sweden.
E-mail: peter.aronsson@hum.vxu.se

Søren Bitsch Christensen, adjunkt (lecturer), Ph.D.
Dansk Center for Byhistorie, Aarhus Universitet, Nørrebrogade, DK-8000 Århus C, Denmark. E-mail: hissbi@hum.au.dk

Ole Degn, arkivar/seniorforsker (archivist and senior researcher), dr. phil.
Landsarkivet for Nørrejylland, Ll. Sct. Hansgade 5, DK-8800 Viborg, Denmark. E-mail: degnio@post3.tele.dk

Atle Døssland, førsteamanuensis (associate professor), cand. philol.
Høgskulen i Volda, Boks 500, N-6101 Volda, Norway. E-mail: atd@hivolda.no

Finn-Einar Eliassen, førsteamanuensis (associate professor), dr. philos.
Avd. for samfunnsfag, Høgskolen i Vestfold, Postboks 2243, N-3103 Tønsberg, Norway. E-mail: finn-einar.eliassen@hive.no

Peter Henningsen, ekstern lektor (external lecturer), cand. mag.
Institut for Historie, Københavns Universitet, Njalsgade 102, DK-2300 København S, Denmark. E-mail: henningsen@mail.tele.dk

Poul Holm, professor, dr. phil.
Center for Maritim og Regional Historie, Syddansk Universitet, Niels Bohrs Vej 9, DK-6700 Esbjerg, Denmark. E-mail: pho@hist.sdu.dk

Ragnhild Høgsæt, førsteamanuensis (associate professor), cand. philol.
Institutt for historie, Samfunnsvitenskapelig fakultet, Universitetet i Tromsø, N-9037 Tromsø, Norway. E-mail: raghoe@sv.uit.no

John P. Maarbjerg, adjunct professor, Ph.D.
University of Connecticut, Stamford. One University Place, Stamford, CT 06901, USA. E-mail: john.maarbjerg@yale.edu

Jørgen Mikkelsen, arkivar/seniorforsker (archivist and senior researcher), Ph.D.
Landsarkivet for Sjælland m.m., Jagtvej 10, DK-2200 København N, Denmark. E-mail: jm@lak.sa.dk

Bjørn Poulsen, professor, dr. phil.
Historisk Institut, Aarhus Universitet, Nørrebrogade, DK-8000 Århus C, Denmark. E-mail: hisbp@hum.au.dk

Øystein Rian, professor, dr. philos.
Historisk institutt, Universitetet i Oslo, Postboks 1008, Blindern, N-0315 Oslo, Norway. E-mail: oystein.rian@hi.uio.no

Åke Sandström, docent (assistant professor), fil.dr.
Högskolan på Gotland, Cramérgatan 3, S-621 57 Visby, Sweden. E-mail: ake.sandstrom@hgo.se

Harald Winge (†), cand. philol.
Leder af Norsk Lokalhistorisk Institutt (Head of the Norwegian Institute of Local History), 1986-1999.